STALINISM RE\

STALINISM REVISITED

The Establishment of Communist Regimes in East-Central Europe

Edited by
VLADIMIR TISMANEANU

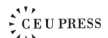 C E U PRESS

Central European University Press
Budapest–New York

© 2009 by Vladimir Tismaneanu

Published in 2009 by

Central European University Press
An imprint of the
Central European University Share Company
Nádor utca 11, H-1051 Budapest, Hungary
Tel: +36-1-327-3138 or 327-3000
Fax: +36-1-327-3183
E-mail: ceupress@ceu.hu
Website: www.ceupress.com

400 West 59th Street, New York NY 10019, USA
Tel: +1-212-547-6932
Fax: +1-646-557-2416
E-mail: mgreenwald@sorosny.org

ISBN 978-963-9776-63-0 Paperback

LIBRARY OF CONGRESS CATALOGING-IN-PUBLICATION DATA

Stalinism revisited : the establishment of communist regimes in East-Central Europe / edited by Vladimir Tismaneanu.
  p. cm.
Includes bibliographical references and index.
ISBN 978-9639776555 (hardcover)
1. Europe, Eastern—Politics and government—1945-1989. 2. Communism—Europe, Eastern—History—20th century. 3. Europe, Eastern—Foreign relations—Soviet Union. 4. Soviet Union—Foreign relations—Europe, Eastern. 5. Europe, Eastern—History—20th century. 6. Stalin, Joseph, 1879-1953. I. Tismaneanu, Vladimir. II. Title.

DJK50.S72 2009
947.0009'045—dc22

2009042289

Printed in Hungary by
Akaprint Kft., Budapest

Table of Contents

Part Three

STALINISM AND HISTORIOGRAPHY

Part Four

NATIONAL OR REVOLUTIONARY
BREAKTHROUGHS?

VLADIMIR TISMANEANU

Introduction

Understanding the nature, dynamics, and consequences of Stalinism in Eastern and Central Europe remains an urgent scholarly and moral task. The present volume compiles the proceedings of the conference "Stalinism Revisited: The Establishment of Communist Regimes in the former Soviet Bloc" (29–30 November 2007, Washington, D.C., USA). The event was envisaged as an opportunity for synthesis and comparison under the favorable circumstances of temporal distance and new available sources. The two decades that have passed since the 1989 watershed brought about an archival upheaval[1] and, consequently, a scholarly explosion within the field of communist studies. The result was an opportunity for reinforcing and/or retesting many of the assertions produced in academia throughout the years of both the Cold War and the immediate post-communist euphoria. Equally significant, a certain sense of closure and atonement at the local level, created new motivations for coming to terms with the first decade of communism's existence in the area, one fundamentally defined by trauma and repression. The year 2007 symbolized a historical threshold that marked six decades since the establishment of communist regimes in Eastern Europe (though it can be argued that this process took place earlier in some countries, such as Bulgaria, and later in other, e.g., Czechoslovakia). The experience of recent years shows that the 21st century is still following upon the footsteps of the previous one. In many respects, it is only a formal convention to speak of a new century. Once Daniel Chirot stated that in the 21st century "the fundamental causes of revo-

---

[1] What Sheila Fitzpatrick defined as "an abrupt and radical transformation of the universe of sources and the conditions of access to information" in her "Introduction" to *Stalinism: New Directions* (London: Routledge, 2000), p. 3.

lutionary instability will be moral."[2] If one concurs, then the study of Eastern Europe's Stalinization remains an important source of pedagogically and cathartically rich examples for the present.

The initial premise behind the above-mentioned event was that we are now better equipped for understanding and interpreting the complex circumstances behind the Stalinist expansion in Eastern Europe. We had in mind such dynamics as the early history of the Cold War, the Stalinist revolutionary project in the region, the participation of local communist elites, the impact of Titoism on these elites, the rivalries between "Muscovites" and "home communists," and the first attempts at constructing, via the Cominform (the Information Bureau of the Communist and Workers' Parties, founded in 1947), a Moscow-centered supra-governmental communist organization. Additionally, many contributors historiographically contextualized the problems singled out in their papers. The volume, subsequently, attained a retrospective facet as well. It familiarizes the reader with the domestic scholarly literature from the various Eastern European countries dealing with the aspects of the establishment of communist regimes in the region. One could also argue that this book discusses and revisits the main hypotheses regarding the inception of the Soviet Bloc as formulated in the classic work on the topic by Zbigniew Brzeziński.[3]

It should be noted, however, that our intention was not to produce a grand narrative about the first decade of the communist experience in Eastern Europe. We purposely chose to create a composite framework reflective of the fragmented discourse about the various political and historical issues discussed. The volume highlights the political, ideological, and personal variables that characterized the post-1945 decade. It emphasizes the complexities, ambiguities and contradictions which affected both the rationality of the actors involved and the predictability of historical events. Consequently, the volume embraces a multi-directional perspective, mirroring the tremendous diversity of domestic and international processes present in each of the cases in the individual papers.

---

[2] Daniel Chirot, "What Happened in Eastern Europe in 1989?" in Vladimir Tismaneanu ed., *The Revolutions of 1989: Rewriting Histories* (London/New York: Routledge, 1999), p. 39.

[3] Zbigniew K. Brzeziński, *The Soviet Bloc, Unity and Conflict* (Cambridge, MA: Harvard University Press, 1967).

The comparative method is the common denominator for all contributions and a fundamental feature of the work itself. It is the direct result of the overall thesis, unanimously adopted by all the authors, namely, that there was no unique path to Stalinization in Eastern Europe. There was no master plan that was designed some evening in the Kremlin by Stalin and his inner circle. Alternatively, however, one would be mistaken to believe that this possibility was not *une idée fixe* for Stalin and the other Moscow magnates. Eastern Europe did indeed become a *cordon sanitaire* for the fatherland of socialism. There may not have been (as far as we know) any blueprints clearly stating USSR's intentions in the region. The increasingly perceived reality of communist takeover during those years is nevertheless an indicator of Stalin's concerted actions of domination over Eastern Europe. Subsequently, four axes of analysis can be identified in the volume: (a) the heterogeneous nature of communization; (b) the role of the "Moscow Center" in the interplay between *Sovietization* and *satellitization*; (c) the ambivalent symbiosis between continuity and change in the societies upon which the communist regimes applied themselves; and (d) the (*il*)logic of Stalinism's infernal reign of terror, purge, co-option, manipulation, and indoctrination, its consequences and legacies in the region.

Despite the multifariousness of the first decade of the communist experience in the region, the researcher can certainly rely on one valid generalization: it all happened along the lines of a presupposed set of ideological premises (maybe not so distinct at the time, but obvious by means of historical hindsight). What these countries experienced was not merely institutional import or imperial expansion. They went through what one could label, using Stephen Kotkin's wording, a "civilizational"[4] transfer that transplanted a secular eschatology (Marxism-Leninism), a radical vision of the world (capitalist encirclement

---

[4] Stephen Kotkin, *The Magnetic Mountain* (Berkeley: University of California Press, 1995), pp. 225–37; Stephen Kotkin, "1991 and the Russian Revolution: Sources, Conceptual Categories, Analytical Frameworks," *The Journal of Modern History*, Vol. 70, No. 2 (June, 1998): 384–425; and "The State— Is It Us? Memoirs, Archives, and Kremlinologists," *Russian Review*, Vol. 61 (January 2002): 35–51. For further commentary of this view, see also Astrid Hadin, "Stalinism as a Civilization: New Perspectives on Communist Regimes," *Political Studies Review*, Vol. 2 (2004): 166–84.

and the touchstone theory or proletarian internationalism formulated by Stalin in the 1920s), and, ultimately, an alternative idea of modernity (based upon anti-capitalism and state managed collectivism) self-identified as infallibly righteous; in other words, Stalinism. The latter was a fanatic, pre-established idea of how society should be, in the name of which the movement dispensed with as many human lives as needed while frantically pacing radical transformation. The personality cult (and the ensuing post-Stalin patrimonialism) combined with the intrinsic and increased traditionalistic outlook of communism (as "a lived system"[5]) spun Bolshevism utterly and irrevocably out of control in each and every case of these countries. As in the case of the Soviet Union, in Eastern Europe Stalinism itself was the revolution:[6] it broke through the already frail structures of the *ancien régime* and laid the groundwork of state socialism in each of the region's countries.

The period of communist takeover and of "high Stalinism" in the region was fundamentally one of institutional and ideological transfer based upon the premise of radical transformation and of cultural revolution. This is why it is important to clarify first the bedrock of this historical process and then put the preliminary conclusions into a comparative, regional, cross-country perspective. As recent scholarship on a variety of topics related to the 1944–48 period has shown, there certainly was a strategic orientation for these multiple takeovers (i.e., Sovietization). At the same time, a series of local developments appeared providing each of the cases with a distinctive character in the process. The early history of post-war East European communism can be divided in two distinct periods: (a) 1944–47, that of Leninist takeover

---

[5] Karen Dawisha, "Communism as a Lived System of Ideas in Contemporary Russia," *East European Politics and Societies*, Vol. 19, No. 3 (Summer 2005): 463–93.

[6] The initial formulation along these lines came from Hugh Seton-Watson, *The East European Revolution* (New York: Praeger, 1951). Kenneth Jowitt added both conceptual and comparative flesh to this idea in his various articles and books throughout the years, first in his published PhD thesis *Revolutionary Breakthroughs and National Development: The Case of Romania, 1944–1965* (Berkeley: University of California Press, 1971). Of course, for the Soviet Union, Stephen Kotkin and later Amir Weiner, with his *Making Sense of War: the Second World War and the Fate of the Bolshevik Revolution* (Princeton, NJ: Princeton University Press, 2001), are maybe the most significant advocates of this idea.

and accelerated annihilation of democratic pluralism in the region's countries; (b) 1948–53, that of communist transformation and offensive development, characterized by institutional and ideological transfer (Sovietization), cultural regimentation, domestic terror, and international bi-polarism (Andrei Zhdanov's "Two Camps" theory). The fateful years 1944–48 must be also understood in the context of the prior developments during the Second World War. One has to take into account the domestic politics framework of each of the region's countries. What I have in mind are issues such as the rise of the extreme right and of anti-Semitism, nationalities policies, and the activity of local communist parties, especially of the Comintern. At the end of the Second World War, a new state system was emerging. It was the product of two simultaneous processes: *Sovietization* and *satellitization*. The "Iron Curtain" was mainly the result of the alternation of what Caroline Kennedy-Pipe called "strategies of occupation and of consolidation."[7]

The field of communism studies presently boasts quite a few case studies (some more general, others more topical) of the Bolshevization of Eastern Europe (1944–53).[8] They are accompanied by important

---

[7] Caroline Kennedy-Pipe, *Stalin's Cold War: Soviet Strategies in Europe, 1943 to 1956* (Manchester: Manchester University Press, 1995).

[8] Some examples are: for Poland, Krystyna Kersten, *The Establishment of Communist Rule in Poland, 1943–1948*, translated and annotated by John Micgiel and Michael H. Bernhard, foreword by Jan T. Gross (Berkeley: University of California Press, 1991) or Padraic Kenney, *Rebuilding Poland: Workers and Communists, 1945–1950* (Ithaca, NY: Cornell University Press, 1997); for Hungary, Peter Kenez, *Hungary from the Nazis to the Soviets: The Establishment of the Communist Regime in Hungary, 1944–1948* (Cambridge: Cambridge University Press, 2006) or László Borhi, *Hungary in the Cold War, 1945–1956: Between the United States and the Soviet Union* (Budapest: CEU Press, 2004); for Yugoslavia, Aleksa Djilas, *The Contested Country: Yugoslav Unity and Communist Revolution, 1919–1953* (Cambridge, MA: Harvard University Press, 1991) or Carol S. Lilly, *Power and Persuasion: Ideology and Rhetoric in Communist Yugoslavia, 1944–1953* (Boulder, CO: Westview Press, 2001); for Czechoslovakia, Bradley F. Abrams, *The Struggle for the Soul of the Nation: Czech Culture and the Rise of Communism* (Lanham, MD: Rowman & Littlefield, 2004) and the still relevant Karel Kaplan, *The Short March. The Communist Takeover of Czechoslovakia 1945–1948* (London: C. Hurst, 1987); for Romania, Vladimir Tismaneanu, *Stalinism for All Seasons: A Political History of Romanian Communism* (Berkeley: University of California Press, 2003) and Robert Levy, *Ana Pauker: The Rise and Fall of a Jewish Communist* (Berkeley: University of California Press, 2001); for Bulgaria, the

collective volumes on the nature and facets of Stalinism as the cornerstone model for Soviet-type socialism.[9] There is, however, only a limited list of titles that deal with both general and specific issues related to the impact and manifestations of Stalinism in the region. Two contributions of such character do stand out, with the caveat that over a decade has passed since their publication: François Fejtö, *Histoire des démocraties populaires, tome 1: L'Ere de Staline (1945–1953)* (Paris: Seuil, 1992) and Norman Naimark & Leonid Gibianskii eds., *The Establishment of Communist Regimes in Eastern Europe, 1944–1949* (Boulder, CO: Westview Press, 1997). The last ten years, however, brought about no such books focused on this specific part of Europe. We believe that the present collective effort fills this void within the scholarly literature. The conference and the volume were imagined along the lines previously sketched by two other significant academic projects that came about at the time, for very similar research purposes as those of the event organized thirty years later in Washington, D.C. The more significant of the two was the 1975 conference on Stalinism organized at the Rockefeller Foundation's conference center in Bellagio, Italy, and which had as result the seminal volume edited by Robert C. Tucker, *Stalinism: Essays in Historical Interpretation* (New York: Norton, 1977). The second, more area studies focused, is the series of seminars devoted to the topic of communist power in Eastern Europe (1944–49), held at the School of Slavonic and East European Studies at the University of London (1974–76) and which resulted in the influ-

---

classical volume by Nissan Oren, *Bulgarian Communism: The Road to Power, 1934–1944* (New York: Columbia University Press, 1971), of which findings have been significantly enriched by Vesselin Dimitrov's *Stalin's Cold War: Soviet Foreign Policy, Democracy and Communism in Bulgaria, 1941–48* (New York: Palgrave Macmillan, 2008); for East Germany, Gareth Pritchard, *The Making of the GDR, 1945–53: From Antifascism to Stalinism* (Manchester: Manchester University Press, 2000) or Catherine Epstein, *The Last Revolutionaries: German Communists and their Century* (Cambridge, MA: Harvard University Press, 2003).

[9] Four such volumes published in recent years come to mind: Sheila Fitzpatrick ed., *Stalinism...*; David L. Hoffmann ed., *Stalinism: The Essential Readings* (Malden, Mass: Blackwell Publishing Inc., 2003); Harold Shukman ed., *Redefining Stalinism* (London: Frank Cass, 2003); and John Keep & Alter Litvin, *Stalinism: Russian and Western Views at the Turn of the Millennium* (New York: Routledge, 2004).

ential volume edited by Martin McCauley, *Communist Power in Europe 1944–1949* (Barnes & Noble Books, 1977) (among the contributors were Hugh Seton-Watson, George Schöpflin, and Norman Davies). We identified with these two projects' commitment to methodological re-assessment, comparative bias, transnational grasp, and non-linear/self-complacent argumentation.

The structure of the present volume provides grounds for both re-interpretation and an input of fresh insights and research. It contains three types of contributions: (a) general analyses of phenomena associated with the category of Stalinism; (b) case studies focusing upon aspects of establishment of communist regimes in each of the Eastern European countries; (c) historiographical evaluations of the literature dealing with the targeted period of time. The authors focus on the following issues: the relationship between domestic and external factors; factionalism and ideological orthodoxy; institution-building as part of the post-war European outlook; terror and transformism; and the impact of the first decade in subsequent dynamics within the Soviet bloc and after its dissolution.

Therefore, the key-issues to be dealt with are: interpretations of Stalinism in the light of the similarities and dissimilarities among the new regimes and their individual path to power; the Cominform and the emerging bloc (dis)unity (the genesis of the Titoist challenge and the birth of "national communism"); the role of local communist leaders, the little Stalins as it were (e.g., Rákosi, Gheorghiu-Dej, Chervenkov, Ulbricht, Gottwald); the incumbent legacies of early post-war communism on later developments within state socialism; and the present perceptions of the Stalinist experience. Additionally, the reader will also find four articles concentrated upon particular elements of Romania's transformation into a communist regime. The explanation for such bias is, in a way, a sub-plot in the justification of the present project. Besides the intention of constructing a comparative and general framework, the conveners of the conference[10] conceived the event as

---

[10] Professor Vladimir Tismaneanu (Director of the Center for the Study of Post-Communist Societies at Government and Politics Department, University of Maryland, College Park), Mr. H.R. Patapievici (President of the Romanian Cultural Institute, Bucharest), and Dr. Christian Ostermann (Director of the Cold War International History Program at Woodrow Wilson International Center for Scholars).

a chance for reinserting the Romanian case in the Anglo-American academic map.[11] Under circumstances of a rejuvenation of communism studies in Romania[12] and considering the existent scholarship dealing with the Romanian case,[13] I believe it is high time to re-introduce the Romanian case to the general debates about communist takeovers and the impact of Stalinism on Eastern Europe. The importance of this pioneering enterprise is heightened by the fact that three of the researchers included in the volume were members/experts of the PCACDR,[14] their contributions being integral parts of the Commission's *Final Report*. It should be noted, however, that this slight Romanian bias does not dilute the overall focus of the volume on regime-change, societal transformation, and international positioning across the entire Soviet Bloc.

The first part of the volume provides a diagnosis of the blueprint model implemented in Eastern Europe in the first post-1945 decade. Kenneth Jowitt argues that the idea of transformation in Stalinist regimes was based upon a "castle" mentality, in the sense of minimizing "the contact with the old data," while simultaneously pursuing revolutionary breakthroughs. This practice not only destroyed the elites, but also shattered institutions and the very potential for political opposition. According to him, Stalinism obliterated, absorbed, and sub-

---

[11] Significantly, the excellent volume by Naimark & Gibianskii does not have any contribution dealing with the Romanian case.

[12] Signaled among other things by the publication of the *Final Report* of the Presidential Commission for the Analysis of the Communist Dictatorship in Romania (PCACDR). It first appeared in e-format on December 2006, when the Romanian President Traian Băsescu officially condemned the communist regime as "illegitimate and criminal," in a speech during a joint session of the Romanian Parliament. The *Final Report* was published in volume format in November 2007 at Humanitas publishing house.

[13] Among the names that come to mind are Henry Roberts, Ghiţă Ionescu, Robert King, Ken Jowitt, Gail Kligman, Katherine Verdery, Robert Levy, Michael Shafir, Dionisie Ghermani, Catherine Durandin, Walter Bacon, William Crowther, Daniel Nelson, Stephen Fischer-Galati, Mary Ellen Fischer, etc.

[14] Cristian Vasile was the scientific secretary, Dragoş Petrescu was member, Dorin Dobrincu was co-editor of the Commission's final report (along with Vladimir Tismaneanu and Cristian Vasile). Another conference participant, professor Virgil Târău, was expert of the Commission. Vladimir Tismaneanu was the president of the investigatory body.

stituted both the state and the public. However, Jowitt insists that pre-communist political culture was only reinforced by Stalinist rule in the region. The danger for the present, incumbent on the legacy of the ambivalent communist past, is that Eastern Europe can become "Europe's ghetto." In the second article of the first section of the book, Vladimir Tismaneanu emphasizes the centrality of the culture and politics of purge to Stalinism. He argues that communist dictatorships were established on sheer terror, permanent propaganda warfare, and personalized power. Subsequently, their fundamental weakness was the chronic deficit of legitimacy. Stalinism imposed a different structure of commitment and consent. One which was based upon the unification of victim and torturer, the abolition of the traditional moral taboos and the codification of different set of communal values, with different prescriptions and prohibitions ("socialist ethics"). The ideologization of morality led to a specific (*il*)logic of authority consolidation that turned Leninism into a political religion. An exterminist hubris complemented communism's proselytic reach over Eastern Europe. The third contribution of Part One analyzes the origins and the intensity of the Cold War. Mark Kramer emphasizes the importance of domestic politics in the USSR, which, along with Stalin's external ambitions, were the decisive factor shaping Soviet ties with Eastern Europe. Stalin's heightened repressive campaigns and xenophobic appetites at home reflected themselves in his embrace of a harder line *vis-à-vis* Eastern Europe. The direct consequence of these developments was the abandonment of initial initiatives for cooperation with the United States and Britain. An important section of Mark Kramer's paper deals with the impact of Stalin's rift with Yugoslavia, his attempts to cope with the split and to mitigate the adverse repercussions upon the "monolithic unity" of the newly born Soviet bloc. Alfred J. Rieber follows a similar path, in the sense that he examines the relationship between the expansion of Soviet influence and the inception of the Cold War and the theoretization and instrumentalization of the idea of a "popular democracy" at the level of the communist elite in the USSR. According to the author, the concept became an illusion because of (a) the incapacity of the local communist parties to adapt to certain rules of the parliamentary game; (b) the perceived hostility of Soviet representatives toward non-communist members of the post-war communist governments; and (c) the internationalization of internal conflicts in this region's countries.

Part Two turns to individual cases of communist takeovers. It opens with an autobiographical piece by Thomas W. Simons, Jr. By presenting his personal experience and background in American foreign policy, Simons constructs a big picture of the US attitude toward Eastern Europe during the Cold War. The author makes a very important observation in relation to the history of the bi-polar period in the 20th century. The US had no strategic interest in that part of Europe and its involvement there remained rather ideological. The causes of this situation lay in the lessons of the Second World War, as learnt differently by Americans and Soviets. The 1944–47 crisis, in Simons' opinion, was one of perceiving appeasement of tyranny vs. democratic capitalism, on one side, and degeneration of capitalism vs. socialism, on the other. The region then became "a canary in the mineshaft for Americans." Agnes Heller's contribution investigates, using the case of Hungary, the nature of the legitimacy deficits that plagued the communist regimes in Eastern Europe. She identifies two factors of difference when comparing the Eastern European "periphery" and the "Moscow center": the initial position and the speed of transformation. Communist parties in the region were faced with two impossibilities: one of escaping the label of alienness, and second, that of not being able to produce charisma out of fear as Stalin had done in the Soviet Union. She then turns to the Hungarian case, showing how the mid-1940s period imprinted upon its generation a "nostalgia of the beginning" in contrast with the Rákosi years. This set the ground for the legitimacy of the post-1953 Nagy government, which basically relied on this generation's hope for wiping the slate clean. She then concludes by contrasting the 1953 moment with the 1956 one. She points out that the former was still one dominated by consensus (the *no*'s hid the conflicting *yes*'s) over the necessity to reject Stalinism as outwardly illegitimate. John Connelly's contribution analyzes the paradox of the German communist regime, which despite not having gone through a Stalinist revolution (to the extent that all the other countries in question here did), it "succeeded" in becoming one of the foremost Stalinist regimes within the Soviet bloc. The paper shows, in contrast with some of the literature on the topic, that the GDR turned to Soviet-style socialism at an early date. Moreover, Connelly also emphasizes and certifies the importance of studying the SED dictatorship in the context of the overall transformations within what became the Soviet bloc. The East German structures of centralized rule can be fully understood only in comparison with the other cases in Eastern Europe. Antoni and Bartłomiej Kaminski propose a different point of view for the interpretation of the imposition of Soviet-style government in Poland. First, they argue for the identification of pre-1945 stages in the process of takeover, namely the Nonaggression Pact in 1939 and the 1941 Teheran conference. Furthermore, they go on to state that from 1939 on a coherent plan of imposing Soviet domination over Poland can be outlined. The two authors notice though the lack of a full-fledged Stalinization of Poland after 1947, which in its turn signals the incomplete transition to socialism of this country. Antoni and Bartłomiej Kaminski stress that this phenomenon would later prove to be an Achilles heel for the entire Soviet bloc. Poland turned into a source of constant crisis that affected the entire region and which ultimately peaked with the Solidarity movement.

Part Three contains both analyses of some aspects of the communization process and historiographical reviews of these issues. János Rainer draws attention to two periods in the study of the Stalinist period in Hungary. The first, during the 1980s, was characterized by weak conceptual employment. The pre-1956 years were used to legitimate Kádár's rule. Evidently after 1989, the memory of 1956 and Stalinism played a key part in Hungary's change of system. Moreover, as Rainer further states, the theory of totalitarianism became the framework of interpretation. This situation gradually changed; presently, new research on social and cultural history is altering the ethical commitment typically attached to the academia in the 1990s. Additionally, János Rainer summarizes some of the most important points of reconsideration on the basis of the inevitable archival "epiphanies" with reference to the Stalinist years in Hungary. Bogdan Iacob's paper similarly adheres to the call for new directions. The author argues for the clarification of the Stalinist model of academia and cultural revolution under circumstances of its application upon the Romanian case. Using the example of the Romanian Academy's "reform," and particularly that of the "historical front," he accentuates the double dichotomy of destruction–reconstruction/change–continuity at the level of the higher education and of the historical-production in the first decade of the communist regime in Romania. The study concludes by pointing to two directions that ultimately intersect, namely, that of institutional and paradigmatic shift. The third contribution, by Ekaterina Nikova, proposes a revision of the long-established tenet of a supposedly more benign communist transformation of Bulgaria. By making use of the avalanche of new materials and sources about the Stalinist period, she stresses "the true meaning of communist political violence." The latter imposed a *modus operandi* that explains the later peculiar features of Bulgarian communism: the preservation of a strong grip upon society, economic adventurism, and grotesque megalomaniac distortions in all spheres of life. Nikova concludes by stating that the people's democracy was a stillborn child and that, despite the leftist equalitarian tradition, the domestic factor in Bulgaria had minimal influence on the unfolding of the events of those early years. In the same vein, Dorin Dobrincu pursues in his article a disenchanted approach of Romania's anticommunist armed resistance. He provides the reader both with a detailed presentation of the historical phenomenon itself and a historiographical record of the topic in the domestic literature. He identifies two periods (1944–7 and 1948 – the early 1960s) differentiated from the standpoint of both the domestic and the international context. In contrast with many of his peers, he questions the existence of a clear political commitment of the resistance leaders. He does however minutely describe the partisanships of some of these groups. One of his main ideas is that the partisans' leaders were mostly people invested with an important symbolic capital in the action areas, but mostly unknown on the country's territory as a whole. By means of comparative history, Dobrincu also dispels the impression of the uniqueness of the phenomenon (apparent in most local scholarly output). He proposes a re-historicization of the topic in a regional context as the only solution which would not breed the same anticommunist myths that often find themselves on the wrong side of the barricades with democratic values.

The last part of the book looks into the role of domestic politics and tradition in the establishment of a communist regime and into the legacy of those years in the later stages of the communist experience in Eastern Europe. In the case of Czechoslovakia, Bradley Abrams marks two distinct stages: that of the Czechoslovak road to socialism (1945–47) and that of "the Czechoslovak road from socialism to Stalinism" (1948–53). The first is reflective of the domestic desires for radical social change and the domestic political actors' emulation of the Soviet Union and/or conformity to the latter's plans. The second is characterized by the turn toward similar developments as in other countries of the region: party recruitment, nationalization, collectivization, purges in the bureaucracy, army and elsewhere, and, finally, show trials. Nevertheless, this notional difference was the origin of the Czechoslovak specificities, throughout the country's history as a Soviet bloc member. The second paper in this section of the volume is Cristian Vasile's analysis of the early history of the Propaganda and Agitation Department in Romania. It focuses upon the role of this institution in the development of a discourse regarding culture, arts, education and in the harassment of the more or less refractory intellectuals and artists. Cristian Vasile discusses the mechanisms by which the guidance of the regime's politics of culture effectively became synonymous with political censorship. Using newly declassified archival materials, he contrasts the dynamics of the Romanian *agitprop* networks with those established in the Soviet Union both before and after Stalin's accession to power. One important aspect of this article is the attention paid to the local institutionalization of propaganda in the country. Additionally, the author does not shy away from raising the alternate question about the readiness of large numbers of Romanian intellectuals in accepting the ideological terms set up by communist cultural policies. Svetozar Stojanovic develops, in his contribution to Part Four, an interesting typology of Stalinisms. His taxonomy relies upon the internal dynamics of Yugoslav communism in the aftermath of the split with the Soviet Union. A culmination of a few elements distinguishes the Yugoslav case from the countries in the Soviet bloc: the pre-communist period (in parliametary opposition, underground, under foreign occupation, and not in power); the anti-fascist and civil war/revolution; and the idealism in relation to the Soviet Union during the immediate post-war period. Subsequently, by 1948, important practical differences with Moscow had already accumulated despite a complete Stalinization of the Yugoslav Communist Party's ideology. After the Tito–Stalin split, Yugoslavia ironically turned more orthodox than the Moscow center. It generated a vicious circle of self-enlarging and self-justifying mass terror that indiscriminately targeted both the uninformed Stalinists and the informed ones. Stojanovic points to three main deviations from the original model, each corresponding to specific periods in the history of the federation and of its relations with the Soviet Union: diffusive Stalinism, anti-Stalinist Stalinism, and Jugo-Stalinism (based upon an-

tifacist patriotism). Dragoş Petrescu closes the last part of the volume
with an reconsideration of Gheorghiu Dej's internationalism and com-
mittment to Soviet objectives. By means of examining the most representative moments of the Romanian Workers' Party history from 1948
to 1965, with the related identity-discourses promoted at the level of
its leadership, Petrescu evaluates the phenomenon of building a new
political community in communist Romania. After a period of random
terror conducted by the state against the majority of its citizens, by
1964, this phenomenon turned into an all-encompassing nation-building process. The contribution emphasizes not only the similarities in
the emplotment of the "Nation" between Gheorghiu-Dej and his successor, Nicolae Ceauşescu, but it also examines the equivalence in the
former's political discourse employe during the inter-war period.

The editor would like to express his gratitude to H.R. Patapievici,
President of the Romanian Cultural Institute, and to Mircea Mihăieş,
the Institute's Vice-President, who have enthusiastically embraced the
idea of a series of conferences on seminal political-intellectual issues,
in Washington, D.C., with the purpose of strengthening and developing the already existent connections between the Romanian scholarly
community and American academia. The contributors are also grateful to Ivo Banac (who presented a reconsideration of some of the main
points developed in his seminal book *With Stalin against Tito: Cominformist splits in Yugoslav Communism*, Cornell University Press, 1988),
Claudiu Secaşiu (who presented a paper on "The Destruction of the
Democratic Anti-Communist Opposition in Romania and the Trials
of 1947–1948") and Virgil Ţârău (who presented a paper on "The
November 1946 Elections and the Consolidation of the Communist
Power in Romania".) Charles Gati, Charles King, and Christian Ostermann were superb discussants for the conference panels, offering
excellent insights and enriching suggestions. Special thanks to Bogdan
Cristian Iacob, a graduate student at the History Department of the
Central European University and project coordinator on behalf of the
Romanian Cultural Institute. He decisively contributed to the success-
ful organization of the conference and the subsequent editorial efforts
in putting together this volume.

Part One

STALINISM REVISITED
AND
THE TAKEOVER MODEL

KEN JOWITT

Stalinist Revolutionary Breakthroughs in Eastern Europe

According to Franz Schurman, a revolutionary breakthrough makes a return to the *status quo ante* impossible. Otto Kirchheimer, in his seminal article "Confining Conditions and Revolutionary Breakthroughs," adds substantially to Schurman's definition noting that a revolutionary breakthrough may occur with the "old data" remaining, "though absorbed in a new context and thereby deprived of its confining nature." I take his point to be that while all social change is partial, some social change is decisive in radically revising who authoritatively defines the institutions of power at all levels of society. Successful revolutions insure that the "old data," e.g., former elites, institutions, and ideologies, when not liquidated, are "privatized" by the "new data."

The immediate question, then, is what did Stalinist revolutionaries in Eastern Europe face in 1948? What did the "old data," the confining conditions and the status quo consist of? And, of course, what were the character defining features and consequences of revolutionary breakthroughs in that area?

One must begin by respecting the substantial differences between the Austro-Hungarian and Ottoman Empires. One could spend countless hours arguing over these differences, or, more likely, invidiously juxtaposing the positive features of the former with the negative features of the latter, or one could simplify by comparing a *Rechtstaat* with a Patrimonial state. I won't do even that, because for my purposes the similarities between the two empires (and the Russian) are more important than their differences. All three empires subordinated and minimized individual identity in favor of collective identities—voluntary association to absolute hierarchies, and rejected political integration based on citizenship roles to political domination based on elite status.

More specifically, the region possessed a certain *gestalt*, a composite of the following elements, which is not to say that each country possessed each feature, or in equal measure. There were monarchies, often imported in genuinely neocolonial fashion; armies, in most cases ineffectively controlled by civilian governments; governments undisciplined by an independent public for the simple reason that none existed, or if they did were disorganized to the point of being easily manipulated, or fragile enough to be ignored.

There were ethnic groups, categoric in nature. Ethnicity was whole, not a role, an essence, not a dimension of one's identity. Ethnic groups occupied particular niches—some privileged, others pariahs—in an invidious but complementary division of ethnic labor. And of course, there were peasants, in Marx's vivid imagery, "sacks of potatoes," subject to taxation, conscription, coercion, and contempt laced with a touch of elite fear. These masses of peasants made up the quasi-national social ghetto in each country; what appeared to be an almost non-biodegradable bit of "old data" confronting any serious agent of social change.

Finally, the political elites of the area usually borrowed status from outside their own culture revealing not only their sense of cultural inferiority but also their effective disconnection from any source of organized indigenous socio-political power. "Limbo" political elites, contemptuous of their own, and held in contempt by those they aped; and consequently, unable and unlikely to generate enough power to successfully oppose external opponents.

This then was the *gestalt*, the "old data" confronting Stalinist revolutionaries in Eastern Europe. To this general pattern, and to all the genuinely diverse, singular configurations that deviated from this Eastern European *gestalt*, Stalin responded in a unique manner. He authorized and authored a set of geographically contiguous replica regimes throughout the area, regimes that duplicated the features of his own Soviet regime. Stalin and his Eastern European loyal retainers created "castle" regimes in each country, regimes based on "distance," "difference," and "dominance."

Stalinist regimes in Eastern Europe created political "moats" between themselves and their societies. They distanced themselves by employing political violence of a distinct type, Terror. Its point was to minimize contact with the "old data," thereby reducing the likelihood of the "old data" contaminating or infiltrating the "castle," itself, the guarded space within which novel revolutionary beliefs, institutions, and practices were to be articulated, initiated, and ultimately generalized.

The emphasis on difference complemented the one on distance and served much the same purpose, i.e., to prevent backsliding and identification with the "old data," whether they were family ties, religious, cultural, or even to some extent languages. The point was not only to emphasize the differences between the "new data" and the "old" but also to concretize those differences. Learn Russian, even marry a Russian, identify with the Soviet Union not your own "bourgeois-peasant-aristocratic" country, and of course enjoy the privileges of being a dominant "castle" elite. After all, castles are not just fortresses; they are, as one eminent student of Norman history notes, "residential fortresses," within which members of the New Class lived well (unless or until they were liquidated).

Dominance was ideally achieved by negating any and all real or potential points of political opposition. Revolutionary breakthroughs are distinct, precisely because their perspective is social not narrowly political, because they destroy institutions, not only elites, and because they address (often in a paranoid fashion) the potential for, not just the reality of, opposition. The agent of these breakthroughs was the secret police whose goal was fear and obedience, not persuasion and legitimacy. As for the social scope and ruthless quality of Stalinist revolutionary breakthroughs one has only to look at collectivization.

Within the bloc the exception to the Stalinist *gestalt* was Poland. Undoubtedly, the social, cultural, and perhaps most importantly, psychological origins of Poland's uniqueness were in the Western Territories. If Yalta "made" Eastern Europe Stalinist, Tehran "unmade" it. At the end of World War II, over five million young, unmarried, tough Polish males moved, aptly enough, west, into the former German territories. In those frontier environs not yet subject to the neo-traditional rule of either the Communist Party or the Roman Catholic Church, a new "protestant" culture of rugged individualism was nurtured and matured, one that would be the core of Solidarity.

In addition to this unique development, the peasantry was not effectively collectivized, nor was the Roman Catholic Church "deprived of its confining nature." Consequently, the breakthrough in Poland was indecisive. Poland was a "Bukharinite" experiment that failed.

Politically, the Stalinist revolutionary "castle" definition and projection of power accomplished the following: the elimination of monarchies, the subversion of the military's professional integrity and national purpose, the destruction of all but heterocephalous and heteronomous political parties, and, with one exception, the negation of an autonomous, let alone independent, political role for Roman Catholic Churches.

Socially, collectivization (not industrialization) stands out as the signature feature of Stalinist revolutionary breakthroughs. Following the Soviet example, Stalinist regimes in Eastern Europe murderously "mashed" their peasant sacks of potatoes thereby making impossible a return to the *status quo ante*. Peasants didn't disappear; peasant society did! With collectivization Stalinist revolutionaries had broken through what other change oriented regimes had been broken by; namely, the "old data" peasant society and its accompanying institutions, elites, beliefs, and practices.

Ethnicity's place in these countries was primarily affected by World War II, though Stalin manipulated ethnicity in a number of countries to serve his imperial design of maximizing allegiance to, and dependence on, Moscow Centre.

Institutionally, the feature of Stalinist breakthroughs with the longest half-life was the elimination of the quasi-public domains in these countries and the neutering of the state as the official locus of political life. The Party destroyed, absorbed, and substituted for both the state and public: cadres ruled, subjects obeyed, citizens disappeared.

Internationally, the tendency of East European elites to look externally for sources of prestige, identity, and power continued in the formal sense but underwent a radical shift in political geography from West to East. The Soviet ideological reference was reinforced by a Soviet presence in the armies, parties, economies, and even families of East European regimes.

The most peculiar feature of Stalinist rule was its unintentional reinforcement of pre-communist political culture. Stalinist rule destroyed the institutional, ideological, and elite "old data," but its "castle format" and *modus operandi* insured that the culture it meant to destroy was reinforced. In crucial respects Stalinist regimes were quite familiar to East European societies and the latter reacted to them in a predictable way.

The "distance," "difference," and "dominance" so sought after by Stalinist regimes essentially, if not practically, absolutized the suspicion, opposition, and disconnection between Party and society. I say Party because the state, as already noted, lacked both independent status and power, making the idea of State Socialism nonsense. In effect, Stalinist regimes created "ghetto" societies, populations that feared and avoided "trouble," i.e., anything political. The social and personal device used to deflect regime attention, reduce regime suspicion, and shield one's own inner thoughts was dissimulation. Dissimulation permitted a master–slave relation of dominance and obedience to operate practically on a routine basis.

The Party's negative evaluation of existing society combined with the built-in ambivalence typical of a Leninist party towards its ideal constituency, the working class, along with the Soviet demand for near uniformity and loyalty meant that East European Stalinist parties were more an extension of the Soviet polity towards which they were deferential than their own societies which they treated in a decidedly uncivil manner.

The Stalinist unintentional reinforcement of the "old data" affected the economic realm as well. The Stalinist emphasis on "storming" was antithetical to methodical rational economic production and acquisition, and ran counter to an understanding of time as an impersonal continuous measure and discipline. Instead, "storming" was consistent with a peasant mode of economic activity, and a corresponding sense of time as urgent harvesting activity followed by *kavehane*-like passivity.

Stalinist breakthrough regimes were obviously not the only experience Eastern Europe had with Leninist rule. Khrushchev and Brezhnev brought substantial development changes to their regimes' internal organization, to regime-society relations, societies that themselves had changed in major ways.

Khrushchev's regime and its counterparts in Eastern Europe had two notable features. The Khrushchevian ideological conclusion that class war was no longer the defining feature of regime-society relations was momentous. In the long run it marked (as Mao correctly noted) the beginning of the end of Leninist rule in the Soviet Union and Eastern Europe, and its neotraditional routinization. Politically, and in line with his ideological innovation, Khrushchev did succeed in ending the Terror and making the secret police a part of, rather than apart from, the Party. But he failed in his political-ideological attempt to square the cadre–citizen circle with his notions of party and state of the whole people. The emergence during the Khrushchevian era of political organizations purportedly representing a newly participant society and *party aktiv* were, to borrow a phrase from the Irish singer, Mary Black, "looked at closely, counterfeit mostly." Khrushchev's changes were substantial, not essential. Predictably, the cadres opposed any dilution of their power and Brezhnev's coup was a testimony to their success. Parties throughout the region maintained their monopoly of political rule, definition, and space.

With all predictable and significant variations a new political *gestalt*, Brezhnevian neotraditionalism, emerged in Eastern Europe consisting of the ideological rejection of class war, the subordination and integration of the secret police within the Party, and the success of the Party cadres in maintaining their superior status. In the 1980s all East European regimes were debilitated by the absence of any heroic task to justify and discipline their claim to political superiority. The consequence was institutional corruption marked by varying degrees of nepotism and the disaggregation of parties into coteries of "big men" leaders and "small boy" clients; the most remarkable contemporary instance of formerly charismatic parties undergoing neotraditional routinization. Regime "parasites" treated their economies and Western aid as "booty," and created "scavenger" societies whose major feature was personalism, egos largely unrestrained by external discipline, conscience, or transcendent beliefs. During the last two decades of Leninist rule, communist parties exercised a "lazy monopoly" over amoral societies.

Consequently, with the region wide collapse of Leninist regimes, due largely to Gorbachev's radical attempt to relativize the Party's and the Soviet Union's political status, I could not find any political, any socio-political, any psychological, and certainly not any ethical identity at the mass level to initiate, organize, lead, let alone institutionalize anything like a liberal market democracy. I fully expected Eastern Europe to be the site of wildcat ethnic violence, demagogues, social suspicion, and counterfeit democratic states weakly connected to fragmented societies, mimicking and depending on the West.

I was wrong. Fortunately, for my own ego's sake, for the right reason. A number of critics were quick and correct to point out that the "colonels, cardinals, and demagogues" I expected to politically pre-dominate in the post-communist period failed in good measure to ap-pear. However, the question is why? In the concluding pages of my article, "The Leninist Legacy," I pointedly asked whether in light of the cumulative negative Leninist legacies—Stalinist, Khrushchevian, and Brezhnevian—there was any "...point of leverage, critical mass of civic effort—political, cultural and economic—that can add its weight to civic forces in Eastern Europe and check the increasing frustration, desperation, fragmentation and anger that will lead to country and re-gion wide violence?" My answer was yes, Western Europe! If Western Europe were to "adopt" Eastern Europe the negative outcome I fore-saw could be avoided. And that is precisely what happened. The EU "adopted" Eastern Europe.

In his book, *Neoiogabia*, the Romanian social theorist Dobroge-anu-Gherea somewhat whimsically suggested that the best thing that could happen to Romania would to become a French province. Well, with admission to the EU ("France") "Romania" (Eastern Europe) did just that! Still, one should ask how decisive the "Western" civic breakthrough has been? The current absence of an anti-Western inter-national ideology centered in a powerful country that appeals to and resonates with the ethnic, social, cultural, religious, and psychologi-cal realities of the eastern part of Europe makes it impossible to say. Should a novel, unexpected anti-Fukuyama like development occur in the future, the best way to prevent Eastern Europe from rejecting its newly acquired Western identity is to prevent it now from becoming an EU ghetto.

VLADIMIR TISMANEANU

Diabolical Pedagogy and the (Il)logic of Stalinism in Eastern Europe

"I am too busy defending innocents claiming their innocence
to waste my time with guilty individuals claiming their guilt."
(Paul Eluard refusing to sign a petition against the hanging
of Czech surrealist poet Zavis Kalandra)

"Lucreţiu Pătrăşcanu died as a soldier serving his political
ideals which he pursued through darkness, underground,
and palaces, tenaciously, fiercely and fanatically."
(Petre Pandrea)

In order to understand the dynamics of the Stalinist experiment in
Eastern Europe, one needs to take into account the prevailing role of
direct Soviet intervention and intimidation.[1] Local communist formations were pursuing the Stalinist model of systematic destruction of
non-communist parties, the disintegration of civil society, and the mo-
nopolistic occupation of the public space through state-controlled ideological rituals and coercive institutions.[2] The overall goal was to build
a passive consensus based on unlimited commitment to the ideocratic
political program of the ruling elite. The true content of the political
regime is described by the "cult of personality" system. The personal-
ization of political power, its concentration in the hands of a demigod,

---

[1] For one of the most illuminating and still valid interpretations of the dynam-
ics of the Soviet bloc, see Zbigniew Brzeziński, *The Soviet Bloc: Unity and
Conflict*, revised and enlarged edition (Cambridge, MA: Harvard University
Press, 1967).

[2] For a detailed discussion, see Vladimir Tismaneanu, *The Crisis of Marxist Ideology in Eastern Europe: The Poverty of Utopia* (London/New York: Routledge,
1988).

led to forcible religious adoration and the masochistic humiliation of its *subjects*. The symbolic vehicle for this moral and political regimentation was the Stalinist definition of internationalism as unbounded allegiance to the USSR (the "touchstone theory"). To keep strict control over all mechanisms that guaranteed social reproduction and preserved the matrix of domination in such a system, the party had to play the central role. Based on my own research in the Romanian Communist Party's archives, it appears that no segment of the body social, economic, cultural, as well as no repressive institution escaped continuous and systematic party intervention. Even during the climatic years of the Terror (1948–53), the secret police served as the party's obedient instrument and not the other way around. Ideological purity and revolutionary vigilance were imposed as main political imperatives. Political police, cast in the Soviet mold and controlled by Soviet advisers, took care to fulfill the ideological *desiderata*. The political content of that ideology in its radical incarnation (the first five years) was sheer terror and permanent propaganda warfare waged within a personalized dictatorship embodied by local "little Stalins."

The main weakness of this system was its chronic deficit of legitimacy. Under mature Stalinism, both in the Soviet Union and in Eastern Europe, autocratic despotism managed to ruin the functioning of the party as an autonomous institution—its potential for "charismatic impersonalism" intrinsic to Leninism as an organizational model. This last phenomenon explains the neotraditionalist features of Stalinism. If one is to follow Ken Jowitt's argument, the mutation of the definition of revolutionary heroism (initially belonging to the Party, but now the prerogative of one)—cancelled the fundamental characteristic of novelty to Leninism as an ideo-political form of aggregation.[3] In this monolithic structure dominated by the revolutionary phalanx, the plans to reshape man, nature, and society were frantically pursued. Stalinism as a political religion overturned traditional morality: good and evil, vice and virtue, were drastically revalued.[4] The goal was to create a sys-

---

[3] Kenneth Jowitt, *New World Disorder: The Leninist Extinction* (Berkeley/Los Angeles: University of California Press, 1992), pp. 1–12.

[4] For political religions, see Emilio Gentile, *Politics as Religion* (Princeton: Princeton University Press, 2006); Michael Burleigh, *Sacred Causes: The Clash of Religion and Politics, from the Great War to the War on Terror* (New York: HarperCollins, 2007). An interesting debate on the relationship between morality

tem that managed to unify victim and torturer, to abolish the traditional moral taboos and set a different code, with different prescriptions and prohibitions. The dramaturgy of show trials with their "infernal pedagogy"[5] was a crucial component of this system based on universal fear, duplicity, and suspicion.

The "oceanic feeling," the ecstasy of solidarity, the desire to dissolve one's autonomy into the mystical transindividual entity of the Party, aptly described by Arthur Koestler, was the emotional ground for a chiliastic type of revolutionary commitment.[6] In his conversations with Czeslaw Milosz, Aleksander Wat formulated a memorable evaluation of the phenomenon:

> communism is the enemy of interiorization, of the inner man [...] But today we know what exteriorization leads to: the killing of the inner man, and that is the essence of Stalinism. The essence of Stalinism is the poisoning of the inner man so that it becomes shrunken the way headhunters shrink heads—those shriveled little heads—and then disappears entirely [...] The inner man must be killed for the communist Decalogue to be lodged in the soul.[7]

Community, defined in terms of class, was the antipode of the execrated egotism of the bourgeois individual. The self had to be denied in order to achieve real *fraternité*. Generations of Marxist intellectuals hastened to annihilate their dignity in this apocalyptical race for ultimate certi-

---

and Marxism-Leninism was put forward by Steven Lukes, "On the Moral Blindness of Communism," *Human Rights Review*, January–March (2001): 113–24; Vladimir Tismaneanu, "Communism and the Human Condition: Reflections on the *Black Book of Communism*," pp. 125–34; John Rodden, "'It Should have Been Written Here': Germany and *The Black Book*," pp. 144–64.

[5] This term adapted from Annie Kriegel, *Les grands procès dans les pays communistes: La pédagogie infernale* [The great trials of the communist countries: the infernal pedagogy] (Paris: Guillmard, 1972).

[6] Norman Cohn, *The Pursuit of the Millennium: Revolutionary Messianism in Medieval and Reformation Europe and its Bearing on Modern Totalitarian Movements* (New York: Harper and Row, 1961); Arthur Koestler, *The Invisible Writing* (London: Macmillan, 1969).

[7] Aleksander Wat, *My Century: The Odyssey of a Polish Intellectual* (Berkeley: University of California Press, 1988).

tudes.[8] The whole heritage of Western skeptical rationalism was easily dismissed in the name of the revealed light emanating from the Kremlin. The Age of Reason was thus to culminate in the frozen universe of rational terror. The subject, the human being—totally ignored at the level of the philosophical discourse—was eventually abolished as a physical entity in the vortex of the "great purges." Jochen Hellbeck, correctly remarked, in his analysis of autobiographies during Stalinism, that "an individual living under the Bolshevik system could not conceivably formulate a notion of himself independently of the program promulgated by the Bolshevik state. An individual and the political system in which he lived cannot be viewed as two separate entities."[9] These images were more than metaphors, since metaphor suggests an ineffable appearance of reality, whereas what happened under Stalin was awfully visible and immediate. It can hardly be denied that Stalinism is the antithesis of the Western humanist legacy and should be described as such.

At the same time, François Furet and Pierre Hassner are right to emphasize the nature of Leninism/Stalinism as a pathology of universalism, a derailed (*devoyé*) offspring of the Enlightenment. Naturally, it would be preposterous to restrict ourselves to mere ethical condemnation. But it would not be, by any means, commendable to gloss over the moral implications of Stalinism, or, echoing a famous essay by the young Georg Lukács, the dilemmas of "Bolshevism as a moral problem." It is important, when pondering the fate of Marxism in the 20th century, to grasp the split of personalities, the clash between lofty ideals and palpable practices, and the methods of the Stalinist terrorist pedagogy in its endeavor to produce a new type of human being whose loyalties and beliefs would be decreed by the party. Revenge of history on its worshipers—thus could the terrorist psychosis of the Stalinist massacres be depicted. To quote Alvin W. Goulder's perceptive interpretation: "The central strategy of the Marxist project, its concern with seeking a remedy to *unnecessary* suffering, was thus in the end susceptible to a misuse that betrayed its own highest avowals. The root of the

---

[8] See François Furet, *Le Passé d'une Illusion: Essai sur l'idée communiste au XXe siècle* (Paris: Robert Laffont/Calmann Lévy, 1995).

[9] Jochen Hellbeck, "Fashioning the Stalinist Soul: The Diary of Stepan Podlubnyi, 1931–1938," *Janrbücher für Geschichte Osteuropas*, No. 2 (1997); and "Working, struggling, becoming: Stalin-era autobiographical texts," *Russian Review*, No. 60 (July 2001), pp. 340–59.

trouble was that this conception of its own project redefined pity... The human condition was rejected on behalf of the historical condition."[10] As Koestler once pointed out (in his 1938 letter of resignation from the exiled German Communist Writers' Union), for Lenin it was not enough to smash his enemy—he wanted to make him look contemptible. Rajk, Pătrăşcanu, Slansky, Ana Pauker, Vladimir Clementis, Kostov, Geminder, London, Rudolf Margolius, etc.—all of them had to be portrayed as despicable scoundrels and scurrilous vermin. Yesterday heroes were today's scum.[11] Especially after 1951, the Stalinist anti-Western, anti-intellectual, and anti-Titoist obsessions merged with an increasingly rabid anti-Semitism:

> Stalin feared that other peace champ countries would follow the independent Yugoslav model and break away from the influential sphere of the Soviet Union. He instigated the terror of political trials to uncover "enemies" within each Communist Party in order to discourage dissent. Victims were sought out and accused of connection with Tito's opposition attitudes and treachery. In later cases, the Soviets turned to Zionism and its supposed link with Western imperialism as the cause of the Communist betrayal. The show trial was a propaganda arm of political terror. Its aim was to personalize an abstract political enemy, to place it in the dock in flesh and blood and, with the aid of a perverted system of justice, to transform abstract political-ideological differences into easily intelligible common crimes. It both incited the masses against the evil embodied by defendants and frightened them away from supporting any potential opposition.[12]

The magic impact of power in classical Stalinism would have been unthinkable in the absence of ideology. They breed and feed upon each other; power derives its mesmerizing force from the seductive potential of ideology. Man is proclaimed omnipotent, and ideology supervises the identification of abstract man with concrete power. Veneration of power is rooted in contempt for traditional values, including those as-

---

[10] Alvin W. Gouldner, *Against Fragmentation: The Origins of Marxism and the Sociology of intellectuals* (New York: Oxford University Press, 1985), pp. 260–1.

[11] See the two volumes of Koestler memoirs: Arthur Koestler, *Arrow in the Blue* (London: Macmillan Collins, 1952) and *The Invisible Writing: the Second Volume of an Autobiography: 1932–40* (New York: Macmillan, 1954).

[12] Ivan Margolius, *Reflections of Prague: Journeys through the 20th Century* (London: Wiley, 2006), p. 153.

sociated with the survival of reason. It is important therefore to repress the temptation of critical thought, since reason is the enemy of total regimentation. In one of his late aphorisms, Max Horkheimer hinted at the philosophical revolution provoked by Marxism. Defending the dignity of the individual subject becomes a seditious undertaking, a challenge to the prevailing myth of homogeneity: "however socially conditioned the individual's thinking may be, however necessarily it may relate to social questions, to political action, it remains the thought of the individual which is not just the effect of collective processes but can also take them as its object."[13] Political shamanism, practiced by alleged adversaries of any mysticism, thwarts the attempts to resist the continual assault on the mind. Marxism-Leninism, which was the code name for the ideology of the *nomenklatura*, aimed to dominate both the public and the private spheres of social life. Man, both as an individual and as a *citoyen*, had to be massified. The cult of violence and the sacralization of the infallible "party line" created totally submissive individuals for whom any crime ordered by the upper echelons was justified in the name of the "glowing tomorrows." As in the case of the ideologically-driven Eichmann, Stalin's "willing executioners" acted on the base of what Hannah Arendt diagnosed as "thoughtlessness."[14]

A climate of fear is needed to preserve monolithism. To cement this frail cohesion, the Stalinist "warfare personality" contrived the diabolical figure of the traitor:

> the characteristically paranoid perception of the world as an arena of deadly hostilities being conducted conspiratorially by an insidious and implacable enemy against the self finds highly systematized expression in terms of political and ideological symbols that are widely understood and accepted in the given social milieu. Through a special and radical form of displacement of private affects upon public objects, this world-image is politicized. In the resulting vision of reality, both attacker and intended victim are projected on the scale of large human collectivities.[15]

---

[13] Max Horkheimer, *Dawn and Decline* (New York: Seabury Press, 1978), p. 239.

[14] Hannah Arendt, *The Life of the Mind* (New York: Harcourt Brace Jovanovich, 1978), p. 45.

[15] Robert C. Tucker, *The Soviet Political Mind. Stalinism and Post-Stalin Change* (revised edition), (New York: W.W. Norton & Company Inc., 1971), pp. 40–1.

In the fullest Girardian sense, scapegoating[16] fed the utopia of a society freed of exploitation, antagonism and the imperative of necessity. The origin of this exclusionary logic is of course Lenin's combatant, intransigent Manichaeism (*kto kogo*).[17] Who are the enemies? Where do they come from? What are their purposes? Providing answers to these questions was the main function of the show trials. Maintaining vigilance and preserving the psychology of universal anguish, those were the tasks Stalin had assigned to the masterminds of successive purges. No fissures are admitted in the Bolshevik shield, no doubt can arise that does not conceal some mischievous stratagems aimed at undermining the system. Time and again the refrain was harangued by restless sycophants: we are surrounded by sworn enemies, we are invincible only inasmuch as we are united. Expressing dissenting views necessarily means weakening the revolutionary avant-garde. Breaking ranks is considered a mortal sin, and suspiciousness is the ultimate revolutionary virtue. When acquiescence is the golden rule, it takes great moral courage to assume the status of the rebel. In the homogenous space of totalitarian domination, opposition amounts to crime and opponents are treated as mere criminals. They incarnate the figure of difference and are therefore seen as outcasts. Ostracization leads ultimately to the mental emancipation, the autonomy of the mind acquired by Solzhenitsyn's *zeks*, the population of Stalin's *gulag*. The barbed wire is thus the symbol of a new kind of boundary: that between absolute victims and relative accomplices of evil. The whole tragedy of communism lies in the core tenets that condition its political practice: the vision of a superior elite whose utopian goals sanctify the most barbaric methods; the denial of the right to life of those who are defined as "degenerate parasites and predators," the deliberate de-humanization of the victims, and what Alain Besançon correctly identifies as the ideological perversity at the heart of totalitarian thinking: the falsification of the idea of good (*la falsification du bien*).

---

[16] James G. Williams ed., *The Girard Reader* (New York: Crossroad Publishing, 1996), pp. 97–141. The same type of mechanism is present in the process of imagining the categories of "saboteur" and "kulak" after 1929 in the USSR.

[17] For the significance of this question in the Leninist mindset, see Martin Amis, *Koba the Dread: Laughter and the Twenty Million* (New York: Hyperion, 2002); Robert Service, *Lenin: A Biography* (Cambridge, MA: Harvard University Press, 2000).

The image of man as a mechanism put forward by French *philoso-phes* found its strange echo in this all-pervading technology of social-ly-oriented murder. That was the acme of radical utopianism, when nothing could deter or resist the perpetual motion of foul play. Marxist eschatology was substituted through Stalinist demonology. Igal Halfin eminently presents the process by which, through cyclical purges in the Soviet Union (one can consider their embryonic stage as 1920–21), Marxist eschatology morphed into a demonology that reached its discursive, hyper-transformist, and criminal maturity with the Sec-ond Socialist Transformation triggered by the *pyatiletka* unleashed to build socialism in one country.[18] The public discourse was saturated with frightening images of deviators, heretics, spies, agents, and other scoundrels. A phenomenology of treason was devised to justify carnage and there was no paucity of intellectuals to support this morbid sce-nario. A lingering sentiment that there was after all something moral in the Bolshevik utopianism, plus the exploitation of anti-Fascist emo-tions, led to a persistent failure to acknowledge the basic fact that from its inception, Sovietism was a criminal system.

In Stalin's mind the purges were means of political consolidation and authority-building, a springboard for newcomers and time-servers. They were bound to secure the human basis for effective control over society. In one of his most poignant essays published before World War II in *Partisan Review*, Phillip Rahv put forward a thorough interpreta-tion of the mechanism that led to the "great terror":

> these are trials of the mind and of the human spirit... In the Soviet Union, for the first time in history, the individual has been deprived of every conceivable means of resistance. Authority is monolithic: prop-erty and politics are one. Under circumstances it becomes impossible to defy the organization; to set one's will against it. One cannot escape it: not only does it absorb the whole of life it also seeks to model the shapes of death.[19]

---

[18] Igal Halfin, *From Darkness to Light: Class, Consciousness, and Salvation in Revolutionary Russia* (Pittsburgh: University of Pittsburgh Press, 2000); *Ter-ror in my soul: Communist Autobiographies on Trial* (Cambridge, MA: Harvard University Press, 2003); *Intimate Enemies: Demonizing the Bolshevik Opposi-tion, 1918–1928* (Pittsburgh: University of Pittsburgh Press, 2007).

[19] Philip Rahv, *Essays on Literature and Politics, 1932–1972* (Boston: Houghton Mifflin, 1978), p. 288.

Without the purges the system would have looked radically different. In other words, both victims and beneficiaries of the murderous mechanism were lumped together by this sacrificial ritual. For some of the Bolshevik militants liquidated or deported during the great purge, the terrorist ordeal amounted to *necessary* self-deprecation and self-abasement. Moreover, it was an opportunity to attain the long-expected absolutism for those moments of "derailment" when they had dared to oppose Stalin. Zbgniew Brzeziński systematically listed long ago the main objectives of the purge: "the cleansing of the party, the restoration of its vigor and monolithic unity, the elimination of enemies, and the establishment of the correctness of its line and the primacy of the leadership."[20] An entire phenomenology came about in the process of massacring society and it was regrettably generously reproduced by too many intellectuals, who had accepted such morbid practices. Nostalgia, or the hope for elusive crumbs of morality within the communist utopia, combined with a Machiavellian exploitation of anti-fascist sentiment, led to numerous intellectuals' resilient failure to come to terms, or acknowledge, the criminal nature of the soviet experiment.

The problem with Leninism (as evinced in 1918 by Karl Kautsky and Rosa Luxemburg) was the sanctification of ultimate ends, and thus the creation of an amoral universe in which the most terrible crimes could be justified in the name of the radiant future. In practice, the elimination of politics seemed a logical terminus, for the Party was the embodiment of an extremist collective will.[21] This fixation on ends and the readiness to use the most atrocious means to attain them is a feature of many ideological utopias, but in the Leninist experience it reached grotesquely tragic limits. No less important, the appeals of communism were linked to the extraordinary power of its ideology (and the core myth of the Party as carrier of Reason in History). No other revolutionary movement has been as successful as Leninism in turning the gnostic creed into a self-hypnotizing weapon. Leninist militants worldwide believed in the myth of the Party with an ardor comparable only to the illuminates of religious millennial sects. It is impor-

---

[20] Zbigniew Brzeziński, "The Pattern of Political Purges," *Annals of the American Academy of Political and Social Science*, Vol. 317, The Satellites in Eastern Europe (May, 1958): 79–87.

[21] A.J. Polan, *Lenin and the End of Politics* (Berkeley: University of California, 1984).

tant to insist on both the ideological and institutional foundations of
Leninism when we try to fathom the mystery of Leninism's endurance
in the twentieth century. The myth of the Party as the repository of historical wisdom and rationality is the key to grasping the dynamics and
finally the decay and extinction of Leninism.[22] The key of the latter
phenomenon lies in the ideo-political complex of the Party as *locus* of
historical reason and knowledge. Leninism, in its various phases, was
what Ken Jowitt coined as a "catholic moment" in history, when "a
universal 'word' becomes institutional 'flesh,' an authoritatively standardized and centered institutional format dominates a highly diverse
set of cultures." The Althusserian interpretation remains valid only if
one performs a phraseological inversion: Leninism was a new type of
praxis of philosophy. The explanation of its longevity in the 20th century can therefore be found in "the promise of the Great October Revolution [...] of a Soviet Union as socialist hierophany."[23]

The biographies of the ideological elites in Soviet-type regimes
were usually colorless and lacked any moment of real distinction.
Speaking about Eastern Europe, one would notice that the ideological watchdogs were recruited from the Muscovite factions of the ruling
parties. In Hungary, József Révai, who had once been one of Lukács's
most promising disciples, became the scourge of intellectual life. Révai
was a member of the Hungarian delegation to various Cominform
meetings and enthusiastically implemented the Zhdanovist strategy. In
Romania, the tandem Iosif Chişinevschi/Leonte Răutu forced the national culture into a mortal impasse. Similar denial of genuine national
traditions and an apocryphal sense of internationalism were promoted
by ideological bureaucracies in Czechoslovakia (Vilem Kopecky, Jiri
Hendrich)[24] and East Germany (Gerhart Eisner, Albert Norden, Kurt

---

[22] Jowitt, *op. cit,* pp. 249–83.

[23] Jowitt, *op. cit,* pp. 250–62.

[24] For a detailed description of the position of "party intellectuals" within the
general Czechoslovak debates over national identity in the post-1945 period,
under circumstances of a widespread perception among the elites of the interwar republic as a compromised state project, see Bradley F. Abrams, *The
Struggle for the Soul of the Nation: Czech Culture and the Rise of Communism*
(Lanham, MD: Rowman & Littlefield, 2004).

Hager).[25] All devices were convenient when it came to uprooting the vicious deviationist temptations. "Bourgeois nationalism" was fused with "rootless cosmopolitanism" in the diabolical figure of the malignant enemy. In the meantime, socialist nationalism was thriving. The members of the ideological army were willingly officiating the rites of the cult. Deprived of their own personality, they were glad to identify with and invest in Stalin's superpersonality. After the terrorist dissolution of the ego it was normal for the *apparatchiks* to project themselves into Stalin's myth as an institutionalized superego.

The Cominform emerged in September 1947 as the first attempt to institutionalize the *satellitization* of Eastern Europe, and it represented an initiative to contain and annihilate the centrifugal trends within world communism (the "domesticist" temptation and the search for a "national path to socialism" championed by militants as different as Gottwald, Gomulka, or Pătrăşcanu). It laid the foundation for future frameworks of supra-governmental domination and ideological hegemony from the part of the CPSU. Paradoxically, the Cominform, brought about the first instance of dissent and revisionism from a "party-state" (the Titoist "heresy"). In Tito's case there was a significant level of ambivalence: he enthusiastically supported Stalin's new orientation (Zhdanov's "two camp theory"), but thought the moment was propitious for furthering his own hegemonic agenda in Southeastern Europe (the Balkans). One could call such a "syndrome" a strategy of *parallel hegemonism*. The irony of the situation was that the break between the two leaders happened at a time when Soviet and Yugoslav visions over class struggle at the world level were mirror images of each other. In 1947–48, Tito underestimated the level of total monopoly of power achieved by the Kremlin tyrant and he fancied himself as the beneficiary of certain leverage in regional decision-making. Ivo Banac excellently diagnosed the paradox: "the dramatic denoument of 1948 was directly connected with Stalin's fears that Yugoslavia began to take on a role of regional communist center and the inherent potential provocations against the West that such position entailed."[26] Indeed,

---

[25] Catherine Epstein, *The Last Revolutionaries: German Communists and their Century* (Cambridge, MA: Harvard University Press, 2003).

[26] Ivo Banac, *With Stalin against Tito: Cominformist Splits in Yugoslav Communism* (Ithaca: Cornell University Press, 1988), p. 29.

the leader of the League of Communists in Yugoslavia (until 1952 the Yugoslav Communist Party) carried along with his plans of creating a communist Danubian confederation (which was to incorporate Yugoslavia, Bulgaria, and Romania)[27] while simultaneously persevering in the assimilation of the Albanian Communist Party (which in 1948 became the Albanian party of Labor).

The conflict with Yugoslavia and Tito's excommunication from the Cominform in June 1948 gave the signal for the beginning of dramatic purges within Eastern European communist parties. It also indicated that Moscow's hegemony could not completely suppress domestic tendencies even within the most pro-Soviet communist factions. In Stalin's view, it was a particularly dangerous time, when the imperialists had decided to intensify their aggressive actions against the budding "people's democracies" and the threat of a new world war was looming large, no country or leader should be allowed to engage in national communist experiments. Those identified as nationalists could be charged with the most fantastic sins. After all, the sole principle of legitimation for the ruling communist parties in the Soviet bloc was their unreserved attachment to the Soviet Union, their readiness to carry out unflinchingly all of Stalin's directives. The harshness of Stalin's reaction can be explained by the fact that the CPS (Communist Party of the United States) leadership reactivated the geopolitical motif of "capitalist encirclement." In this vein, the end of the Second World War triggered a new imperialist offensive against communism in general and against "the young popular democracies" in particular, which, according to Stalin, signaled an imminent global armed conflict. Under the circumstances, any national-communist temptations had to be nipped in the bud. Therefore, within the various countries of the Soviet bloc, party leaders would be allowed to enjoy the adoration of their subordinates, but their cults were only echoes of the true faith: unswerving love for Stalin. In the words of Wladyslaw Gomulka, the

---

[27] During his trip to Moscow, via Bucharest, in January 1948, Georgi Dimitrov visited his old friend Petre Pandrea (Pătrăşcanu's brother-in-law) and talked about issues related to the emerging conflict between Tito and Stalin. They knew each other from the early 1930s Berlin where Pandrea studied law and Dimitrov was active with the Comintern's Balkan Bureau. See Petre Pandrea, *Memoriile mandarinului valah* (Bucharest: Albatros, 2000).

cult of the local leaders "could be called only a reflected brilliance, a borrowed light. It shone as the moon does."[28]

Links with Tito, of course, were used as arguments to demonstrate the political unreliability of certain East European leaders (e.g., László Rajk in Hungary, who fought in the Spanish Civil War and had maintained friendly relations with members of Tito's entourage). It is worth discussing in this context the following analysis of forced confessions proposed by Erica Glaser Wallach, Noel Field's foster daughter, whose parents had been themselves members of the medical units associated with the International Brigades in Spain:

> That depends on you, confess your crimes, cooperate with us, and we shall do anything in our power to help you. We might even consider letting you go free if we are satisfied that you have left the enemy camp and have honestly contributed to the cause of justice and progress. We are no man-eaters, and we are not interested in revenge. Besides you are not the real enemy; we are not interested in you but in the criminals behind you, the sinister forces of imperialism and war. You do not have to defend them; they will fight their own losing battle. People like you we want to help—and we do frequently—to find their way back to a normal life and a decent place in society... You want to know what a capitalist snake looks like? Take a look at her, at that bag of filth standing over there. You will never see such a low and abominable creature... Take that dirty smile off your face, you American stooge... You are a prostitute! That's what you are. Worse than that: prostitutes sell only their bodies: you sold your soul. For American dollars, stinking American dollars...[29]

---

[28] Brzeziński, *op. cit*, p. 65.

[29] Erica Wallach, *Light at Midnight* (New York: Doubleday, 1967), quoted by Ivan Margolius, *Reflections of Prague: Journeys through the 20th Century* (London: Wiley, 2006), p. 193. A personal element: my mother and Erica Wallach were friends during the Spanish Civil War when my mother worked as a nurse under the supervision of Doctor Glaser, Erica's father. In as much as I know, during the 1951–52 investigations at the Party Control Commission in Bucharest, my mother was questioned regarding her Glaser Slansky connections. During World War II, both my parents worked for Radio Moscow's Romanian service, which was part of the Balkan Department subordinated to the Central-East European Section headed by Rudolf Slansky. For show trials and the psychology of true believers, see Egon Balas, *Will to Freedom: A Perilous Journey Through Fascism and Communism* (Syracuse: Syracuse University Press, 2000), p. 219.

Domesticism, according to Zbigniew Brzeziński, was an exaggerated, even if frequently unconscious, "preoccupation with local, domestic communist objectives, at the expense of broader, international Soviet goals."[30] It was not an elaborate philosophy of opposition to Soviet hegemony, but a conviction on the part of some East European leaders, like Gomulka in Poland, Lucreţiu Pătrăşcanu in Romania, and Traicho Kostov in Bulgaria, that national interests were not necessarily incompatible with the Soviet agenda and that such purposes could therefore be pursued with impunity. Henceforth, the Cominform's main task—if not its only task—was to suppress such domestic ambitions. The fulfillment of the Stalinist design for Eastern Europe included the pursuit of a singular strategy that could eventually transform the various national political cultures into carbon copies of the "advanced" Soviet experience. Local communist parties engaged in frantic attempts to imitate the Stalinist model, transplanting and sometimes enhancing the most repulsive characteristics of the Soviet totalitarian system. The purpose of the show trials that took place in the people's democracies was to create a national consensus surrounding the top communist elite and to maintain a state of panic and fear among the population. According to George H. Hodos, a survivor of the 1949 László Rajk trial in Hungary, those frame-ups were signals addressed at all potential freethinkers and heretics in the satellite countries. The trials also "attempted to brand anyone who displayed differences of opinion as common criminal and/or agent of imperialism, to distort tactical differences as betrayal, sabotage, and espionage."[31]

But those trials were not a simple repetition of the bloody purges that had devastated the Soviet body politic in the 1930s. Between 1949 and 1951 the main victims of the trials were members of the "national communist elites", or "home communists," as opposed to doctrinaire Stalin loyalists. Koci Xoxe, Traicho Kostov, Lucreţiu Pătrăşcanu, Wladyslaw Gomulka, and László Rajk had all spent the war years in their own countries. They had participated in the anti-Nazi resistance movement. Unlike their Moscow-trained colleagues, they could invoke a source of legitimacy from direct involvement in the partisan movement.

---

[30] Brzeziński, *op. cit*, p. 52.
[31] Goerge H. Hodos, *Show Trials: Stalinist Purges in Eastern Europe, 1948–1954* (New York: Praeger, 1987), pp.11–2.

Some of these "home-grown" communists may have even resented the condescending attitudes of the "Muscovites," who relied on their better connections with Moscow and treated the home communists like junior partners. Stalin was aware of those factional rivalries and used them to initiate the permanent purges in the satellite countries.

In the early 1950s Stalin became increasingly concerned with the role of the Jews as carriers of a "cosmopolitan world view" and as "objective" supporters of the West. For the communists, it did not matter whether an individual was "subjectively" against the system, but rather what he or she might have thought and done by virtue of his or her "objective" status (coming from a bourgeois family, having studied in the West, belonging to a certain minority, and so forth). While there is growing and impressive literature dealing with Stalin's anti-Semitism during the later years of his reign, there is a regrettable scarcity of either analysis or interpretation regarding the salience of anti-Semitism as a defining feature of post-1948 political culture in the East European satellites. In a general assessment about the specifics of anti-Semitism in the Soviet Union, William Korey made in 1972 an interesting observation:

> Anti-Jewish discrimination had become an integral part of Soviet state policy ever since the late thirties. What it lacked then was an official ideology rationalizing the exclusion of Jews from certain positions or justifying the suspicion focused upon them. First during 1949–1953, and then more fully elaborated since 1967, the "corporate Jew," whether "cosmopolitan" or "Zionist," became identified as the enemy. Popular anti-Semitic stereotyping had been absorbed into official channels, generated by chauvinist needs and totalitarian requirements. [...] The ideology of the "corporate Jew" was not and is not fully integrated into Soviet thought. It functions on a purely pragmatic level— to fulfill limited, though clearly defined, domestic purposes. This suggests the possibility that it may be set aside when those purposes need no longer be served.[32]

While the specter of a massive pogrom loomed over the Soviet Jewish population, in the people's democracies, the struggle against "rootless

---

[32] William Korey, "The Origins and Development of Soviet Anti-Semitism: An Analysis," p. 135, *Slavic Review*, Vol. 31, No. 1. (March, 1972): 111–135. A year later, Korey developed his article into a book: William Korey, *The Soviet Cage: Anti-Semitism in Russia* (New York: Viking, 1973).

cosmopolitanism" allowed certain local leaders to engage in an elite purge against the "Muscovite" factions dominated by communists of Jewish extraction (many of whom had fled fascism and had sought refuge in the Soviet Union between the two wars).[33] The elimination of those otherwise totally loyal Stalinists reached a spectacular level in Czechoslovakia, where the chief defendant was Rudolf Slansky, who until September 1951 had been the General Secretary of the ruling communist party and in that capacity had presided over the ruthless persecution of communists and non-communists. Since the trial had to confirm Stalin's conviction about the existence of a worldwide conspiracy determined to unsettle the communist bloc, there was no way to exonerate any of the defendants. Furthermore, the anti-Semitic charges were bound to appeal to procommunist chauvinistic prejudices in the whole region.

A purge-trial that was a direct consequence of the Slansky events in Czechoslovakia was that of Paul Merker, member of the Central Committee of the SED since 1946. His initial downfall came about because of his relationship during the Second World War with Noel Field and Otto Katz (included in the group tried and executed in Prague in 1951). However, the crux of the accusations against Merker was his opinions and positions on the Jewish question in post-1945 Germany. In 1952, the SED's Central Party Control Commission produced a document that detailed Merker's errors and the mischief. Unsurprisingly it was entitled "Lessons of the Trial against the Slansky Conspiracy Centre." It insisted that Merker was involved in "the criminal activity of Zionist organizations," which, allied with "American agents," aimed at destroying the "people's democracies" in Eastern Europe. Additionally, it also claimed that Merker tried "winning over SED comrades of Jewish descent."[34] During interrogation (both by Stasi and

---

[33] "Rootless cosmopolitanism" alternated with a hardly veiled anti-Semitic version, that is, "cosmopolitanism of kith and kin." On the phases of state and public anti-Semitism in the Soviet Union and under Stalin, in particular, see: Zvi Gitelman, *A Century of Ambivalence: The Jews of Russia and the Soviet Union, 1881 to the Present* (New York: Schocken Books, 1988); and Amir Weiner, *Making Sense of War: The Second World War and the Fate of the Bolshevik Revolution* (Princeton, NJ: Princeton University Press, 2001).

[34] Merker himself was not of Jewish origin, but other high-profile people associated by the Stasi (and NKVD) to his trial were Lex Ende, Leo Bauer, or

NKVD), Merker was stamped with the label of *Judenknecht* (servant of the Jews). In an interesting twist, even after the 1954 resolution of Noel Field case, Merker was not released. On the contrary, now his whole trial was focused on his alleged collaboration with the Jewish capitalist/cosmopolitan circles. He was sentenced to eight years in prison in 1955, but was released in 1956 without ever being fully rehabilitated. Nevertheless, Merker and his spouse never attempted to flee to West Germany afterwards. Adopting an exemplarily Rubashov-like attitude, Merker stated: "In the trial against me, I did without a defense lawyer in order to help keep the proceedings absolutely secret." Again, the (*il*) logic of Stalinism was at work: "He had made efforts to prevent "enemies of the DDR" from using his case, and he and his wife had been and would remain silent about the case."[35] His trial, sentence, and interrogation minutes were indeed kept secret, becoming known only after the fall of the Berlin Wall.

In May, 1952, the Romanian media announced the elimination of three members of the Politburo, two of whom had been the leaders of the party's Moscow *émigré* center during World War II. All three had been party secretaries and had shared absolute power with the leader of the domestic faction, Gheorghe Gheorghiu-Dej. Ana Pauker, a veteran communist leader who long had been lionized by international

---

Bruno Goldhammer. See Dorothy Miller, "The Death of a 'Former Enemy of the Working Class'—Paul Merker," *Radio Free Europe Research/Communist Area*, GDR/15, May 14, 1969.

[35] Paul Merker was in Mexico City from 1942 until 1945 and through his articles in *Freies Deutschland* was the only one member of the KPD's Politbüro who insisted on the central role of anti-Semitism in Nazi Germany and on the special status of the Jews among Hitler's victims. This was in sharp contrast with Walter Ulbricht's writings and public stances on the nature of fascism, of Germany's war crimes, and of collective responsibility. Moreover, after 1948, Merker was sharply diverging from the Soviet policy of refusing special status and retribution to Jews among Hitler's victims. For the definitive work on Paul Merker's case, see Jeffrey Herf, "East German Communists and the Jewish Question: The Case of Paul Merker," *Journal of Contemporary History*, Vol. 29, No. 4 (October, 1994): 627–61; but also Jeffrey Herf, *Divided Memory: The Nazi Past in the Two Germanies* (Cambridge, MA: Harvard university Press, 1997); and Jeffrey Herf, "The Emergence and Legacies of Divided Memory: Germany and the Holocaust after 1945," in Jan-Werner Müller ed., *Memory and Power in Postwar in Europe: Studies in the Presence of the Past* (Cambridge: Cambridge University Press, 2002), pp. 184–205.

communist propaganda as an impeccable communist fighter, lost her job as Minister of Foreign Affairs and was put under house arrest. Her Muscovite ally, the Hungarian-born Vasile Luca, was accused of economic sabotage during his tenure as Minister of Finance and collaboration with the bourgeois police during the party's underground activity. Luca was arrested and died in prison in the early 1960s. The third member of the group, Teohari Georgescu, a home communist and former Minister of Internal Affairs whose principal fault consisted in his close association with the Pauker–Luca faction, was also jailed but was soon released, though never reinstated in party positions. The Romanian case is the perfect example of country dynamics determined by party factionalism and sectarianism. It can be said that the more marginal and less historically representative a communist party was, the more profound its sectarianism was. The Romanian Communist Party (RCP), torn apart by internal struggles among its three centers[36] during the underground period, preserved a besieged fortress mentality even after World War II. Given that in the pre-1945 period mutual accusations had usually resulted in the expulsion of the members of the defeated faction, once the party was in power, the effects of the continued struggles were catastrophic. Once established as a ruling party, the RCP projected a vision based on exclusiveness, fierce dogmatism, and universal suspicion at the national level. The mystique of the party called for complete abrogation of its members' critical faculties. As Franz Borkenau put it, communism, "a Utopia based upon the belief in the omnipotence of the 'vanguard,' cannot live without a scapegoat, and the procedures applied to detect them, invent them, become only more cruel and reckless."[37] For all practical purposes, the political history of the international communist movement is the history of continuous purges of different factions branded by the victors as "anti-party deviations." Those defeated in party power struggles were labeled factionalists, whereas the winners were lionized as champions of the "holy cause" of party unity.

---

[36] For a detailed explanation of power struggles in the 1930s and 1940s, see the chapter "A Messianic Sect: The Underground Romanian Communist Party, 1921–1944," in my book *Stalinism for All Seasons: A Political History of Romanian Communism* (Berkeley: University of California Press, 2003).
[37] Franz Borkenau, *World Communism: A History of the Communist International* (Ann Arbor: University of Michigan Press, 1962), p. 178.

Whereas the Slansky trial and the "doctors' plot" seem to represent the limits of the Stalinist systems irrationality, the purge of the Pauker–Luca–Georgescu group appears more an expression of domestic revolutionary pragmatism. The latter process was accompanied by massive purges of the Jewish Democratic Committee and in the Hungarian Committee, suggesting a concerted campaign of weakening the Moscow faction. In the Byzantine schemes that devoured the Romanian communist elite, the mystical internationalism of the Comintern period was gradually replaced by a cynical position embellished with nationalist, even xenophobic, motifs. Gheorghiu-Dej and his acolytes not only speculated about Stalin's anti-Semitism but did not hesitate to play the same card.[38] The stakes were absolute power, and the Jewishness of rivals was an argument that could be used with the Soviet dictator. If the national Stalinists were the prime beneficiaries of Stalin's warning not to transform the party from a "social and class party into a *race* party"[39] they were neither its initiators nor its architects. No less caught up in the same perverse mechanism of self-humiliation than their Polish and Hungarian colleagues, the Romanian Stalinists—Gheorghiu-Dej, Chişinevschi, and Ceauşescu, as much as Ana Pauker and Vasile Luca—were willing perpetrators of Stalin's designs. They were allowed by the Soviet dictator to gain autonomy not from the center but from another generation of the center's agents. It was indeed a sort of moment of emancipation, but one that signaled the fact that Moscow sanctioned the coming of age of a new Stalinist elite in Romania. The history of the Stalinist ruling group in various other East-Central European countries is strikingly similar. There is the same sense of political predestination, the same lack of interest in national values, the same obsequiousness *vis-à-vis* the Kremlin.

---

[38] For details on this interpretation of the events, see Robert Levy, *Ana Pauker: The Rise and Fall of a Jewish Communist* (Berkeley: University of California Press, c2001). For a critique, see Pavel Campeanu, Ceauşescu, *The Countdown* (New York: Columbia University Press, 2003).

[39] "Note Regarding the Conversation of I.V. Stalin with Gh. Gheorghiu-Dej and A. Pauker on the Situation within the RCP and the State of Affairs in Romania in Connection with the Peace Treaty," No. 191, February 2, 1947, in *Vostochnaia Evropa v dokumentakh arkhivov, 1944–1953*, edited by Galin P. Muraschko, Albina F. Noskowa, and Tatiana V. Volokitina, Vol. I, 564–5 (Moscow, 1997). See also "Stenograma şedinţei Biroului Politic al CC al PMR din 29 noiembrie 1961," pp. 14–6.

An indicator of the *continuous* Stalinist nature of the Romanian regime, of its permanent purge *mentalité*, is Leonte Răutu's fateful longevity within the highest power echelons, the high priest of a cultural
revolution *à la roumaine*.[40] A prominent party veteran of Bessarabi-
an-Jewish origin, perfectly fluent in Russian, he was the architect of
anti-cultural politics of Stalinism in Romania. Until his removal from
the Political Executive Committee in the summer of 1981, he was the
epitome for a *perinde ac cadaver* commitment to the Marxist-Leninist
cause. He was the most significant figure of the category of "party intellectuals," who produced, reproduced, and instrumentalized ideological
orthodoxy. A professional survivor prone to the most surreal dialectical
acrobatics, Leonte Răutu adjusted and took advantage of the regime's
gradual systemic degeneration, making the successful transition from
the position of professional revolutionary to that of a cunning and slip-
pery bureaucrat always ready to hunt down heretics among party ranks
and within the society as whole. Born in 1910, Răutu joined the RCP
in 1929 (while still a student in mathematics at Bucharest University)
and in the 1930s he became head of the propaganda and agitation department. In Doftana Prison he entered in direct contact with Gheorghiu-Dej and Ceauşescu. In the following years he became the editor
of *Scanteia*, the party's illegal newspaper. In 1940 he left Romania and
took refuge to the USSR, becoming the director of the Romanian section of Radio Moscow. He returned to the country at the same time
as Ana Pauker, Vasile Luca, Valter Roman, etc., where he initiated a
domestic version of Zhdanovism. In one of his most vehemently Zhda-
novite speeches, "Against Cosmopolitanism and Objectivism in Social
Sciences," [41] Răutu declared war on everything that was valued in the
national culture:

> The channels by which cosmopolitan views become pervasive, especially
> among intellectuals, are well known: servility to and kowtowing bour-
> geois culture, the empty talk of the so-called community of progressive

---

[40] For a detailed presentation of Leonte Răutu's role in the power politics of
Romanian communism see Vladimir Tismaneanu and Cristian Vasile, *Per-
fectul Acrobat: Leonte Răutu, Măştile Răului* (Bucharest: Humanitas, 2008).

[41] This article was published both in the Central Committee official journal
Lupta de clasă, No. 4, October 1949, and as a brochure at the R.W.P. Publishing house in 1949.

scientists and the representatives of reactionary, bourgeois science, national nihilism, meaning the negation of all that is valuable and progressive for each people in their culture and history, the contempt for the people's language, hate against the building of socialism, the defamation of all that is new and developing, replacing the *partiinost* with bourgeois objectivism, which ignores the fundamental difference between socialist, progressive culture and bourgeois, reactionary culture.[42]

After 1953, he pursued a seemingly more balanced approach as defense mechanism in the context of de-Stalinization. His main weapon in these changing times was that of *manipulation*. The individual was always a tool with no distinct personality (being rather a complex of acquired/ascribed features); when s/he displayed the will for autonomous action, s/he became victim of the diabolical logic of the purge (an excellent example for this situation is the career of Mihai Beniuc, the "little tyrant from the Writers' Union" as veteran communist poet Miron Radu Paraschivescu once called him). Răutu's cynicism and opportunism were flagrantly apparent in 1964 when Răutu, the same individual who directed the Sovietization of Romanian culture, initiated a strident campaign against the academia, whom he unmasked and accused of "having forgotten the true national values" and of "shamelessly showing fealty to even the slightest Soviet achievement." Leonte Răutu's career was fundamentally characterized by an extraordinary capacity of siding with those in power within the RCP. He first became a favorite of Ana Pauker and Vasile Luca, obtaining his position at Radio Moscow and his initial nominations in Romania because of this connection. By 1952, he knew when to jump into Dej's boat, being, along with Miron Constantinescu, the author of the May–June Plenary Session resolution, the text on which the purge proceedings were based (what came to be known as "the June nights"). His inquisitorial contribution to the Pauker case was not the first (see his involvement into unmasking Pătrășcanu's intellectual "crimes") and would not be the last type of such activity. In 1957, he could be found again on the prosecutor's bench during the party action against Chișinevschi-Constantinescu (these events are often labeled in Romanian historiography as "a failed de-Stalinization"). After the downfall of the two, who previously were direct competitors in the struggle for supremacy in administering

---

[42] Tismaneanu and Vasile, *op. cit.*, p. 224.

and ruling the cultural front, Răutu became the unchallenged patriarch of communist politics of culture. With the exception of the moment when he had to share power with Grigore Preoteasa, Răutu created an apparatus manned by mediocre individuals, whose ego would only equal their incompetence (e.g., M. Roller or P. Țugui). The biography and actions of Leonte Răutu are the perfect expression of the perverse game of Stalinist masks. Dissimulation, ethical posturing and hypocrisy were the only constants of the apparatchik's existence, a full-blown retreat from any moral imperative. Răutu was the incarnation of the diabolical anti-logic of Stalinism: an individual experiencing an irresistible process of personal decomposition based upon the unswerving subordination to the party leader beyond considerations such as reason, honor and dignity.

The mind of the Stalinist elites in Eastern Europe was impressively revealed by the Polish journalist Teresa Toranska in a series of interviews conducted in the early 1980s with some of the former leaders of the Polish communist party. The most striking and illuminating of the interviews is with the former Politbüro member and Central Committee Secretary Jakub Berman, who tried to defend the options and actions of his political generation. According to Berman, Polish communists were right in championing Stalin's policies in Poland because, he claimed, the Soviets guaranteed his country's social and national liberation. The leaders of the Soviet-bloc communist parties were convinced, like Lenin the moment he founded the Bolshevik party, that the people needed an external force to enlighten and teach them, and that without such a vanguard party there was no hope of true emancipation. Berman was convinced that a day would come when mankind would do justice to this chiliastic dream of global revolution, and all the atrocities and crimes of Stalinism would be remembered only as passing incidents: "I am nonetheless convinced that the sum of our actions, skillfully and consistently carried out, will finally produce results and create a new Polish consciousness; because all the advantages flowing from our new path will be borne out, must be borne out, and [...] there will finally be a breakthrough in mentality which will give it an entirely new content and quality."[43]

---

[43] Teresa Toranska, "*Them*": *Stalin's Polish Puppets* (New York: Harper & Row, 1987), p. 354. Marci Shore has provided excellent characterizations of Jakub

In his absolute belief that history was on his and his comrades' side, Berman was not alone. His was a mindset characteristic of the communist elites in all Soviet satellite countries. Such (*il*)logic explains the frenzy of submission syndrome: the readiness to engage in any form of self-debasement and self-deprecation as long as such gestures were required by the Party.[44] The East European communist leaders were seasoned militants for whom Stalin's personality was an example of correct revolutionary conduct. They admired the Soviet leader's intransigence and his uncompromising struggle against oppositional factions, and they shared his hostility to the West. They believed in the theory of permanent intensification of the class struggle and did their best to create a repressive system where all the critical tendencies could be immediately weeded out. Their minds were Manichean: socialism was right, capitalism was wrong, and there was no middle road between the two. During their communist underground service, the Soviet-bloc communists had learned to see Stalin's catechistic formulations as the best formulations of their own thoughts and beliefs. They fully internalized a diabolical pedagogy based upon a belief in being ordained as both juror and executioner, for their legitimacy drew from a frantic obedience to the *vozhd*. When Stalin died, his East European disciples suffered like orphans: more than their parties' supporter, they lost their protector, the very embodiment of their highest dreams, the hero they had come to revere, the symbol of their vigor, passion, and boundless enthusiasm.

The logic of Stalinism excluded vacillation and hesitation, numbed critical reasoning and intelligence and instituted Soviet-style Marxism as a system of universal truth inimical to any form of doubt. The mech-

---

Berman, detailing his career from his role during the murky history of interwar Polish communism and its relationship with Moscow during the Great Purge and the Second World War to his involvement in Gomulka's purge trial in the early 1950s up until his resignation in 1957 from the Polish United Workers' Party and retirement in 1969. Another issue that requires clarification is whether Berman's prominent role in the Stalinist purges prevented the duplication of a Slansky-type of trial in Poland. See Marci Shore, "Children of the Revolution: Communism, Zionism, and the Berman Brothers," *Jewish Social Studies*, Vol. 10, No 3, (Spring/Summer 2004, New Series): 23–86; and Marci Shore, *Caviar and Ashes: A Warsaw Generation's Life and Death in Marxism, 1918–1968* (New Haven: Yale University Press, 2006).

44 Vladimir Tismaneanu, *Ghilotina de scrum* (Bucharest: Polirom, 2002).

anism of permanent purging, the basic technique of Stalinist demonology, was the modern equivalent of the medieval witch-hunt. It was
eagerly adopted by Stalin's East European apprentices and adapted for
their own purposes. Echoing Stalin's fervid cult, East European leaders
engineered similar campaigns of praise and idolatry in their own countries. The party was identified with the supreme leader, whose chief
merit consisted in having correctly applied the Stalinist line. The solutions to all disturbing questions could be found in Stalin's writings,
and those who failed to discover the answers were branded "enemies of
the people." Members of the traditional political elites, members of the
clergy, and representatives of the nationalist intelligentsia who had refused to collaborate with the new regimes were sentenced to long term
prison terms following dramatic show trials or cursory camera trials.
That was the first stage of the purges in Eastern Europe. After 1949
the purges fed upon the communist elites themselves, and through
them many faithful Stalinists experienced firsthand the effects of the
unstoppable terrorist machine they had helped set in motion. According to Leszek Kolakowski, the purges had an integrative function, contributing to the destruction of the last vestiges of subjective autonomy and creating a social climate where no one would even dream of
criticism: "the object of a totalitarian system is to destroy all forms of
communal life that are not imposed by the state and closely controlled
by it, so that individuals are isolated from one another and become
mere instruments in the hands of the state. The citizen belongs to the
state and must have no other loyalty, not even to the state ideology."[45]
The communist victims belonged to a category described by Stalinist legal theory as "objective enemies." They were people who once in
their lives may have expressed reservations about the sagacity of Soviet
policies, or, even worse, may have criticized Stalin personally. Stalinism
functioned on the basis of an exhaustively repressive strategy displaying
pedagogical ambitions and vaunting itself as the triumph of the ethical
spirit and of egalitarian collectivism. Nicolas Werth enunciated, along
these lines, the following diagnosis:

---

[45] Leszek Kolakowski, *Main Currents of Marxism, Vol. II: The Golden Age* (Oxford: Oxford University Press, 1978), p. 85

throughout Stalin's dictatorship of a quarter of a century, repressive phenomena varied, evolved, and took on different forms and scope. They reflected transformations of the regime itself in a changing world. This adaptable violence was characterized by various levels of intensity, continual displacements, shifting targets, often unpredictable sequences, and excesses that blurred the line between the legal and extralegal.[46]

Maniacal purging consummate with self-devouring was both the praxis and the theoretical "legitimation" of this extremist and exterminist system. To paraphrase the title of a famous novel of Stalin's era, this is *How the Steel Was Tempered.*

---

[46] Nicolas Werth, "Strategies of Violence in the Stalinist USSR", p. 75, in Henry Russo ed., *Stalinism & Nazism. History and Memory Compared* (London: University of Nebraska Press, 2004), pp. 73–95.

EASTERN EUROPE

MARK KRAMER

Stalin, Soviet Policy, and the Consolidation of a Communist Bloc in Eastern Europe, 1944–53

Soviet policy in Eastern Europe during the final year and immediate aftermath of World War II had a profound impact on global politics.[1] The clash of Soviet and Western objectives in Eastern Europe was submerged for a while after the war, but by March 1946 the former British Prime Minister Winston Churchill felt compelled to warn in his famous speech at Fulton, Missouri, that "an Iron Curtain has descended across the Continent" of Europe. At the time of Churchill's remarks, the Soviet Union had not yet decisively pushed for the imposition of Communist rule in most of the East European countries. Although Communist officials were already on the ascendance throughout Eastern Europe, non-Communist politicians were still on the scene. By the spring of 1948, however, Communist regimes had gained sway throughout the region. Those regimes aligned themselves with the Soviet Union on all foreign policy matters and embarked on Stalinist transformations

---

[1] The term "Eastern Europe," as used in this chapter, is partly geographic and partly political in its designation. It includes some countries in what is more properly called "Central Europe," such as Czechoslovakia, Hungary, Poland, and what became known as the German Democratic Republic (or East Germany). All four of these countries were under Communist rule from the 1940s until 1989. The other Communist states in Europe—Albania, Bulgaria, Romania, and Yugoslavia—are also encompassed by the term "Eastern Europe." Countries that were never under Communist rule, such as Greece and Finland, are not regarded as part of "Eastern Europe," even though they might be construed as such from a purely geographic standpoint. The Soviet Union provided some assistance to Communist guerrillas in Greece and considered trying to facilitate the establishment of Communist regimes in both Finland and Greece, but ultimately decided to refrain from moving directly against the non-Communist governments in the two countries.

of their social, political, and economic systems. Even after a bitter rift emerged between Yugoslavia and the USSR, the other East European countries remained firmly within Moscow's sphere.

By reassessing Soviet aims and concrete actions in Eastern Europe from the mid-1940s through the early 1950s, this chapter touches on larger questions about the origins and intensity of the Cold War. The chapter shows that domestic politics and postwar exigencies in the USSR, along with Joseph Stalin's external ambitions, decisively shaped Soviet ties with Eastern Europe. Stalin's adoption of increasingly repressive and xenophobic policies at home, and his determination to quell armed insurgencies in areas annexed by the USSR at the end of the war, were matched by his embrace of a harder line *vis-à-vis* Eastern Europe. This internal-external dynamic was not wholly divorced from the larger East–West context, but it was, to a certain degree, independent of it. At the same time, the shift in Soviet policy toward Eastern Europe was bound to have a detrimental impact on Soviet relations with the leading Western countries, which had tried to avert the imposition of Stalinist regimes in Eastern Europe. The final breakdown of the USSR's erstwhile alliance with the United States and Great Britain was, for Stalin, an unwelcome but acceptable price to pay. Although he initially had hoped to maintain a broadly cooperative relationship with the United States and Britain after World War II, he was willing to sacrifice that objective as he consolidated his hold over Eastern Europe.

The chapter begins by describing the historical context of Soviet relations with the East European countries, particularly the events of World War II. The wartime years and the decades preceding them helped to shape Stalin's policies and goals after the war. The chapter then discusses the way Communism was established in Eastern Europe in the mid- to late 1940s. Although the process varied from country to country, the discussion below highlights many of the similarities as well as the differences. The chapter then turns to an event that threatened to undermine the "monolithic unity" of the Communist bloc in Eastern Europe, namely, the acrimonious rift with Yugoslavia. The chapter discusses how Stalin attempted to cope with the split and to mitigate the adverse repercussions elsewhere in Eastern Europe. The final section offers conclusions about Stalin's policy and the emergence and consolidation of the East European Communist regimes.

The analysis here draws extensively on newly available archival materials and memoirs from the former Communist world. For many years after 1945, Western scholars had to rely exclusively on Western archives and on published Soviet, East European, and Western sources. Until the early 1990s, the postwar archives of the Soviet Union and of the Communist states of Eastern Europe were sealed to all outsiders. But after the demise of Communism in Eastern Europe in 1989 and the disintegration of the Soviet Union two years later, the former Soviet archives were partly opened and the East European archives were more extensively opened. Despite the lack of access to several of the most crucial archives in Moscow—the Presidential Archive, the Foreign Intelligence Archive, the Central Archive of the Federal Security Service, and the Main Archive of the Ministry of Defense—valuable anthologies of documents pertaining to Soviet-East European relations during the Stalinist era, including many important items from the inaccessible archives, have been published in Russia over the past decade.[2] Many other first-rate collections of declassified documents have been published or made available on-line in all of the East European countries. It is now possible for scholars to pore over reams of archival materials that until the early 1990s seemed destined to remain locked away forever. In the West, too, some extremely important collections of documents pertaining to Soviet policy in Eastern Europe in the 1940s and early 1950s have only recently become available. Of particular note are declassified transcriptions of Soviet cables that were intercepted and decrypted by U.S. and British intelligence agencies. This chapter takes advantage of the documents that are now accessible, without overlook-

---

[2] Of the many document collections that have appeared, two are particularly worth mentioning, both published as large two-volume sets: T.V. Volokitina et al. eds., *Vostochnaya Evropa v dokumentakh rossiiskikh arkhivov, 1944–1953*, 2 vols., Vol. 1: *1944–1948 gg.* and Vol. 2: *1949–1953 gg.* (Novosibirsk: Sibir'skii khronograf, 1997 and 1999); and T.V. Volokitina et al. eds., *Sovetskii faktor v Vostochnoi Evrope, 1944–1953: Dokumenty*, 2 vols., Vol. 1: *1944–1948* and Vol. 2: *1949–1953* (Moscow: ROSSPEN, 1999 and 2002). The situation in the former East-bloc archives is far from ideal (especially in Russia), but the benefits of archival research usually outweigh the all-too-frequent disappointments and frustrations. For an appraisal of both the benefits and the pitfalls of archival research, see Mark Kramer, "Archival Research in Moscow: Progress and Pitfalls," *Cold War International History Project Bulletin*, No. 3 (Fall 1993), pp. 1, 15–34.

ing the valuable sources that were available before the collapse of the
Soviet bloc.

The Historical Setting

The Bolshevik takeover in Russia in November 1917 and the conclusion of the First World War a year later radically altered the political
complexion of East-Central Europe.[3] Under the Versailles Treaty and
other postwar accords, many new states were created out of the remnants of the Austro-Hungarian, Ottoman, and Tsarist empires. Some
of these new entities—Czechoslovakia, Yugoslavia, Estonia, and Latvia—had never existed before as independent states. Others, such as
Poland and Lithuania, had not been independent since the pre-Napo-
leonic era. Germany, which since Bismarck's time had been the most
dynamic European country, was relegated to a subordinate status by
the allied powers. The new Bolshevik government in Russia was able
to maintain itself in power but was badly weakened by the vast amount
of territory lost to Germany in the closing months of the war (some of
which was recovered after Germany's defeat) and then by the chaos
that engulfed Russia during its civil war from 1918 to 1921. The extent of Soviet Russia's weakness was evident when a military conflict
erupted with Poland in 1919–20. The Soviet regime was forced to cede
parts of Ukraine and Belorussia to Poland, a setback that would have
been unthinkable only five years earlier.[4] Although the Red Army re-
claimed some of the forfeited territory after World War I ended, the
new Soviet state was still a good deal smaller along its western flank
than the Tsarist empire had been.[5]

---

[3] Aviel Roshwald, *Ethnic Nationalism and the Fall of Empires: Central Europe,
the Middle East, and Russia, 1914–1923* (New York: Routledge, 2001); Ruth
Henig, *Versailles and After, 1919–1933*, rev. ed. (New York: Routledge, 1995);
and Erwin Oberländer ed., *Autoritäre Regime in Ostmittel- und Südosteuropa,
1919–1944* (Paderborn: F. Schöningh, 2001).

[4] See the useful collection of documents on the postwar settlement signed in
March 1921 in Bronisław Komorowski ed., *Traktat Pokoju między Polską
a Rosją i Ukrainą, Ryga 18 marca 1921: 85 lat później* (Warsaw: Oficyna
Wydawnicza Rytm, 2006).

[5] Dieter Segert, *Die Grenzen Osteuropas: 1918, 1945, 1989—Drei Versuche im
Westen anzukommen* (Frankfurt am Main: Campus, 2002), pp. 29–68.

During the interwar period, attitudes toward the Soviet Union differed widely among the countries of Eastern Europe.[6] The repressive policies and revolutionary rhetoric of the Bolshevik government, and the fierce competition for influence waged by the Germanic states and Tsarist Russia in Eastern Europe since the late eighteenth century, shaped many people's perceptions of the newly constituted USSR. Some East European leaders in the 1920s and 1930s sensed a more ominous threat from the Soviet Union than from Germany. Several nations, especially the Poles, had bitter memories—memories rekindled by the 1920 Russo-Polish War—of Russia's armed intervention against them during their struggles for independence in the nineteenth and early twentieth centuries. The different religious, ethnic, and cultural backgrounds of these peoples also had long separated them from their Russian neighbors. Moreover, the violent tyranny of the short-lived Soviet republic in Hungary under Béla Kun in 1919 had aroused widespread antipathy, particularly among Hungarians and Romanians, toward the Communist system that had been established in Russia.

Among other peoples in the region, however, sentiments toward the Soviet Union were distinctly warmer or at least not as hostile. The Czechs and the Serbs had traditionally relied on Russia as a counterweight against German expansion, and the Bulgarians were still grateful for Russia's assistance in liberating them from the Turks in 1873. The influence of pan-Slavism continued to prevail among many Serbs, Croats, Czechs, and Bulgarians, prompting them to look favorably upon their fellow Slavs in the Soviet Union.

---

[6] For a solid overview of this period, see Joseph Rothschild, *East-Central Europe between the Two World Wars* (Seattle: Washington University Press, 1974). Other useful accounts include Alan Palmer, *The Lands Between: A History of East-Central Europe Since the Congress of Vienna* (London: Weidenfeld and Nicolson, 1970); Hugh Seton-Watson, *Eastern Europe Between the Wars, 1918–1941*, rev. ed. (Cambridge: Cambridge University Press, 1962); Hans Hecker and Silke Spieler, *Nationales Selbstverstandnis und Zusammenleben in Ost-Mitteleuropa bis zum Zweiten Weltkrieg* (Bonn: Kulturstiftung der Deutschen Vertriebenen, 1991); Antony Polonsky, *The Little Dictators: The History of Eastern Europe Since 1918* (London: Routledge & Kegan Paul, 1975); Hans-Erich Volkmann ed., *Die Krise des Parlamentarismus in Ostmitteleuropa zwischen den beiden Weltkriegen* (Marburg/Lahn: J.G. Herder-Institut, 1967); and Wayne S. Vucinich, *East Central Europe Since 1939* (Seattle: Washington University Press, 1980).

Nevertheless, even for these normally friendly East European nationalities, developments in the interwar period had engendered discord with Moscow. In the case of Bulgaria, tensions had developed after a foiled Communist assassination attempt against King Boris; in the
case of Czechoslovakia, relations had deteriorated as a result of the assistance given by the Czechoslovak Legion to the anti-Bolshevik forces
during the Russian Civil War and of Czechoslovakia's subsequent participation in the French-sponsored Little Entente. The entrenchment
of Stalinism in the USSR, as the human toll of forced collectivization,
de-kulakization, purges, and deportations of non-Russian minorities
reached new heights in the 1930s, further eroded Czechoslovakia's
pro-Moscow inclinations and made the prospect of an alliance with
Moscow far less palatable.

The fear that many in Eastern Europe had of the Soviet Union
intensified throughout the 1930s, despite the growing realization of the
threat posed by Germany. Even after Adolf Hitler's dismemberment of
Czechoslovakia and annexation of the Sudetenland had raised alarm
about German intentions toward the whole region, the Nazi regime's
strong opposition to Soviet Communism (and Hitler's policies toward
the Jews) ensured at least tacit support for Germany from large segments of the Hungarian, Slovak, Romanian, and other East European
populations. Poland and Romania still rejected any form of military alliance with the Soviet Union, even though both had readily entered
into such an arrangement with Great Britain and France.[7]

The situation in Eastern Europe took a sharp turn for the worse
in August 1939, when the Soviet Union and Nazi Germany signed a
Non-Aggression Pact and soon thereafter concluded a secret protocol to the Pact. Under the terms of the secret protocol, the two signatories divided Eastern Europe into spheres of influence and pledged
not to interfere in each other's sphere. In mid-September 1939, Soviet troops set up a brutal occupation regime in eastern Poland and
moved en masse into the three Baltic states, where they forced the lo-

---

[7] I.I. Kostyushko ed., *Vostochnaya Evropa posle Versalya* (St. Petersburg: Aletei-
ya, 2007); Anita Prażmowska, *Eastern Europe and the Origins of the Second
World War* (New York: St. Martin's Press, 2000); Anita Prażmowska, *Britain,
Poland, and the Eastern Front, 1939* (New York: Cambridge University Press,
1987); and Hans Roos, *Polen und Europa: Studien zur polnischen Aussenpolitik
1931–1939* (Tubingen: Schutz Verlag, 1957), pp. 320–61.

cal governments to comply with Moscow's demands and eventually replaced them with puppet governments that voted for "voluntary" incorporation into the Soviet Union. The same pattern was evident in the formerly Romanian territories of Bessarabia and northern Bukovina, which the Soviet Union annexed in June 1940. The only major impediment to the expansion of Soviet rule came in Finland, where the entry of Soviet troops sparked a brief but intense war that exposed severe weaknesses in the Red Army. Although the vastly outnumbered Finnish forces eventually had to surrender, the four months of combat in 1939–1940 inflicted devastating losses on the Red Army, including the deaths of at least 126,875 soldiers and wounding of 264,908.[8]

Meanwhile the German army, which had already established control over the whole of Czechoslovakia in early 1939, moved southward into the Balkans, occupying Yugoslavia and Greece in April 1941. From that vantage point, Nazi officials were able to compel the governments in Romania, Hungary, and Bulgaria to accede to the Axis alliance. These latter three East European states had sought to remain neutral before war broke out between Germany and the Soviet Union, but they soon found themselves having to align more and more closely with Germany for both economic and politico-military reasons.

This trend accelerated sharply after Hitler launched Operation "Barbarossa" in a full-scale attack on the Soviet Union in June 1941. Although Bulgaria did not actually join in the fighting against Sovi-

---

[8] See the secret report on the "lessons of the war with Finland" presented by People's Commissar of Defense Kliment Voroshilov on 28 March 1940 to the VPK(b) Central Committee, "Uroki Voiny s Flnlyandiei," in Arkhiv Prezidenta Rossiiskoi Federatsii (APRF), Fond (F.) 3, Opis' (Op.) 50, Delo (D.) 261, Listy (Ll.) 114–158; reproduced in *Novaya i noveishaya istoriya* (Moscow), No. 4 (July–August 1993): 104–22. For other important declassified documents pertaining to the Soviet–Finnish Winter War, as well as reassessments of the war, see N.L. Volkovskii, ed. *Tainy i uroki zimnei voiny: Po dokumentam rassekrechennykh arkhivov* (St. Petersburg: Poligon, 2000); A.E. Taras, *Sovetsko-finskaya voina, 1939–1940 gg.: Khrestomatiya* (Minsk: Kharvest, 1999); Carl Van Dyke, *The Soviet Invasion of Finland, 1939–40* (London: Frank Cass, 1997); V.N. Baryshnikova *et al.* eds., *Ot voiny k miru: SSSR i Finlyandiya v 1939–1944 gg.: Sbornik statei* (St. Petersburg: Izdatel'stvo S.-Peterburgskogo Universiteta, 2006), pp. 47–172 and the very useful bibliography on pp. 425–51; and M.I. Semiryaga, "'Asimmetrichnaya voina': K 50-letiyu okonchaniya sovetsko-finlyandskoi voiny (1939–1940 gg.)," *Sovetskoe gosudarstvo i pravo* (Moscow), No. 4 (1990): 116–23.

et forces, it supported Germany in numerous other ways, prompting Moscow to declare war on Bulgaria in September 1944. The Hungarian and Romanian governments, for their part, dispatched troops to fight alongside the Nazis against the Red Army, and the Romanians quickly managed to regain Bessarabia.[9] The Hungarian army, despite suffering heavy losses, fought to the end against the Soviet Union. Detachments of Slovak troops from the German-supported state in Slovakia also took up arms against the USSR, and many of the Polish units resisting the Nazi occupation subsequently fought the Red Army as it crossed the interwar frontier along the Pripet Marshes into Polish territory.[10] Czech soldiers, on the other hand, sided with the advancing Soviet troops, as did the Communist-led partisans in Yugoslavia and Bulgaria. Pro-Communist factions of the anti-Nazi resistance movements in most of the other countries under German occupation also received assistance and close supervision from the Soviet government and were often led by Moscow-trained émigrés. These Communist factions, having benefited from their identification with the nationalist cause and from their combat experience, served as the core of the region's Communist parties once the war was over. Their actual contribution to the victory over Germany was exiguous at best (German occupying forces were able to neutralize the resistance movements through the use of unbridled violence), but the partisans successfully fostered the myth afterward that they played a crucial role in helping the Red Army to defeat the Wehrmacht.[11]

---

[9] Nicholas Dima, *From Moldavia to Moldova: The Soviet–Romanian Territorial Dispute* (Boulder, CO: East European Monographs, 1991), ch. 2. This book is a revised version of Dima's *Bessarabia and Bukovina: The Soviet–Romanian Territorial Dispute* (Boulder, CO: East European Quarterly Monographs, 1984).

[10] See Nikolai Bulganin's on-site report on this fighting in "Tov. Vyshinskomu," Telephone Cable (Top Secret), 3 November 1944, in Arkhiv Vneshnei Politiki Rossiiskoi Federatsii (AVPRF), F. 07, Op. 5, Papka (P.) D. 119, LI. 8–9.

[11] For an excellent account of the Germans' ruthless suppression of the resistance movements, see Mark Mazower, *Hitler's Empire: How the Nazis Ruled Europe* (New York: Penguin Books, 2008).

Stalin and the New Postwar Context

Nine consequences of the pre-1945 period are crucial in understanding the evolution of Soviet policy toward Eastern Europe after World War II:

First, Stalin and other leading Soviet officials were determined to ensure that, at a minimum, Eastern Europe would be converted after the war into a protective zone against future invasions from European armies and a safeguard against the threat of revived German militarism.[12] The history of Russia's (and later the Soviet Union's) vulnerability to foreign invasion—from the Napoleonic Wars to the final year of World War I to the Russo-Polish War of 1919–20 to Hitler's invasion in June 1941—and in particular the incursions by Germany, deeply colored the perceptions of Stalin and his subordinates. Protection of socialism at home, as they saw it, would require acquiescent border-states, especially because the territory of the Soviet Union at war's end had been expanded westward to the former boundaries of the old Tsarist empire and even into regions that had never been un-

---

[12] This is evident from the preliminary materials released from Stalin's personal archive (*lichnyi fond*), parts of which were transferred in 1999 from the Russian Presidential Archive to the former Central Party Archive, now known as the Russian State Archive for Social-Political History. (Unfortunately, nearly all of the files in Stalin's *lichnyi fond* pertaining to foreign policy, military affairs, and foreign intelligence are still off-limits in the Presidential Archive.) Vladimir Pechatnov's two-part article, based on privileged access to still-classified files, sheds fascinating light on Stalin's views about foreign affairs at the outset of the Cold War. See "'Soyuzniki nazhimayut na tebya dlya togo, chtoby slomit' u tebya volyu...': Perepiska Stalina s Molotovym i drugimi chlenami Politbyuro po vneshnepoliticheskim voprosam v sentyabre-dekabre 1945 g.," *Istochnik* (Moscow), No. 2 (1999): 70–85; and "'Na etom voprose my slomaem ikh anti-sovetskoe uporstvo...': Iz perepiski Stalina s Molotovym po vneshnepoliticheskim delam v 1946 godu," *Istochnik* (Moscow), No. 3 (1999): 92–104. See, for example, the accounts in N.S. Khrushchev, *Vremya, lyudi, vlast'—Vospominaniya,* 4 vols. (Moscow: Moskovskie novosti, 1999), Vol. 2, pp. 313–82; and James F. Byrnes, *Speaking Frankly* (New York: Harper and Brothers, 1947), pp. 30–1. I cross-checked the published version of Khrushchev's memoirs with the full, 3,600-page, marked-up Russian transcript of Khrushchev's memoirs, which was given to me by Khrushchev's son Sergei. I also listened to the original recordings of Khrushchev's reminiscences, copies of which are now stored at both Columbia University and Brown University.

der Tsarist rule.[13] The experiences of the interwar years, most notably with Poland, Romania, and Hungary, and Stalin's feelings of betrayal and humiliation when Hitler broke the Nazi–Soviet Pact and
launched an all-out war against the USSR, had further convinced the
Soviet leader that he must prevent the reemergence of hostile regimes
anywhere along the Soviet Union's western flank. This objective did
not necessarily require the imposition of Communist regimes in the
region (at least in the short term), but it did presuppose the formation
of staunchly pro-Soviet governments.

Other considerations pointed Stalin in the same direction. The Soviet leader viewed the establishment of a secure buffer zone in Eastern
Europe as the best way to obtain economic benefits from the region,
initially in the form of reparations and resource extraction.[14] From
eastern Germany alone, the Soviet Union extracted some 3,500 factories and 1.15 million pieces of industrial equipment in 1945 and
1946.[15] Similar amounts of industrial facilities, manufacturing equipment, and transport systems (especially railroad cars) were taken from
Hungary.[16] In addition, Stalin regarded the East European countries
as a foundation for the eventual spread of Communism into France,
Italy, and other West European countries that in his view would be in-

---

[13] "I. V. Stalin o rechi U. Cherchillya: Otvety korrespondentu 'Pravdy'," *Pravda*
(Moscow), 14 March 1946, p. 1. The Soviet Union in 1939–40 re-annexed
the Baltic states and, following the war, acquired further territory from Poland, Germany (East Prussia), Czechoslovakia, Hungary, Romania, and Finland.

[14] See, for example, Stalin's comments in "Zapis' besedy tov. I. V. Stalin s
pravitel'stvennoi delegatsiei Vengrii, 10 aprelya 1946 g.," Transcript of Conversation (Top Secret), 10 April 1946, in APRF, F. 558, Op. 1, D. 293, LI.
2–16.

[15] Data cited in speech by A.A. Kuznetsov, VKP(b) Central Committee Secretary, to a closed meeting of the VKP(b) Department for Propaganda and Agitation, 9 December 1946, in Rossiiskii Gosudarstvennyi Arkhiv Sotsial'no-
Politicheskoi Istorii (RGASPI), F. 17, Op. 121, D. 640, L. 5.

[16] "Azon vállalatok jegyzéke, amelyeket a szovjet hatóságok teljesen vagy rész-
ben leszereltek és gépi berendezésüket elszállították, amelyek nem szerepel-
nek a jóvátételi listán," List Prepared for the Hungarian Minister of Industry, 1945, in Magyar Országos Levéltár (MOL), Küm, Szu tük, XIX-J-1-j,
31. doboz, IV-536/5, 116/45; and "Feljegyzés az ipari miniszternek leszerelt
gyárakról," Memorandum to the Hungarian Minister of Industry, 27 June
1945, in MOL, XIX-F-1-b 44. doboz, ikt. sz. n.

creasingly "ripe for socialism" as the benefits of the system elsewhere became more apparent.[17]

These diverse objectives—military, economic, and political—led almost inevitably to the sweeping extension of Soviet military power into Eastern Europe, for Stalin had increasingly come to believe, in the oft-cited comment recorded by Milovan Djilas, that "whoever occupies a territory [after the war] also imposes on it his own social system. Everyone imposes his own system as far as his army has power to do so."[18] Even though Stalin did not set out to establish full-fledged Communist regimes in Eastern Europe overnight, he wanted to ensure that he alone would determine the parameters for political change in the region—an objective that required a large-scale Soviet military presence throughout Eastern Europe.

Second, in contrast to the experience of the interwar years, the Soviet Union after the war possessed sufficient military and political power to establish dominance over Eastern Europe. In 1919 the Soviet government had been compelled to watch helplessly as Béla Kun's Communist regime was overthrown in Hungary, and in March 1921 the Soviet Union was forced to cede parts of Belarus and Ukraine to Poland. But by the time World War II ended and the Red Army had driven back the Nazi invaders and occupied most of Eastern Europe, the Soviet Union was able to use its armed forces to give support to Communist parties and pro-Moscow forces throughout the region. Complementing the USSR's vastly greater military strength was the direct political influence that Moscow had gained by overseeing the rise of Communist parties in all the East European countries, including even the countries in which Communist influence had traditionally

---

[17] Silvio Pons, "Stalin, Togliatti, and the Origins of the Cold War in Europe," *Journal of Cold War Studies*, Vol. 3, No. 2 (Spring 2001): 3–27, esp. 11–7.

[18] Quoted in Milovan Djilas, *Conversations with Stalin* (New York: Harcourt, Brace & World, 1962), p. 90. The official transcript of Stalin's conversation with Djilas in April 1944 includes comments very similar, but not identical, to the remark transcribed by Djilas. See "Zapis' besedy I. V. Stalina i V. M. Molotova s predstavitelyami narodno-osvobozhditel'noi armii Yugoslavii M. Dzhilasom i V. Terzichem, 25 aprelya 1944 g.," Transcript of Conversation (Top Secret), 25 April 1944, in AVPRF, F. 06, Op. 6, P. 58, D. 794, LI. 10–8.

been negligible or non-existent.[19] The loyalty of these parties to Moscow was unquestioned, for most of the top East European Communist officials had been trained in Moscow and owed their careers to the Soviet Union. The large majority of Hungarian, Polish, Czech, East German, and Bulgarian Communist party leaders, who later gained ascendance in their countries under Soviet auspices, had been living as émigrés in the USSR since the late 1920s and 1930s.[20] Many of them had little choice but to serve as informants for the Soviet state security apparatus. After gaining power, they more often than not remained steadfastly loyal to their Soviet mentors—a situation sharply contrasting with the hostility Moscow faced in the interwar period.

Third, although Soviet power in Eastern Europe in relative terms was much greater after World War II than during the interwar years, the reverse was true for the East European countries. The independence and relative buoyancy of the East European countries in the first decade after World War I had been possible only because the traditional rivals for overarching power in the region—Germany and Russia— had been temporarily eclipsed. By the mid-1930s, the revival of both Germany and Russia (in the form of the Soviet Union) was well under way, and the East European countries were increasingly impotent and fractioned. The wartime fighting in Europe exacted its heaviest toll in the eastern half of the continent. The territory stretching from Germany to the western regions of the Soviet Union suffered untold devastation and bloodshed. With the defeat of Germany in 1945, a power vacuum opened up in Eastern Europe, which the Soviet Union was both determined and able to fill. Power relationships are always reciprocal, but in 1945 the Soviet-East European relationship was overwhelmingly one-sided. The establishment of Soviet dominance in the region at the end of World War II was due as much to East European weakness as to Soviet strength.

Fourth, the stance adopted by the United States and Great Britain toward Eastern Europe during World War II undoubtedly bolstered a

---

[19] See the discussions of individual countries in Norman Naimark and Leonard Gibianskii eds., *The Establishment of Communist Regimes in Eastern Europe, 1944–1949* (Boulder, CO: Westview Press, 1997).

[20] The major exceptions to this rule were Władysław Gomułka and Edward Gierek of Poland, Gustáv Husák of Slovakia, and Gheorghe Gheorgiu-Dej and Nicolae Ceauşescu of Romania.

perception among Soviet leaders that the USSR would enjoy a secure sphere of influence in the region after the war.[21] High-level U.S. officials repeatedly sought to defer allied consideration of future political arrangements for Eastern Europe until the postwar negotiations, despite the reality that was taking shape on the ground. This posture led to a series of U.S. and British concessions on Eastern Europe starting at the December 1943 Teheran Conference, where British Prime Minister Winston Churchill and U.S. President Franklin D. Roosevelt acquiesced in Stalin's demands for an East-West division of military operations in Europe and a shift in the postwar Soviet-Polish border back to the Curzon Line.[22]

Significant as these concessions may have been, the real turning point came during the Warsaw uprising of August-September 1944, when the non-Communist Polish resistance (*Armia Krajowa*, or AK) had risen against the Nazis in the expectation that thousands of Soviet troops, who had already reached the outskirts of Warsaw, would aid in the liberation of the Polish capital.[23] A broadcast on Radio Moscow

---

[21] V.O. Pechatnov, *Stalin, Ruzvel't, Trumen: SSSR i SShA v 1940-kh gg.— Dokumental'nye ocherki* (Moscow: TERRA-Knizhnyi klub, 2006). For a still useful assessment, see Vojtech Mastny, *Russia's Road to the Cold War: Diplomacy, Warfare, and the Politics of Communism, 1941–1945* (New York: Columbia University Press, 1979), pp. 279–312.

[22] Jacek Tebinka, *Polityka brytyjska wobec problemu granicy polsko-radzieckiej, 1939–1945* (Warsaw: Wydawnictwo Neriton, 1998); Keith Eubank, *Summit at Teheran: The Untold Story* (New York: William Morrow, 1985), pp. 445–70; Detlef Brandes, *Grossbritannien und seine Osteuropaischen Allierten 1939–1943* (Munich: Oldenbourg, 1988), esp. pp. 487–563.

[23] For valuable collections of documents and perceptive commentaries, see Piotr Mierecki *et al.* eds., *Powstanie Warszawskie 1944 w dokumentach archiwów Służb specjalnych* (Warsaw: Instytut Pamięci Narodowej, 2007); and Jan Ciechanowski ed., *Na tropach tragedii—Powstanie Warszawskie 1944: Wybór dokumentów wraz z komentarzem* (Warsaw: BGW, 1992). For other recent assessments of the Warsaw uprising and its implications, see Włodzimierz Rosłoniec, *Lato 1944* (Kraków: Znak, 1989), esp. pp. 172–99; and Tadeusz Sawicki, *Front wschodni a powstanie Warszawskie* (Warsaw: PWN, 1989). Soviet policy during the uprising has come under scrutiny in specialized Russian journals, though primarily by military officers and official military historians who want to absolve the Red Army of any "blame." See, for example, the introduction to the two-part series "Kto kogo predal—Varshavskoe vosstanie 1944 goda: Svidetel'stvuyut ochevidtsy," *Voenno-istoricheskii zhurnal* (Moscow), Nos. 3 and 4 (March 1993 and April 1993): 16–24 and 13–21,

International on the eve of the uprising had exhorted the AK forces to take up arms, declaring that "the time for action has arrived." But when the fighting actually began, the Red Army refrained from intervening and instead waited for two months on the banks of the Vistula (Wisła) River before attacking the Germans. By that time, the Polish AK fighters had either surrendered or been annihilated. The motivation behind Moscow's delay became evident when Stalin also blocked the attempts of Allied planes to airlift supplies and weapons to the Polish resistance forces from bases in Soviet-occupied territory.[24] U.S. and British officials strongly protested the Soviet leader's actions, but took no concrete measures in retaliation. Nor did they take any action when Soviet troops, after driving out the Germans, began tracking down and destroying the surviving AK units.[25] Stalin evidently interpreted the Western reaction to imply that, except for verbal protestations, the

---

respectively. Each part contains a newly declassified document. For other intriguing materials from the Soviet side, see "Varshavskoe vosstanie 1944 g.: Dokumenty iz rassekrechennykh arkhivov," *Novaya i noveishaya istoriya* (Moscow), No. 3 (May–June 1993): 85–106, which includes seven detailed situation reports transmitted in September and October 1944 by Lieut.-General K.F. Telegin of the 1st Belorussian Front to the head of the Red Army's Main Political Directorate, Col.-General A.S. Shcherbakov, who in turn conveyed the reports directly to Stalin. For a recent English-language overview of the Warsaw uprising, see Norman Davies, *Rising '44: The Battle for Warsaw* (New York: Viking, 2004). Davies's book is solid and well-researched, but is marred by numerous factual errors. Moreover, his decision to anglicize Polish names makes his account unduly confusing (and the publisher's relegation of three separate sets of notes to the back of the book compounds the difficulty). Fortunately, these problems are not present in a Polish translation of Davies's book, *Jak powstało Powstanie '44*, trans. by Elżbieta Tabakowska (Kraków: Znak, 2005). The Polish edition corrects most of the factual errors and places the notes with the text itself, making it much easier to follow.

[24] The goal of allowing the AK to be destroyed is spelled out candidly in "Instruktsiya predstavitelyu Soveta Narodnykh Komissarov Soyuza SSR pri Pol'skom Komitete Natsional'nogo Osvobozhdeniya," Directive of the USSR Council of Ministers (Secret) to the Soviet envoy Nikolai Bulganin, 2 August 1944, in AVPRF, F. 06, Op. 6, P. 42, D. 551, Ll. 3–6.

[25] On these campaigns, see the documents in Gosudarstvennyi Arkhiv Rossiiskoi Federatsii (GARF), F. R-9401, Op. 2, D. 67, many of which are reproduced in A.F. Noskova *et al.* eds., *NKVD i pol'skoe podpol'e, 1944–1945: Po 'Osobym papkam' I. V. Stalina* (Moscow: Institut slavyanovedeniya i balkanistiki, 1994).

West would not and indeed could not deny him a "free hand" in Eastern Europe after the war.[26]

This perception almost certainly increased after Churchill's efforts to arrange formal postwar "spheres of responsibility" with the USSR at his October 1944 meeting in Moscow, and after Roosevelt's announcement at the Yalta conference in early 1945 that all U.S. troops would be withdrawn from Europe no more than two years after the war. The Soviet Union, in the meantime, was rapidly creating *faits accompli* with its tanks and artillery in Romania, Bulgaria, Hungary, Slovakia, and Poland. Any lingering doubts Stalin may have had about U.S. policy toward Eastern Europe were presumably dispelled when the United States held back its own troops for several weeks to permit the Red Army to be the first to enter Berlin and Prague, two events whose political significance was not fully appreciated in Washington. (This was especially true of Prague, which U.S. troops could have entered rapidly and with minimal bloodshed. A U.S. drive toward Berlin would have required much heavier losses, something the U.S. public would have resisted so long as those costs could be borne by the Red Army instead.) Thus, long before the fighting was over, Soviet leaders had many reasons to conclude—accurately, as later events proved—that the Western countries ultimately would not pose a serious challenge to Soviet military and political hegemony in Eastern Europe.

Fifth, the role that Soviet troops played in liberating most of the East European states from Nazi occupation contributed in four ways to Soviet dominance in the region: First, it evoked at least temporary gratitude from some nations in Eastern Europe, particularly the Czechs and Bulgarians. Second, it induced the new East European regimes to continue to look to Moscow for protection against German "revanchism," a threat that was especially acute in Czechoslovakia and Poland inasmuch as these two states had been granted westward adjustments of their borders into former German territory (to help make up for the territory they had lost to the USSR) and had expelled millions of ethnic Germans from within their new boundaries.[27] Third, it

---

[26] See, for example, Stalin's comments in "Zapis' besedy tov. I. V. Stalina s predstavitelyami pol'skoi pravitel'stvennoi delegatsiei vo glave s S. Mikolaichikom," 9 August 1944 (Secret), in APRF, F. 558, Op. 1, D. 358, Ll. 12–6.

[27] Poland's borders were shifted westward to the Oder and Neisse (Odra and Nysa) Rivers, and several million ethnic Germans were expelled from the

provided the Soviet armed forces with a well-established military presence in the region. Fourth, it enabled the Soviet Union to ensure that Communist officials and labor activists would lead the renascent East European bureaucracies and trade unions, which served as a foothold for the subsequent Communist takeovers.

These four factors ensured preponderant Soviet influence over the coalition governments that were established in the region in 1945–1947. If Stalin's only goal had been to establish a secure buffer zone along the western flank of the USSR, the war was far more important than any peace treaties in allowing him to achieve it. To gauge the importance in later years of the Soviet Union's role in the liberation of Eastern Europe from Nazi rule, one might simply note that the two countries in the region that could claim (rightly or wrongly) to have played a major part in their own liberation during the war—Albania and Yugoslavia—were also the only two East European countries that managed to break away from the Soviet bloc before 1989.

Sixth, in several East European countries the Soviet Union's role in World War II was not favorably received. In Poland, for example, the 1939 Nazi–Soviet Pact, which resulted in the partition of the Polish state, had engendered deep and lasting resentment toward Moscow. The Soviet occupation of eastern Poland from September 1939 to June 1941 was extraordinarily harsh—far harsher indeed than the Nazis' occupation of western Poland during that same period.[28] Soviet troops and security forces undertook wholesale deportations and mass killings, including the massacre of more than 20,000 Polish officers near Katyń

---

new Polish territory in Silesia, Pomerania, and West Prussia. Czechoslovakia received back the Sudetenland in western Bohemia, and some 3.1 million Germans were forcibly transferred out, resulting in great bloodshed and cruelty. For a thorough reassessment of the border changes and expulsions, drawing on new archival materials, see Philipp Ther and Ana Siljak eds., *Redrawing Nations: Ethnic Cleansing in East-Central Europe, 1944–1948* (Boulder, CO: Rowman & Littlefield, 2001).

[28] Piotr Chmielowiec ed., *Okupacja sowiecka ziem polskich 1939–1941* (Warsaw: Instytut Pamięci Narodowej, 2005); Keith Sword, ed., *The Soviet Takeover of the Polish Eastern Provinces, 1939–41* (New York: St. Martin's Press, 1991); and Jan T. Gross, *Revolution from Abroad: The Soviet Conquest of Poland's Western Ukraine and Western Belorussia* (Princeton, NJ: Princeton University Press, 1988). This assessment, of course, does not apply to the situation after 1941, when the Nazis embarked on the mass extermination of Jews and Gypsies.

Forest in March 1940. They also engaged in widespread looting, raping, and other atrocities. The Soviet government's actions during the 1944 Warsaw uprising came as a further blow to Polish nationalist aspirations. Compounding the tensions between the Soviet Union and Poland was the USSR's postwar annexation of the Polish provinces east of the Curzon Line, which shifted Poland's borders 200 kilometers to the west.[29]

Equally bitter feelings toward Moscow existed in the Soviet zone of Germany (after 1949, East Germany), where the defeat inflicted by the Soviet Union and the brutal postwar occupation by the Red Army obviously made it difficult for the indigenous Socialist Unity Party to gain even a semblance of popular support.[30] Soviet leaders were well aware that for many years the Soviet Union would not be able to "count on the sympathies of the East German people in the way we would have liked."[31] Partly for this reason, Stalin in December 1948 instructed the leaders of the Socialist Unity Party of Germany (SED, the name for the Communist party in Eastern Germany from April 1946 on) to be content with an "opportunistic policy" that would entail "moving toward socialism not directly but in zigzags and in a roundabout way." He said they must avoid any temptation to adopt a "premature path toward a people's democracy."[32] In an earlier conversation, Stalin had even suggested that the SED could bolster its popular support by allowing former Nazis to join its ranks.[33] The leaders of the SED were dismayed by this last idea, and they politely though firmly declined to go along with it after Stalin raised it. Nonetheless, the very fact that

[29] Piotr Eberhardt, *Polska granica wschodnia, 1939–1945* (Warsaw: Spotkania, 1992). See also I.I. Kostyushko ed., *Materialy "Osoboi papki" Politbyuro TsK RKP(b)-VKP(b) po voprosu sovetsko-polskikh otnoshenii, 1923–1944 gg.* (Moscow: Institut slavyanovedeniya i balkanistiki RAN, 1997), pp. 133–37.

[30] Norman M. Naimark, *The Russians in Germany: A History of the Soviet Zone of Occupation, 1945–1949* (Cambridge, MA: Harvard University Press, 1995).

[31] Khrushchev, *Vremya, lyudi, vlast'*, Vol. 2, p. 326.

[32] "Zapis' besedy tov. I. V. Stalina s rukovoditelyami Sotsialisticheskoi edinoi partii Germanii V. Pikom, O. Grotevolem, V. Ul'brikhtom," Transcript of Conversation (Top Secret), 18 December 1948, in APRF, F. 558, Op. 1, D. 303, Ll. 53–79, quoted from L. 69.

[33] "Zapis' besedy tov. I. V. Stalina s rukovoditelyami Sotsialisticheskoi edinoi partii Germanii V. Pikom, O. Grotevolem, V. Ul'brikhtom," Transcript of Conversation (Top Secret), 31 January 1947, in APRF, F. 558, Op. 1, D. 303, Ll. 1–23, quoted from L. 11.

Stalin would have broached such a peculiar step was indicative of his realization that the SED was nearly bereft of public backing.

Similar hostility toward the Soviet Union was evident in the other East European countries. In a conversation with Soviet Foreign Minister Vyacheslav Molotov in April 1947, the Hungarian Communist leader Mátyás Rákosi acknowledged that Hungary's new foreign policy orientation and social order were inherently fragile because "the Hungarian nation's traditional fear of Russians still persists."[34] One of Stalin's closest associates, Nikita Khrushchev, made the same point later in his memoirs, describing Hungary and Romania as "our involuntary allies." Khrushchev added:

> It was only natural that there should have been some resentment on their part left over from the war and the first years after the war. The Romanians and Hungarians had been dragged into the war against us by Hitler. Therefore, our army, as it pursued the retreating Hitlerite invaders back into Germany, had attacked and defeated these other countries as well... Because of the lingering hard feelings and even antagonism on the part of our allies, we found it difficult to achieve the desired degree of monolithic unity within the socialist camp.[35]

Given the initial reluctance of most of the East European states to subordinate their foreign policies to Soviet preferences indefinitely, Stalin increasingly sensed that his goal of maintaining a pliant buffer zone would require the imposition of direct Communist rule throughout the region. This realization came at the same time that Stalin had begun to restore a brutal dictatorship at home, undoing the liberalization of the wartime years.

Seventh, the "political cultures" of the East European peoples— that is, their historically-molded political values, beliefs, loyalties, practices, and expectations—were not amenable to the political *system* of Soviet Communism.[36] In the interwar period, all the East European so-

---

[34] "Zapis' besedy tov. Molotova s Matyashom Rakoshi," Transcript of Conversation (Top Secret), 29 April 1947, in RGASPI, F. 17, Op. 128, D. 1019, Ll. 8–22, quoted from L. 14.

[35] Khrushchev, *Vremya, lyudi, vlast'*, Vol. 2, pp. 345–46.

[36] Cf. the excellent volume edited by Archie Brown and Jack Gray, *Political Culture and Political Change in Communist Societies*, 2nd ed. (London: Macmillan, 1979). On different conceptions of "political culture," see Richard

cieties except Czechoslovakia had experienced one form or another of dictatorship, but none of them had exhibited much popular support for a Communist alternative. Indigenous Communist parties, when permitted to organize, were generally of negligible importance in pre-1939 East European politics. Even in Czechoslovakia, which, as the lone industrialized state in the region before the war, had by far the largest Communist party, only about ten percent of the vote went to Communist candidates in pre-war parliamentary elections.[37] Although electoral support for the Communist party in Czechoslovakia increased dramatically after 1945—reaching 38 percent in the May 1946 elections—it still represented only a minority of the country. The Communist share of the vote in the 1946 elections was larger in the Czech lands than in Slovakia (where the Slovak Communist Party trailed far behind the Slovak Democratic Party), but even among Czechs the 1946 voting results were due less to an intrinsic rise of support for Communism than to the bitter disillusionment many Czechs felt toward the West for what they saw as the "betrayal" at Munich in September 1938, as well as the gratitude they felt toward the Soviet Union for its part in the defeat of Nazi Germany.[38] Moreover, Czechoslovakia was an anomaly in Eastern Europe; in no other country in the region except Bulgaria had pre-war Communist parties garnered more than trifling support; and in several countries, especially Romania, Hungary, and Poland, Communism was widely regarded as antithetical to traditional beliefs and values.[39]

Despite the enormous impact of World War II on the political cultures of Eastern Europe, popular attitudes toward the Communist

---

W. Wilson, "The Many Voices of Political Culture: Assessing Different Approaches," *World Politics*, Vol. 52, No. 2 (January 2000):) 245–73; Lucian W. Pye and Sidney Verba eds., *Political Culture and Political Development* (Princeton, NJ: Princeton University Press, 1965); and Dennis Kavanagh, *Political Culture* (London: Macmillan, 1972).

[37] *Zprávy Statního úřadu statistického* (ZSUS), Vol. II, Prague, 1921, p. 2; ZSUS, Vol. VI, 1925, p. 76; ZSUS, Vol. X, 1929, p. 87b; and ZSUS, Vol. XVI, 1935, p. 72.

[38] See Bradley F. Abrams, *The Struggle for the Soul of the Nation: Czech Culture and the Rise of Communism* (Lanham, MD: Rowman & Littlefield, 2004).

[39] For a useful discussion, see R.V. Burks, "Eastern Europe," in Cyril E. Black and Thomas P. Thornton eds., *Communism and Revolution: The Strategic Uses of Political Violence* (Princeton, NJ: Princeton University Press, 1964), pp. 77–116.

parties after the war changed surprisingly little in most countries. The destructiveness and horrors of the war, to be sure, had thoroughly discredited the sociopolitical structures of the interwar period and had spawned a general desire for far-reaching social change. Leftist parties had a favorable milieu in which to operate and seek electoral support. Nonetheless, the longing of most East Europeans for a sharp break with the pre-war order—a sentiment that was evident in France, Great Britain, and Italy as well—did not translate into support for a Soviet-imposed version of Communism. The popularity of the East European Communist parties had increased as a result of their participation in the anti-Nazi resistance and their advocacy of radical change, but in only a few countries (Albania, Yugoslavia, and Czechoslovakia) was this increase of major importance. Without direct or implicit Soviet military backing, the Communist parties would not have been able to gain power in Eastern Europe except in Albania and Yugoslavia and perhaps eventually in Czechoslovakia. Indeed, in most of the East European countries the Communists would have been of little or no political consequence: In Hungary, for example, the Communist party received only 17 percent of the vote in the 1945 elections (despite Soviet browbeating), and in Poland, as Khrushchev admitted, "the recognition which the Party received from the working-class and the people was never very deep-rooted or widespread."[40] Much the same was true of Romania and Eastern Germany.

Furthermore, even if popular support for Communism had been stronger, the puissant sense of nationalism underlying the political cultures of all the East European states guaranteed that external domination by the Soviet Union would not be accepted easily. Even in Czechoslovakia, the willingness of the Communist Party to subordinate all its domestic and foreign positions to those of Moscow alienated large numbers of otherwise sympathetic voters, especially after the contrast between Czechoslovakia's democratic heritage and the Stalinist dictatorship in the USSR had become apparent. The

---

[40] Khrushchev, *Vremya, lyudi, vlast'*, Vol. 2, p. 319. On Hungary, see Peter Kenez, *Hungary from the Nazis to the Soviets: The Establishment of the Communist Regime in Hungary, 1944–1948* (New York: Cambridge University Press, 2006).

consequences of nationalist sentiments throughout the region were enormous: More than anything else, the Soviet Union's role in establishing Communist regimes, and the continued subordination of those regimes to Soviet preferences and policies, thwarted efforts by the East European governments to acquire genuine legitimacy among their populations.

Eighth, for both geographical and historical reasons, Soviet leaders attached special importance to East Germany, Poland, and Czechoslovakia after the war. The northern part of Eastern Europe had been the traditional avenue for Germany's *Drang nach Osten*, and after 1945 Poland and Czechoslovakia provided crucial logistical and communications links between Moscow and the Group of Soviet Forces in Germany (later renamed the Western Group of Forces). Thus, the perceived threat from West Germany appeared more exigent in those two states and in East Germany, and to a lesser extent in Hungary, than it did in Romania, Bulgaria, Albania, or Yugoslavia. Moreover, the potentially dynamic economies of East Germany, Poland, and Czechoslovakia, and the consequent ability of those states to become military powers in their own right—as the vital Northern Tier of what was later to become the Warsaw Pact—ensured that they were regarded from the outset by Soviet leaders as the key countries in Eastern Europe. Threats to Soviet relations with the Northern Tier countries, especially with East Germany, were always viewed with particular concern.

Ninth, the subordination of the East European states to Soviet power enabled the Soviet Union to set the "political agenda" for the region. Territorial disputes and other conflicts that were so common before 1945—such as those between Poland and (East) Germany, Hungary and Romania, Czechoslovakia and Poland, Bulgaria and Yugoslavia, and Bulgaria and Romania, as well as the general phenomenon of "Balkanization"—ceased to be as important in an era of Soviet hegemony. These sorts of conflicts were not totally absent during the Communist era, as the Hungarian–Romanian and Bulgarian–Yugoslav disputes illustrate; but they tended to be submerged and contained by Soviet power. To that extent, Soviet control of Eastern Europe imposed a form of ostensible order on the region that could not have existed during the interwar period.

Domestic Political Trends in the USSR and Their Implications for Policymaking *vis-à-vis* Eastern Europe

The Second World War had both short-term and long-term political effects in the Soviet Union that were important for policymaking toward Eastern Europe. In the years leading up to the war and during the fighting itself, Stalin ordered mass deportations of many national and ethnic groups from their homelands to desolate sites in Siberia, the Arctic, or Central Asia.[41] In the swaths of the western USSR that fell under German occupation, Stalinist political controls were temporarily replaced by equally harsh German rule. Elsewhere in the Soviet Union, the war brought a tightening of some political strictures (e.g., a drastic increase in the penalties for job-changing and absenteeism) but also a cessation of the violent mass terror of 1937–39 and a relaxation of some of the long-standing restrictions on peasants, religious believers, and artists. As the fighting drew to a close, many ordinary Soviet citizens were hoping that the privations of the wartime years would cease and that life would genuinely improve as the country recovered from its vast human and material losses.[42] But Stalin himself came to fear, soon after the war ended, that the Soviet Union was dangerously vulnerable to political "contamination" from outside, as soldiers and refugees returned home after having been exposed to the "alien ideas" and superior living standards in the West. To ward off this threat and reassert tight control, Stalin brought back a series of draconian restrictions and reinvigorated the internal security organs, using them to send more prisoners to the gulag. By 1946 many of the repressive measures of the prewar period were being revived—a trend that accelerated over the next six years with a resumption of political purges (albeit selectively), further mass deportations of national groups, a vicious anti-Semitic campaign, and other brutal policies. Although Stalin by the end of his

---

[41] N.L. Pobol' and P.M. Polian eds., *Stalinskie deportatsii, 1928–1953* (Moscow: Mezhdunarodnyi Fond Demokratiya—Izdatel'stvo Materik, 2005).

[42] See Elena Zubkova, *Poslevoennoe sovetskoe obshchestvo: Politika i povsednevnost', 1945–1953* (Moscow: ROSSPEN, 2000). See also the declassified documents compiled by Elena Zubkova in *Sovetskaya zhizn', 1945–1953* (Moscow: ROSSPEN, 2003).

life had not returned to mass terror, Soviet citizens' hopes of enjoying somewhat greater political freedom proved to be in vain.

Part and parcel of Stalin's effort to solidify his own political control and to shield Soviet society from Western influence was his push for ever greater conformity in Eastern Europe. His initial goal of creating a secure buffer zone against possible military threats did not require the imposition of Communist systems in Eastern Europe, but as he became increasingly worried about the political/ideological "threat" from the West he sought to close potential channels of "contamination" in Eastern Europe. To this end, he pressed the local Communist leaders to "intensify [their] class struggle," reversing his earlier emphasis on a step-by-step approach.[43] By late 1946 and early 1947, he began urging the East European Communist leaders to abandon their cooperation with non-Communist parties and to take "bolder actions" to ensure the "Communists' victory."[44] Unlike in November 1945, when the Soviet Union permitted free elections in Hungary that ended in a humiliating setback for the Communist party, Soviet leaders in 1946 and 1947 abetted the falsification of elections in Poland, Romania, and Hungary in favor of the Communists.[45] By the same token, Stalin in mid-1947 prohibited the East European countries from taking part in the Marshall Plan.[46]

Stalin's shift to a harder line in Eastern Europe was spurred not only by his desire to establish a firmer barrier against "hostile" Western influences but also by his determination to crush underground nationalist movements in the newly annexed regions of the western USSR. From the mid-1940s through the mid-1950s the Soviet army and internal security organs devoted an extraordinary amount of effort and resources to a fierce—but, at times, only partly successful—struggle

---

[43] "Zapis' besedy tov. Molotova s Matyashom Rakoshi," LI. 8–22.

[44] See, for example, "Zapis' besedy I. V. Stalina s G. Georgiu-Dezh i A. Pauker, 2 fevralya 1947 g.," Transcript of Conversation (Top Secret), 2 February 1947, in RGASPI, F. 17, Op. 128, D. 903, LI. 89–95.

[45] See, for example, G.P. Murashko and A.F. Noskova, "Sovetskii faktor v poslevoennoi Vostochnoi Evrope, 1945–1948 gg.," in L.N. Nezhinskii ed., *Sovetskaya vneshnyaya politika v gody "kholodnoi voiny" (1945–1985): Novoe prochtenie* (Moscow: Mezhdunarodnye otnosheniya, 1995), pp. 93–4.

[46] For relevant declassified evidence, see Volokitina et al. eds., *Vostochnaya Evropa v dokumentakh rossiiskikh arkhivov*, Vol. 1, Docs. 224, 226, and 227.

against underground nationalist "bandits" and resistance fighters in western Ukraine, Lithuania, Estonia, Latvia, and western Belarus.[47] Even after Soviet MVD (Ministry of Internal Affairs) units wiped out the main guerrilla forces by the early 1950s (a process accompanied by great cruelty and bloodshed, especially through mid-1948), some of the underground national movements survived.[48]

The emergence of these armed resistance groups deeply angered Stalin, who demanded a "merciless campaign to eradicate them." He frequently and harshly criticized the Ukrainian, Lithuanian, Belarusian,

---

[47] Countless declassified materials about the Soviet campaign against underground nationalist movements (and against nationalist sentiment in general) are available in the archives of Belarus, Estonia, Latvia, Lithuania, and Ukraine (Kyiv and L'viv). In Moscow, the bulk of documents about this topic in the Presidential Archive and the State Archive of the Russian Federation (in Fond R-9478, "Glavnoe upravlenie po bor'be s banditizmom MVD SSSR, 1938–1950 gg.") are still classified, but many important items have been released since 1992. For some valuable samples of the enormous quantity of newly available documentation outside Russia, see "Vsem nachal'nikam UO NKVD Latv. SSR," Report No. 1/90ss (Top Secret), directive for the Latvian NKVD, 14 July 1945, in Latvijas Valsts Arhīvs (LVA), Fonds (F.) 1822, Apridos (Apr.) 1, Lietas (Li.) 244, Lapa (La.) 165; "Ob usilenii politicheskoi raboty, povyshenii bol'shevistskoi bditel'nosti i boevoi vyuchki v istrebitel'nykh batal'onakh zapadnykh oblastei USSR: Postanovlenie TsK KP/b/u," 18 April 1946 (Strictly Secret/Special Dossier), in *Tsentral'nyi Derzhavnyi Arkhiv Hromads'kykh Ob'ednan' Ukrainy* (TsDAHOU), F. 1, Op. 16, Sprava (Spr.) 50, LI. 44–50; "O nedostatkakh v rabote organov MVD, MGB, Suda, i Prokuratury po bor'be s narushitelyami sovetskoi zakonnosti v zapadnykh oblastyakh USSR: Postanovlenie TsK KP/b/u," 24 July 1946 (Strictly Secret), in *TsDAHOU*, F. 1, Op. 16, Spr. 50, LI. 92–104; "O nedostatakh bor'by s narusheniyami sotsialisticheskoi zakonnosti i merakh po ikh ustraneniyu: Postanovlenie No. Soveta ministrov Ukrainskoi SSR i Tsentra'lnogo Komiteta KP(b)U," 24 August 1946 (Top Secret), in *TsDAHOU*, F. 1, Op. 16, Spr. 50, LI. 122–32; and "Sekretaryu TsK KP(b) Latvii tov. Kalnberzin," Report No. 00293 (Top Secret) from Lieut.-Colonel A. Boikov, head of the military tribunal of the Latvian Internal Affairs Ministry, 26 May 1948, in LVA, F. 1219s, Apr. 8, Li. 102, La. 86–93.

[48] "Spravka o sostoyanii bor'by s ostatkami bandounovskogo podpol'ya v zapadnykh oblastyakh USSR," Memorandum No. 49/a (Top Secret), May 1952, from F. Golynnyi, deputy head of the UkrCP CC Administrative Department, in *TsDAHOU*, F. 1, Op. 190, Spr. 72, LI. 81–93. See also "Spravka," Informational Memorandum (Top Secret) from N. Koval'chuk, Ukrainian minister of state security, 23 April 1952, in *TsDAHOU*, F. 1, Op. 190, Spr. 72, LI. 94–6.

Estonian, and Latvian party leaders and internal security forces for their failure to destroy the clandestine nationalist organizations in their respective republics. Stalin repeatedly ordered the union-republic governments to finish off the task as soon as possible, but his injunctions initially had little effect, as underground nationalist fighters continued to challenge the Soviet regime. The Soviet leader eventually concluded that the task of combating the guerrilla movements would be greatly facilitated if the Soviet Union could enlist the help of several East European countries, notably Czechoslovakia, Poland, Romania, and what became East Germany. Before the East European countries came under Communist rule, Soviet proposals for joint operations against resistance fighters in the western USSR often were abortive or resulted in only limited help. In western Ukraine, for example, local party officials complained in early 1946 that they were "not receiving the timely assistance [they] needed" from Polish troops and security units and that this was "posing grave complications."[49] Soviet leaders came to believe that wider and more sustained deployment of the East European security forces against "hostile, anti-Soviet elements" along the border with the USSR would be infeasible unless Communists gained sway in those countries. This perception reinforced Stalin's growing inclination to press ahead with the establishment of Communist rule in Eastern Europe.

Stalin's judgment on this particular matter proved to be correct. Once Communist regimes were in place in Eastern Europe, joint campaigns against the anti-Soviet guerrillas became far more efficacious, as was underscored in a top-secret analysis prepared by the deputy chairman of the Soviet State Security (KGB) apparatus:

> Direct contacts were established among the [East-bloc] state security organs [in the late 1940s], and they began to convene periodic meetings of their senior officials. As a result of this cooperation, the state security organs of the USSR, Romania, and Poland arranged joint measures to

---

[49] "Pro seryozni nedoliky v roboty orhaniv MVS ta partiinykh orhanizatsii po likvidatsii reshtkiv band ta pidpillya ukrains'kykh burzhuaznykh natsionalistiv v zakhidnykh oblastyakh ukrains'koi RSR: Postanovka TsK KP Ukrainy," Memorandum (Top Secret) to the Ukrainian Communist Party Central Committee, 4 December 1953 (Top Secret), in *TsDAHOU*, F. 1, Op. 190, Spr. 87, Ll. 174–81.

liquidate the bands of the [Ukrainian] underground and to safeguard their borders. [...] Cooperation among the state security organs of the USSR, Poland, Czechoslovakia, and the GDR contributed to the [USSR's] successful struggle against Ukrainian, Belorussian, Lithuanian, Latvian, and Estonian nationalists. With the help of the state security organs of Poland, Czechoslovakia, and the GDR, all of which provided valuable operational means of studying nationalist organizations and their agents as well as means of uncovering lines of communications and their control mechanisms, the Soviet state security organs were able to infiltrate agents into the underground nationalist centers, recruit a number of spies within the nationalist organizations (OUN, NTS, etc.), establish control over the channels for setting up agent networks and over their communications, and achieve other aims.[50]

Although armed partisan groups in the western USSR were not fully extirpated until the mid-1950s, the turning point in the Soviet government's struggle against clandestine nationalist organizations came with the ascendance of Communist governments in Eastern Europe. This factor alone would have given Stalin a powerful incentive to encourage the East European Communist leaders to "act more boldly" in their "bid for power."[51]

The Entrenchment of Communist Rule in Eastern Europe

The emergence and consolidation of Communist regimes in Eastern Europe proceeded at varying rates.[52] In Yugoslavia and Albania, the

---

[50] See the lengthy, top-secret textbook compiled by Lieutenant-General V.M. Chebrikov *et al.*, *Istoriya sovetskikh organov gosudarstvennoi bezopasnosti*, No. 12179 (Moscow: Vysshaya Krasnoznamennaya Shkola Komiteta Gosudarstvennoi Bezopasnosti, 1977), pp. 485, 486.

[51] "Zapis' besedy I. V. Stalina s G. Georgiu-Dezh, 10 fevralya 1947 g.," Transcript of Conversation (Top Secret), 10 February 1947, in RGASPI, F. 558, Op. 1, D. 361, LI. 67–71.

[52] For a first-rate, concise overview, see L.Ya. Gibianskii, "Problemy Vostochnoi Evropy i nachalo formirovaniya sovetskogo bloka," in N.I. Egorova and A.O. Chubar'yan eds., *Kholodnaya voina, 1945–1963 gg.: Istoricheskaya retrospektiva—Sbornik statei* (Moscow: OLMA-PRESS, 2003), pp. 105–36. See also N.E. Bystrova, *SSSR i formirovanie voenno-blokogo protivostoyaniya v Evrope, 1945–1953 gg.* (Moscow: Kuchkovo Pole, 2007); and the essays

indigenous Communist parties led by Josip Broz Tito and Enver Hoxha had obtained a good deal of political leverage and military strength
through their participation in the anti-Nazi resistance during World
War II. Tito's and Hoxha's partisan armies had also fought against
their domestic rivals throughout the war and were able to gain control
of their countries as the fighting came to an end. Once in power, they
quickly moved to establish Stalinist regimes that were closely modeled
on the Soviet system.

In Bulgaria and Romania, Soviet troops who had occupied the
countries in the late summer of 1944 enabled Communist-dominated
governments to assume power in late 1944 and early 1945. The Bulgarian and Romanian Communist parties had been of negligible influence prior to and during World War II, but the presence of Soviet
military forces on Bulgarian and Romanian territory shifted the balance of political power sharply in favor of the Communists during the
final months of the war.[53] The new, Soviet-backed governments in both
countries initially took the form of coalitions in which non-Communist
parties were allowed to take part. But that arrangement was mostly
cosmetic, intended to forestall any immediate frictions with the United
States and Britain. No sooner had the governments in both countries
been set up then the Communists began methodically eliminating their
potential opponents, paving the way for Stalinist transformations.[54]

---

in Norman M. Naimark and Leonid Gibianskii eds., *The Establishment of
Communist Regimes in Eastern Europe* (Boulder, CO: Westview Press, 1997).
Older monographs on this subject that remain exceptionally useful are Hugh
Seton-Watson, *The East European Revolution*, 3rd ed. (New York: Praeger,
1956); Zbigniew K. Brzeziński, *The Soviet Bloc: Unity and Conflict*, rev. ed.
(Cambridge, MA: Harvard University Press, 1967); and R.V. Burks, *The Dy-
namics of Communism in Eastern Europe* (Princeton, NJ: Princeton University
Press, 1961).

[53] See Mito Isusov, *Politicheskiyat zhivot v Bulgariya, 1944–1948* (Sofia: Univ.
Izdatelstvo "Sv. Kliment Okhridski," 2000); Lyubomir Ognyanov, *Dur-
zhavno-politicheskata sistema na Bulgariya, 1944–1948* (Sofia: Izdatelstvo na
Bulgarskata akademiya na naukite, 1993); and Flori Stănescu and Dragoş
Zamfirescu eds., *Ocupaţia sovietică in România: Documente, 1944–1946* (Bu-
charest: Vremea, 1998). See also the relevant documents in Volokitina *et
al.* eds., *Vostochnaya Evropa v dokumentakh rossiiskikh arkhivov*, 2 vols.; and
Volokitina *et al.* eds., *Sovetskii faktor v Vostochnoi Evrope*, 2 vols.

[54] Isusov, *Politicheskiyat zhivot v Bulgariya*; pp. 190–227, 258–342; Ognyan,
Durzhavno-politicheskata sistema na Bulgariya, pp. 137–201; and Ioan Scur-

In the eastern zone of Germany, the Soviet occupation forces and administrators did not move immediately after the war to establish a Communist system, and Stalin (as noted above) repeatedly urged the leaders of the SED to adopt a "cautious approach." From the beginning, however, the Soviet occupation authorities took a number of steps that—perhaps unintentionally—ensured that the SED would eventually gain preeminent power. By the time the East German state, known as the German Democratic Republic (GDR), was formally created in October 1949, a Soviet-style polity was firmly entrenched in East Berlin under Walter Ulbricht.[55] Stalin by that point had largely abandoned any further hope of creating a unified German polity and had overcome his ambivalence about the desirability of setting up a Communist system in the GDR.

Elsewhere in the region—in Hungary, Poland, and Czechoslovakia—events followed a more gradual pattern. Local Communists who had spent many years in the Soviet Union returned to their native countries after World War II and worked jointly with fellow Commu-

---

tu ed., *România—viaţa politică în documente: 1945* (Bucharest: Info-Team, 1994). On the process of forced collectivization in Bulgaria (a country that was predominantly agrarian in 1945), see Kalin Iosifov, *Totalitarnoto nasilie v bulgarskoto selo (1944–1951) i posleditsite za Bulgariya* (Sofia: Univ. izdatelstvo "Sv. Kliment Okhridski," 2003).

[55] For a comprehensive account of the Soviet role in the eastern zone of Germany, see Naimark, *The Russians in Germany*. See also Stefan Creuzberger, *Die sowjetische Besatzungsmacht und das politische System der SBZ* (Köln-Weimar: Böhlau Verlag, 1996). Some extremely important collections of declassified East-bloc documents regarding Soviet policy in Germany during this period have been published over the years. See Georgii Kynin and Jochen Laufer eds., *SSSR i germanskii vopros, 1941–1949: Dokumenty iz Arkhiva vneshnei politiki Rossiiskoi Federatsii*, 3 vols. (Moscow: Mezhdunarodnye otnosheniya, 1996, 1999 and 2004); Rolf Badstubner and Wilfried Loth eds., *Wilhelm Pieck—Aufzeichnungen zur Deutschlandpolitik, 1945–1953* (Berlin: Akademie Verlag, 1994); Bernd Bonwetsch, Gennadii Bordyugov, and Norman Naimark, eds., *SVAG: Upravlenie propagandy (informatsii) i S. I. Tyul'panov* (Moscow: Rossiya Molodaya, 1994); and Elke Scherstjanoi ed., *Das SKK-Statut: zur Geschichte der Sowjetischen Kontrollkommission in Deutschland, 1949–1953* (Munich: K.G. Saur, 1998). For valuable memoirs by former Soviet and East German officials, see K.I. Koval', *Poslednii svidetel': "Germanskaya karta" v kholodnoi voine* (Moscow: Rosspen, 1997); M.I. Semiryaga, *Kak my upravlyali germaniei: Politika i zhizn'* (Moscow: Rosspen, 1995); and Erich W. Gniffke, *Jahre mit Ulbricht* (Cologne: Verlag Wissenschaft und Politik, 1966).

nists who had stayed at home during the war and had taken part in the anti-Nazi resistance (or had kept a low profile). In all three countries, the resurgent Communist parties played a leading role in the formation of what initially were broad coalition' governments that carried out extensive land redistribution and other long overdue economic and political reforms. The reform process, however, was kept under tight Communist control, and the top jobs in the ministry of internal affairs went exclusively to Communist party members. From those posts, they could oversee the purging of the local police forces and armies, the execution of alleged "collaborators," the control and censorship of the mass media, and the intimidation and ouster of non-Communist ministers and legislators.

With the backing of the Soviet Army, the Communist parties in these countries gradually solidified their hold through the sedulous use of what the Hungarian Communist party leader Mátyás Rákosi later called "salami tactics."[56] The basic strategy in each case was outlined by Stalin in 1946 when he told the Polish Communists that "there is no need to rush." He urged them to "move gradually toward socialism by exploiting elements of the bourgeois democratic order such as the parliament and other institutions." The aim of these incremental steps, Stalin said, would be to "isolate all your enemies politically," to "resist the constant pressure from reactionary circles," and to lay the groundwork for a "decisive struggle against the reactionaries."[57]

Moscow's role in the Communization of the region was strengthened in September 1947 by the establishment of the Communist Information Bureau (Cominform), a body responsible for binding to-

---

[56] Mátyás Rákosi, "Népi demokráciánk útja," *Társadalmi Szemle* (Budapest), No. 3 (March 1952), pp. 115–49. On p. 134, Rákosi declares that "'Salami Tactics' ("*Szalámi taktikának*"), as we called this approach, involved the cutting out of reaction in slices from the Smallholders' Party." Rákosi originally presented these remarks to a session of the higher party school of the Hungarian Workers' Party on 29 February 1952. He provides a remarkably candid description of the strategy and tactics used by the Hungarian Communists in their gradual seizure of power.

[57] "Zapis' besedy tov. I. V. Stalina s B. Berutom i E. Osubka-Moravskim, 24 maya 1947 g.," 24 May 1947 (Top Secret), in Arkhiv Prezidenta Rossiiskii Federatsii (APRF), Fond (F.) 558, Opis' (Op.) 1, Delo (D.) 355, Ll. 330–62, reproduced in Volokitina *et al.* eds., *Vostochnaya Evropa v dokumentakh rossiiskikh arkhivov*, Vol. 1, pp. 443–63.

gether the East European Communist parties (as well as the French
and Italian Communist parties) under the exclusive leadership of the
Soviet Communist Party.[58] Because the Cominform was formally created a few months after the U.S. secretary of state, George Marshall,
made his historic speech at Harvard University proposing a European
Recovery Program (i.e., the Marshall Plan), some Western analysts
have speculated that the enunciation of the plan is what spurred Soviet leaders to set up the Cominform.[59] Archival materials that have
recently come to light in both Russia and Eastern Europe contravene
this notion. It is now clear that Soviet planning for an organization like
the Cominform began in the early part of 1946 (and possibly earlier),
long before the Marshall Plan was even contemplated, much less announced.[60] The establishment of the Cominform was motivated not
by the Marshall Plan but by Stalin's growing conviction that the East
European states must conform to his own harsh methods of dictatorial

---

[58] For a meticulously documented analysis of the origins of the Cominform,
see L.Ya. Gibianskii, "Kak voznik Kominform: Po novym arkhivnym materialam," *Novaya i noveishaya istoriya* (Moscow), No. 4 (July–August 1993), pp.
131–52. See also G.M. Adibekov, *Kominform i poslevoennaya Evropa, 1947–
1956 gg.* (Moscow: Rossiya molodaya, 1994). The voluminous files of the
Cominform, from 1947 to 1956, have been available for research since early
1994 in Fond 575 at the former Central Party Archive (now known as the
Russian State Archive of Socio-Political History) in Moscow. Declassified
materials from the Cominform conferences held in 1947, 1948, and 1949
are available in Grant Adibekov *et al.* eds., *Soveshchaniya Kominforma, 1947,
1948, 1949: Dokumenty i materialy* (Moscow: ROSSPEN, 1998).

[59] See, for example, Michael Cox and Caroline Kennedy-Pipe, "The Trag-
edy of American Diplomacy? Rethinking the Marshall Plan," *Journal of Cold
War Studies*, Vol. 7, No. 1 (Winter 2005), pp. 97–134; Vladislav Zubok and
Constantine Pleshakov, *Inside the Kremlin's Cold War: From Stalin to Khrush-
chev* (Cambridge, MA: Harvard University Press, 1996), pp. 103–7; Vojtech
Mastny, *The Cold War and Soviet Insecurity: The Stalin Years* (New York:
Oxford University Press, 1996), pp. 27–8; Scott Parrish, "The Turn toward
Confrontation: The Soviet Response to the Marshall Plan, 1947," CWIHP
Working Paper No. 9 (Washington, D.C.: Cold War International History
Project, March 1994), pp. 32–6; and William C. Taubman, *Stalin's American
Policy: From Entente to Détente to Cold War* (New York: W.W. Norton, 1982),
pp. 215–45. For more nuanced views, see Martin Schain ed., *The Marshall
Plan: Fifty Years After* (New York: Palgrave, 2001).

[60] L.Ya. Gibianskii, "Forsirovanie sovetskoi blokovoi politiki," in Egorova and
Chubar'yan eds., *Kholodnaya voina*, pp. 137–86.

rule. Stalin's determination to prevent any further "contamination" from the West in the USSR necessitated the Stalinization of Eastern Europe.

The final step in the establishment of Communist regimes in Eastern Europe came with the seizure of power by the Communist Party of Czechoslovakia (*Komunistická strana Československa,* or KSČ) in February 1948. From that point on, "People's Democracies" allied with the Soviet Union were in place all over Eastern Europe. Although the USSR ultimately withdrew its support for the Communist insurgency in Greece and refrained from trying to establish a Communist government in Finland or even a Soviet–Finnish military alliance, Soviet power throughout the central and southern heartlands of the region was now firmly entrenched.

The Split with Yugoslavia

Despite the formation of Communist regimes in Eastern Europe, the June 1948 Cominform summit revealed the emergence of a schism in the Soviet bloc. Yugoslavia, which had been one of the staunchest postwar allies of the Soviet Union, was expelled from the Cominform and publicly denounced. Tension between the Soviet Union and Yugoslavia had been developing behind-the-scenes for several months and had finally reached the breaking point in March 1948. The rift stemmed from substantive disagreements, domestic political maneuvering, and a clash of personalities.[61] Documents released since 1990 indicate that

---

[61] The origins of the Soviet–Yugoslav split are much better understood now than before 1991, thanks to newly declassified archival materials collected by Leonid Gibianskii and other researchers in Moscow, Belgrade, and other East European capitals. See, for example, Leonid Gibianskii, "The Origins of the Soviet–Yugoslav Split," in Naimark and Gibianskii eds., *The Establishment of Communist Regimes in Eastern Europe,* pp. 291–312; Jeronim Perović, "The Tito–Stalin Split: A Reassessment in Light of New Evidence," *Journal of Cold War Studies,* Vol. 9, No. 2 (Spring 2007): 32–63; and L.Ya. Gibianskii, "Ot 'nerushimoi druzhby' k besposhchadnoi bor'be: Model' 'sotsialisticheskogo lagerya' i sovetsko-yugoslavskii konflikt," in L.Ya. Gibianskii, ed., *U istokov "sotsialisticheskogo sodruzhestva": SSSR i vostochnoevropeiskie strany v 1944–1949 gg.* (Moscow: Nauka, 1995), pp. 137–63. For an insightful and more extended analysis, see A.S. Anikeev, *Kak Tito ot Stalina ushel:*

the level of animosity between the two countries by mid-1948 was even greater than Western analysts had previously thought.

The most serious differences between Moscow and Belgrade had arisen over policy in the Balkans.[62] Stalin was increasingly wary of Tito's efforts to seek unification with Albania and to set up a Yugoslav-dominated federation with Bulgaria—an issue that figured prominently in the final face-to-face meetings between Stalin and Tito, in May–June 1946.[63] Although the relationship between the two leaders in mid-1946 was not yet acrimonious, it deteriorated over the next year. Stalin was

---

Yugoslaviya, SSSR i SShA v nachal'nyi period "kholodnoi voiny" (Moscow: Institut slavyanovedeniya RAN, 2002), esp. pp. 86–206. For a good sample of the newly available documentation, see "Sekretnaya sovetsko-yugoslavskaya perepiska 1948 goda," *Voprosy istorii* (Moscow), Nos. 4–5, 6–7, and 10–11 (1992): 119–36, 158–72, and 154–69, respectively; as well as the multitude of relevant documents in Volokitina *et al.* eds., *Vostochnaya Evropa;* and Volokitina *et al.* eds., *Sovetskii faktor v Vostochnoi Evrope.* The materials released in the early 1990s were discussed extensively in a number of articles at the time, including I. Bukharkin, "Konflikt, ktorogo ne dolzhno bylo byt' (iz istorii sovetsko-yugoslavskiikh otnoshenii)," *Vestnik Ministerstva inostrannykh del SSSR* (Moscow), No. 6 (31 March 1990): 53–7; L.Ya. Gibianskii, "U nachala konflikta: Balkanskii uzel," *Rabochii klass i sovremennyi mir* (Moscow), No. 2 (March–April 1990): 171–85; I.V. Bukharkin and L.Ya. Gibianskii, "Pervye shagi konflikta," *Rabochii klass i sovremennyi mir* (Moscow), No. 5 (September–October 1990): 152–63; L.Ya. Gibianskii, "Vyzov v Moskvu," *Politicheskie issledovaniya* (Moscow), No. 1 (January–February 1991): 195–207; and the related series of articles by L.Ya. Gibianskii, "K istorii sovetsko-yugoslavskogo konflikta 1948–1953 gg.," in *Sovetskoe slavyanovedenie* (Moscow), No. 3 (May–June 1991): 32–47 and No. 4 (July–August 1991): 12–24; and *Slavyanovedenie* (Moscow), No. 1 (January–February 1992): 68–82 and No. 3 (May–June 1992): 35–51.

[62] For an insightful discussion of this issue, see L.Ya. Gibianskii, "Ideya balkanskogo ob"edineniya i plany ee osushchestvleniya v 40-e gody XX veka," *Voprosy istorii* (Moscow), No. 11 (November 2001): 38–56.

[63] "Zapis' besedy generalissimus I. V. Stalina s marshalom Tito" (Secret), 27 May 1946, in APRF, F. 558, Op. 1, D. 397, Ll. 107–10. The secret Yugoslav transcript of these talks, from Arhiv Josipa Broza Tita (AJBT), F. Kabinet Maršala Jugoslavije (KMJ), I–1/7, pp. 6–11, was published in *Istoricheskii arkhiv* (Moscow), No. 2 (1994): 24–8, along with valuable annotations by Leonid Gibianskii. The two transcripts are complementary for the most part, rather than duplicative. For more on Moscow's concerns about the Balkan issue, see several dozen top-secret cables and reports to Stalin and Foreign Minister Vyacheslav Molotov in Arkhiv vneshnei politiki Rossiiskoi Federatsii (AVPRF), F. 0144, Op. 30, Papka (Pa.) 118, D. 10.

especially irritated by Tito's failure to consult with Moscow and to wait for Stalin's explicit approval before taking any steps *vis-à-vis* Bulgaria and Albania. After Yugoslavia neglected to obtain Soviet approval for a treaty it signed with Bulgaria in August 1947, Stalin sent a secret cable to Tito denouncing the treaty as "mistaken" and "premature."[64] Tensions increased still further over the next several months as Yugoslavia continued to pursue unification with Albania, despite Moscow's objections.[65] Under pressure from Stalin, Tito promised in January 1948 not to send a Yugoslav army division to Albania (as Yugoslavia had tentatively arranged to do after deploying an air force regiment and military advisers in Albania the previous summer to prepare the country to "rebuff Greek monarcho-fascists"). This concession, however, failed to alleviate Stalin's annoyance. In February 1948, Soviet Foreign Minister Vyacheslav Molotov warned Tito that "serious differences of opinion" about "relations between our countries" would persist unless Yugoslavia adhered to the "normal procedures" of clearing all actions with Moscow beforehand.[66] Concerns about following "normal procedures" were at least as salient as any substantive disputes in the bilateral exchanges over the Balkans.

A few other points of contention had also emerged between the Soviet Union and Yugoslavia in the early postwar years. In particular, Tito was far more willing than Stalin to provide military and financial assistance to Communist guerrillas in "gray-area" countries, notably in Greece.[67] On other issues, too, the Yugoslav leader had occasionally

---

[64] "Shifrtelegramma" No. 37-443-506 (Strictly Secret), from Stalin to Tito, 12 August 1948, in AJBT-KMJ, I-2/17, L. 70.

[65] See the valuable collection of declassified documents from the Soviet foreign ministry archive in "Stranitsy istorii: Konflikt, kotorogo ne dolzhno bylo byt' (iz istorii sovetsko-yugoslavskikh otnohenii)," *Vestnik Ministerstva inostrannykh del SSSR* (Moscow), No. 6 (31 March 1990): 57–63, esp. 57 and 59.

[66] "Iz telegrammy V. M. Molotova A. I. Lavrent'evu dlya peredachi I. Broz Tito 31 yanvarya 1948" and "Iz telegrammy V. M. Molotova A. I. Lavrent'evu dlya peredachi I. Broz Tito 1 fevralya 1948 g," both of which are reproduced in the valuable collection of declassified documents from the Soviet foreign ministry archive in "Stranitsy istorii: Konflikt, kotorogo ne dolzhno bylo byt'," pp. 57 and 59, respectively.

[67] For useful analyses of the Yugoslav, Soviet, and Bulgarian roles in the Greek civil war, see Peter Stavrakis, *Moscow and Greek Communism, 1944–1949* (Ithaca: Cornell University Press, 1989); Jordan Baev, *O emfylios polemos*

objected to what he regarded as the Soviet Union's excessively conciliatory policies toward the West—an ironic position in view of subsequent developments. Nonetheless, the disagreements between the two sides, important though they may have been, were hardly sufficient in themselves to provoke such a bitter and costly schism. For the most part, the Yugoslav Communists had been unstinting in their support for Stalin and the Soviet Union until early 1948. Indeed, the steadfast loyalty of Yugoslavia on almost all issues—loyalty that was spontaneous and not simply coerced—was evidently one of the major factors behind Stalin's decision to seek an abject capitulation from Belgrade as an example to the other East European countries of the unwavering obedience that was expected.[68]

Far from demonstrating Soviet strength, however, the split with Yugoslavia revealed the limits of Soviet coercive power—economic, political, and military. The Soviet Union and its East European allies imposed economic sanctions against Yugoslavia and adopted a number of political measures to destabilize and precipitate the collapse of Tito's regime. But the economic pressure came to naught when Yugoslavia turned to the West and to Third World countries for economic assistance and trade (including supplies of energy and key raw materials) and when Tito rebuffed Moscow's attempts to force Yugoslavia to pay for hundreds of millions of rubles' worth of aid supposedly provided by the USSR in the first few years after the war.[69]

---

sten Ellada: Diethneis diastaseis (Athens: Filistor, 1996); Vladislav Zubok and Constantine Pleshakov, Inside the Kremlin's Cold War: From Stalin to Khrushchev (Cambridge, MA: Harvard University Press, 1996), pp. 56–7; and Artiom Ulunian, "The Soviet Union and the Greek Question, 1946–53: Problems and Appraisals," in Francesca Gori and Silvio Pons eds., The Soviet Union and Europe in the Cold War, 1943–53 (London: Macmillan, 1996), pp. 140–58. Among many examples of the Soviet leadership's relatively cautious approach, see "Beseda tov. Zhdanova s Zakhariadisom," 22 May 1947 (Top Secret), Rossiiskii Gosudarstvennyi Arkhiv Sotsial'no-Politicheskoi Istorii (RGASPI), F. 17, Op. 128, D. 1019, LI. 35–6.

[68] This point is well illustrated by the documents in "Stranitsy istorii: Konflikt, kotorogo ne dolzhno bylo byt'," pp. 57–63. See also "Krupnoe porazhenie Stalina—Sovetsko-yugoslavskii konflikt 1948–1953 godov: prichiny, posledstviya, uroki," Moskovskie novosti (Moscow), No. 27 (2 July 1989): 8–9.

[69] "Tovarishchu Stalinu I. V. ," Memorandum No. 12-s (Top Secret) from A.A. Gromyko, M.A. Men'shikov, A.M. Vasilevskii, A.G. Zverev, and B.P. Beshev to Stalin, 18 December 1950, with attached draft resolution of the

Soviet efforts to encourage pro-Moscow elements in the Yugoslav government, Communist party, and army to launch a coup against Tito proved equally ineffective when the Yugoslav leader liquidated the pro-Moscow factions in these bodies before they could move against him.[70] The Soviet and East European governments broke diplomatic relations with Yugoslavia, annulled the bilateral treaties of friendship, cooperation, and mutual assistance they had signed with Belgrade over the previous few years, and inundated Yugoslavia with radio broadcasts condemning Tito as a "fascist" and a "traitor to the socialist cause." The broadcasts also exhorted the Macedonians and other ethnic groups to "rise up against the oppressive regime" and claimed (falsely) that widespread violent turmoil had broken out in Yugoslavia and within the Yugoslav army.[71] The broadcasts were intended to demoralize the Yugoslav population and to spark social disorder, but they actually had the opposite effect of uniting the country more solidly behind Tito.

Nor was Stalin any more successful when he attempted to rely on covert operations to undermine the Yugoslav government. The Soviet state security and intelligence organs devised a multitude of secret plots to assassinate Tito, including several as late as 1953 that involved a notorious special agent, Josif Grigulevich, who had been posing under aliases as a senior Costa Rican diplomat in both Rome and Belgrade. The idea was for Grigulevich (codenamed "Max") either to release deadly bacteria during a private meeting with the Yugoslav leader or to

Communist Party Central Committee and draft note to the Yugoslav government, in APRF, F. 3, Op. 66, D. 910, Ll. 167–74, reproduced in T.V. Volokitina *et al.* eds., *Sovetskii faktor v Vostochnoi Evrope, 1944–1953*, 2 vols., Vol. 2: *1949–1953* (Moscow: ROSSPEN, 2002), pp. 429–33.

[70] U.S. Central Intelligence Agency (CIA), "National Intelligence Estimate: Probable Developments in Yugoslavia and the Likelihood of Attack upon Yugoslavia, through 1952," NIE-29/2 (Top Secret), 4 January 1952, p. 3, in Harry S. Truman Library (HSTL), President's Secretary's Papers, Intelligence File, 1946–53, Central Intelligence Reports File, 1946–53, Box 213: National Intelligence Estimates.

[71] CIA, "Memorandum: Analysis of Soviet and Satellite Propaganda Directed to or about Yugoslavia," 00-F-125 (Top Secret), 1 September 1950, pp. 1–6, in HSTL. President's Secretary's Papers, Intelligence File, 1946–53, Central Intelligence File, 1946–53, Box 211: Memoranda 1950–52.

fire a concealed, noiseless gun at Tito during an embassy reception.[72] Other plots, devised as early as the summer of 1948, envisaged the use of Bulgarian, Romanian, Hungarian, and Albanian intelligence agents acting at the behest of the Soviet Union. In addition to these covert operations directed against Tito, the Soviet and East European intelligence agencies spirited a large number of saboteurs and subversives into Yugoslavia to foment social chaos, disrupt economic activity, and incite a popular uprising against Tito's government.[73] Soviet-bloc officials also smuggled in huge quantities of newspapers and leaflets in the various national languages of Yugoslavia urging "all true Communists"

---

[72] For a description of the bizarre plots involving Grigulevich, see the handwritten memorandum from S.D. Ignat'ev, chief of the State Security Ministry, to Stalin, in APRF, F. 3, Op. 24, D. 463, LI. 148–9. The full text of the memorandum is transcribed in Dmitrii Volkogonov, "Nesostoyavsheesya pokushenie: Kak sovetskii agent Maks gotovilsya k terroristicheskomu aktu protiv Tito," *Izvestiya* (Moscow), 11 June 1993, p. 7, which was the first publication to mention this scheme. It is discussed far more fully in the book by the late head of the Stalin-era covert operations branch of the Soviet foreign intelligence service, Pavel Sudoplatov, *Spestoperatsii: Lubyanka, Kreml', 1930–1950 gody* (Moscow: Olma-Press, 1998), pp. 528–32. On other plots to assassinate Tito, see Marko Lopušina, *KGB protiv Jugoslavije* (Belgrade: Evro, 2001), pp. 69–75; Christopher Andrew and Vasili Mitrokhin, *The Sword and the Shield: The Mitrokhin Archive and the Secret History of the KGB* (New York: Basic Books, 1999), pp. 355–8; and the first-hand observations in Khrushchev, *Vremya, lyudi, vlast'*, Vol. 3, p. 119.

[73] See, for example, "Protokol za zasedanieto na plenuma na TsK na BKP, sustoyal se na 16 i 17 yanuari 1950 godina," 16–7 January 1950 (Top Secret), in *Tsentralen Durzhaven Arkhiv* (TsDA), F. 1-B, Op. 5, arkhivna edinitsa (a.e.) 55, LI. 15–20; and "Stenogramma ot suveshchanie na aktivistite na sofiiskata organizatsiya na BRP(k) po makedonskiya vupros," 9 October 1948 (Secret), in *TsDA*, F. 214b, Op. 1, a.e. 71, LI. 66–117. See also CIA, "National Intelligence Estimate: Probability of an Invasion of Yugoslavia in 1951," NIE-29 (Top Secret), 20 March 1951, p. 3, in HSTL, President's Secretary's Papers, Intelligence File, 1946–53, Central Intelligence Reports File, 1946–53, Box 213: National Intelligence Estimates. The East European state security forces also sought to disrupt alleged rings of spies and subversives in their own countries and "turn" them so that they could be used as double agents against Yugoslavia. See, for example, "Predlozhenie otnosno: Realiziranata v D. S.—G. Dzhumaya razrabotka 'Izmennik,'" 10 February 1949 (Strictly Confidential), in *TsDA*, F. 1-B, Op. 7, a. e. 1560, LI. 1–4.

to "expose and remove the Tito–Ranković clique."[74] In the end, however, all of these clandestine schemes proved infeasible or were thwarted by the Yugoslav state security forces, which remained firmly beholden to Tito.

The ineffectiveness of political, economic, and covert pressure against Yugoslavia left Stalin with the unattractive option of using large-scale military force, an option he never ultimately pursued. Stalin's hesitation about launching an invasion of Yugoslavia evidently stemmed from many factors, including the prospect that Soviet troops would encounter staunch Yugoslav resistance, the burden of deploying large numbers of Soviet soldiers at a time when the Soviet armed forces were already overstretched, the transport and logistical problems of crossing Bulgaria's mountainous terrain into Yugoslavia, the possibility of provoking a war with the West (a concern that became more acute after the United States and its European allies began forging closer political, economic, and even military ties with Yugoslavia), and a belief that Tito could be ousted by non-military means.[75] If Yugoslavia had

---

[74] "Informatsiya ob organizatsii nelegal'nogo rasprostraneniya na territorii Yugoslavii izdanii yugoslavskikh politemigrantov," Memorandum No. 61ss (Top Secret) from V.G. Grigor'yan to V.M. Molotov, 22 August 1951, in RGASPI, F. 82, Op. 2, D. 1379, Ll. 106–10.

[75] General Béla Király, the commander of Hungarian ground forces in 1949–1950, later claimed that the vigorous U.S. response to North Korea's attack against South Korea in June 1950 was the main thing that caused Stalin to abandon plans for an invasion of Yugoslavia. See Béla Király, "The Aborted Soviet Military Plans against Tito's Yugoslavia," in Wayne S. Vucinich ed., *At the Brink of War and Peace: The Tito–Stalin Split in a Historic Perspective* (New York: Brooklyn College Press, 1984), pp. 273–88. Király may be correct about the *short-term* impact of the U.S. intervention in Korea on Stalin's calculations, but declassified materials reveal that the Soviet leader was emboldened after China intervened in the war and the U.S. military effort bogged down. At a top-secret conference in Moscow in January 1951, Stalin declared that the U.S. failure to defeat China and North Korea demonstrated that "the United States is unprepared to start a third world war and is not even capable of fighting a small war." See the declassified notes of Stalin's remarks at the conference, transcribed in C. Cristescu, "Strict Secret de importanţă deosebită—Ianuarie 1951: Stalin decide înarmarea României," *Magazin istoric* (Bucharest), Vol. 29, No. 10 (October 1995): 15–23. Király's argument is further belied by the concrete evidence of Soviet and East European military preparations for a possible invasion of Yugoslavia. Before the Korean War broke out, Soviet and East European preparations for armed

been adjacent to the Soviet Union or had been located in the center of Eastern Europe rather than on the periphery, Stalin might have been quicker to rely on armed force. Khrushchev, who took part in deliberations about the matter, later said he was "absolutely sure that if the Soviet Union had shared a border with Yugoslavia, Stalin would have resorted to military intervention."[76]

It is conceivable, of course, that if Stalin had lived longer, he would eventually have ordered Soviet troops to occupy Yugoslavia. There is considerable evidence that in the final two years of his life he was seeking the capability for a decisive military move in Europe, possibly against Yugoslavia. Initially, from 1948 through mid-1950, the Soviet Union and its East European allies made only limited preparations for military contingencies *vis-à-vis* Yugoslavia.[77] Declassified U.S. intelligence documents reveal that, as of January 1950, the combined armed

---

intervention in Yugoslavia were minimal, whereas at the height of the Korean War, in 1951–52, the Soviet-bloc states were engaged in a massive military buildup, which would have been of great use for an invasion of Yugoslavia.

[76] Khrushchev, *Vremya, lyudi, vlast'*, Vol. 3, p. 118.

[77] See, for example, CIA, "Estimate of the Yugoslav Regime's Ability to Resist Soviet Pressure During 1949," ORE 44-49 (Top Secret), 20 June 1949, in HSTL, President's Secretary's Papers, Intelligence File, 1946–53, Central Intelligence Reports File, 1946–53, Box 215: O.R.E.; CIA, "The Possibility of Direct Soviet Military Action during 1949," ORE 46-49 (Top Secret), 3 May 1949, p. 4, in HSTL, President's Secretary's Papers, Intelligence File, 1946–53, Central Intelligence Reports File, 1946–53, Box 215: O.R.E.; and László Ritter, "War on Tito's Yugoslavia? The Hungarian Army in Early Cold War Soviet Strategy," Working Paper of the Parallel History Project on NATO and the Warsaw Pact, February 2005. Ritter skillfully debunks the claims made by Béla Király about alleged Soviet preparations in 1948–50 for an invasion of Yugoslavia, but Ritter's impressive analysis contains a few important shortcomings. First, he focuses so much on Király's account that he fails to give due weight to the crucial changes that occurred in the final two years of Stalin's life. Second, Ritter refers to East-bloc planning and preparations for a "counteroffensive" against Yugoslavia (and against Western countries that might join Yugoslavia in attacking the Soviet bloc), but he fails to acknowledge that planning and preparations for a "counterattack" would be just as useful in carrying out an invasion of Yugoslavia. Nothing about these preparations was inherently "defensive." Third, Ritter focuses solely on Hungary and does not discuss the buildup and preparations under way in Romania and Bulgaria, two countries (especially the latter) that would have played far more important roles than Hungary in any prospective Soviet-bloc incursion into Yugoslavia.

forces of the four Soviet-bloc countries adjoining Yugoslavia (Albania, Bulgaria, Hungary, and Romania) numbered only 346,000 troops organized in 28 divisions, or roughly the same size as Yugoslavia's army of 325,000 soldiers in 32 divisions.[78] Even though Hungary, Bulgaria, and Romania had been receiving substantial inflows of Soviet-made weaponry and equipment, none of the 28 East European divisions had attained a high level of combat readiness. The documents also indicate that the Soviet Union at that point had only a token number of troops still deployed in Bulgaria and Albania and only four to six ground divisions (numbering 60,000 to 90,000 troops) in Romania and Hungary, equipped with roughly 1,000 battle tanks.[79] Moreover, only one of the Soviet units, the 2nd Guards Mechanized Division, which had been relocated from Romania to Hungary in mid-1949, was actually deployed near the Yugoslav border.[80]

The East-bloc divisions arrayed against Yugoslavia as of early 1950 would have been sufficient for relatively limited contingencies, but they fell well short of the quantity and quality of forces needed to achieve decisive military results in the face of stiff Yugoslav resistance. The U.S. Central Intelligence Agency (CIA) concluded in May 1950 that the East European armies at their existing force levels would be "incapable of waging offensive war" unless they received much greater Soviet backing. An invasion of Yugoslavia, the CIA estimated, would require "a minimum of 25–30 Soviet divisions plus overwhelming air and

---

[78] CIA, "NIE: Probable Developments in Yugoslavia and the Likelihood of Attack upon Yugoslavia, through 1952," pp. 4–5.

[79] Figures derived from CIA, "Possibility of Direct Military Action in the Balkans by Soviet Satellites," Special Evaluation No. 40 (Top Secret), 29 July 1950, p. 2, in HSTL, President's Secretary's Papers, Intelligence File, 1946–1953, Central Intelligence Reports File, 1946–53, Box 219, Special Evaluation Reports; and "Appendix, Table 1: Soviet Forces Estimated to Be Stationed in the Satellites July 1954," in "National Intelligence Estimate: Probable Developments in the European Satellites Through Mid-1956," NIE 12-54 (Top Secret), 24 August 1954, p. 19, in Dwight D. Eisenhower Library, White House: National Security Council Staff: Papers, 1948–61, Executive Secretary's Subject File Series, Box 1, Miscellaneous File.

[80] "Review of the Military Situation in Hungary: The Likelihood of an Immediate Offensive against Yugoslavia Discounted," Memorandum (Secret) from G.A. Wallinger, British ambassador to Hungary, to the Foreign Office, 11 August 1950, in The National Archives of the United Kingdom, FO 371/87865, p. 4.

armored support." Anything short of that, the agency added, "would probably result in a prolonged stalemate."[81]

Nonetheless, even though Soviet and East European military preparations for a possible invasion of Yugoslavia were initially modest, the mobilization of East-bloc forces that could have been used against Yugoslavia increased drastically during the final two years of Stalin's life. This shift, which began in late 1950, reached a feverish pace after Stalin summoned the East European Communist party leaders and defense ministers to Moscow for a meeting on 9–12 January 1951 that was held in complete secrecy and was not disclosed at all in public afterward. Stalin and his chief political and military aides (Molotov, Georgii Malenkov, Lavrentii Beria, the Military Minister Marshal Aleksandr Vasilevskii, and the chief of the Soviet General Staff Army-General Sergei Shtemenko) took part in the meeting, as did the principal Soviet military advisers assigned to the countries around Yugoslavia. The full stenographic transcript of this four-day conclave has not yet been released from the Russian archives, but detailed notes taken by some of the East European participants reveal that Stalin used the sessions to call for a huge expansion of all the East-bloc armed forces, including those in the countries contiguous with Yugoslavia.[82] Soviet

---

[81] CIA, "Evaluation of Soviet–Yugoslav Relations (1950)," ORE 8-50 (Top Secret), 11 May 1950, p. 5, in HSTL, President's Secretary's Papers, Intelligence File, 1946–53, Central Intelligence Reports File, 1946–53, Box 216: O.R.E./1950.

[82] The most extensive notes were taken by the Romanian defense minister, Emil Bodnăraş, and by the Hungarian Communist party leader, Mátyás Rákosi, both of whom recorded Stalin's comments and provided many other details of the proceedings. Bodnăraş's notes were declassified in the 1990s and published in a monthly Romanian historical journal. See Cristescu, "Strict Secret de importanţă deosebită," pp. 15–23. Rákosi's detailed account, evidently based on the contemporaneous notes he was able to take with him to Moscow in 1956, can be found in his memoirs, *Visszaemlékezések*, Vol. 2: *1940–1956* (Budapest: Napvilág Kiadó, 1997), pp. 860–6, esp. 860–2. A shorter account, attributed to the Czechoslovak defense minister, Alexej Čepička, was published by the historian Karel Kaplan in *Dans les archives du Comité Central* (Paris: Albin Michel, 1978), pp. 164–6. See also the brief but interesting retrospective comments of Edward Ochab in Teresa Torańska, *Oni* (London: Aneks, 1985), pp. 46–7. Although Ochab was not the leader of the Polish United Workers' Party in 1951, he attended the conference in place of Bolesław Bierut, the party leader, who apparently was ill. Because

leaders had been emphasizing the need for sharply increased military deployments since early 1950 in their discussions with Bulgarian and Romanian officials, and at the January 1951 conference Stalin extended this demand to the whole Soviet bloc and laid out a much more compressed timetable—a timetable suitable for a crash war effort.[83]

Stalin opened the meeting on 9 January by declaring that it was "abnormal for [the East European countries] to have weak armies." He already knew from Soviet military and intelligence personnel that the East European armed forces were in woeful shape. This assessment was amply corroborated on 9 January when each of the East European defense ministers presented a status report indicating that his country's military forces were "currently unable to meet the requirements of a war."[84] Stalin warned his guests that "this situation must be turned around" as soon as possible. "Within two to three years at most," he declared, the East European countries must "build modern, powerful

---

Stalin had not yet decided how far he would go in allowing East Germany to deploy a regular army, no East German officials took part in the conference. Albania also was not represented at the conference, but Stalin and several other high-ranking Soviet officials met in Moscow in early April 1951 with the Albanian Communist leader, Enver Hoxha, and the chief of the Albanian General Staff, General Bekir Baluku, and discussed the need to strengthen the Albanian armed forces, particularly by equipping them with more tanks and combat aircraft. For a summary transcript of the meeting, see "Zapis' besedy I. V. Stalina s E. Khodzei, 2 aprelya 1951 g.," Memorandum of Conversation (Top Secret), 2 April 1951, in APRF, F. 558, Op. 1, D. 249, LI. 90–7, reproduced in T.V. Volokitina *et al.* eds., *Vostochnaya Evropa v dokumentakh rossiiskikh arkhivov, 1944–1953*, 2 vols., Vol. 2: *1949–1953 gg.* (Novosibirsk: Sibirskii khronograf, 1998), pp. 504–9. The transcript tallies surprisingly well with the account of this meeting in Hoxha's memoirs, *With Stalin: Memoirs*, 2nd ed. (Tirana: 8 Nëntori Publishing House, 1981), pp. 201–19. According to the transcript, Hoxha told Stalin that the Albanian army already numbered 150,000–175,000 troops plus 218,000 reserves, but these figures, compared to U.S. intelligence estimates, are much too high even if the Albanian security forces are included with the army.

[83] On the earlier demands, see, for example, "Protokol za zasedanieto na plenuma na TsK na BKP, sustoyal se na 16 i 17 yanuari 1950 godina," L. 18. Stalin provided similar "advice" to the Hungarian authorities in the last few months of 1950. See "Tovarishchu Stalinu Iosifu Vissarionovichu," 31 October 1950 (Top Secret), letter from Mátyás Rákosi to Stalin, in APRF, F. 558, Op. 1, D. 293, LI. 80–2.

[84] Cristescu, "Strict Secret de importanţă deosebită," p. 18.

armies" consisting of more than 3 million soldiers. More than 1.2 million of these troops were to be deployed in peacetime in fully "combat-ready" condition, "poised to go to war" at very short notice.[85] Another 1.85 million to 2 million military reserves in Eastern Europe were to be trained and equipped for rapid mobilization in the event of an emergency.[86] Stalin's blunt remarks at the conference clearly indicated that he believed a large-scale military confrontation in Europe was coming in the near future, and that he wanted to make sure that the Soviet and East European armed forces would be successful in any campaign they might undertake. Stalin was pleased that the United States had "failed to cope with even a small war in Korea" and that U.S. troops would "be bogged down in Asia for the next two to three years." "This extremely favorable circumstance," he argued, would give the East-bloc countries just enough time to complete a massive buildup of their armed forces.[87]

Initially, most of the East European officials were caught off-guard by the onerous task Stalin was assigning them. The Polish national defense minister, Marshal Konstanty Rokossowski, insisted that the force levels set for Poland could not be achieved "before the end of 1956." Poland, he said, would find it "enormously difficult" to complete such a large buildup in the short amount of time Stalin was proposing.[88] The Bulgarian Communist Party leader, Vulko Chervenkov, expressed similar reservations. Stalin replied that "if Rokossowski [and Chervenkov] can guarantee that there will be no war by the end of 1956, then [a scaled-back program] might be adopted, but if no such guarantee can be offered, then it would be more sensible to proceed" with a crash buildup. This rebuke made clear to the East European leaders that Stalin was not there to bargain with them over the terms of the expansion and modernization of their armed forces. Although many of the East Europeans remained uneasy about the strain their countries would en-

---

[85] *Ibid.*, pp. 17–8.

[86] *Ibid.*, p. 19. These figures, which were stipulated by Soviet Defense Minister Marshal Aleksandr Vasilevskii and approved by Stalin, come from the documents transcribed by Bodnăraş. I have adjusted them slightly to take account of Albania's projected troop levels, which were not specified at the meeting.

[87] *Ibid.*, p. 20.

[88] Rákosi, *Visszaemlékezések*, Vol. 2, p. 861.

dure from the pace and magnitude of the envisaged buildup, they knew they had no choice but to comply with Stalin's wishes.[89]

No sooner had the conference ended than the East European governments embarked on programs to fulfill the inordinately ambitious numerical goals established for them by the Soviet High Command, which also oversaw a crash buildup of the Soviet Union's own armed forces. The troop strength of the Soviet military had been cut precipitously after World War II, declining to only 2.9 million soldiers by 1948 from a wartime peak of nearly 12 million. During the final two years of Stalin's life, the size of the Soviet armed forces nearly doubled, reaching 5.6 million troops as of March 1953.[90] These new forces, many of which were equipped with the latest weaponry, were almost entirely located in the westernmost portion of the Soviet Union, including hundreds of thousands of combat troops who could have been assigned to any possible contingencies against Yugoslavia. The number of Soviet ready reserves also sharply increased, giving the Soviet General Staff the capacity to deploy more than 10 million combat troops within thirty days of war mobilization.[91] The sheer scale and rapidity of this peacetime military buildup were unprecedented, especially in a country that not yet fully recovered from the damage of World War II. The vast expansion of the Soviet armed forces in 1951–53 allowed for military deployments that would have been infeasible in 1948–50.

In Eastern Europe, too, the results of the crash military buildup were evident almost immediately. By January 1952 the combined armed forces of the four East-bloc countries bordering on Yugoslavia had expanded to 590,000 troops in 38 divisions, or nearly double the

---

[89] *Ibid.*, pp. 862–3, 865. See also Cristescu, "Strict Secret de importanţă deosebită," pp. 17–20.

[90] "Spravka-doklad G. K. Zhukova o sokrashchenii vooruzhenykh sil," Report to the CPSU Presidium (Top Secret), 12 August 1955, in *Voennye arkhivy Rossii* (Moscow), No. 1 (1993): 280–1; and "Zapiska G. Zhukova i V. Sokolovskogo v TsK KPSS," Report to the CPSU Presidium (Top Secret), 9 February 1956, in *Voennye arkhivy Rossii* (Moscow), No. 1 (1993): 283–8.

[91] North Atlantic Treaty Organization (NATO), "Report by the Standing Group to the North Atlantic Military Committee on Estimate of the Relative Strength and Capabilities of NATO and Soviet Bloc Forces at Present and in the Immediate Future," M.C. 33 (Top Secret—Cosmic), 10 November 1951, pp. 21–5, in NATO Archives (Brussels), C8-D4.

size of the Yugoslav army, which had not increased at all since 1950.[92] The East European armies continued to grow at a breakneck pace during the final year of Stalin's life, reaching the target goal of roughly 1.2 million soldiers. Furthermore, the quality of the weapons deployed by the Bulgarian and Romanian armed forces (and to a lesser extent by the Hungarian and Albanian armies) improved a great deal, whereas the opposite was the case for the Yugoslav army, which was no longer receiving any new armaments, spare parts, munitions, or support equipment from its erstwhile supplier, the USSR. Although Yugoslavia by the early 1950s had begun receiving small amounts of weapons and military-related equipment from a few Western countries, these items were hardly enough to make up for the loss of Soviet-made weaponry, communications gear, and spare parts.[93] In early 1952, U.S. intelligence analysts reported that the Yugoslav armed forces were plagued by grave weaknesses, including the "insufficient quantity and obsolescence of much of [their] equipment," a "lack of spare parts and of proper ammunition," a "severe shortage of heavy weapons, particularly of antitank artillery, antiaircraft artillery, and armor," and the "lack of experience of the [Yugoslav] general staff in the tactical and technical utilization of combined arms."[94] Thus, even as the Soviet and East European armed services were rapidly expanding and gearing up for a military confrontation in Europe, the Yugoslav army was declining and was unfit for combat.

---

[92] CIA, "NIE: Probable Developments in Yugoslavia and the Likelihood of Attack upon Yugoslavia, through 1952," p. 5.

[93] Some aspects of the Western military supplies to Yugoslavia were reported at the time—though not always accurately—in the American press. See, for example, "U.S. Arms Delivered to Yugoslavia for Defense of Her Independence," *The New York Times*, 20 June 1951, pp. 1, 7. For more on this issue, see Anikeev, *Kak Tito ot Stalina ushel*, pp. 189–203; Lorraine M. Lees, *Keeping Yugoslavia Afloat: The United States, Yugoslavia, and the Cold War* (University Park, PA: Pennsylvania State University Press, 1997), pp. 81–119, esp. 98–111; Franklin Lindsay, *Beacons in the Night: With the OSS and Tito's Partisans in Wartime Yugoslavia* (Stanford, CA: Stanford University Press, 1993), pp. 334–6; and Beatrice Heuser, *Western Containment Policies in the Cold War: The Yugoslav Case, 1948–53* (New York: Routledge, 1989), pp. 117–24, 155–72, esp. 160–4.

[94] CIA, "NIE: Probable Developments in Yugoslavia and the Likelihood of Attack upon Yugoslavia, through 1952," p. 4.

The military buildup in the Soviet bloc was ostensibly intended to deter or, if necessary, repulse an attack from outside, but the Soviet General Staff assumed that scenarios involving a war against the North Atlantic Treaty Organization (NATO) were not really separable from contingency plans for an invasion of Yugoslavia.[95] Soviet and East European preparations for a massive "counterattack" against enemy forces could just as easily have been adapted for an incursion into Yugoslavia if Stalin had eventually decided to launch one. As part of the post-January 1951 buildup, the USSR provided each of the East European countries with dozens of Tu-2 high-speed bomber aircraft, which would have played a crucial role in any coordinated East-bloc move against Yugoslavia.[96] Stalin had emphasized to the other leaders at the January 1951 conference that "you will need to have a bomber force, at least one division per country initially, to carry out offensive operations."[97] As a further boost to the East European countries' offensive capabilities, the Soviet Union supplied large quantities of Il-10 ground-attack aircraft for airborne assault forces, which would have spearheaded an attempt to seize strategic positions in Yugoslavia, including fortifications around Belgrade.[98]

Moreover, under Soviet auspices the armed forces of the four East-bloc states adjoining Yugoslavia conducted war games in 1951 and

---

[95] "O deyatel'nosti organov Severo-atlanticheskogo Soyuza v svyazi s sozdaniem atlanticheskoi armii i remilitarizatsiei zapadnoi Germanii," Intelligence Memorandum (Top Secret), forwarded by the Soviet Communist Party Politburo to the leaders of the East European countries, February 1951, in Český Národní Archiv (ČNA), Archiv Ústředního vyboru Komunistické strany Československa (Archiv ÚV KSČ), F. 100/24, Svazek 47, Archivní jednotka 1338. I am grateful to Oldřich Tůma for giving me a copy of this document. Vojtech Mastny cites the document in his first-rate analysis of Soviet and East-bloc responses to NATO during the early years of the alliance, "NATO in the Beholder's Eye: Soviet Perceptions and Policies, 1949–56," CWIHP Working Paper No. 35 (Washington, DC: Cold War International History Project, March 2002).

[96] "Appendix, Table 3: Estimated Satellite Air Forces, July 1954," in CIA, "NIE: Probable Developments in the European Satellites Through Mid-1956," p. 19. Bulgaria received three divisions of Tu-2 bombers totaling 120 aircraft, and Hungary and Romania each received one division of 40 bombers.

[97] Cristescu, "Strict Secret de importanță deosebită," p. 20.

[98] Nicolae Balotescu *et al.*, *Istoria aviației române* (Bucharest: Editura Științifică și enciclopedică, 1984), pp. 375, 380–1.

1952 that envisaged "forward deployments" and "large-scale offensive operations" to encircle and destroy enemy troops on Yugoslav territory. The Hungarian army in its exercises was specifically responsible for "seizing the Belgrade area" and other strategic sites in Yugoslavia.[99] This task, though depicted in the context of a counterattack against an enemy occupier, obviously would have been an integral part of any joint Soviet–East European campaign to invade and occupy Yugoslavia. The Romanian and Bulgarian armed forces conducted similar exercises near their projected entry routes into Yugoslavia.[100] The Romanian government supported its army's preparations in June 1951 by forcibly deporting more than 40,000 civilians from the Banat and Oltenia regions along the Yugoslav border to the forbidding reaches of the Bărăgan Steppe.[101] This mass deportation, which was closely coordinated with leaders in Moscow, was intended to remove "hostile elements" and "Titoist sympathizers" who might otherwise hinder Romanian military operations against the "reactionary Yugoslav state."[102] The Romanian army subsequently stepped up its maneuvers in the cleared-out regions,

---

[99] See the guidelines for the Hungarian army's war game held on 8–12 May 1951, Report No. 02609 (Top Secret) from Endre Matekovits, 7 May 1951, divided into four parts, "Feladat tisztázása," "Vázlat a front feladatáról," "Köveztetések," "Tájékoztató jelentés," plus a planning map, in Hadtörténelmi Levéltár, Magyar Néphadsereg iratai (HL MN), 1951/T/24/2 őrzési egység (ő.e.), pp. 207–26, document provided by László Ritter.

[100] Mircea Chirițoiu, *Între David și Goliath: România și Iugoslavia în balanța Războiului Rece* (Iași: Demiurg, 2005), pp. 132, 135, 138–41. See also Gheorge Vartic, "1951–1953: Ani fierbinți din istoria Războiului Rece în relatarea generalului (r) Ion Eremia, opozant al regimului stalinist din România," in *Geopolitică și istorie militară în perioada Războiului Rece* (Bucharest: Editura Academiei de Înalte Studii Militare, 2003), pp. 84–5.

[101] Silviu Sarafolean ed., *Deportații în Bărăgan, 1951–1956* (Timișoara: Editura Mirton, 2001), esp. the 39-page introductory essays; Rafael Mirciov, *Lagărul deportării: Pagini din lagărul Bărăganului, 1951–1956* (Timișoara: Editura Mirton, 2001); and Chirițoiu, *Între David și Goliath*, pp. 247–8. The book edited by Sarafolean includes a remarkably detailed, 590-page list of those who were deported.

[102] "Zapis' besedy s A. Pauker," Memorandum No. 70-k (Secret) from S. Kavtaradze, Soviet ambassador in Romania, to Soviet Foreign Minister A. Vyshinskii, 1 March 1951, in AVPRF, F. 0125, Op. 39, P. 198, D. 76, LI. 234–5; and "Zapis' besedy s A. Pauker," Memorandum No. 166-k (Secret) from S. Kavtaradze, Soviet ambassador in Romania, to Soviet Foreign Minister, A. Vyshinskii, 11 July 1951, in AVPRF, F. 0125, Op. 39, P. 190, LI. 33–6.

simulating large-scale thrusts across the border. By learning how to "organize and command large-scale offensive operations in difficult conditions on the ground and in the air," how to "concentrate forces that are superior in troop strength and equipment to break through enemy defenses," and how to "distribute forces for the optimal structure of attack," high-ranking East-bloc military officers gained the training they needed for a prospective invasion of Yugoslavia.[103]

The rapid military buildup in the Soviet Union and Eastern Europe and the experience derived from war games meant that, from mid-1952 until Stalin's death, the Soviet-bloc forces confronting Yugoslavia posed a daunting military threat to Tito's regime. NATO intelligence analysts reported in late 1951 that the East European armies were acquiring "significant offensive capabilities" against Yugoslavia, even without Soviet support.[104] A number of highly classified U.S. intelligence assessments in the early 1950s, which kept close track of military developments in the USSR and the four Communist countries surrounding Yugoslavia, warned that "the groundwork is being laid for a possible invasion of Yugoslavia" and that a full-scale Soviet and East European "attack on Yugoslavia should be considered a serious possibility."[105] Although U.S. intelligence analysts believed that such an attack was "unlikely" in the near term, they concluded as early as March 1951 that if Soviet and East European forces embarked on a concerted offensive against Yugoslavia they would be able to occupy the country, destroy the Yugoslav army, and, over time, quell all guerrilla resistance:

---

[103] "Feladat tisztázása," p. 210.

[104] NATO, "Estimate of the Relative Strength and Capabilities of NATO and Soviet Bloc Forces," p. 22.

[105] See CIA, "NIE: Probable Developments in Yugoslavia and the Likelihood of Attack upon Yugoslavia, through 1952"; CIA, "NIE: Probability of an Invasion of Yugoslavia in 1951"; and CIA, "National Intelligence Estimate: Review of the Conclusions of NIE-29 'Probability of an Invasion of Yugoslavia in 1951,'" NIE-29/1 (Top Secret), 4 May 1951, in HSTL, President's Secretary's Papers, Intelligence File, 1946–53, Central Intelligence Reports File, 1946–53, Box 213: National Intelligence Estimates. See also CIA, "National Intelligence Estimate: Soviet Capabilities and Intentions," NIE-3 (Top Secret), 15 November 1950, pp. 17–8, in HSTL, President's Secretary's Papers, Intelligence File, 1946–53, Central Intelligence Reports File, 1946–53, Box 213: National Intelligence Estimates.

The continuing military build-up in the neighboring Satellite states (increase in armed forces, stockpiling, re-equipment, gasoline conservation, stepping-up of war industry, etc.) has reversed the previous balance of military strength between the Satellites and Yugoslavia and has given the Satellites the capability of launching a major invasion of Yugoslavia with little warning. [...] Combined Soviet-Satellite forces could successfully invade Yugoslavia, overcome formal military resistance, and eventually render guerrilla operations ineffective.[106]

This judgment was reinforced by the immense expansion of the East-bloc armies following the January 1951 conference.

To be sure, the Soviet bloc's growing *capacity* to invade Yugoslavia did not necessarily signal an *intention* to move in. U.S. intelligence agencies in 1952 deemed it "unlikely" that the Soviet bloc would embark on an all-out military attack against Yugoslavia by the end of the year. Western intelligence assessments in 1951–52 pointed out that the various signs of Soviet and East European preparations for an invasion—the "rapid increase in the capabilities of the armed forces" in the four East-bloc states contiguous with Yugoslavia, the fact that the East European "countries adjacent to Yugoslavia have evacuated the majority of the civilians from key border areas," the unrelenting Soviet and East European "propaganda [and] psychological preparations" designed to "justify an attack on Yugoslavia," the increased registration for compulsory military service in the four East-bloc states adjoining Yugoslavia, the "recurrent concentrations of [East-bloc] troops along the Yugoslav border," and the increasing frequency of border incidents coupled with "rumors from Cominform circles of an impending attack on Yugoslavia"— did "not necessarily reflect a Soviet intention to launch an attack upon Yugoslavia" in the near term.[107] U.S. intelligence analysts noted that these actions might simply be part of a larger Soviet-bloc effort to gear up for an East–West war in Europe, rather than being directed specifically against Yugoslavia. The analysts also surmised that if the USSR genuinely intended to invade and occupy Yugoslavia, it would wait to do so until "the Bulgarian, Romanian, and Hungarian armed forces [...] complete their reorganization and reach maximum effectiveness"

---

[106] CIA, "NIE: Probability of an Invasion of Yugoslavia in 1951," pp. 5–6.
[107] See the sources adduced in notes 77, 79, and 105 *supra*.

at the end of 1953 and until the Albanian military reached a similar state in mid-1954.[108] Stalin's death in March 1953 came well before the reorganization of the East European armies was completed.

Thus, even though Stalin toward the end of his life was overseeing a huge expansion of the East-bloc armed forces and was thereby "laying the groundwork" for an invasion of Yugoslavia (regardless of whether that was the main purpose of the buildup), it is impossible to say what he actually would have done if he had lived another few years.[109] Despite the Soviet bloc's extensive military preparations, and despite Moscow's efforts to stir acute fears in Yugoslavia of a looming Soviet–East European attack, the available evidence suggests that Stalin never firmly decided—one way or the other—about military intervention in Yugoslavia.

Reconsolidation of the Soviet Bloc

Short of actually launching an all-out invasion, the Soviet Union had to put up, at least temporarily, with a breach in the Eastern bloc and the strategic loss of Yugoslavia *vis-à-vis* the Balkans and the Adriatic Sea. Other potential dangers for Moscow also loomed. Yugoslavia's continued defiance raised the prospect that "Titoism" would spread and "infect" other East European countries, causing the Soviet bloc to fragment and even to collapse. To preclude any further challenges to Soviet control in Eastern Europe, Stalin instructed the local Communist parties to carry out new purges and political trials and to eliminate anyone who might be seeking to emulate Tito. The repressions took a particularly severe toll in Bulgaria, Czechoslovakia, and Hungary.[110]

---

[108] CIA, "NIE: Probable Developments in Yugoslavia and the Likelihood of Attack upon Yugoslavia, through 1952," p. 5.

[109] The quoted phrase comes from CIA, "NIE: Probability of an Invasion of Yugoslavia in 1951," p. 5.

[110] Mito Isusov, *Stalin i Bulgariya* (Sofia: Universitetsko Izdatelstvo Sv. Kliment Okhridski, 1991), pp. 171–218; George H. Hodos, *Show Trials: Stalinist Purges in Eastern Europe, 1948–1954* (New York: Praeger, 1987); Wolfgang Maderthaner, Hans Schafranek, and Berthold Unfried eds., *"Ich habe den Tod verdient": Schauprozesse und politische Verfolgung im Mittle- und Osteuropa 1945–1956* (Vienna: Verlag für Gesellschaftskritik, 1991); and Adam B. Ulam, *Titoism and the Cominform* (Cambridge, MA: Harvard Univer-

The political purges that swept through Eastern Europe in 1949–54 differed fundamentally from the repressions that took place earlier, in 1944–48. The earlier crackdowns were targeted predominantly against non-Communists, whereas the purges in 1949–54 were focused mostly on Communists, including many high officials who had avidly taken part in the initial repressions. The show trials of Communist leaders were intended not only to root out anyone who might strive for a degree of autonomy from Moscow, but also to instill a general sense of fear in society. Both of these goals contributed to the mobilization of the East-bloc countries for war. The sudden discovery of alleged Titoist and Western "spies" in the ruling organs of the Communist parties created a war psychosis and fostered the perception that no one—not even those who seemed to be unwaveringly loyal—could really be trusted. Stalin had used this same approach in the USSR in the late 1930s when he wanted to secure the home front in the face of an approaching war. By early 1951 he once again believed that an armed conflict was nearing, and he therefore was transferring Soviet methods to the East European countries so that they could uproot the "Titoist fifth columns" in their midst.

Within the Soviet Union, the drive against potential "fifth columnists" and the mobilization for war entailed a violent anti-Semitic campaign, preparations for a sweeping high-level purge (perhaps targeted against Molotov, Anastas Mikoyan, and Beria), and ruthless counter-insurgency operations in the western areas of the country. All of these policies, to one degree or another, were adopted in Eastern Europe under Soviet supervision. The pronounced anti-Semitic overtones of the East European show trials, for example, were directly patterned on Stalin's own anti-Semitic repressions. As the East-bloc Balkan countries geared up for a military confrontation, they also carried out mass deportations along their borders with Yugoslavia and arrested tens of thousands of people each year. In Romania alone, 6,635 people were

---

sity Press, 1952), pp. 145–202. See also Vladimir Zelenin, "Sovetsko-yugoslavskii konflikt 1948-ogo goda i Repressii v Vostochnoi Evrope," *Novoe vremya* (Moscow), No. 31 (July 1989): 34–5. There is no longer any doubt that Stalin and his aides directly supervised the purges in Eastern Europe, especially the most spectacular of the show trials. See, for example, the relevant documents in Volokitina *et al.* eds., *Vostochnaya Evropa*, Vol. 2; and Volokitina *et al.* eds., *Sovetskii faktor v Vostochnoi Evrope*, Vol. 2.

arrested by the Securitate in 1950, 19,235 in 1951, and 24,826 in 1952.[111] The aim of the deportations and arrests was not only to ensure that strategically vital border areas would be free of "Titoist sympathizers" and other "enemies of the people," but also to forestall any possibility of internal disruption. The deportations were larger in Romania than elsewhere, but the same basic policy was adopted in all of the countries adjoining Yugoslavia.

Stalin's efforts to prevent a spillover from Yugoslavia and to promote a common anti-Tito front had the desired effect. Soviet influence in Eastern Europe came under no further threat during his lifetime. From the late 1940s through the early 1950s, all the East-bloc states embarked on crash industrialization and forced collectivization programs, causing vast social upheaval yet also leading to rapid short-term economic growth. The drastic expansion of the East European armed forces in the early 1950s required an ever greater share of resources to be devoted to the military and heavy industry, with very little left over for consumer output. However, because ordinary citizens in the Soviet bloc were largely excluded from the political sphere and were forbidden to engage in political protest, they had no choice but to endure a sharp decline in living standards and many other hardships, both material and intellectual. No conflict between "viability" and "cohesion" yet existed in the Communist bloc, for Stalin was able to rely on the presence of Soviet troops, a tightly-woven network of state security forces, the wholesale penetration of the East European armies and governments by Soviet agents, the use of mass purges and political terror, and the unifying threat of renewed German militarism to ensure that regimes loyal to Moscow remained in power.[112] By the early 1950s, Stalin had established a degree of control over Eastern Europe to which his successors could only aspire.

---

[111] "Dinamica arestărilor efectuate de către organele Securității Statului in anii 1950-31.III.1968," Statistical Report (Top Secret) to the director of the Securitate, 17 April 1968, in Consiliul Național pentru Studierea Arhivelor Securității, Dosar 9572, Vol. 61, Foaie 1. See also Vladimir Tismaneanu, *Stalinism for All Seasons: A Political History of Romanian Communism* (Berkeley: University of California Press, 2003), pp. 19–24.

[112] The notion of a trade-off between "viability" and "cohesion" is well presented in James F. Brown, *Relations Between the Soviet Union and Its East European Allies: A Survey*, R-1742-PR (Santa Monica, CA: RAND Corporation, 1975).

ALFRED J. RIEBER

Popular Democracy: An Illusion?

From the classic formulations of Marx and Engels to the end of the communist system in Eastern Europe, Marxist theoreticians and communist party leaders wrestled with the dual problem of defining and managing the transition from bourgeois democracy to socialism. During the brief period leading up to the establishment of communist regimes in Eastern Europe, the terms "new democracy" or "popular democracy" entered the communist political vocabulary in order to identify an intermediate stage in the transition that would substitute for the dictatorship of the proletariat. At the end of the war, throughout Europe, not only in the East, new forms of politics and structural changes in society and the economy were being introduced. At different times in the period from 1945–48 attempts were made in France, Italy, the Soviet zone in Germany, and several countries in Eastern Europe to create or re-create a unified party of the left. Almost everywhere in the post-war years coalitions of "anti-fascist" parties, i.e., those not tainted by collaboration with the German and Italian occupiers, came to power with communists occupying ministerial posts for the first time. Nationalization of industries, agrarian reforms (especially in Eastern Europe), and widespread purges of the collaborationist administrations, police and armed forces from France to Romania contributed to weakening the old elites.

The full range of Soviet territorial war aims emerged gradually during the war, becoming clear at the Yalta Conference in February 1945. In contrast, Stalin continued to appear uncertain about the political and socio-economic changes that might take place after the war within the Soviet sphere of influence to say nothing of Europe as a whole. He refrained from making *ex cathedra* pronouncements on the crucial question of the transition to socialism that might have been expected from the author of *Socialism in One Country*. Moreover, from the abolition of the Comintern in 1943 to the establishment of the Cominform in 1947 there was no acknowledged international communist center to coordinate the activities of local communist parties.[1] During the same period, as the archives now show, Stalin's orders to his army commanders and his advice to local communists do not add up to a clear and consistent policy. The picture is one of trial and error informed by a Marxist perception of the world. The aim of this essay is to throw further light on this murky subject by following two lines of investigation: first, to sketch in the torturous historical evolution of communist praxis and theory on the transition; and second, to inquire into the extent to which popular democracy, as a variant of the transition, was a viable option for the communist parties of Eastern Europe, with special reference to Romania.

A thoughtful post-Soviet Russian analysis poses the question of whether popular democracy was a myth or reality.[2] Tipping my own hand, I have posed the question somewhat differently: was the concept and implementation of popular democracy an illusion in the sense of being "a perception which fails to give the true character of an object perceived." Or to foreshadow even more sharply my conclusion: was popular democracy conceived as a possible alternative transition born of particular circumstances that combined Stalin's views of revolution, the experience of a near catastrophic anti-fascist war in an alliance with western liberal democracies and the dangers of incipient civil wars in the western borderlands of the Soviet Union? As circumstances changed in the postwar years, and changed rather rapidly, the possibilities inherent in popular democracy also changed. They diminished. And the concept was rendered illusory.

---

[1] At a meeting between Stalin and Georgi Dimitrov in June 1943 it was decided to create a Department of International Information of the Central Committee in order to maintain contact with foreign communist parties. But by the end of the war its contacts had taken on "an episodic character" and information about their activities was "with rare exceptions insufficient." *Rossiiskii gosudarstvennyi arkhiv sotsial'no-politicheskoi istorii* (RGASPI), f. 17, op. 128, d. 51, pp. 35–7.

[2] T.V. Volokitina, G.P. Murashko, and A.F. Noskova, *Narodnaia demokratiiia: mif ili realnost'? Obshchestvenno-politicheskie protsessy v Vostochnoi Evrope, 1944–1948* (Moscow, 1993).

Ideological Foreshadowing

To pursue briefly the first question, one only has to recall the poverty of theory about the dictatorship of the proletariat in the classic formulations to understand in part the dilemma shared by all the Russian Social Democrats in the pre-revolutionary period and the Bolsheviks once in power. The Paris Commune was more of an inspiration than a model. Plekhanov was the first to toy with the idea of the hegemony of the proletariat in the bourgeois democratic revolution, but he then retreated from its implications. However ingenious Lenin's invention of a democratic dictatorship of the proletariat and peasantry in 1906–07, he soon abandoned it. Trotsky's uninterrupted revolution was useful up to the point of taking power, but not in consolidating it. Theory withered, albeit without dying, under the terrible exigencies of civil war and intervention. NEP was another improvisation. Stalin confronted the problem of whether any of this experience was of use in conceiving transitions within societies undergoing revolution outside the boundaries of the Soviet state. One thing was clear throughout the debates and discussions. The nature of the transition was inseparably linked to the character of the revolution that preceded it.

Clues to Stalin's thinking on revolution and transition are already apparent in the year 1917.[3] He continued to grope for the right formula during the twenties and thirties. In his first major address to a Comintern Congress, the Sixth in 1928, he argued that in countries with weak capitalism and feudal remnants such as "Poland, Romania, etc." where the peasantry would play a large role in the revolution, "the victory of the revolution in order that it can lead to a proletarian dictatorship can and probably will demand some intermediate stages in the form, let us say, of a dictatorship of the proletariat and peasantry."[4] But these were still straws in the wind.

---

[3] For Stalin's ambivalence toward the Provisional Government before Lenin returned to Finland Station, see Robert Service, *Stalin: A Biography* (London: Macmillan, 2004), pp. 120–2.

[4] I.V. Stalin, *Sochineniia*, Vol. 9 (Moscow 1946–52): 155–6. To drive home his point Stalin repeated his prediction of the future course of revolution in Poland and Romania three times in the same speech. *Nota bene* that Stalin revised Lenin's early formula by omitting the term "democratic" from his definition of the transition.

By 1934 it was clear even to Stalin that the left turn of the Comintern and denunciation of the social democrats as social fascists had
led to a face off with fascism in a blind alley. His decision to appoint
Georgi Dimitrov, the hero of the Leipzig trial, as head of the Comintern opened the door to the Popular Front strategy that paved the way
for the introduction of the Popular Democracy in the postwar period.
But from the outset Stalin took a more cautious view of the possibility of cooperation between communists and social democrats, not to
speak of other liberal democratic parties in the struggle against fascism. Ironically, Stalin's skepticism was aimed more at the West European workers whom he believed had been seduced by the fruits of
parliamentary democracy and imperialism.[5] His skepticism proved
doubly ironic. On the one hand, the Popular Front proved to have
greater appeal to both communists and social democrats in Czechoslovakia, France and Spain than in Eastern Europe. On the other hand,
the postwar development of a popular front cum popular democracy
strategy in France and Italy and even Czechoslovakia, developed more
fully in the direction of genuine coalitions and democratic practices
and came under Soviet fire at the first Cominform meeting. Who was
here guilty of nurturing illusions?

The outbreak of the Spanish Civil War was the first real test of both
a Popular Front movement and a Popular Front government. Stalin's
response was startling. In a famous letter to Largo Caballero, the socialist president of the Spanish Republic, Stalin, Molotov and Voroshilov
defined a path for the Spanish revolution that differed from the Russian
"due to different social, historical and geographical [sic] conditions and
to the different international situations which Russia had to face. It is
quite possible," they concluded, "that in Spain the parliamentary way
will prove more appropriate toward revolutionary development than was

---

[5] Stalin's comments on Dimitrov's letter of July 1, 1934 in Alexander Dallin
and F.I. Firsov eds., *Dimitrov and Stalin, 1934–1943: Letters from the Soviet
Archives* (New Haven: Yale University Press, 2000), p. 13. For Dimitrov's
relations with Stalin, see Vesselin Dimitrov, *Stalin's Cold War: Soviet Foreign
Policy, Democracy and Communism in Bulgaria, 1941–1948* (London: Palgrave
Macmillan, 2007). I am grateful to Dr. Dimitrov for sharing a manuscript
version of his book with me.

the case in Russia."[6] At the same time, Stalin sought to fashion a similar policy in China. He urged a coalition between communists and nationalists, and sent arms, Soviet advisers and fighter pilots to support the resistance against "Japanese fascism." Dimitrov was the first to suggest that the defense of republican liberties in Spain and China were opening skirmishes in the coming general war against fascism. For him each struggle represented in its own way a creative application of popular front tactics.[7] In both cases the Dimitrov-Stalinist variant proved illusory. In Spain, it was a result of military defeat, albeit accompanied by serious in-fighting among the republican forces. In China, Mao was forging his own version of the transition, calling it the "New Democracy." In exile in Moscow the leaders of the Spanish Communist Party were unrepentant in defending their tactics. And Stalin neither reproached nor purged them. Was this an endorsement?

---

[6] E.H. Carr, *The Comintern and the Spanish Civil War* (New York: Pantheon, 1984), pp. 20–1, 86–7. The original version of the letter appeared in *Guerra y Revolucion en Espana* (Moscow, 1971), pp. 96–7. Dimitrov's analysis was theoretically more precise, arguing for "something new in politics, a special state with a people's (popular) democracy," a "special form of democratic dictatorship of the working class and peasantry," thus fully restoring Lenin's formula of 1905. *Kommunisticheskii internatsional. Kratkii istoricheskii ocherk* (Moscow, 1969), pp. 439–40. See also G. Dimitrov, *Selected Works* (Sofia, 1968), Vol. I, pp. 76, 93–5, 97–9, 102–4. But there was no unanimity within international communism on the transition. Palmiro Togliatti, a Comintern representative in Spain, adopted a more subtle position calling the struggle "a national revolutionary war" against external fascist domination and a struggle for autonomy of the nationalities (Catalan and Basque). Palmiro Togliatti, *Opera*, Vol. 4 (Turin, 1977): 139–54. Spanish Communists at the local level were more inclined to insurrectionary class warfare. Burnett Bolloton, *The Spanish Revolution: The Left and the Struggle for Power during the Civil War* (Chapel Hill: University of North Carolina Press, 1979), pp. 54–6, 59–60; Mikhail Koltsov, *Ispanskii dnevnik*, second edition (Moscow, 1958). The three different emphases adumbrated positions taken after World War II: Togliatti edging his way toward Eurocommunism on the right; the Yugoslav, Greek, and Albanian communists embracing an insurrectionary strategy on the left; and Dimitrov, warily supported by an ever skeptical Stalin, seeking a middle ground as applied in Romania, Bulgaria, Czechoslovakia, Poland, and, above all, Finland.

[7] *Kommunisticheskii internatsional*, No. 14 (August 1936). For Soviet aid, M.I. Sladkovskii, *Istoriia torgovo-ekonomicheskikh otnoshenii SSSR s Kitaem, 1917–1974* (Moscow, 1977), p. 138; and *Na kitaiskoi zemle: Vospominaniia sovetskikh dobrovol'tsev, 1925–1944 gg.,* second edition (Moscow, 1977), pp. 175–6.

An answer depends how one interprets Stalin's laconic endorsement of the parliamentary approach. To anticipate, Spain and China from 1936–38 proved to be prototypes of a model that evolved further from 1944 to 1949 in Eastern Europe. To gain perspective, it may be argued that Stalin's invocation of a parliamentary way to socialism in foreign countries corresponded to his simultaneous calls for democracy inside the Soviet Union.[8] His aims were similar: to mobilize the masses under the leadership of the party in order to advance the transition to socialism. Domestically, this meant unleashing repression from below in order to eliminate any obstacle, real or imagined, to rapid industrialization. Abroad this meant expanding the influence of the party by placing it at the head of a broad anti-fascist coalition that would assume governmental responsibilities and carry out radical socio-economic reforms through legal parliamentary means. In both cases the goal was to compensate for the minority status and end the isolation of the Communist Party without losing control over the process of building socialism. In this respect the parliamentary path took Lenin's formula of 1906–07 as a point of departure. But in Stalin's hands it underwent a radical transformation.

From Popular Front to United Front

Although the Popular Front tactics had not led to the establishment of a Popular Democracy, it had not entirely lost its appeal to Stalin as a means of opposing fascism without isolating the Soviet Union or exposing the international movement to the blandishments of Trotsky's uninterrupted revolution. However, in 1937–38 the growing signs of weakness in the policy of collective security and his exaggerated, indeed pathological fears of deviation and subversion among the European communist parties forced him back to a position of autarchy in foreign affairs and a murderous purge of the Comintern. Litvinov was removed as foreign commissar and many of his close colleagues purged, but he was held in reserve. Several of his associates like Ivan Maiskii who continued to serve in London and G.Ia. Surits, formerly

---

[8] For the domestic link, see Wendy Z. Goldman, *Terror and Democracy in the Age of Stalin: The Social Dynamics of Repression* (Cambridge: Cambridge University Press, 2007), especially chapter 3.

in Paris, and B.E. Shtein, formerly in Rome, retained posts in the Foreign Commissariat. Dimitrov's position was precarious. But he kept his office at the cost of participating in the purge of his subordinates, only occasionally, if fatefully, rescuing a few endangered individuals like Tito. When Stalin burned his bridges he always left one span intact. He was able to cross over again following the Nazi attack on the Soviet Union by proclaiming the war as one of "all freedom loving peoples against fascism." Revolutionary rhetoric disappeared. A "united" not "popular" front was proclaimed. Alliances with the West were concluded; Litvinov was sent to Washington. Stalin planned to abolish the Comintern, but to retain Dimitrov as *de facto* coordinator of communist parties and to resurrect the concept of popular democracy in such a way as to fit different national conditions.

Stalin gave Dimitrov three reasons for his decision to abolish the Comintern. First, it would make clear the distinction between the separate tasks of the communists in seeking to overthrow the governments of fascist states while supporting the governments of the western liberal democracies. Second, it refuted "the lie" that communist parties were the agents of a foreign state by presenting themselves as national workers parties. Third, it would ease the way for the broad masses to join or sympathize with these parties.[9] Question remained open, however, what would be the exact means of forging an alliance of anti-fascist parties in the occupied countries of Europe and then of taking power and presenting a program of broad socio-economic change that would be the foundation for a popular democracy?

As the Red Army began to take the offensive following the battle of Kursk in June 1943 and then by early 1944 approached the pre-1940 borders of the Soviet Union, Stalin let drop a few hints of the kind of governments he envisaged in the liberated territories. Having created two postwar planning commissions, he instructed the one headed by Maxim Litvinov "to prepare its work ignoring the possibility of serious social upheavals (*perevoroty*) and taking its point of departure from the existing social structure."[10] What is striking about Stalin's initial think-

---

[9] Ivo Banac ed., *The Diary of Georgi Dimitrov, 1933–1949* (New Haven: Yale University Press, 2003), entry for May 21, 1943, pp. 275–6.

[10] Arkhiv vneshnei politiki Rossiiskoi federatsii (AVP RF), f. 0512, op. 2, p. 8, d.4, l. 31. In analyzing the conclusions of the Litvinov and Maiskii commissions, the Russian historian Aleksei M. Filitov emphasizes their overwhelm-

ing about transitional postwar governments in the Soviet sphere was
his adherence to a modified model of his previously defined parliamentary path. This emerges clearly in his policy toward Romania.

Romania as a Test Case of Popular Democracy

As the Red Army approached the 1940 boundary of Romania in April
1944, Stalin signed an order of the State Defense Committee (GOK)
to the General Staff of the Second Ukrainian Front that set down the
guidelines for the occupation of the country. The population was to
be informed that the Soviet forces had no intention of acquiring any
part of Romanian territory or changing the social structure of the country. The order specified that the Soviet entry into Romania had as its
sole aim the destruction of German forces and end the domination of
Nazi Germany over the country. It contained fifteen specific articles
concerning the behavior of the army in maintaining order. The Soviet
command was instructed that "All the existing Romanian organs of
power and the economic and political structure existing in Romania
will be maintained without change." There would be no interference
with public or private worship. "The Romanian state order (*poriadok*)
will not be destroyed and a Soviet regime will not be introduced."[11]

In attempting to detach Romania as well as Hitler's other allies,
Finland, Hungary, and Bulgaria, the Soviet Union did not insist on
unconditional surrender, or the establishment of a Soviet military administration which would have placed these countries under the immediate and full control of Moscow. Rather it sought, in consultation
with its Western Allies, to negotiate armistice agreements initially with

---

ingly "non-ideological character" although they interpreted a postwar soviet
sphere of influence in broad terms, implying the likelihood of Soviet intervention in order to establish "broad democracy" and an "Eastward" orientation. Aleksei M. Filitov, "Problems of Post-War Construction in Soviet
Foreign Policy Conceptions During World War II," in Francesca Gori and
Silvio Pons eds., *The Soviet Union and Europe in the Cold War, 1943–53* (New
York/Houndmills: Blasingstoke, 1996), pp. 14–5.
[11] Order of the State Committee of Defense, April 10, 1944 in T.V. Volokitina
et al eds., *Vostochnaia Evropa v dokumentakh Rossiiskikh arkhivov, 1944–1953*
(Moscow–Novosibirsk, 1997) (VE) Vol. I, No. 4, pp. 53–6.

governments that were not communist dominated. In the case of Romania the armistice conditions were harsh, the implementation often harsher and the overall effect clearly intended not only to compensate for the destruction of lives and property by the Romanian Army in Ukraine but also to reorient Romania's economy toward the Soviet Union. However, once again, the instructions of the Soviet Foreign Ministry to its representatives on the Allied Control Commission for Romania made clear that its functions were limited to supervising the armistice agreement and working with the Romanian administration to maintain civic order in areas up to one hundred kilometers from the front line.[12] In his three diplomatic interventions in Romania from November 1944 – February 1945 Andrei Vyshinskii repeatedly sought to work out a compromise with the non-communist Romanian leaders. The three Romanian governments during that period were all headed by a non-communist Romanian general. The key ministries were in non-communist hands.

The objectives of Soviet policy at this time were to unify the country in its reversal of fronts against the Germans, to reassure the Allies that there was no intention of sovietizing Romania (or Eastern Europe), and to legitimize the Communist Party after years of forced illegality, enabling it to develop a mass base. The key to success of this policy was a unified government which included all the non-fascist parties thereby excluding the possibility of an opposition. In Stalin's eyes opposition could only mean obstruction at best and subversion at worst. It was tantamount to undermining the war effort by implicitly endorsing Goebbels' line that the Grand Alliance was unnatural and doomed to splinter. "Free elections" meant that only "anti-fascist parties" could take part and then preferably under the banner of a united electoral bloc.[13]

---

[12] AVP RF, f. Vyshinskogo op. 5, p. 47, pp. 8–13. These instructions corresponded to Soviet members of the ACC in Finland and Hungary. For Finland, see RGASPI f. 77, d. 39, pp. 19, 20, 21; and for Hungary, see Kirk to Secretary of State, March 1, 1945, National Archives (NA), State Department, 740.001 119 Control (Hungary), Box 3796, folder 1.

[13] The Soviet authorities did not dictate this approach but they did attribute the problems facing the Hungarian Communists in 1947 to not adopting it. In April Molotov told Rákosi, "I think you made a big mistake in 1945 when at the time of parliamentary elections you did not enter into a united

In order to secure legitimacy for the communists, Stalin promised the Romanians the return of all of Transylvania. It was a shrewd move that provided the Romanian Army with a strong incentive to fight against the Hungarians and Germans; it strengthened the appeal of the Communist Party as a national party (Romanian opinion always having preferred the incorporation of Transylvania to the recovery of Bessarabia if the choice became necessary); and at the same time it adhered to his nationality policy for disputed territories on the frontiers of multicultural states.[14] What then happened to radicalize and accelerate the transition in Romania?

My answer to that question is given in greater detail elsewhere.[15] Briefly, the reasons may be summarized as follows. The Romanian governments up to February 1945 were evasive and slow in meeting the armistice terms. The Soviet forces made fulfillment difficult by their policy of expropriation. This heightened tensions between Moscow and Bucharest. But the key factor in the communist advance to power was the result of a complex internal struggle for power between the "historic parties," the National Liberals and National Peasants on the one hand and on the other hand the National Democratic Front composed of the Communists, Ploughman's Front, Social Democrats and Hungarian Peoples Alliance (MADOSZ). Their political conflict threatened to erupt in civil war. Each side appealed to its putative great power protector, respectively the West and the Soviet Union thus internationalizing the struggle and raising the stakes. The creation of a government of the National Democratic Front in February 1945 did not end the political struggle, which continued for two years. Nor did it begin the process of a socialist transformation of Romania. The agrarian reform of May

---

bloc with other parties [...] If you had entered as a bloc, then you would not have the situation where one party [the Smallholders] received a majority." Conversation of V.M. Molotov with M. Rákosi, RGASPI, f. 17, op. 128, d. 1019, l. 27.

[14] His decision reversed the recommendations of the Litvinov Commission which proposed the creation of a separate Transylvanian state in a federated union with Hungary and Romania, an ingenious if wholly unrealistic solution. Stenographic Protocol No. 7, June 8, 1944 AVP RF, f. 0512, op. 2, p. 8, pp. 176–88.

[15] Alfred J. Rieber, "The Crack in the Plaster: Crisis in Romania and the Origins of the Cold War," *Journal of Modern History*, Vol. 76, No. 1 (March 2004): 62–106.

1945 created 400,000 new peasant households but this merely complicated the subsequent campaign for collectivization. Similarly, the Soviet policy of creating joint stock companies with Romanian firms tended to strengthen capitalism as an unintended by-product.

The fierce political struggle that engulfed the country in 1945 and 1946 is well known. The communists employed every means, legal and illegal, mass persuasion and violence, to eliminate the historic parties and gain control of parliament. Stalin had never excluded violence from the parliamentary path, but he was still advising caution in January 1945 on the eve of Yalta.[16] By contrast, the Romanian communists were pushing the envelope. Their supporters were drawn from predominantly unskilled and low skilled workers with a weak political consciousness. They were particularly susceptible not only to slogans of social egalitarianism but also to violent means by direct assaults on property owners or political competitors. They represented a fertile field for the party recruiters who had no experience in the institutions of parliamentary democracy. Moreover, the party was still relatively small compared to the Social Democrats or even MADOSZ and could only maintain its strong position in the National Democratic Front with the support of the Soviet representative on the ACC.[17] But the Soviet representatives revealed at times that they were not pleased with the violent tactics of the Romanian communists which threatened to provoke a civil war and immensely complicate Soviet–Western relations.[18]

---

[16] During a visit of Ana Pauker and Gheorghiu-Dej to Moscow in January, Stalin advised them to concentrate on agrarian reform but to avoid the issue of nationalizing industry; "to try not to scare and not to alienate the bourgeois [anti-German] elements but to work toward establishing a National Front government." Dimitrov, *Diary*, entry of January 1945, pp. 350–1.

[17] Volokitina, *Narodnaia demokratiia*, pp. 65–6. In the spring of 1945 the Communist Party numbered 35,000, while the Social Democrats had 400,000 and MADOSZ 225,000. Ibid.

[18] During the February 1945 crisis the Soviet representative on the ACC, V.P. Vinogradov, pleaded with his American and British colleagues to help avoid civil war. Transcript Allied Control Commission, February 21, 1945, AVP RF, f. 453, d. 1870ll. 15–6. He was replaced by General I.Z. Susaikov, who took a tougher line, but also confided to the American political representative Berry that "he is going to save his head at all costs and this probably means he is going to close his eyes to the tactics used by the Romanian communists to maintain their position." *Foreign Relations of the United States* (FRUS), 1945, V, pp. 558–601. Quotation on p. 600.

The real economic transformation and political conformity to a revised, monolithic model of popular democracy only took place after 1948, although the political opposition to communism had been eliminated long before that. Romania was a classic case of what Stalin meant by a transition through parliamentary means. Civil war and the danger of foreign intervention were avoided. But this was not the case throughout Eastern Europe.

The Insurrectionary Model

There were two basic methods of promoting military victory and laying the foundations for the transition to socialism through the creation of New or Popular Democracies: the insurrectionary and the parliamentary. Both exhibited several variations. It is important to state clearly that these were not consciously designed, fully worked out models emanating from either the Soviet center or the local parties. Rather, they emerged in the course of World War II in response to a complex mix of factors: military, geographic, political and ideological. The two tendencies were supposed to complement one another. But the inherent tension between them developed into a deep contradiction. A comprehensive comparison of these factors on a European scale is not possible here. But some preliminary conclusions may be drawn.

Early in the war both Churchill and Stalin had urged the peoples of occupied Europe to rise up against the common enemy. But for Stalin, no less than for Churchill, insurrection was a military measure. Its purpose was to disrupt the enemy rear, sabotage war production, and—paramount for Stalin—to force the Germans to withdraw front line units from the Eastern front in order to relieve pressure on the Red Army. But favorable conditions for insurrection did not exist uniformly throughout Europe. Where they did, as in Yugoslavia, Albania, Greece, and in Asia, China, insurrection, or, as it became known, the partisan movement, gave rise to civil war mainly between a communist and nationalist resistance which effectively blocked a parliamentary path to socialism.[19] Where they did not, as in France, Italy, and

---

[19] For the impact of civil wars in the Soviet borderlands on Stalin, see Alfred J. Rieber, "Civil Wars in the Soviet Union," *Kritika*, Vol. 1 (2003): 129–62.

Czechoslovakia (up to the moment of liberation), there was no civil war between the communist and nationalist resistance, but instead political cooperation that made possible the postwar opening to a parliamentary path. There was a second variation of the parliamentary path in Romania, Hungary, Finland, and Germany where there was no effective resistance movement, to say nothing of an insurrection, but also few signs of political cooperation between communists and non-communist, anti-fascist parties. Here Stalin showed a willingness to cut deal with former allies of Hitler, whether captured German generals, Admiral Horthy, General Antonescu, or Marshal Mannerheim in order to remove Hitler or detach his satellites by getting them to sign a separate peace and then turning them against Germany. He was also willing to accept, at least initially, postwar governments in which the communists were not dominant and, with the exception of Romania, to permit postwar elections that were relatively free.

With the end of the war, the primary task of the National Front shifted to preparing the transition to socialism. Under wartime conditions and with the dissolution of the Comintern, the local communist parties developed along more strongly national lines. The French and Yugoslav parties represented the opposite ends of the spectrum of variations, with Romania and Bulgaria somewhere between them. What ideological guidance would the Soviet Union give to define more clearly the options facing the national parties?

Theory and Practice

Looking to Stalin as the fount of Marxist-Leninist theory could only have disappointed the true seeker. The Soviet leader's comments on the nature of the emerging state systems in Eastern Europe were scattered, vague and open to interpretation. For instance, meeting with the Polish communists in May 1946 he declared: "the democracy in Poland, Yugoslavia and partly in Czechoslovakia is a democracy that brings you close to socialism without the need to establish a dictatorship of the proletariat." Stalin went on to explain that the dictatorship of the proletariat had been necessary in France during the Commune and in Russia after November 1917 because of the powerful opposition of the bourgeoisie. But in Poland the capitalists had been compromised by collaboration with the Germans, and "doubtless" the Red Army had helped to remove them. Stalin invoked Lenin's authority for an alternative path to socialism. He even went so far as to insist that the Polish government needed a "tame opposition" to disarm the underground and criticize it without planning to overthrow it.[20] Much of what he said in this long and revealing interview had to do specifically with Poland. Its relevance for other East European states became clearer as he conducted interviews with their communist representatives.

In the case of Bulgaria, Stalin advised Dimitrov in September 1946 that the new Bulgarian constitution should be "a people's constitution." But in order to "avoid frightening the *strata who do not belong to the working class*; draw up a constitution more to the right than the Yugoslav one." He also urged the formation of a Labor Party uniting all other working strata including the Agrarians. It would serve as a "*convenient mask* for the present period." He then repeated his advice to the Polish communists: "All this will contribute to your peculiar transition to socialism—without a *dictatorship of the proletariat.*" He hammered home the point that "it is necessary to use different methods and forms and *not copy the Russian Communists* who in their time were in an entirely different position."[21] Despite his frank advice to the local communists, Stalin chose even at this point not to codify his thoughts. Instead, he encouraged or allowed (it is not clear which) prominent figures in the foreign policy establishment and among his own secretariat to sketch out their version of the parliamentary path and the new or popular democracy.

Within the Foreign Commissariat this task was assigned to the Litvinov and Maiskii commissions on planning for postwar Europe and in his Secretariat the burden, as it came to be, was assumed by Eugene Varga.[22] In addition, a third commission headed by the more influen-

---

[20] Record of conversation between Stalin and Boleslaw Bierut and Eduard Osobka-Morawski, May 24, 1946 in (VE) Vol. I, No. 151, pp. 443–63. Quotation on pp. 456–7.

[21] Dimitrov, *Diary*, entry September 2, 1946, pp. 413–4, italics as in original.

[22] Litvinov and Varga were personal friends. Conversations with Ivy Litvinov, Februrary 1966. They also had ties to other moderate communists like Imre Nagy whose ideas on a gradual path to socialism were influenced by Bukharin and introduced, abortively, twice in Hungary, in 1945 and 1956. Miklos Molnar and Laszlo Nagy, *Imre Nagy: Reformateur ou revolutionnaire?* (Paris, 1959), pp. 18–20, 24–7, 38, 46–9.

tial Klim Voroshilov dealt mainly with the postwar German question. Its conclusions reinforce the argument that the Soviet leadership intended to pursue a policy of postwar collaboration with the Western powers as the best means of maintaining Soviet security in Central and Eastern Europe.[23] The Litvinov and Maiskii commission reports both reflected elements that would re-surface in the Varga debates. They assumed a growing contradiction between British and American interests as the main representatives of imperialism. They envisaged a division of three spheres of influence in Europe (and not a division into two blocs). They stressed vital state interests over ideological issues which they down-played but did not ignore. Finally, they did not exclude the possibility of external intervention in the name of imposing "broad democracy in the spirit of the people's front."[24]

The first systematic attempt to define the prerequisites and variations in the emerging popular democracies was undertaken by Boris

---

[23] Voroshilov expressed concern that the Western governments might not be committed to the idea of a united Germany after the war. He was convinced that the preservation of good relations among the wartime allies was the sole guarantee that the Germans "cannot for their own ends exploit differences among the allies or even minor disputes that might arise in the course of the occupation. Precisely for this reason, there ought to be a unified [allied] consultative organ empowered to reach agreements on all important questions concerning the whole of Germany before these measures would be announced to the German government for implementation." He repeatedly emphasized the need to demonstrate to the Germans "the absence of any disagreements or tension" among the allies. AVP RF, f. 0512, op. 2, p. 8, d.4, pp. 116–8. As the Soviet representative and head of the ACC in Hungary, Voroshilov followed the same line. According to General Miklos, the head of the provisional Hungarian government in March 1945, "Pushkin [the Soviet political adviser to the ACC] has forbidden the Communist Party to agitate against the government and Voroshilov himself has stressed that civil strife will not (repeat not) be tolerated." Kirk to Secretary of State, March 1, 1945, NA, State Department, Control Hungary, 740.001 119, Box 3796, folder 1.

[24] For the most complete analysis, see Aleksei Filitov, "Problems of Post-War Construction in Soviet Foreign Policy Conceptions during World War II," in Francesca Gori and Silvio Pons eds., *The Soviet Union and Europe in the Cold War, 1943–53* (New York and London: St. Martin's Press, 1996) especially pp. 12–7. The fact that most of their recommendations were ignored, except for those by Maiskii on reparations, lay at the basis of Litvinov's bitter disillusionment as expressed to Western journalists. Vojtech Mastny, *Russia's Road to the Cold War* (New York: Columbia University Press, 1979).

Nikolaevich Ponomarev, then deputy director of the Marx–Engels–
Lenin Institute and member of the Comintern aparatus and Department of International Information of the Central Committee, a leading party historian and theoretician whose career extended into the
1980s. In a report to the Department of International Information on
November 9, 1945, he analyzed the changing circumstances underpin-
ning the "democratic transformation in the liberated countries" of Europe. For him the key questions were who held power and what was
the structure of the economy. He declared that the democratic forces
were best organized and actively committed to the struggle for national liberation in countries where the communist parties had the greatest
influence among the popular masses. But the process of democratization differed in countries liberated or occupied by the Red Army—
Yugoslavia, Bulgaria, Poland, Czechoslovakia, Austria, Romania,
Hungary, and Finland. Countries liberated by the Allies constituted a
second group—France, Italy, Belgium, Greece, Holland, Norway, etc.
Ponomarev rejected the concept being promoted by the Department
of Propaganda of the Central Committee that countries in the first
group should be called "revolutionary-democratic dictatorships of the
proletariat and peasantry." This was an outdated formula put forward
by Lenin in 1906–07 under very different circumstances. Today, he insisted, "the existence of a socialist country changes everything."[25] This
formula could not be applied to any of the countries in the first group.
The new basis for power in these countries was the national liberation
committees and a bloc of political parties including the communist,
socialist and agrarian that shared one "absolute" condition, the absence of any ties with the German occupation. Ponomarev admitted
that external politics and internal conditions required the inclusion of
reactionary individuals (like Mikolajczek in Poland and Grol in Yugoslavia) and shifts in the composition of these government. But this
did not affect their basic character. The second important question
was who controls the army? Here Ponomarev distinguished between
the armies of wartime allies, Yugoslavia, Poland, and Czechoslovakia,
where the army was being reconstructed on a wholly new basis to create an "army of a new type." In Bulgaria, Romania, and Hungary the

---

[25] Report of B.N. Ponomarev "On the democratic transformations in the liberated countries of Europe," RGASPI, f. 17, op. 128, d. 749, pp. 136–7.

old army remained in place but was reformed in a radical way through purges. Then, first Bulgaria followed by Romania, constructed a new army out of the anti-fascist participants in the national liberation struggle. In Hungary reactionaries constituted a more significant part of the army than in Romania.[26]

On the subject of the economy Ponomarev celebrated the destruction of the landlord class in Eastern Europe. He acknowledged that mistakes had been made, especially in Poland and Romania. He denied that there was any intention of collectivizing the peasantry; "it does not appear on the agenda." The formation of cooperatives was important to overcome poverty in the countryside and to forestall rumors of collectivization. In industry the picture was more checkered. While in Poland and Yugoslavia seventy to eighty percent was under state control, the majority of firms in other countries were in private hands; they faced "very great difficulties." The old bourgeoisie had been deprived of the commanding heights of the economy though some had elected to participate in the new life of the state. Foreign trade was reoriented toward the Soviet Union, depriving the western capitalists of influence, especially in Romania.[27]

At the level of politics Ponomarev insisted that "no single democratic party was predominant (*imeet dlia sebia preimushchestva*). Any talk of the dictatorship of the communists was the fruit of reactionary fabrications." The struggle for democratization, as Ponomarev called it, had not ended, or even diminished but was intensifying. The reaction was linked to the plutocracy, or German collaborationism or English and American capital supported by the old state apparatus except in Yugoslavia and Bulgaria where the old state apparatus had been smashed. The tactics of the reaction was to "break up the democratic bloc." The recent pattern was to introduce bearers of bourgeois reaction from abroad who had no record of collaborating like "Gemeto" in Bulgaria or Grol and Šubašić in Yugoslavia. When they failed to delay the transformation, they and their supporters turned to sabotage either by quitting the government as Šubašić and Grol in Yugoslavia, and Petkov in Bulgaria, or by blocking legislation as in Romania where king refused to sign decrees. Another tactic was to isolate the peasant masses from the Communists, then cut

---

[26] *Ibid.*, pp. 140–1.
[27] *Ibid.*, pp. 146–9.

them off from other parties and declare that the communists cannot rule alone. This was similar, Ponomarev reminded his audience, to the tactics of the Second International and the Mensheviks. Even at this late date Ponomarev identified the international reaction primarily with the Vatican "never to be underestimated," and "the main enemy," the British Labor Party, linked to the Second International.[28] The Soviet leadership was still less concerned, clearly, with the United States. Ponomarev found it necessary to repeat that the question of establishing Soviet power and Soviet democracy was not on the agenda; "this task is not worth considering (*ne stoit*) and we should keep this in mind when we are dealing with the spontaneous (*neposredstvennym*) processes unfolding in these countries."[29] Ponomarev's authoritative analysis still left open many questions, implying that the tempo and range of the transformation would differ in each country depending on local circumstances.

The Varga Debates and Popular Democracy

A second stage in the attempt to define the character of the popular democracies centered on the Varga debates.[30] Evgenii Varga's controversial book on capitalism, published in 1946, started things off. A former member of the Béla Kun Soviet government in Hungary in 1919, Varga had emigrated to the Soviet Union and fashioned a successful career despite his early associations with several of Stalin's most prominent political enemies including Trotsky and Bukharin. In 1927 at the height of the Bukharin–Stalin entente, Varga was appointed director of the newly created Institute for World Economics and World Politics, where he remained in charge for the following twenty years. His knowl-

---

[28] *Ibid.*, pp. 156–62.

[29] *Ibid.*, pp. 165–7, 170. An edited version of his remarks were published in *Bol'shevik*.

[30] Stalin characteristically constructed ideological or policy statements in such a way as to suggest the possibility of multiple interpretations. The "correct" one was left unclear and could be the subject of "diskussia" by specialists until Stalin decided on which side to come down. For insights into this process, see Alexei Kojevnikov, "Rituals of Stalinist Culture at Work: Science and Intraparty Democracy circa 1948," *Russian Review*, Vol. 57 (January 1998): 25–52; and Yuri Slezkine, "N.Ia. Marr and the National Origins of Soviet Ethnogenetics," *Slavic Review*, Vol. 55 (Winter 1996): 26–62.

edge of western languages and economic theory earned him the reputation of one of the leading specialists on capitalism. He also became a member of Stalin's private secretariat, which may help explain how he survived the purges that carried off his former associate Béla Kun. As late as 1943 Stalin praised Varga's report at the Academy of Sciences and, according to Dimitrov, found it *"good, Marxist. Any criticisms of that report in the CC secretariat are no longer valid."*[31] At the end of the war he published volume one of a projected two volume work on *Changes in the Economy of Capitalism Resulting from the Second World War.*[32] His work, together with that of his colleagues in the Institute, became the storm center of a controversy which involved several scientific institutes, the leading theoretical organs of the party, and high ranking figures in the party hierarchy. The entire affair, which dragged on for several years until in 1949 when Varga publicly recanted his views, casts additional light on the relationship between the concept of popular democracy or, as Varga called them, "democracies of the new type" and Soviet foreign policy.[33] Dimitrov, who had worked with him in the Comintern, considered him a man "of proven worth" with whom, it may be assumed, he shared similar perspectives on the transition to socialism.[34]

Three major intertwined themes ran through Varga's analysis. First, during the war the massive intervention of the state in the economies of Great Britain and the United States had given capitalism a new lease on life. The introduction of various forms of regulation, price setting, rationing, allocations of resources, and technological in-

---

[31] Dimitrov, *Diary*, entry May 13, 1943, p. 273.

[32] E.S. Varga, *Izmeneniia v ekonomike kapitalizma v itoge vtoroi mirovoi voiny* (Moscow, 1946). The projected second volume on political questions was never published. An excellent summary and commentary is Frederick C. Barghoorn, "The Varga Discussion and Its Significance," *American Slavic and East European Review*, Vol. 7 No. 3 (October, 1948): 214–36. But see also R.S. "The Discussions on E. Varga's Book on Capitalist War Economy," *Soviet Studies*, Vol. 1, No. 1 (June 1949): 28–40. An economist's analysis is Evsey D. Domar, "The Varga Controversy," *The American Economic Review*, Vol. 40 No. 1 (March, 1950): 132–51. For the connections with foreign policy, see Jerry F. Hough, "Debates about the Postwar World," in Susan Linz ed., *The Impact of World War II on the Soviet Union* (London, 1985), pp. 253–81.

[33] Hough, "Debates," pp. 266–74, is particularly informative on this.

[34] Dimitrov, *Diary*, p. 76, entry September 16, 1938 and p. 273, entry May 13, 1943.

novation represented the interests of the bourgeoisie as a whole and
not merely the monopolies. Varga foresaw that "the issue of a larger
or smaller share in running the state will form the main content of
the political struggle between [...] the bourgeoisie and proletariat."[35]
His point echoed faithfully Stalin and Dimitrov's views on the possibility of a parliamentary path to socialism. Second, in the post-war
period the imperialist rivalry between the two leading capitalist powers
would intensify but would not necessarily threaten the Soviet Union
in the short run. The war had increased not only the military power of
the Soviet Union but also its prestige among progressive circles in the
West who would act as a damper on aggressive, anti-Soviet policies.[36]
Moreover, the United States as the dominant capitalist power would
challenge the war-torn colonial powers of Western Europe for their external markets. This would aggravate the normal rivalry among imperialist powers. In Varga's words: "American policy now aspires above
all to crush the English colonial empire in order to seize for American capital equal conditions in a real struggle for the whole world."
It was even possible in his eyes that a Western bloc forming under
British aegis might become an instrument for defending the overseas
colonies against the U.S. Varga did not deny the common elements
linking Great Britain and the U.S. nor the possibility that the two Anglo-Saxon powers might scrape together an anti-Soviet bloc. But he
considered that less likely. The implication was strong that the Soviet
Union would not have to face another cycle of capitalist encirclement.
It could then revive its policy of the 1930s of playing one set of imperialist powers against another in order to relieve the pressure on its
own internal development, in the first instance building socialism and
in the second building communism. This theme also echoed Stalin's
views on two levels. First, he recognized, indeed exaggerated, his own
tactical skill in devising ways of aligning the Soviet Union with one
group of capitalist powers against another.[37] Second, although war

---

[35] Varga, *Izmeneniia*, p. 318.

[36] Ibid., pp. 318–9. Certain of Varga's associates placed greater emphasis on
the imperialist rivalry.

[37] Stalin boasted to the Yugoslav communist Andrija Hebrang how he had improved on Lenin's strategy of dealing with the capitalist states: "But now it
turns out that one group of bourgeoisie goes against us and another with us.
Earlier, Lenin did not think that it was possible to maintain an alliance with

was inevitable as long as capitalism survived, as he restated the Marxist truism in his election speech, Stalin refuted the prospect of a war between the Soviet Union and the western power as a provocation that encouraged anti-communist, oppositionist elements in Eastern Europe.

Varga's third closely related theme was that wartime changes in the essential structure of capitalist society had produced in Eastern European economies "democracies of a new type." These were a more advanced form of state capitalism than in Western countries. It "is not the apparatus of coercion of the big bourgeoisie, but a democratic state, based on the broad mass of toilers."[38] Following a discussion in which his basic positions were attacked, Varga boldly elaborated the political implications of his economic analysis. In an article published in the journal of his Institute he declared:

> Today, thirty years after the victory of the Great October Revolution, *the struggle in Europe is becoming in its historical development more and more a struggle for the tempos and forms* of the transition from capitalism to socialism. Although the Russian way, the Soviet system, is undoubtedly the best and fastest method for transition from capitalism to socialism, historical development, as Lenin predicted theoretically, shows that other ways are also available for the achievement of this goal.[39]

Here was a historical materialist explanation of an alternative to the dictatorship of the proletariat. This is precisely what Stalin had been saying to Dimitrov and others for the previous several years. In fact, it is no exaggeration to conclude that Varga's book and his defense in the face of criticism was a sophisticated Marxist-Leninist interpretation of Stalin's immediate post-war policy in Eastern Europe.

Placed in a larger historical perspective, Varga's ideas echoed Bukharin and foreshadowed Khrushchev. Bukharin had initiated

---

some powerful bourgeois [states] and to fight with another. We succeeded in doing that; we were guided not by emotions but by reason, analysis and calculation." Conversation of Stalin with A. Hebrang, January 9, 1945, in *Vostochnaia Evropa* Vol. I, No. 37, pp. 132–3.

[38] Varga, *Izmeneniia*, p. 291.

[39] E. Varga, "Sotsialism i kapitalism za tridtsat let," *Mirovoe khozaistvo i mirovoe politika*, Vol. 10 (October 1947): 4–5. This was rather late to be still defending the separate path!

the theory of the stabilization of capitalism at higher organizational and technological levels as a result of growing state intervention during World War I. Although he did not live to witness it, the experience of World War II, as interpreted by Varga, reinforced Bukharin on the recuperative powers of capitalism. Faced with the prospect of diminishing revolutionary opportunities, Bukharin had advocated a united front in order to prevent the isolation of the communist parties and consequently a "tragedy" for the working class. He anticipated a new wave of revolutionary upheavals in the future arising from the external contradictions of capitalism in the form of another imperialist war. This is not to ignore differences between post-war Varga and pre-war Bukharin. For example, in his publications right after the war Varga soft pedaled Bukharin's views on the importance of "national independence" movements—only to revive and proclaim them after Stalin's death when he was rehabilitated and much honored. He also stopped short of making the prediction that had caused Bukharin so much trouble, of the imminent outbreak of an imperialist war. But these were refinements. The main thrust and theoretical foundations of their analyses had much in common. So did the implications of their theories for a foreign policy of accommodation, peaceful coexistence and *détente* with the West.

In the first round of discussions in May 1947 over Varga's book, the critics mainly nibbled at the edges, ending up in what Evsey Domar called "sterile" arguments over whether or not capitalism had entered a new phase after the war. But Varga was taken to task for having underestimated the importance of the new democracies. He was forced to retreat from his position that they were forms of state capitalism rather than a transition stage to socialism. This was one of his most vulnerable arguments. State capitalism, as his critics pointed out, had been rejected in the 1920s as a revisionist definition of NEP. In the peoples' democracies of the 1940s, it suggested a closer relationship with the economies of Western capitalists than with the Soviet Union.[40] Still, the atmosphere at the discussion was collegial rather than hostile.[41] Varga was certainly not alone. His Institute colleagues, while not un-

[40] R.S., "The Discussions on E. Varga's Book," pp. 33–4; Barghoorn, "The Varga Controversy," p. 232.
[41] Domar, "The Varga Controversy," p. 148.

equivocally endorsing all his views, defended him from the criticism that he had slighted international politics and the internal situation of capitalist countries.[42]

The implications of the Varga discussion for the course of Soviet foreign policy were not immediately clear, although Varga proved vulnerable to attack on his position that the struggle between socialism and capitalism had been suspended within the coalition during the war. In the eyes of his critics he had failed to give sufficient weight to conflicts among the wartime allies. And he had left unanswered the question of how long the struggle could remain suspended.[43] Varga was not prepared to wade into these deep waters. There was much that was "esoteric" in the debate; policy alternatives were not confronted openly. Nor could they be, given the sensitivity of these issues and Stalin's acknowledged monopoly on their ultimate meaning and implementation. In 1947 and 1948 a series of crises within the governments and societies of Eastern Europe forced a reassessment of the theory of transition and the definition of popular democracy.

The Monolithic Model

Following the establishment of the Cominform and the expulsion of Tito from its ranks, Dimitrov reformulated the concept of a people's democracy followed by harsh attacks on Varga and his associates. In several works published in 1947, Varga and I.P. Trainin faithfully had followed Stalin's line that the doctrine of the dictatorship of the proletariat was not applicable to the new democracies in the early postwar years.[44] Dimitrov, however, reemphasized the essential resemblance of the people's democracies to the Soviet state. Popular democracy was redefined as another form of the dictatorship of the proletariat. The critics now piled on. They accused Varga and Trainin of having neglected the "decisive role" of the proletariat and communist parties in the states of Eastern Europe. Still, they did not completely identify the

---

[42] Barghoorn, "The Varga Discussion," p. 229.

[43] *Ibid.*, pp. 230–1.

[44] The key texts are analyzed by Samuel L. Sharp, "New Democracies: A Soviet Interpretation," *American Perspective*, Vol. 1, No. 6 (November 1947): 368–81.

Soviet and East European experiences. The reorganization of the national fronts and the establishment of the hegemony of the communist parties was viewed as a process moving toward the establishment of a dictatorship of the proletariat, implying an evolution but one that had acquired a rapid and unequivocal movement. These exquisite refinements retained the idea that the main difference from the Bolshevik revolution was, as Stalin had pointed out, the absence of civil war, but attributed this solely to the presence of the Red Army.[45] Clearly, Stalin's decision to accelerate the transition and to reject interpretations that emphasized separate paths stemmed from two sources of perceived danger. One was the magnetic power of a revitalized western capitalism embodied in the Marshall Plan and the other was the potential political attraction of a separate Yugoslav path. Stalin viewed the Marshall Plan as an attempt to create a Western bloc and isolate the Soviet Union.[46] Yugoslavia was even more of a problem. In a document prepared by the Foreign Department of the Central Committee for the Soviet leadership, the Yugoslavs were accused of "devoting themselves exclusively in 1945–47 to the practical tasks of building and strengthening a new government." Tito had failed to speak of communism as the final goal and had limited the party and the people to "the attainment of a genuine popular democracy."[47] To be sure, the Soviet attack on Tito was multifaceted and the charge of following a separate path was absurd on the face of it; but Stalin did not always take appearances for reality. Stalin abandoned the more moderate and gradual concept and policy of a transition when he believed that economic pressure from the capitalist west and political deviation within the popular democracies would jeopardize Soviet control over the borderlands. Only a more rapid incorporation of the Soviet model could do that. Yet even then,

---

[45] H. Gordon Skilling, "'People's Democracies,' in Soviet Theory," *Soviet Studies*, Vol. 3, No. 1 (1951–52): 26–30. His critics also rejected Varga's formula that the state apparatus had not been demolished as in the Soviet Union but "is being reorganized by means of uninterrupted inclusion in it of partisans of the new regime." *Ibid.*, p. 31.

[46] Conversation of Stalin with delegation of Czechoslovak government, July 9, 1947, VE, Vol. I, pp. 672–3, No. 227.

[47] Memo of Department of Foreign Policy of the Central Committee to M.A. Suslov, March 18, 1948, ibid, Vol. I, pp. 790–1, No. 267.

the Soviet model would remain a stage ahead in the march to full communism.[48]

To return to the initial question: why was the concept of popular democracy an illusion? To be sure the concept evolved over time. But before 1944–45 it was wholly abstract insofar as there did not exist any government based upon its principles, if we exclude the Spanish Republic from 1936–38, which was only a prototype. After 1948 the concept of popular democracy was virtually the equivalent of the Soviet model. Therefore, we are left with that brief period of attenuated opportunity in the early post World War II years.

Stalin's perception of a post-war world in which the transition to socialism in the sphere of Soviet influence would evolve under the leadership of communist parties within coalition governments operating within a parliamentary form over a long period of time, at least ten years, while a continuation of the wartime alliance would delay the revival of Germany and Japan until the USSR could recover from the devastation of World War II was based on a number of conditions that proved to be unrealistic. There were, it seems to me, three principal conditions that could not be met. First, his grand design required the local communist parties to accept certain rules of the parliamentary game for which they were not suited either by training, ideology, or experience. Second, it required the Soviet representatives in Eastern Europe no less than Stalin himself to accept as genuine the protestations of friendship and cooperation by the non-communist members of the coalition governments, instead of accepting the hostile evaluations of their motives by the local communist parties which more easily fit into Stalin's personal and ideological world view. Third, it required the non-communist parties to avoid internationalizing their internal con-

---

[48] The concept of popular democracy did not lose all its value as a device for making hierarchical distinctions within the socialist camp. For example, in Stalin's discussions with Soviet economists in 1950, he not only defined popular democracy as a less developed form of the dictatorship of the proletariat than the Soviet Union, but also explicitly excluded the People's Republic of China from this category, placing it instead under the old Leninist rubric of "democratic dictatorship of the proletariat and peasantry." *RGASPI*, f. 17, op. 133, d. 41, l.6, as quoted in Ethan Pollock, "Conversations with Stalin on Questions of Political Economy," Working Paper No. 33, Woodrow Wilson Center (Washington, D.C., July 2001), p. 45.

flicts with the communists by drawing in the Western powers whose representatives were also predisposed to interpret every move by a local communist party as Moscow inspired. Taken separately these were very large requirements. Entangled as they were, they created insurmountable obstacles to a moderate interpretation of the course of post-war capitalism and the evolution of popular democracy.

Part Two

THE ESTABLISHMENT OF COMMUNIST REGIMES IN CENTRAL AND EASTERN EUROPE

Thomas W. Simons, Jr.

Eastern Europe between the USSR and the West: Reflections on the Origins and Dynamics of the Cold War

Where I Came In

I was actually born in 1938 during the Munich crisis, so I could almost say, with the 17th-century English political philosopher Thomas Hobbes, that fear and I are twins, even if the Cold War and I are not. But I did come of age during the mean early years of the Cold War, from the Berlin Blockade to the Cuban Missile Crisis. I am of the generation that learned in school to get under door jams to survive a Soviet nuclear attack. So when I entered the U.S. Foreign Service in 1963 I hoped to work in and on the Cold War.

I also brought with me into the Service an interest in Eastern Europe that was unusual at the time. I had studied in Paris and Vienna, and in Vienna the East is near: there is an old saying that Asia begins at the Landstrasse, and I lived two blocks away. But even before that, as a 7-year-old in Calcutta with my diplomat parents in 1945, I had been gripped by a film about the destruction of Warsaw six years before: Chopin mixed on the soundtrack with the whine of Stukas. When I was a student in Paris in 1956 crowds of French youths vented their outrage at the Soviet reconquest of Budapest by storming the Communist Party headquarters at the Carrefour de Châteaudun. The next spring a friend and I drove around Austria's Burgenland looking for James Michener's bridge at Andau where the Hungarian refugees had come across the previous fall, and I was warned off my first minefield by Hungarian border guards. So when I entered the Service I wanted to work not just on the Cold War, but on the Cold War in precisely this part of the world.

Although we did not know it then, 1963 was actually a kind of turning point. Perhaps, as someone once said, 1963 was the last year when the sun didn't give you cancer. But it was certainly the year the Cold War turned a corner into something different from what it had been when I was growing up. I took my oath on July 15. Five weeks before, on June 10, President Kennedy had given the speech at American University that signaled the turn as far as U.S. policy was concerned. Three weeks later, on August 5, the U.S., the USSR, and Britain would sign the Limited Test Ban Treaty, the first major step toward strategic arms control. So while East–West hostility was still the order of the day, it was a somewhat hopeful time; change was in the air.

Yet when I started to work on the Cold War as a diplomat a few years later, the men at whose knees I learned the trade had already lived through two rounds of a characteristic Cold War cycle that began with hope and ended with Soviet actions which then crushed that hope. Here I would like to suggest a framework for our discussion about the Cold War's first decade that encompasses all five of its decades, from World War II through to the end in 1990. I will argue that each Cold War decade witnessed an attempt to get beyond the foundations of hostility that were laid in the 1940s; that only the last effort, in the 1980s, succeeded, and then only in very paradoxical fashion; and that when the previous attempts failed, they failed because the foundations of hostility were very strong among elites in the U.S. and the Soviet Union. I will also argue that the core foundations of the Cold War were *ideological*, on both sides, and that they proved indispensable to both sides until near the very end.

What I Inherited

My mentors in the Service, then, were already the survivors of two cycles that began with efforts to extend the basics of East–West competition beyond its foundational ideologies, but ended by locking them back in. And Eastern Europe had been central to both cycles.

During World War II, when these men had been the age I was then, the states of the Grand Alliance were in systemic competition with each other, but they had found a common interest in defeating Nazi Germany that forced them to set aside or adjust elements of their ideologies, their "principled approaches," as the Soviets used to say, in order to win. They had in fact won, and their success had aroused hope that the enlarged definitions of principle they had been forced to tinker out could be carried forward into the post-war world.

My mentors had shared some of that hope. Many had fought in the war; and just after the war a number had served in the West German provinces as political advisors or interrogators with their newly minted Russian language. Several of them had been serving in Eastern Europe as the Iron Curtain descended. Dick Davies, who became our Ambassador to Poland in the 1970s, once told me that when he joined our Embassy in Warsaw in 1947 it was enormous, because we staffed it to be a bridgehead for Poland's democratization. And then the curtain had come down. (By his account the Embassy came to look a little like Baghdad's Green Zone after that.) Davies recalled that he was in the Polish Sejm, the parliament, when it made Soviet Marshal Rokossowski first a Polish citizen, then a Marshal of Poland, and finally Polish Minister of Defense. By the Sejm's own rules, each law needed three readings, and they did them all in one session, nine votes in all. Bailiffs went up and down the aisles urging deputies to stand and vote yes, shouting that resistance was futile; more and more did so; and at the end only one old peasant party deputy in felt boots still kept his seat (and was never heard from again). I was intrigued by how punctiliously the old Republican Sejm's legal requirements were observed; Davies himself still steamed with outrage.

That kind of outrage went deep, and it made reasoning hard. Later on I had the privilege of friendship with Poland's late great Jan Nowak Jeziorański, and he once told me that when he joined Radio Free Europe in the late 1940s he quickly realized that America had no *strategic* interest in Eastern Europe. For Americans like my bosses and me, though, it was hard to grasp the implication, which was that U.S. interests were in fact *ideological*. We did not feel particularly ideological ourselves—we thought we were pragmatic (for that is the American ideology)—and it was hard for us to see that the Cold War started because American and Soviet elites drew contradictory lessons from Hitler's rise and defeat, and that these lessons were rooted in the ideologies that had presided over the very births of the states they governed.

To be sure, some geopolitical thinking was present on both sides. Some thought was given to how heavily Eastern Europe's resources might weigh in the geopolitical scales. Chiefly, though, such thinking was filtered into the prevailing ideological interpretations of the world crisis that emerged gradually—between 1944 and 1947—in Washington and Moscow. For the Americans, the crisis was caused by *appeasement of tyranny*—that was the lesson of Munich, when I was born—and it had been overcome by the productive power of democratic capitalism. For the Soviets, the crisis was caused by the degeneration of capitalism, and it had been overcome by their might, and they were mighty because they were *socialist*. For the Americans, the watchword was "No more Munichs"; for the Soviets, it was "No more isolation for the socialist motherland."

For the Soviets, that made Eastern Europe crucial: binding Eastern Europe to themselves actually *created* the socialist camp that would preserve them from isolation forever. For Americans like my mentors, though, once the Cold War came Eastern Europe shrank to the function of the canary in the mineshaft of Soviet intentions. It might be freed or caged, but it was important only because of what it told you about the Free World's great Soviet adversary.

My mentors then lived through a second cycle of hope and disappointment, in the 1950s. In this one Eastern Europe was still central, but again only as the canary in the mineshaft. The trouble was that its chirp kept rising toward a scream. These men were now advancing through the middle ranks of the Service, and they had their hopes raised once again, by Stalin's death, by the spirit of Geneva, by the Austrian State Treaty of 1955. But those hopes were then buried again by Khrushchev's blustering and Khrushchev's crises, by Budapest, by Berlin I and Berlin II, and finally by the Cuban Missile Crisis of 1962. And that was the paradigm that greeted me in 1963, when I came in.

The 1960s

Where the Soviets actually were I had no idea: they were purposely opaque in any case, and the paradigm was by now so well-worn that it seemed good enough for government work, as the saying goes. But in fact the 60s then taught us that some important things had changed. Western Europe had recovered, it now seemed secure against subversion, and it was also starting to chafe first at American tutelage and then at American neglect as the Vietnam War got in high gear after 1965. After Cuba, the Soviets embarked on a huge strategic arms buildup—"never again Cuba"—and the U.S. developed anti-ballistic missiles to vitiate it. There were thus real incentives to go beyond confrontation, new reasons to start processes of interaction and negotiation that might keep the confrontation manageable. The superpower elites had now lived with the threat of nuclear incineration through a whole decade—the student in the room next door to me in Harvard graduate school fled to Western Massachusetts during one of the Berlin crises to avoid just that—and it had been topped off by one frightful crisis. In the process the elites of the two countries had discovered their first common interest since World War II. Then it had been to defeat Hitler; now it was to avoid nuclear war. So they began to fumble toward strategic arms control negotiations.

As it turned out, the new beginnings of the 1960s were more creative and also more robust than those of the previous decade. Creativity brought paradox. By nailing down the division of Europe in Budapest and Berlin, the Soviets made it easier for Westerners to be subversive with clear consciences. Westerners could now promote connections between societies—exchanges, trade, people-to-people contacts—as a way under and around the political division, just because they could count on the Soviets to set limits to how far the East Europeans could go. The Soviets now had their own distraction—the jockeying for leadership primacy that followed Khrushchev's ouster in 1964—and they proved willing to lengthen the East Europeans' leash to accommodate such contacts. On the American side, this even generated a degree of ideological thaw. It was in these middle 60s that Zbigniew Brzeziński tried to transmute the multiplying societal interactions into a new concept, called bridge-building, which he promoted outside and inside government as an "alternative to partition." Like most of Brzeziński's ideas, the Soviets considered it subversive, and with good reason; but it also represented a significant departure in American thinking.

Alas, this cycle too ended with brutal Soviet action that sent everyone back to their ideological ramparts. The Soviet leadership's post-Khrushchev distraction ended August 21, 1968, with the invasion of Czechoslovakia. My wife and I had just arrived in Warsaw, having passed through Prague and fleetingly savored the springtime of the peoples still going on there, and we were awakened that morning by the roar of Polish planes taking off southward. It was the "socialist camp" in action indeed.

In the end, I think, that aging and not particularly bloodthirsty Soviet leadership was unwilling to tolerate the Czechoslovak refusal to enforce orthodoxy, because it came to see that refusal as a danger to everything. Whatever they told their troops about the German threat, they defined the real threat ideologically. As Kádár warned Dubček at the time, "Don't you really know who you're dealing with?" And Dubček didn't. The proof of the pudding for me is that this fear was then given ideological form in the so-called Brezhnev Doctrine, proclaiming the duty of fraternal assistance to threatened socialist regimes. It was a diminishment—formulating a "line" usually means that the roots of a policy are drying up—but it was also a return to roots.

For my mentors in the American government, it ended a third cycle of dashed hopes. They had been there before. In Warsaw, my new Ambassador Walter Stoessel had been Washington's workhorse policy deputy all through the crisis, and when I asked if Washington policymakers had been surprised he said they had expected it so often only to see the Soviets draw back that when it finally happened they were surprised. But they had expected it. And at that point, for us Eastern Europe shrank once again back into its now-familiar role of canary in the mineshaft of Soviet intentions. Another East European effort to become an actor had failed; the region was once again important to us only because it told us better than Moscow itself how the wind was blowing from Moscow.

The 1970s

As with the Cuban Missile Crisis, crushing the Prague Spring did not end everything. The U.S. was still bleeding in Vietnam and still developing ABMs, the Soviets were still driving toward strategic parity, and nuclear war still seemed to both elites a danger to be avoided through negotiation: strategic arms talks began a year later. They were bilateral *par excellence*, and this grated on Europeans still chafing at American tutelage and neglect. In Budapest, the spring after Prague, the Soviets sought to tap into this West European restlessness with a renewed call for a European security conference. But then that fall of 1969 they also decided to risk military confrontation with China. Over the next years the Nixon Administration then had the wit to wrap strategic arms control, China, and European security together into a single diplomatic negotiating package that was intended to relieve what it saw as mounting pressure on the U.S. global geopolitical position.

But all this required incessant negotiation, many balls in the air all the time—even more balls once the Middle East was included—and negotiation with an ideological adversary had to be justified in ideological terms. Ever since Lenin the Soviets had had "peaceful coexistence" to fall back on for this purpose, so justification was mainly a U.S. problem. It was never entirely solved, but not for want of trying. Kissinger explained strenuously and at length that negotiation was essential to American strength, because the public would not support defense unless it was convinced no effort had been spared to reach agreements. Every year a foreign policy report to the nation elaborated that thought. There was even a "Nixon Doctrine" that justified hiving off defense tasks to allies.

And of course there were major achievements to point to, and I enjoyed my modest but growing role in the effort. I was in the last talks with China in Warsaw, and when both sides—without prior coordination—suggested sending a high-level emissary to a capital, you could feel the earth move: it was the origin of Kissinger's 1971 secret visit to Beijing. When I returned from Warsaw to Washington, I worked on conventional arms talks and what became the Conference on Security and Cooperation in Europe, or CSCE; I was in fact one of two or three people in town who thought CSCE could be a good thing, just as later, under Reagan, I was one of three who thought the Soviets could ever withdraw from Afghanistan. But then I have a sanguine temperament. Reporting on the Polish workers' revolt in 1970 I was thrilled, because to me it was a blow for liberty, and I was then shocked to hear that "Washington" was mainly afraid the Poles would screw up *détente*; yet I understood.

But it turned out that very many influential Americans did *not* understand, or did not *want* to understand, and the same was true in Moscow. In both capitals *détente*'s mounting achievements brought mounting ideological backlash. Parts of each elite were seized with fear that something fundamental was being lost in the rush to agreement with the adversary, and in the end those fears brought détente down.

Yet the process was not straightforward, because in each elite an attempt was made to carve out enough space for the Good Old Cause to allow the negotiation track to move forward at the same time, without damaging the Cause itself.

It happened first in the U.S. Following the great strategic arms control agreements of 1972 the Soviets expected to move on from "military *détente*" to "political *détente*," by which they meant ratification of the postwar status quo in Europe through CSCE and a whole new era of economic cooperation that would allow them to modernize the creaking socialist economies without reform. Instead, American skeptics promptly loaded down further strategic arms control with difficult new requirements, as a condition for ratifying the SALT I Interim Agreement, and they then made both East–West economic relations and CSCE hostage to Soviet concessions in a field that had not bulked very large before, a field that was central only to the American ideology. That field was human rights. This hostage-taking was what the Jackson–Vanik Amendment and Basket III in CSCE meant.

Upping the ante in this way slowed détente's brisk pace to a slow grind that frustrated the Soviets, and this in turn was followed by the Soviet version of the same impulse: only their pendant to negotiations was support for national liberation in the Third World. Like human rights for the U.S., "national liberation" had been a string in the Soviet ideological bow since their Revolution, at least for use outside the "socialist camp." But now on top of Vietnam, Portuguese decolonization opened up a whole new range of opportunities in Africa, and that string became thicker and tougher, and as *détente* soured, U.S. complaints had less and less resonance. Working in our Moscow Embassy in 1976, I watched the 25th Party Congress on TV, and marveled as the Politburo's white-haired ideological watchdog Mikhail Suslov leapt from his seat to cheer some wild African freedom fighter, to the point of ripping out his interpretation earphone. I also warned my Soviet friend, the Afghanistan expert, that we Americans had learned something about the limits of our power in Vietnam, but we were perfectly capable of unlearning it if the Soviets kept it up in Africa.

Kissinger was warning them too, but the Soviets did keep it up in Africa anyway, and then went into my friend's bailiwick in Afghanistan, and this brought down even the ark of the *détente* covenant, the SALT II Treaty that had been laboriously negotiated and signed in

1979. Defending *détente* had badly weakened President Ford in his struggle for the Republican nomination against Reagan in 1976, and President Carter continued the effort, but only by reinforcing the new human rights stress and thereby trying to demonstrate that we were faithful on essentials, so we were not really negotiating anything essential away. But *détente* was now a diminished thing for Americans, discredited ideologically and with fewer and fewer successes to shore it up politically. With Afghanistan, Carter had to withdraw the SALT II Treaty from Senate consideration. A fourth cycle of hope and bitter disillusionment was at an end.

The 1980s

I would argue that the decade of the 1980s broke the mold by reversing the cycle. Once again change started on the American side; with a leadership cadre now deep into its 70s, the Soviets clung to the achievements of *détente* amid total ideological immobility. And I was now in the middle of things. I served as State Department Director for Soviet Affairs in the first Reagan Administration, beginning in 1981, and then in the second as the policy workhorse deputy for both the Soviet Union and Eastern Europe—Stoessel's old job in 1968—until 1989. Only now the movement was dialectical, and started with disillusionment rather than with hope. Bitterly disappointed by Afghanistan and its own debilities, the U.S. returned massively to its ideological roots, to the "freedom agenda" that is as old as the Republic, and that had ushered us into the Cold War. And I saw up close how this return to origins, together with a little help from the Soviets, from Solidarity, and from circumstances, actually freed up U.S. policy for negotiation in good faith and good conscience, really for the first time in the Cold War.

It is of course also true that the first fruit of this ideological restoration was a two-year standstill in serious U.S.–Soviet negotiations, between 1981 and 1983, and that in a nuclear-armed world this hiatus frightened many. But during those years the Administration made enough progress on its real priorities—our domestic economy, our military power, and our morale—to respond creatively when the peace and nuclear freeze movements then forced a return to negotiations, and then when the new Gorbachev leadership came on the scene in

Moscow in 1985. We had been lucky that the decrepit Soviet leadership had been so immobile during its first term; but we were now ready.

As had been true since 1956, Eastern Europe was not playing much of a role. It is true that the Solidarity crisis in Poland had been one factor driving Americans back onto their "freedom agenda." But while historians dispute who was responsible for the martial law that ended it in December 1981, the characteristic first reaction of the U.S. Government was to blame the Soviets: for Americans, in other words, the Poles themselves were still the canary in the mineshaft. Enduring under martial law, Solidarity was then one factor rubbing Gorbachev's nose in the burdens of empire, just as Ceauşescu's crazed self-isolation in Romania was another. But the Soviets were still confident enough in the system (including Eastern Europe's economic dependence on them) to end the raw materials subsidies that had undergirded their empire there since Khrushchev. Had they been more worried about Eastern Europe they would not have done so. The main impulses for Soviet change were domestic.

Under those impulses, though, Soviet change now took the form of serious ideological adjustment, really for the first time in the Cold War. The Americans were hunkering down on their native ideology and were finally able to negotiate successfully. Having hunkered down on theirs without success in the early 1980s, the Soviets under Gorbachev felt they had to revamp it if they were to negotiate. They now fought for "all-human values" rather than the victory of the proletariat; they wanted to be part of a "common European house"; the enemy was not so much capitalism as their "enemy image" in the West.

Like the American effort to justify détente in the 1970s, this Soviet revamping was only partly successful. While the Americans marched in lockstep to the negotiating table, the Soviets now dispersed their energies in a score of directions, not all of them compatible. With regard to their "enemy image," however, they were successful: when the end came in 1991, it was not because of Western pressure but because of their own internal contradictions and mistakes. Rallied around its old ideology, the U.S. negotiated so well that the Soviets were unable to blame the Americans for their demise.

Coda

Does this history have anything to tell us today? Let me suggest a few possibilities. I think it tells us that if today's Russians blame the Americans for their problems at home and abroad, as they do, it is not because of the way the Cold War ended, but because of *subsequent*, post-1991 developments. But if the U.S. sticks so adhesively to its "freedom agenda" in the post-Cold-War world, it is no wonder, given the experience described above. And if East Europeans use new Russian aggressiveness under Putin and Medvedev to brighten Western interest in their region, that is no wonder either. The only wonder is that the U.S. seemed to forget, at least for a while, that once you are strong and confident, you then negotiate. But finally, it seems to me, this history does raise an important question for both East Europeans and Americans: the question of whether Eastern Europe can ever be more than the canary in the mineshaft for Americans, if all we have in common is a Russian threat.

AGNES HELLER

Legitimation Deficit and Legitimation Crisis in East European Societies

In the following paper I use the term "legitimation" roughly in its Weberian understanding. A system of domination can be regarded as "legitimate" if at least one part of the population acknowledges it as exemplary and binding, while the other part, most often the majority, does not confront the existing social order with an image of an alternative one as, at least, equally exemplary and more desirable. In Weber's view there are three major sources of legitimacy, namely, the legal order, charisma and tradition.

Dealing with communist systems, I would add first the distinction between the legitimacy of a system (of domination) and the legitimacy of a government, and second two supplementary sources of legitimacy, such as interest and fear. Interest and fear can be termed spurious sources of legitimacy, yet since they can be effective for a long time, they cannot be neglected. Fear can have also two sources. First, fear from Stalinist terror, second, fear from external threat. For example, in the Soviet Union, the first was strong in the thirties, the second during World War II. As far as interest is concerned, it never worked, not even as supplementary source of legitimacy during Stalinism, yet, for example during the second half of Kádár's rule, it did function in Hungary.

I want to say in advance that, whereas Stalinism enjoyed legitimacy in the above described senses in the Soviet Union, especially in Russia and Georgia, it constantly struggled with serious cases of legitimacy deficit in all East European societies, although not in all of them to the same extent. Deficit in legitimacy does not always lead to legitimacy crises, and even in cases of legitimacy crises one has to distinguish between acute and chronic crises, and between the legitimacy crises of the system of domination and the government. It was typical of most

East European totalitarian dictatorships to solve, at least on the surface, chronic crises by changing the government, sometimes successfully (e.g., Gomulka's succession of Ochab), other times not (Gerő replacing Rákosi as first secretary and Hegedűs as prime minister).

The constant legitimacy deficit is due to two factors. One is the initial position, the other is the speed of transformation. The salience of the initial position is obvious. Soviet communism was homegrown, whereas at least in Romania, Hungary, and Poland, it was superimposed. I do not want to dwell on the cases of Bulgaria, Albania, and Czechoslovakia, yet it is well known that communism ultimately took the upper hand in Czechoslovakia in a kind of putsch in 1948. The second factor is the variation on the nature of the starting points for each Eastern European regime. It is particularly interconnected with the problem of speed.

Stalinism is not a special form of domination, but a period within the history of Soviet totalitarianism. I call it "terroristic totalitarianism" because it was during this period that terror became the vehicle of the full establishment and the maintenance of the totalitarian form of domination. Terror was also practiced before Stalin, but mass terror as the means to the full elimination of the possibility of political action was his invention. Only Stalin succeeded with the attempt of legitimation through charisma, which worked only together with terror. Fear feeds faith. More precisely, Stalinist terror succeeded in creating the Leader's charisma; it created love and faith with the power of legitimacy. Although, when talking about East European communist first secretaries, we speak frequently of mini-Stalins, none of whom succeeded in building up their own charisma, for they lived on borrowed charisma.

In order to dwell on the element of speed, I will first present my interpretation of totalitarianism, referring only, however, to its communist incarnation. I call a system of domination totalitarian if pluralism is outlawed by the powers of domination. The power of domination is formally the communist party, in fact the dominating body of the communist party. In the case of Stalinism this equation of power was reduced to the rule of one man, what later acquired the stamp of "personality cult." Pluralism does exist in every modern society, since if there were none there would be no need to outlaw it. But, in the case of our distinctive type of system, the political center has absolute discretion over what is outlawed and what is permitted.

In the Soviet Union classic Stalinism was preceded by an already long period of practice in totalitarian domination. First, the communist party had been cleansed from pluralism; second, all political bodies of the state became homogenized. Stalin came to power in an already totalitarian party and a totalitarian state. It was with the help of those institutions that he "totalized" the whole society, outlawing pluralism also in property ownership, art, science, etc., securing this radical step by incessant waves of purges. At the time, roughly 15 years had elapsed since the seizure of power by the communist party. For example, independent art associations were outlawed in 1929, while "socialist realism" became obligatory in arts only at the Congress of the Writers' Union in 1934. This process, roughly 15 years long, shrunk to 3 years or less in the new communist regimes in Eastern Europe.

One can also argue that the script itself was not entirely faithfully followed. In Hungary for example, the political totalization of the state, in 1948, preceded the totalization of the party during the 1949 purge, which happened simultaneously with the Rajk trial. If only for the reason of speed, chronic legitimation deficit or even crisis could be swept under the carpet yet not avoided. The difference in speed was also characteristic to the short history of Cominform. The so-called third International, the Comintern, was only gradually and slowly totalized through the exclusion of pluralism by the Soviet Party which finally turned Stalinist. In contrast, the Cominform was entirely Stalinized in less than a single year. The Resolution against the Communist Party of Yugoslavia, published in *Rude Pravo*, in the summer of 1948, rapidly led to the expulsion of Tito, the "traitor" (i.e., "a dog on the short leash of American imperialism") of the so-called great family of brotherly parties, and triggered the subsequent Rajk and Kostov trials.

It is not my intention, however, to explain the reasons for the accelerated speed of Stalinization in East-Central Europe. I only wish to discuss its effects on the legitimation of the regimes in the regions. To accomplish the feat, I will turn my attention to the case most familiar to me, that is, Hungary, while also trying to maintain a comparative dimension with references to other Soviet satellite states.

The year 1945 found Hungary in a power vacuum. There was no system of domination yet; only a provisory government which moved from Debrecen to Budapest. The previous Hungarian government, led by the Arrow Cross Nazi party, couldn't have claimed legitimacy for two reasons: on the one hand it represented only the extreme right-wing fringe of the political spectrum; on the other, their coming into power was instrumentalized by Nazi Germany in the context of a collapsing Eastern front. In contrast, and according to my definition of the concept, Admiral Horthy's regime can be seen as legitimate. By 1945, though, because of the collapse of the latter's administration and under circumstances of occupation and failure in the war, one burning political issue was to fill the power vacuum with a government that was supported by tacit consent, for more could hardly be expected. Besides the above reasons, an additional burden for the post-war emerging political establishment was the outcome of the peace conference. Moreover, except for the old social democrats and the few Jews who survived the war, the Hungarian population never accepted the Soviet occupation as "liberation." Yet, since even in 1945 it was believed to be dangerous to speak of occupation in public, people normally spoke about "the front": this happened "before the front," that "after the front." Even those conservative gentlemen who hated the Arrow Cross movement and blamed them for the destruction of Budapest, mourned the sad Hungarian fate of always being on the wrong side. There was, however, a kind of tacit consent that could be regarded as a seed of legitimacy. It was the shared desire to start life again from the ruins.

There were three important events which offered the initial solid ground for legitimacy. First, Hungary elected a legitimate government, second the land reform, a century-old dream of the peasantry, and finally, in 1946, after the most rampant inflation in Hungarian history, the stabilization of the currency. I must stress that these happened under a non-communist government. In the only fair elections in Hungarian history before 1990, the Independent Freeholders' Party received an absolute majority of 57% of the votes, the Social Democratic Party 17.4%, the Communist Party 16%, the Peasant Party 6.8%, and the Democratic Party 1.6%. In fact, the result was a great achievement for the then not yet totalized communist party, one that had to overcome the bad memories from the so-called 1919 Soviet Republic. But they expected more, for in their aspiration for a central political position they would have needed at least the score obtained by their Czechoslovakian counterparts. The government was dominated by the moderate right wing, which agreed, for the country's sake and out of reasons of pure rational calculation, to form a coalition government, although no law had compelled them to do so. Historians agree that, at that time, Hungary's full Sovietization had not yet been decided. In all probability, it was put on the agenda with urgency, after the creation of the Cominform. Rákosi called the year 1948 "the year of the turn," and it was indeed an upswing moment for the newly formed Hungarian Workers' Party. The elimination of the independent social democratic party and the nationalization of industry were executed simultaneously, in the context of a prior nationalization of the banks and mines. Yet, as I already mentioned, interestingly, the Stalinization of the whole political life happened earlier than the Bolshevization of the party. An explanation can be found only if we return to the issue of the party's drive for legitimacy.

The leaders of the communist party, being in minority, began immediately after the first elections to prepare the way for their domination, as the outcome was still open. This happened in four ways. First, the open-endedness of the outcome was emphasized even after the door had been shut. In speeches, newspaper articles, theories were invented about a so-called "peoples' democracy," which had absolutely nothing to do with the dictatorship of the proletariat. That is, the communist leaders denied the preparation of a kind of Soviet regime in Hungary. They assured the population that they were aware of the differences in traditions and circumstances. Second, the party and its leaders (Rákosi, Gerő, and the chief ideologue, Révai) made sure to get the control of all institutions and positions capable of exercising force and violence. They obtained the Ministry of Interior, took control of the police forces, and re-organized the secret police. A bonus feature of the domestic reality for them was that, of course, the Soviet army was also at their disposal. Third, they intervened in the business of the parliamentary parties by ruse and by force. They co-opted one of the leaders of the Freeholders' Party, Tildy, instated him as state president and persuaded him to expel twelve deputies of his own party, the most independent minds of the party. Moreover, the Red Army could circumvent Hungarian law and arrest "enemies." Fourth, they tried to make the communist party more popular, by claiming authorship of all the real achievements of the previous administration. They claimed to have been the initiators of the land reform, the powers which "gave" food to the hungry, and the masterminds behind the stabilization of the currency. They were the defender of the poor, of the needy, of the

"people" in general, they provided theater, concerts, books; they created the new democratic culture. First and foremost, they tried to associate their political image with the ideas of reform and hope.

Such circumstances considered, it is now apparent why they could
not "Bolshevize" the party prior to 1949. They waited first for the
1947 elections, when, in spite of massive fraud, they still remained in
minority. And they needed a populist party to offer legitimacy for their
seizure of power during 1948, the "year of the turn." That is, in Hungary, the legitimation of the party and the legitimation of the system of
domination appeared together on the agenda. And, interesting as it is,
a not yet totalized party proved to be a good legitimating force for the
totalizing politics of their leaders and for the great leap towards a fully
totalized society. Almost all these happened simultaneously, with the
exception of the campaign to collectivize private-owned farms. A similar pattern of post-war development into communism can be observed
in the Polish case as well.

The Hungarian Workers' Party, by 1948, had become a mass party. An intense recruitment activity swelled its ranks, thus allowing for a
consistent claim for populist support. Of those who joined, opportun-
ists, however, were perhaps in the majority. Yet, there remained large
numbers of true believers, in the strictest sense of the word. During
those three years, before 1949, party members entertained the illusion
of party democracy, and perhaps, it was not just an illusion. Those
who read the autobiography of the famous Hungarian economist, János Kornai, understand what I mean. Kornai and other 19–20 year-old
young idealists belonged to the internal staff of *Szabad Nép*, the party's
newspaper. Even after many decades of anti-communism, Kornai recalls those years with sympathy. He and his friends could talk freely,
they wrote what they believed to be true, and no one compelled them
or controlled them. And they were not the only ones. Millions of people saw the rose, with no idea yet of its thorns. This was one of the legitimating forces of the new form of domination, which they only later,
1953–1956, were to make a forceful attempt at destroying.

At this time—before 1948–49, the "year of the turn," of the Rajk
trial and of the party purge—one can find at least a considerable minority that had begun to regard the system of domination as exemplary, even if their referent was more its potential than its reality. The
promise which was suggested by the communist ideology was not, or at

least seemed not to be, merely a superimposed doctrine. Many people sincerely believed in the so-called "people's democracy," in its prospects for real democracy, socialist humanism, freedom and so on. As far as the broad stratum of intellectuals were concerned charisma also worked. Yet it was not charisma that served as the main vehicle of legitimacy. Rákosi's charisma was artificially created, because he himself as a personality had none. This became obvious after 1953. Nevertheless, the chief ideologue, József Révai, did possess considerable personal charisma. Even his very mediocre speeches were perceived to be great and sensational products of Marxist reasoning. Within the social democratic party, the left wing social democratic strategist, the chief promoter of the unification of the two leftist parties in 1948, György Marosán, also boasted significant personal charisma. The strategic actions of these two individuals, described favorable conditions and fuelled a kind of enthusiasm and expectation.

Certainly, the majority of the population remained hostile or at least skeptical. Before 1948, the new system of domination was still in the making, while the old one was not yet *tabula rasa*. One part of society's politically active contingent still found the old Horthy regime exemplary, reservations considered. Losing a war, however, was far from a legitimating bonus. The land reform however had won great popular support, forcing important sections of the right wing to support this policy. Western democracies could have served as an alternative, yet a great part of the right wing, following its populist spirit, was suggesting a so-called third way between capitalism and socialism, and maintained their skepticism toward the West. To sum it up, a smaller part of the Hungarian population, mainly the members of the populist communist party, were legitimated by at least the proposed prospect of a different kind of social and political system, whereas those who cried wolf were, at that time, unable, *en masse*, to come up with an alternative social perspective. Their primary objective was to defend the political status quo produced by the results of the 1945 free elections.

Most people felt, but had not realized what went on behind the political curtain during the preparation of the 1947 election. They knew of course that Béla Kovács had been arrested by the Soviets before the election, but did not grasp its full significance. Although during the second election in 1947 there was massive fraud by the communist party, the outsider noticed only that the right wing had won again. A different kind of right, however, resulted than the one of the 1945 elections. While the Independent Party was a truly independent political force, the Smallholder Party made many compromises with the communists. The government elected in 1947 was still regarded as legitimate by the law, before the constitution. Those who hated and feared the communist party supported the government, while those who expected a freer and better way of life supported the communist party and offered a green light for its experiments. There were after all important empirical signs of improvement. The government could abolish the rationing of most of the foodstuff, the reconstruction of the destroyed cities was well on its way, people's colleges were organized, the tertiary educational system was opened for all.

Before 1948, there was a kind of legitimacy deficit, yet no legitimation crisis. This needs to be said with reservation. For no new system of domination was in place. There was political pluralism, even if it was in retreat and defensive, there was private property. Factories were managed by a *troika*—the owner, the trade union and the workers council—an arrangement which was accepted as democratic; cultural life was thriving. Therefore, legitimacy was not granted to the Soviet type of system of domination. It rather aimed at the capacity of the communist party to improve life and maintain order. The organization of Cominform put an end to this moment of hope.

As I mentioned, the totalization of the communist party, of the political life and of the whole structure of power happened almost simultaneously. No breathing room was granted. The communist party started a permanent propaganda and institutional war, and bombarded the population with an ever expanding list of restrictions, upheavals of social bonds, traditions, customs etc. The speed of change can hardly be emphasized enough. Every change, even for the worse, can become habitual; one can accustom oneself to it. Yet there was no way for the Hungarian population to accustom itself to any of those changes. It would be difficult to even speak about legitimacy deficit. It was a full-fledged crisis, for no one could legitimate a system of domination that was constantly in flux. One could only legitimate the communist party as the mastermind behind all these changes. This situation provided then the psychological background of the tremendous effect of Imre Nagy's speech in June 1953.

Let me enumerate the steps of this permanent upheaval which lasted less than five years. For those five years were the years of Hungarian Stalinism. It was perhaps the briefest of Stalinist periods in Eastern
Europe, but also arguably the most devastating one. Neither its speed
nor its radicalism was primarily due to any kind of internal development, good or bad. It started with the birth of the Cominform and
it ended three months after Stalin's death. Between 1948 and 1953,
everything came from "without," with the mediation of Hungarian
communism. Until 1948, the "without" exerted constraint, defined the
limits, yet did not determined all the steps. The same became the case
after 1953. Stalinism never returned to Hungary, even if totalitarianism
could bring about even more devastating effects, as in the first decade
of Kádár's rule.

I will return now to my definition of totalitarianism: it is a system of domination where pluralism is outlawed. Which type of pluralism is outlawed depends on the leading bodies of the communist party
or on one man. In Stalinism, almost all of pluralisms were outlawed.
Stalinism was a period of Soviet or communist totalitarianism which
is with justification identified by the dictators name. Stalinism is the
terrorist version of totalitarianism, that is, the kind of totalitarianism
which is supported by the permanence of terror. The word "terror" has
two meanings: fear and the exercise of violence. To unpack the term
one has to specify that violence is exercised in this case against non-
combatants. Certain groups of people are selected for extermination,
imprisonment, internment and other punitive measures, yet within
those groups individuals are randomly picked. Random selection in-
flicts general fear, for no one knows who comes next. Terror, however,
is a modern sociopolitical phenomenon, which, already in its cradle,
was associated with virtue. This is also true about Stalinism. The good,
the virtuous Comsomol youth was supposed to declare that "the party
is our reason, honor and conscience." This is the participatory facet in
the exercise of terror—to lend unconditional support to it becomes the
supreme virtue of a young communist soul.

In Hungary, terrorist totalitarianism (i.e., Stalinism) was estab
lished within two years and lasted for another three. The process of
the establishment of Stalinism started roughly at the same time as in
other satellite countries, perhaps with the exception of East Germany.
For example, the so-called unification of the working class, that is the

elimination of the social democratic parties in Czechoslovakia, Poland and Hungary, happened in all these countries in 1948. The Kostov trial in Bulgaria followed quickly after the Hungarian Rajk trial. In the Soviet Union, the stages towards totalitarianism came, so-to-speak, logically, one after another. First the party was subjected to a totalitarian regime, then the political life, then society. But, since in the process of "totalizing" society a pluralism of sorts appeared, or at least was feared to have appeared, within the party ranks, a second wave of totalization of the party took place. This last step required legitimacy through charisma. If there was any kind of pluralism within the inner circle of the ruling party, then the popular support, if there was any, could be divided. Stalin's personal charisma, which was, for some reason, a real one, tolerated no real division. Surely, even Stalin's legitimacy was constantly fed by the servility of those surrounding him, by the flattery of ideological chiefs and by all the panegyrics of writers and poets. Yet, neither of these complementary legitimating forces could generate real charisma around Rákosi, Gottwald, Gheorghiu-Dej, or Bierut, as they did in Stalin's case. Stalin was backed by the glory of the aggrandizement of his country.

The long-term legitimacy of terroristic totalitarianism depends on the charisma of the Leader. To refer to another regime, one can argue that Hitler also had it. As far as the other East European satellite countries are concerned, with perhaps the exception of Dimitrov (who died too early for any real assessment in this sense), none of the communist leaders can be said to have enjoyed such a position. They could not even exercise the condition of a secondary charisma, that is, the legitimating power of nationalism. At the time, Tito was the only communist leader who could boast such opportunity and worth.

To return to the case of Hungary, the society was spared no time to adjust or even internalize a step, when the next already followed. Shortly after the right wing had won the 1947 elections (when the communist leaders hoped in vain that electoral fraud would ensure their victory), the communists simply dissolved the elected parliament, starting with the arbitrary dismissal of Ferenc Nagy, the acting Prime Minister. The communists in power immediately called for new elections, from which the so-called united "National front" unsurprisingly emerged victorious. Political pluralism was over. From this moment on, as Hungarians put it, the population was left only with the right to choose between two white elephants. While the establishment of a single party rule was in motion, the "unification" of the working class took place. Simultaneously, industry was fully nationalized. Moreover, the most important step toward the elimination of private property, the nationalization of industry, happened before the totalization of the party. In the Soviet Union, as we know, the totalization of the party through the outlawing of factions within the party had already been decided under Lenin; under Stalin, only a second purge phase (the show-trials) took place, a completion of the job started earlier. In Hungary, they fused the two stages, mainly because of the specific dynamics at the level of the Cominform. Some leaders of Hungarian communism paid a heavy price as a result of such mixed practices.

The Hungarian story therefore stands out across the whole of Eastern Europe. There were hardly any Stalinist terror trials in Poland. Gomulka was not executed. The Slansky trial in Czechoslovakia, which took place roughly half a year earlier than the final end of Stalinism in Hungary, has, in my mind, not much to do with the Cominform, for it was meant as preparation for the "doctors' plot" (ultimately prevented by the tyrant's death). Before the party purge (out of one million two hundred thousand members, four hundred thousand were expelled), a section of the party membership still believed that they could voice their own opinion. I could, for example, ask the question of the party group leader "why was Trotsky wrong," and nothing happened, I was just enlightened on the issue. Half a year later, no one would dare to ask such a question, not even of themselves. With the purge and the political show trials terror reigned supreme.

Five faithful communists were executed in the Rajk trial. It was a show trial in a double sense: as a means of intimidation and as a trial against Tito. Many hundreds of other communists were arrested. Almost all members of the former social democratic leadership on Hungarian territory were either murdered or imprisoned. The ideological witch hunt against György Lukács was also an essential part of the intimidation campaign—members of the intellectual strata had learned their lesson. Those who did not join the slander campaign were destined to similar indictments. The universities were purged too. All cultural products were closely watched and controlled. Mindszenty had been arrested earlier; now Grósz was added to the corps of imprisoned clergy. Those designated as members of the so-called "former ruling classes" were deported to the countryside, their property and goods confiscated. In fact, seizure of real estate was the main purpose behind the deportations, for the construction of apartment houses had stopped; there were no apartments for the increasing city population, even after the old apartments were divided in several units, and families had to share one apartment. After a relatively successful three-year plan, the party launched a Soviet type five-year plan, focusing on heavy industry. Simultaneously, those identified as *kulaks*, the wealthy and productive peasant farmers were persecuted and imprisoned. Collective farms were established without providing means to cultivate them. Starvation, not just shortage, was the result. Food rationing was restored. The shops did not even receive enough bread or milk to provide the rations. One could still drink cheap rum, but this was hardly compensation. Imagine for a minute: peasants striving for centuries to become free farmers on their own plot. Now, finally, the dream comes true, yet within three years, not more, they lose their land again, they are forced to join, with their land, the collective farms. And in addition they are obliged to jubilate, to express gratitude for their loss as if it were a gain.

Rákosi, Gerő, and Révai maneuvered themselves into an impossible situation. This was the first time when the Soviet system of domination *itself* required legitimacy, not just the government or merely the promise of a new and better life. The communist party tried to establish it through conspicuous references to its great successes and achievements. But the very "achievements," which should have served as the ideological vehicle of legitimacy, became the greatest obstacles for attaining it. The regime, after its Stalinist turn, became merely a bloody tyranny in the service of an alien power. To make matters worse, it also showed a great capacity for irrational decision-making, as it destroyed its own supporting basis.

Fear, as we know, can promote legitimacy whenever it creates faith. In the Soviet Union, it created faith through Stalin's charisma. Yet, Rákosi and the other regional leaders had no such charisma. Fear without charisma does not create faith; on the contrary, it most likely induces the loss of it. The new farmers, who previously supported the party because of its perceived involvement in the land reform, turned away from it when the latter made the push for collectivization. The enthusiasts of the communist party before 1950, whether intimidated or not, now began to lose their faith. In a caustic formulation, all things were bad, yet the essence was good. This essence could not be recaptured, even for those who still believed in it. At the time of the XIXth Party Congress of the Bolshevik Party, there was a chronic legitimation crisis in Hungary. The crisis remained hidden, because of widespread fear. Although no one had any idea what the arrest of Gábor Péter, the former head of the Hungarian Secret Police, the Hungarian *Jezhov*, meant (now we know that it was meant as the prelude to the "doctors' plot trial") no one expected any good from it. Ultimately, the "personality cult" misfired. If Rákosi was praised for everything before, after 1953 he ended up being blamed for everything.

The first premiership of Imre Nagy in 1953 changed the domestic environment almost entirely. Hungarian Stalinism, perhaps the cruelest version of it, was over. One cannot understand the upheaval of 1956, without clarifying the transformations which began in 1953. Imre Nagy and his famous speech restored, at least partially, the legitimacy of the communist party, and through it, the legitimacy of the system of domination. Those communists and former communists who saw the promises betrayed could believe in them again. Even the real enemies of the regime lent some conditional support to the Nagy government. It seemed to be a national government; it adjusted its projects to the Hungarian tradition, it offered people peace. It did not intrude into their private life, taste, religion and else. All this was framed in a discourse of the betrayal of Western democracies that sold Hungary out to the Soviets, leaving it with such government as the best of the available options left.

The new government began to deliver the goods it promised through the revision trials, the rehabilitation of victims, and by closing internment camps. These measures reconfirmed the end of the Stalinist terror. In addition, it declared its support for light industry instead of heavy industry and allowed the peasants to retrieve their plots from the collective farms. This meant three important things. First, the territory of outlawed pluralism became narrower since private ownership of land and even of certain necessary services, became again legal. Second, one could reasonably hope that the system of food rationing would become obsolete, elementary needs would be satisfied, shops would again sell and people buy. Third, Imre Nagy spoke a new, a different language, one radically different from the previous *langue de bois*. Terror spoke a Stalinist language, which prohibited open argument and discussion. The new language allowed it and perhaps even encouraged it. This change implicitly impacted upon the communist ideology itself.

In a certain way, Hungary after 1953 seems a repeat of the Soviet story before Stalin's victory. Pluralism appeared in the ranks of the party itself. The struggle between Nagy and Rákosi was not just a power struggle; it was a clash of two kinds of state-policy. I would not go so far as saying two types of politics. The Hungarian party remained, at least formally, a fully centralized totalitarian party just like the Soviet one had been before the Stalinist turn. The question which remained open was that of policy. The conflict was fought out between a Stalinist policy and a post-Stalinist one, a battle which surfaced in several other People's Democracies after the 20th CPSU(b) Congress. In Hungary, however, the same conflict preceded the 20th Congress. It came even less than a year after the 19th. This means that the Hungarian development was not synchronized with the overall regional one. And, as a result, it had a "national" touch. This was an important aspect with respect to legitimation. In certain other countries, like Romania or Albania, or China, the national aspect, the relative or at least seeming independence later on stabilized a kind of Stalinist post-Stalinism, whereas in Hungary, it was strongly combined with an *ante factum* de-Stalinization. The only comparable development occurred in Poland, much later, since Bierut died only at the time of 20th Congress, and Gomulka succeeded only after Ochab. The conflict between party factions led by Rákosi and Nagy, respectively, was, at the beginning, centered on policy issues. Yet, still Nagy's programs attained the aura of being "national," while also being fashioned as the providing hope and of extraction out of the reign of terror. In the struggle between the two leaders, Rákosi ultimately got the upper hand and Nagy was expelled from the party, but the latter's strong legitimacy destabilized the regime. For his fall did not just come about with the price of a strong de-legitimization of Rákosi, but also against the party that now came to be perceived as Rákosi's turf. The Hegedűs government was seen as merely a puppet of Rákosi.

I cannot emphasize more strongly the importance of language. People began to speak about politics in a non-Stalinist language and this language promoted discourse. It happened first among intellectuals inside and outside the party, then among the party members, in general, and in the country at large. The Khrushchev-initiated reconciliation with Tito in 1955, had only a slight reverberation in Hungary, insofar as it added an extra reason to the increasing demand for state funerals for the victims of show trials (especially László Rajk) and an official apology by the Hungarian party for the Stalinist terror. Yet, a Rajk-type of sympathy for Tito and for his politics did not appear Hungary, as Nagy's program was perceived to be far more radical than the reforms in Yugoslavia. I want to return to the importance of timing. Since the so-called "year of the turn," only five, and since the time of the Rajk trial and the party purge, only four years, passed. For the true believers of the early period, four years were enough to prove that all the promises had been betrayed. For the enemies of the party and of the regime, the change in policy proved that their worst fears had been justified. These two camps met in the middle, namely at the level of agreeing about the utter de-legitimation of Rákosi's party. If shouted from two different directions the two "no's" sounded as one, they reinforced each other. And the focus of those two "no's" was the promise of 1953, the promise that things could be significantly different.

At the beginning of this paper, I defined legitimacy in the following way: *a system of domination is legitimate if a minority regards it as exemplary and binding, and if there is no alternative image or option available for the remaining majority.* I added that there is a difference between the legitimation of a system of domination and of a government. In 1953, Nagy's rule was legitimate even if none of the sources of legitimacy enumerated by Weber fit into the picture. Nagy's government was not legitimated by the non-existing rule of law, Nagy had no personal charisma, at least not at the time when he took up premiership, and in the eye of the beholder he rather disrupted his own tradition than followed it. Nineteen fifty-three was a revolution in the ancient Greek understanding of the word, as a return to the beginning, this time to 1945–46—the years prior to the Stalinization of Hungary. A wise Hungarian politician, Ferenc Deák once said that a wrongly buttoned vest has to be unbuttoned. In 1953, people hoped for the unbuttoning of a wrongly buttoned vest. Four or five years are nothing in the life of a generation, even if they are difficult. They even might, more often than not, turn into just a memory of a bad dream. The generation of mid-1940s was still active. The same generation which experienced and survived the Second World War, the loss of the war, the hardships of the reconstruction, the first hope in a coalition of the so-called democratic forces, in a parliamentary system; the generation which had lived through the times of the land reform, of the projects of social justice, autonomy, the workers councils and the like. Imre Nagy offered the possibility of a new beginning by wiping the slate clean. His government was legitimated by the promise of a return to the starting point. It was originally intended in a peaceful way, step by step. All these developments confirm that the idea of an alternative way of domination was quite concrete at the time, a similar situation with that of 1945–47. That is why the combined "no's" inherently meant also a shared "yes."

Going back now to these "nos," I wish to note some details. One of them was the "no" of the socialists and communists who said "no" to Stalin and his terror regime. The other was that of all the anti-communists, who rejected not just communism but also socialism in all its forms. Nevertheless, they did unite in a "yes" that veiled the intention to return to the beginning, to unbutton the wrongly buttoned vest. The difference in the program, among those involved in the support for the 1956 movement, was already present, yet not to the extent of becoming louder than the common yes. A multiparty system and workers' councils, representation and direct democracy were required almost immediately. Yet the emphasis on the national way of socialist development was replaced by the demand for full independence.

I will try now to summarize the main ideas of the present paper and to insert my conclusions on the Hungarian case in the more regional and historical context created during the first post-war decade. Hungarian Stalinism was never legitimate. It was characterized by a constant, yet permanently hidden, legitimation crisis. It was sitting on "bayonets" even more tenuously than in some other satellite states. The permanence of terror, the constant escalation of it, was not due just to the proximity of Yugoslavia, but also for reasons of exigencies in domestic politics. Fear, without charisma, had to serve as the foundation of the new regime. As a result, however, even most of the communists felt themselves and their ideals betrayed.

I would like to enumerate the main reasons for this hidden legitimacy crisis (some of them negative, while others are positive). On the negative side: Hungary had lost the war, the Soviet Union was regarded not as a liberating, but as an occupying power. Hungarian communism had to deal with the specter of 1919 and found it difficult to ever again take root in the country's political spectrum. Perhaps this is also why, besides protecting themselves, the Hungarian trio, Rákosi, Gerő, Révai (and, additionally, Farkas) secretly decided not to arrest or try Muscovites. On the positive side: Hungary was maybe the only country where, after 1945, free and un-manipulated elections took place; where, for a short time, an authentic, albeit always threatened, parliamentary system was established; and where workers' councils existed in the still privately owned factories. The hope, or project, to return to beginnings, to unbutton the wrongly buttoned vest, was reinforced and can be explained by the reality of the first two post-war years. As a result, not even a considerable minority perceived the Hungarian Stalinist regime as exemplary and binding, and almost everyone cherished an alternative image or idea of a political system (or of its potentiality) which they regarded as exemplary. The prime minister of June 1953 suggested that they were right. The conclusion of 1953 was that any return to Stalinism was illegitimate. It did not matter much that Imre Nagy was himself a loyal communist. He was the symbol of an alternative already entrenched in people's mind, of a muted pluralism that re-surfaced in 1953 and which defined itself in contrast, as *different* in every way from the experiments of the Rákosi years.

Without the promise of the possibility of returning to the beginning (in 1953) no uprising could have turned into a revolution. In 1945, in Hungary, a regime based on popular sovereignty was established. Popular sovereignty was then transformed in 1948 into party sovereignty by violence and force. Nineteen fifty-three signaled an attempt to return people's sovereignty. But how to institutionalize liberties further remained an open question. This is why the political interpretation of the revolution can be so divergent. Returning to what? To the Freedom Party? To social democracy? To the workers' councils? Only to independence one could not return, because it was lost earlier than 1945.

Revolutions are in general not legitimate. The so-called right to revolution is more than problematic; it is at best a moral right. The revolution of 1956 is an exception, for the grounds of its legitimation were laid as early as 1953: it was perceived as a break from an illegitimate capture and a return to a society-wide favored and cherished beginning. Berlin was different, so was Poznan, and despite several similarities, so was Prague. Later on, the Kádár regime began where the Rákosi regime had ended: in a permanent crisis of legitimation. How this legitimation crisis turned from the late sixties onwards into legitimation deficit, is another story.

JOHN CONNELLY

The Paradox of East German Communism: From Non-Stalinism to Neo-Stalinism?

The German Democratic Republic (GDR) figured as one of the world's most orthodox Communist states. This was especially apparent against the background of the Soviet Bloc. As one author has stated of the post-1961 period: "Close Party control over all aspects of national life was more systematically elaborated in the GDR than in any other eastern European state..."[1] While Poland or Hungary gradually liberalized, the East German leadership resisted reform so tirelessly that western commentators have called it "neo-Stalinist."[2] "Neo-Stalinist," when applied to Brezhnev's Soviet Union, referred to a repressive, strictly centralized political regime that had been created in the 1920s, and persisted despite the de-Stalinization of the 1950s. East Germany, however, supposedly never had Stalinism to begin with. At best, most scholars agree, it experienced a mild form of Stalinism. It lagged behind neighboring states in the severity of inner-Party purges, and in the socialization of the economy. In some scholars' views, these anomalies even placed East Germany outside the context of Eastern Europe. The challenge in telling GDR history is to bridge this gap between that country's supposed failure to fully institutionalize Stalinism during its

---

[1] L.P. Morris, *Eastern Europe since 1945* (London: Heinemann, 1984), p. 51.

[2] Dietrich Orlow, *A History of Modern Germany, 1871 to the Present* (Upper Saddle River: Prentice Hall, 2002), p. 298; Bruce Allen, *Germany East: Dissent and Opposition*, 2nd ed. (Montreal: Black Rose, 1991), p. 157. (First ed. was 1989); Alexander Wendt and Daniel Friedhelm, "Hierarchy under Anarchy: Informal Empire and the East German State," *International Organization*, Vol. 49, No. 4 (1995): 714; Jonathan Zatlin, *The Currency of Socialism: Money and Political Culture in East Germany* (Cambridge: Cambridge University Press, 2007), p. 10.

formative years, and the apparent neo-Stalinism of its mature years. How could East Germany become neo-Stalinist if it had never been Stalinist in the first place?

Ironically, the most famous popularizer of East German non-Stalinism was the Socialist Unity Party of Germany's (*Sozialistische Einheitspartei Deutschlands*, SED) foremost Stalinist: Walter Ulbricht. In 1956, in perhaps the most sudden and brazen break with the Cult of Personality, Ulbricht proclaimed that "Stalin cannot be regarded as one of the all-time greats (*Klassiker*) of Marxism-Leninism."[3] The GDR required no de-Stalinization because it had been non-Stalinist. This "fact" became dogma.[4] Ulbricht took credit for sparing East Germans the excesses known in other East Bloc countries, especially bloody inner-Party purges.

Ulbricht's reasoning gained broad acceptance among East German scholars—when they dared address the issue. Best known are the formulations of the economic historian Jürgen Kuczynski. In the early 1980s, self-described dissident, Kuczynski published a book of letters answering questions which he imagined his great-grandson might someday ask—when he became old enough to talk. In one famous letter Kuczynski asked himself through his great-grandson: "Don't be angry, great-grandfather, and don't answer if you don't want to, but I would like to know what you would say about yourself in the 'time of Stalin'." Kuczynski wrote:

> If you would ask me if I was happy as a comrade and scholar in the "time of Stalin" I can only answer: Yes!
> Yes! For I was convinced of the greatness and intelligence of Stalin, and did not feel oppressed in my scholarly work, let alone repressed. But don't forget that the effects of "Stalinism" were slighter in our Party than in the Soviet Union. Our conditions—think of the multi-party system—made the worst crimes impossible, as did the

---

[3] Cited in Martin McCauley, *Marxism-Leninism in the German Democratic Republic* (London: Macmillan, 1979), p. 96.

[4] During a 1966 interrogation, a Stasi officer challenged Robert Havemann: "But you must admit that Stalinism has never existed in the GDR!" Havemann replied that "a comrade from the Central Party Control Commission said the same when I was expelled from the Party." Robert Havemann, *An Alienated Man*, trans. Derek Masters, (London: Davis-Poynter, 1973), pp. 14–5.

influence of several comrades. I need only mention Erich Honecker, Hermann Matern, or Franz Dahlem.[5]

In fact, the SED did have incentives for restraint in its formative years. On the one hand, the Soviet Union was undecided about East Germany's fate, and did not want hasty socio-economic change to preclude a bargain with the West, and perhaps the neutralization of a united Germany.[6] On the other hand, alone among East European Communist Parties, the SED attempted to rule over a population that could vote against it. Until August 1961, East Germans who felt displeased by some measure of their regime could purchase a subway ticket to West Berlin and leave East Germany for good. This state of affairs should have caused the SED to temper its measures in order not to lose the support of its citizens. A loss of too many citizens would cause the First Worker and Peasant State on German Soil to hemorrhage to death.[7]

---

[5] *Dialog mit meinem Urenkel* (Berlin and Weimar, 1983), p. 83. The roles played by Honecker and Matern are not made explicit, and one imagines that their presence in Kuczynski's answer was dictated more by the logic of the 1970s than that of the 1950s.

[6] Georg Hermann Hodos, *Schauprozesse: Stalinistische Säuberungen in Osteuropa 1948–54* (Berlin: LinksDruck Verlag, 1990), p. 189; Dietrich Staritz, *Geschichte der DDR 1949–1985* (Frankfurt am Main: Suhrkamp, 1985), pp. 66–73. This logic of course played a role to some degree in all East European states; see Joseph Rothschild, *Return to Diversity: A Political History of East Central Europe Since World War II*, 2nd ed. (New York: Oxford University Press, 1993), p. 137. Scholars disagree on whether lack of sovereignty should have meant more or less harsh policies within the GDR. Janusz Bugajski and Maxine Pollack write that "The East Berlin regime remained one of the most rigid and illiberal in the bloc, even though the soviet occupation administration was formally dissolved in March 1954 and GDR sovereignty recognized." *East European Fault Lines: Dissent, Opposition, and Social Activism* (Boulder, CO: Westview Press, 1989) p. 23. Philip Longworth on the other hand writes "Even though East Germany was not yet a sovereign state, Ulbricht responded by raising the work norms of the labour force by 10 per cent and inveighing against 'saboteurs'." *The Making of Eastern Europe* (New York: St. Martin's Press, 1992), p. 15.

[7] Bennet Kovrig writes for example that "hemorrhaging through the open sore of Berlin, [the GDR] was at least in the short run a questionable economic asset." *Of Walls and Bridges: The United States and Eastern Europe* (New York: NYU Press, 1991), p. 55.

Scholars in the West have also viewed the East Germany of the Stalin years as a special case, because of its supposed "protracted course" toward socialism.[8] According to Zbigniew Brzeziński, at the time of the founding of the German Democratic Republic in 1949 "internal changes... were lagging behind those in other People's Democracies." Brzeziński quotes the metaphor used by Colonel Tiul'panov of the Soviet Military Administration in Germany (SMAD) to describe East Germany's progress in achieving "socialist transformation." At the Party School in East Berlin in April 1948 Tiul'panov had spoken of the countries of Eastern Europe as of swimmers crossing a river: "Yugoslavia has already reached the other bank [a socialist state]; Bulgaria is taking the last few strokes to reach it; Poland and Czechoslovakia are about in the middle of the river followed by Romania and Hungary, which have gone about a third of the way; while the Soviet Occupation Zone has just taken the first few strokes away from the bourgeois bank." Brzeziński's analysis shows particular sensitivity to East German deviations from official Soviet nomenclature. For example its 1949 constitution proclaimed the GDR a "Democratic Republic" rather than a "People's Democracy."[9] Peter Bender also judges that by 1949 "all the other countries in the Soviet sphere of influence were already 'people's democracies' striving toward Socialism. In East Germany, where the constitution was only 'democratic,' not that of a 'people's democracy,' the building of Socialism was not proclaimed until the summer of 1952."[10]

For varying reasons, scholars in East and West thus concurred in the judgment of the GDR's belated entrance onto the road to

---

[8] Joni Lovenduski and Jean Woodall eds., *Politics and Society in Eastern Europe* (London: Macmillan, 1987), p. 57.

[9] Zbigniew Brzeziński, *The Soviet Bloc: Unity and Conflict* (Cambridge, MA: Harvard University Press, 1967) p. 79. The GDR proved an exception in the wording of standard treaties signed throughout the Bloc in the early 1950s. Instead of treaties of "friendship, cooperation, and mutual assistance" it signed simply treaties of "friendship" with other Bloc countries. Robert L. Hutchings explains the exceptional position of the GDR "by the fact that the remaining treaties were directed against external aggression, particularly by a rearmed German state." "Soviet–East European Relations," in *Consolidation and Conflict 1968–1980* (Madison, 1983), p. 17.

[10] Peter Bender, *East Europe in Search of Security* (London: Chatto and Windus, 1972), p. 12.

socialism. The former emphasized the leadership's relative restraint, the latter official proclamations. A fact often neglected is that these proclamations were meant for external consumption and did not necessarily impinge upon the GDR's internal political logic. To call the GDR simply a "democratic republic" in 1949 was to underscore the Soviet Union's willingness to keep the German question "open." A most extreme example of the tendency to judge the GDR's internal developments by external criteria has been the work of Essen political scientist Wilfried Loth, who has claimed that Stalin actually intended an independent and "anti-fascist democratic" Germany, and, that had the Soviet dictator only lived longer, the GDR would not have become part of the "socialist community of states." By focusing attention on the supposed content of discussions between the SED leadership and Stalin, he pushed consideration of internal developments in the Zone deep into the background, where they assumed a somewhat schematic character.[11] Like most German analysts of East Germany, Loth failed to take East Germany seriously as a member of the Soviet Bloc until after official proclamations accorded the GDR sovereignty in the wake of Stalin's death.

Anglo-American scholarship on Eastern Europe has witnessed a complementary tendency. The GDR's admittedly a-typical development, coupled with the difficulty of describing a German state as East European, have caused some experts on Eastern Europe to disregard the GDR entirely in their considerations of post-war Eastern Europe. Joseph Rothschild writes in the preface to the second edition of his magisterial *Return to Diversity*: "I am also gratified to note that my much criticized decision to omit in-depth coverage of East Germany has been vindicated by history, as that *soi-disant* state has now vanished from the map of Europe."[12]

---

[11] Wilfried Loth, *Stalins ungeliebtes Kind: Warum Moskau die DDR nicht wollte* (Berlin: Rowohlt, 1994), pp. 144, 224–5.

[12] Joseph Rothschild, *Return to Diversity*, p. ix. Robin Okey's *Eastern Europe: 1740–1985* (Minneapolis: University of Minnesota Press, 1991) likewise disregards East Germany. The journalist John Dornberg provides the following explanation for his decision to omit East Germany from his *Eastern Europe: A Communist Kaleidoscope* (New York: Dial Press, 1980): "Until 1945 it was an integral part of the German Reich. It started on the path to separate statehood—a development only reluctantly recognized by West Germany,

What of the tremendous growth of GDR studies that took off after the opening of archives in 1990? What have the over 7,000 scholarly books and articles on the GDR—dozens times more than on any
other Soviet Bloc state—done to enhance our understanding of the
neo-Stalinist GDR? [13] The answer is very little: social historians of East
Germany have hesitated to investigate the repressive dynamic of the regime. They have felt called upon to validate their subjects through a focus on resistance: and arguing that one should not "focus on repression
alone" they have tended to take it for granted. [14] In refuting totalitarian
models, they absolutized them in ways that did little justice to the analyses undertaken by Hannah Arendt or Karl Friedrich and Zbigniew

---

the United States, and most of the world's other Western capitalist democracies as recently as the early 1970s—as the Soviet occupation zone [sic] of
Germany. The path was uncertain and rocky, even in the eyes of East Berlin's mentor, the Soviet Union, which until the mid-1950s could not make
up its mind as to whether that was the course it wanted history to take. East
Germany did not join the United Nations as a separate state, and was not
recognized as such, until 1972. And today its outlook is still so uncertain
that it looks more toward its West German neighbor than towards Poland or
Czechoslovakia, for example. A major share of its Western trade is with West
Germany and is not considered foreign trade at all, going by the name of
'intra-German.' West Germany does not recognize a separate East German
nationhood or citizenship and automatically regards all East German citizens
as its own. The question of reunification has been neither resolved nor laid
to rest on either side of the border. It is a separate state, but not a separate
nation, and as such its position in the context of this book would simply be
out of place." p. viii. Historian of Russia, Abbott Gleason implicitly excludes
East Germany from his discussion of Eastern Europe. See *Totalitarianism:
The Inner History of the Cold War* (New York: Oxford University Press, 1995),
p. 169. Brzeziński of course does include East Germany in his study, as do
Thomas W. Simons, Jr. (*Eastern Europe in the Postwar World* [New York: Palgrave Macmillan, 1991]), and George Schöpflin (*Politics in Eastern Europe*
[Oxford, Cambridge MA: Blackwell, 1993]).

[13] In 2003 Jürgen Kocka spoke of some 7,700 publications. Jürgen Kocka,
"Bilanz und Perspektiven der DDR-Forschung," *Deutschland Archiv*, Vol. 5,
(2003): 764–9.

[14] These are the words of Mary Fulbrook, who wrote that the "focus on repression is not very revealing. It does not tell us very much about degrees of
passive compliance, or acquiescence to their own domination, to be found
among the East German population... Nor does a focus on repression alone
tell us very much about modes of resistance." *Anatomy of a Dictatorship: Inside
the GDR 1949–1989* (Oxford: Oxford University Press, 1995), p. 11.

Brzeziński—which were much more sophisticated than later critics gave them credit for. Take for example the contributors to the influential volume *Die Grenzen der Diktatur*, edited by Ralph Jessen and Richard Bessel, who successively blow over the straw men of "boundless" dictatorial rule (p. 7), of the "unconditional" establishment of dictatorship (p. 130), of "social change [that] was only an effect of the policies of the SED regime" (p. 140) and of a state that could "dominate a society in every aspect at every time." (p. 224).[15] In her own influential study Mary Fulbrook felt it necessary to inform readers that: "there is more to the inner history of the GDR than the Cold War division of Europe and the presence of Soviet tanks."[16] These are the sorts of simplistic ideas about Communist dictatorship that were considered passé in the social history of the Soviet Union, but also of Nazi Germany.[17]

Here we enter the heart of the paradox of post-1989 GDR research in a field dominated by historians of Germany, usually from West Germany, with deep knowledge of the German but not the East European past. In 1990 many were eager to get their hands onto fresh documents for dissertations and *Habilitationen*, but failed to first consult basic literature on Soviet type societies, or even on the GDR.[18] They also failed to integrate into their research studies of society in Nazi Germany, which had likewise seriously compromised ideas of total rule. One reason for this failing was political: to compare the two German dictatorships seemed to imply that they were of a kind. To little avail one hears the endless reminders: "*vergleichen heisst nicht gleichsetzen.*"

In a controversial talk in 2003 one of the deans of German social history, Jürgen Kocka, confirmed the insularity that resulted: "As a

---

[15] Richard Bessel, *Die Grenzen der Diktatur: Staat und Gesellschaft in der DDR* (Göttingen: Vandenhoeck und Ruprecht, 1996).

[16] Fulbrook, *Anatomy of a Dictatorship*, p. 10.

[17] For a summary of this research on Soviet society, largely neglected by students of the German society refashioned on Soviet models, see Daniel Kaiser ed., *The Workers' Revolution in Russia, 1917: The View from Below* (Cambridge: Cambridge University Press, 1987); see also the pieces on Stalinism in *Russian Review*, Vol. 46, No. 3 (1987). For developments in totalitarian theory, see Abbott Gleason, *Totalitarianism: The Inner History of the Cold War* (New York: Oxford University Press, 1995).

[18] For example, the earlier work of Ernst Richert, Martin Jänicke, Kurt Sontheimer, Ekkehart Krippendorf, or Peter-Christian Ludz was largely neglected.

whole, GDR research here in Germany has been highly self-referential and self-contained."[19] This solipsism has also been methodological.[20] He summarized results: "knowledge about the GDR has grown enormously [...] many pictures have been revised." And one could add: concepts made more precise, definitions debated in extraordinary detail: was the GDR Stalinist, did the GDR possess "society," what was the precise neologism that might capture the experience of the population, or the nature of the regime? Was it a "welfare-dictatorship" or a "consensus-dictatorship"?[21]

If it seems strange to imagine a system that was introduced and maintained by force as based on "consensus" then one can perhaps understand why, as Kocka maintains, GDR history has failed to attract interest beyond the field of GDR studies. It has even failed to capture the imagination of the history-consuming public in Germany itself: in December 2007 it was revealed that a majority of schoolchildren in East Berlin and Brandenburg believed the GDR could not be described as a dictatorship.[22] They were ignorant of basic facts of its

---

[19] *Bilanz und Perspektiven.*

[20] See the inspiration drawn by Alf Lüdtke—probably the most influential GDR researcher—of Joan Scott's dictum that "there is no reality beyond language." The authors of this edited volume discuss the "independent dynamic" of language. Alf Lüdtke and Peter Becker eds., *Die DDR und ihre Texte: Erkundungen zu Herrschaft und Alltag* (Berlin: Akadamie Verlag, 1997), p. 11. No doubt this dynamic existed in the GDR as it exists in every place: but this is not what stands out about the GDR in international comparison. Remarkable was the success of the regime in imposing a new vocabulary upon the population in many noticed and unnoticed ways.

[21] The former is a creation of Konrad Jarausch, the latter of Martin Sabrow. See Martin Sabrow, "Der Konkurs der Konsensdiktatur: Überlegungen zum inneren Zerfall der DDR aus kulturgeschichtlicher Perspektive," in Konrad Jarausch and Martin Sabrow eds., *Weg in den Untergang: Der innere Zerfall der DDR* (Göttingen: Vandenhoeck & Ruprecht, 1999), pp. 83–116; Konrad H. Jarausch, "Care and Conformity: The GDR as Welfare Dictatorship," in *Dictatorship as Experience: Toward a Socio-Cultural History of the GDR* (New York: Berghahn, 1999) pp. 47–72.

[22] Only about every third student knew that the GDR had built the Berlin Wall, some 70 percent believed that the Federal Republic was not better than the GDR; more than half refused to deny the statement: "the GDR was not a dictatorship," 60 percent believed that the GDR environment was cleaner than that of the Federal Republic. The ignorance was particularly marked among students of Potsdam. *Berliner Morgenpost*, 28 December 2007.

history, and ignorance was particularly marked in Potsdam, the very city out of which the largest center studying GDR society operated.[23]

Yet perhaps this evaluation is ungenerous. The Potsdam Center was bound to develop deeply nuanced research on GDR society given the apparent calm that governed GDR society over many decades; from 1953 to 1989 the country was not shaken by the upheavals witnessed in neighboring states. It was a case of explaining stability, something historians of society resist with their hesitance to imposing "teleologies" upon "open" historical processes. One productive term for evaluating the apparent stasis was *"Eigen-Sinn"*—a neologism developed by anthropologist Alf Lüdtke to describe the behavior of workers in Imperial and Nazi Germany.[24] As explicated by Thomas Lindenberger, it directs attention to the ways in which meanings are produced by individuals and groups within networks of social relations: "it is supposed to embrace the potential multiplicity of meanings carried by attitudes and actions." Unlike the once popular concepts "resistance" and

---

[23] This is the Zentrum für Zeithistorische Forschung, which grouped former East German historians and social historians from West Germany. Part of the problem may be precisely the theoretical sophistication, taking historians far beyond the limits of standard German vocabulary. In a *public* lecture of 2005, for instance, Center director Martin Sabrow used the term "Dispositiv" to describe Stalinism. This is a word not carried in standard German dictionaries, and, little suspected by the German public, was coined by Michel Foucault to describe "a decidedly heterogeneous ensemble, which embraces discourses, institutions, architectural installations, regulating decisions, laws, administrative measures, scientific statements, philosophical, moral, or philanthropic teachings: in a word that which is spoken and unspoken [...] The dispositiv is the network that connects these elements." Michel Foucault, *Michel Foucault über Sexualität, Wissen und Wahrheit* (Berlin: Merve Verlag 1978), p. 119f. As such, Dispositiv is boundless, arguably of little use for social science analysis. For Sabrow's speech: "Gab es eine stalinistische DDR?" in Martin Sabrow ed., *Zeiträume: Potsdamer Almanach des Zentrums für Zeithistorische Forschung* (Berlin: Transitverlag, 2005), pp. 131–41.

[24] It is derived from the word "Eigensinn," which means stubbornness. Yet taken apart, the word's components mean "one's own sense." For his early usage see Alf Lüdtke, "Die große Masse ist teilnahmslos, nimmt alles hin..." "Herrschaftserfahrungen, Arbeiter-"Eigen-Sinn" und Individualität vor und nach 1933," in H.-J. Busch and A. Krovoza eds., *Psychoanalyse und Geschichte* (Frankfurt, 1989), pp. 105–28. It is ironic that historians would employ a term to describe workers under Nazi rule without wondering what might be learned by comparing the behavior of workers in Nazi Germany and the GDR.

"opposition," the "criterion for using the concept 'Eigen-Sinn' was not the explicitly negative relation to the respective relation to power."[25] It has the virtue of comprehending domination as going beyond the "logic of giving and obeying orders."[26] Yet it also may lead to a form-less history, with no "prejudice" in favor of one question or explanation over another. As described by Lindenberger, it tends to take the SED and its "totalitarian ambition" (*der totalitäre Geltungsanspruch der SED*) for granted, rather than thinking of this ambition as itself requiring ex-planation. Even more than in totalitarian theory, the party is taken for granted rather than considered a subject of historical development.[27]

The essay that follows uses a comparative perspective to explore factors specific to the GDR that permitted the SED to rule the East German population with relatively little challenge, and earn its reputa-tion of being "neo-Stalinist." It will argue that the GDR was well on the way to Soviet-style socialism from an early date, and that in a po-litical sense, it was thus eminently East European: the Soviet Bloc is the context to which it most immediately belonged.[28] The SED leader-ship may have spared itself the sanguinary self-purgation that the Hun-garian, Czech, or Bulgarian parties endured, but East German society was more thoroughly transformed than any other in East Europe in the early post-war years. Because of these transformations, the SED could enforce rule upon a relatively malleable society. Indeed, this so-ciety would provide it with the stuff with which to mold a sturdy Party

---

[25] Thomas Lindenberger, "Die Diktatur der Grenzen," in Thomas Linden-berger ed., *Herrschaft und Eigen-Sinn in der Diktatur* (Berlin: Böhlau, 1999), p. 23.

[26] Lindenberger, *Die Diktatur*, p. 22.

[27] Lindenberger, *Die Diktatur*, p. 25. It is interesting to note that the standard story of the "stalinization" of the SED that is cited in this rather insular litera-ture is really a story of the growth of formal institutions, rather than of Party legitimacy, that is, the projection of power into society. See Andreas Malycha, *Die SED: Geschichte ihrer Stalinisierung 1946–1953* (Paderborn: Ferdinand Schoning, 2000).

[28] Definitions of East Europe vary. In the post-war period, Bulgaria, Romania, Hungary, Poland, Czechoslovakia, and East Germany constituted a common *political* context. The attempt to institute the same Soviet model in these countries makes them a productive context for comparative research. Be-cause of the force used, variations in application of the common model tell us about the specificities of each society.

apparatus. Although the GDR may have lagged in nationalizing the economy, it was foremost in creating structures of centralized rule that in other contexts have been called "Stalinist." A comparative perspective thus reveals East Germany as having been foremost among Stalinist societies, despite the pressures of an open border and Soviet concerns to keep the German question "open." The question that remains to be answered is: with so much incentive to reform, why did the SED fail to do so?

Foundations for Stalinist Socialism

Careful study of the early years of combined Soviet/German Communist rule in East Germany reveals the need to go beneath the surface of official self-descriptions, and to look at the society beneath the upper crusts of SED leadership. Ostensibly restrained "anti-fascist democratic" transition reveals itself as a set of policies which formed a solid base for later construction of socialism. Excepting Yugoslavia, there was not another place in the Eastern Europe of 1945–46 which witnessed policies and events more suited to the creation of a Marxist-Leninist Party, or of a society more suited for socialist transformation.

In no other place could a more thorough exchange of elites take place, because in no other place had elites been more delegitimized than in Germany. It may be true that in Poland pre-war elites had been subjected to a physical destruction unknown to Germans; but many surviving elites (the medical profession, academics, engineers) emerged from the war morally invigorated, and could effectively contest state attempts to unseat or manipulate them. They had taken leading roles in anti-Nazi resistance.[29] East German elites, on the other hand, had

---

[29] The Polish intelligentsia had suffered grievous losses from systematic annihilation by both Soviet and Nazi occupiers. Over one quarter of Poland's professors were killed. Tomasz Szarota, "Upowszechnienie Kultury," in F. Ryszka *et al.* eds., *Polska Ludowa 1944–1950, przemiany społeczne* (Wrocław, 1974), p. 411. Those who remained defended academic autonomy. Poland's rectors for example formed a united front against attempted change in higher educational regulations, and in 1947 achieved the weakening of a proposed statute. A memorial of 1 March 1947 of the professors of Jagiellonian University, many of whom had been sent to concentration camps in 1939,

no choice but to submit to humiliating de-nazification measures. In the Soviet Zone one did not even have to have been an NSDAP member in order to feel these measures' effects. The Soviets defined the origins of "German fascism" economically, and thus the destruction of the old elites' economic power constituted the cornerstone of de-Nazification.[30] In the summer of 1945 a land reform was carried out which expropriated owners of estates exceeding 100 hectares. In many cases people with smaller estates were expropriated as well, especially if they had been denounced for political behavior. Unlike other expropriated groups in East Europe these "Junkers" were forced completely off their property, and were not even left the servants' quarters to live in.[31] To the extent that they were not interned, many then made their way to West Germany. In summer 1946 further extreme measures of expropriation followed a so-called "People's Referendum on Nazi and

spoke of their "honest services for the Fatherland." *Archiwum Uniwersytetu Jagiellońskiego* S III/18. The force of the united professoriate was so great that the one Communist rector—Kuczewski of Gliwice—joined the common protest. Bolesław Krasiewicz, *Odbudowa szkolnictwa wyzszego w Polsce Ludowej w latach 1944–1948* (Wroclaw, 1976), pp. 327–30.

[30] On the economic approach to de-nazification taken in the Soviet Zone, see Sigrid Meuschel, *Legitimation und Parteiherrschaft in der DDR: Zum Paradox von Stabilität und Revolution in der DDR (1945–1989)* (Frankfurt am Main: Suhrkamp, 1992), p. 76.

[31] The "Land Reform" in East Germany was essentially completed by January 1946. In its course 7,160 "Junkers," owning 2,517,358 hectares, and 4,537 "active Nazis or war criminals," owning 131,742 hectares of land, were expropriated. They had to leave their villages and give up all of their possessions, including livestock, machinery, homes, and furniture. Institut für Marxismus-Leninismus beim ZK der SED, *Geschichte der deutschen Arbeiterklasse*, Vol. 6 (Berlin, 1966), p. 89. In Saxony, properties under 100 hectares to be expropriated included those of: "Nazi leaders and all active advocates (*Verfechter*) of the Nazi Party and its formations, as well as all leading persons of the Hitler state, including anyone who during the Nazi period was member of the Reich government or the Reichstag." See "Das Gesetz zur Durchführung der Bodenreform in der Provinz Sachsen," in *Bodenreform: Junkerland in Bauernhand*, (Berlin, 1945), pp. 35–9. The standards for ascertaining who had been an active Nazi varied greatly from place to place; indeed the very make-up of the land reform commissions was quite variable. See reports in *Tagesspiegel* (Berlin), 24 May 1946. Much of the commissions' information stemmed from denunciations. Gregory W. Sandford, *From Hitler to Ulbricht: the Communist Reconstruction of East Germany 1945–46* (Princeton: Princeton University Press, 1983), p. 101.

War Criminals" in Saxony. The success of this referendum, which had garnered over 70 percent "yes" votes, was taken as a sign to proceed with large-scale expropriations of plant and equipment throughout the Zone. Often a compromised past was constructed for entrepreneurs who had become politically undesirable.[32]

---

[32] Owners of large enterprises were considered to have supported the Nazi regime implicitly. As Walter Ulbricht later candidly observed: "The peculiarity of Germany's development was precisely that the leaders of large industry, and the banks, as well the Junkers and the majority of the bureaucracy had become fascists... In Germany there were only a few larger enterprises whose owners were not war criminals." *Zur Geschichte der neuesten Zeit* (Berlin, 1955), p. 273. By March 1947 some 9,281 enterprises had been expropriated and transformed into "people's property." Of those, 3,834 were industrial, accounting for only 8 percent of the total number of enterprises but 40 percent of total production. Sylvia Pohl, "Enteignung der Betriebe in der SBZ," in Alexander von Plato ed., *Auferstanden aus Ruinen: von der SBZ zur DDR (1945–1949)* (Cologne: Rote Fahne, 1979), p. 149. The CDU and LDP objected continuously to the tendentious usage of the term "active Nazi" that had permitted the rising number of expropriations: "Reasons are being sought in order to expropriate enterprises at all costs. If the reasons don't fit, then they're bent until they do. Words like 'supporter and beneficiary,' 'war profiteer,' 'servant of capitalists' interests,' and others are flexible enough to be used according to need." *Tagesspiegel*, 30 March 1947. The SED for example demanded in 1947 the nationalization of movie theaters in Mecklenburg arguing that their owners had contributed to Nazi propaganda by showing films. The LDP protested such collective condemnation, stating that if one were to apply this principle consistently, one would have to accuse every letter carrier of spreading Nazi propaganda, since postage stamps bore Hitler's image. The SED "regretted" that anyone in this "high house" would defend the "bloodied hands of people, who for the sake of profit, had spread an ideology that brought millions of our brothers to their graves." Its resolution carried, despite the combined opposition of CDU and LDP, 42 to 34. Ekkehard Krippendorff, *Die LDPD in der SBZ 1945–48* (Düsseldorf: Droste 1961) p. 110; *Tagesspiegel*, 20 September 1947. In Saxony, factories which had manufactured uniforms were expropriated due to "active service for war criminals." Johann B. Gradl, *Anfang unter dem Sowjetstern: Die CDU 1945–48 in der Sowjetischen Besatzungszone* (Cologne: Verlag Wissenschaft und Politik, 1981), p. 72. During the winter of 1946–47, 45 percent of the craftsmen and small tradesmen in Brandenburg lost their businesses after the "discovery" that they had not been nominal Nazis after all. See report of the CDU at the 17 February 1947 meeting of Central Unity Front Committe, in Siegfried Suckut ed., *Blockpolitik in der SBZ/DDR 1945–1949: Die Sitzungsprotokolle des Zentralen Einheitsfront-Ausschusses* (Cologne, 1986), p. 196.

Equally shattering of old elites were the de-nazifying purges of the public administration. In the course of the first post-war years, up to 80 percent of the judges, lawyers, and school-teachers were removed from practice.[33] Refused reentry into their professions, many of these people made their way westward.[34] The SMAD and SED quickly took over the offices that controlled admission to the professions and to state administration; together they had unmatched competence to mold a new elite. From the very beginning, it was shaped in such a way as to meet the needs of a "workers' and peasants' state." A student of denazification in Mecklenburg-Vorpommern has spoken of "a far-reaching break with political, personal, and socio-economic traditions in the Soviet Zone... Even before the end of 1945."[35]

Kuczynski and others partially base their opinion of East Germany's "lagging behind" in Stalinism on the persistence of a multi-party system. This claim neglects the persistence of multi-party systems in other People's Democracies, well beyond the Stalinist years, as well as the early disappearance of an independent Social Democratic Party in East Germany. Excepting Slovakia, where social democrats had merged with other anti-Tiso forces during wartime resistance, the joining of the SPD and KPD in April 1946 was the earliest such merger in Eastern Europe. In other states social democrats and communists would not be joined for at least two more years. There is no doubt that the merger in the Eastern Zone and East Berlin was achieved with use of force. German social democrats may have mostly favored such unity in 1945, but the initial refusal of the KPD to consider a merger, coupled with German communists' close connections to a widely resented occupying power, tended to alienate Social Democratic Party members. By early 1946, their majority, as demonstrated by an open vote of their West Berlin members, overwhelmingly favored cooperation with the communists, but not amalgamation. In the East, however, the social

---

[33] Staritz, *Geschichte der DDR*, p. 55. The severity of purging varied according to Land, type of administration, and level of administration. Clemens Vollnhals, *Entnazifizierung: Politische Säuberung und Rehabilitierung in den vier Besatzungszonen 1945–1949* (Munich, 1991), pp. 43–55.

[34] On the flight for example of former teachers from the Soviet Zone to the West, see Damian van Melis, "Denazification in Mecklenburg-Vorpommern," *Germany History*, Vol. 13, No. 3 (1995): 357.

[35] *Ibid.*, p. 369.

democrats were left with no choice. After late April, they could either enter the Socialist Unity Party, or reject membership in a political organization altogether. Left with this alternative, the overwhelming majority entered union with the communists, often with the hope that equal representation (*Paritätsprinzip*) in all Party organizations would guarantee the stronger Social Democratic organization greater influence. While it is true that *after* 1948 former social democrats would increasingly be purged from the SED, in the early years it was former social democrats that permitted rapid construction of foundations for socialism in East Germany. They gave the KPD personnel with which to carry out its policies.[36]

SED policies for the most part enjoyed wide support among former social democrats. Decades-old demands of the workers' movement became high Party priorities. One of the most pressing needs in East Germany was to find replacements for the thousands of teachers and jurists who had been dismissed. Crash courses of all sorts were set up to train new officials. In order to insure that they would faithfully serve the new "democratic" Germany, these officials were drawn from strata of society which traditionally had suffered discrimination in Germany: namely "workers and peasants." What former social democrat could oppose a policy that would finally break the "bourgeois education privilege"? In fact, social democrats contributed avidly to the construction of new university faculties that trained the new generation of teachers.

---

[36] The standard explanation for the Soviet rush to merge KPD and SPD was prevention of further growth of the relatively strong Social Democratic Party. In particular, the communist election failure in Austria in the fall of 1945 was taken as a warning sign of what might happen to the KPD should it face elections in Germany. In neighboring Poland and Czechoslovakia, social democratic Parties were more supportive of communists than in East Germany, and advantages could be gained by permitting them independent existence, for example in the apportionment of ministries among the several parties. Wolfgang Diepenthal, *Drei Volksdemokratien: Ein Konzept kommunistischer Machtstabilisierung und seine Verwirklichung in Polen, der Tschechoslowakei und der Sowjetischen Besatzungszone Deutschlands* (Cologne, 1974), pp. 116–21, 168–9. In addition, in the view of Thomas W. Simons, Jr. the absence of a major peasant party—against which Communists in other countries could unite with Social Democrats—contributed to the early merger in East Germany. *Eastern Europe in the Postwar World* (New York: Palgrave Macmillan, 1991), p. 69. He neglects to explain why an independent Social Democratic Party would not have opposed East German Christian Democrats and Liberal Democrats.

In important ways the SED had a head-start. In Poland, Hungary, and Czechoslovakia, social democrats would not be made part of the communist apparatus until 1948/49. This ability to make full use of the labor of a large social democratic organization gave the increasingly Stalinist SED a privileged position in Eastern Europe. The Polish Workers Party (PPR) had decisive influence in all central ministries by early 1947 at the latest, but it still needed to create institutions and a party organization, mostly from the top down. Organizations that helped funnel the energies of social democrats to support "democratic" policies were only just coming into existence in Poland in late 1947. East German counterparts could rely upon loosely directed, mostly spontaneous energies of grass roots organizations. The Party leadership could afford to wait until 1948 to discipline its hierarchy; for the time being the task was simply to create structures that would activate and educate young, socio-culturally uncommitted workers. *They* would not fall victims to the purges that often swept away their teachers. Having created basic organizational forms at an early point (like *Neulehrer* courses, worker-peasant faculties, the Administrative Academy "Walter Ulbricht," a United Trade Union), it could then proceed to perfect them, and make use of them for even more precise forms of social engineering.

Perhaps more important than the early creation of a large Socialist Unity Party was the presence of an institution which supervised and enforced that creation: namely the Soviet Military Administration. It is true that the SMAD did not intend to transfer the Soviet system to East Germany in the early years, but its understanding of the Potsdam accord's "four d's" (democratization, de-nazification, de-militarization, de-cartelization) tended to foreclose alternatives to Soviet-style socialism, even if the word "socialism" was carefully avoided. "Democratization" of the justice system, the police forces, public administration, or education meant the introduction of members of the Party which by definition represented the interests of the majority of the population: the SED. Success in democratization could be measured by the degree of SED domination in any given area; democratization *never* meant anything which opposed SED policy. Direct interference of the SMAD assured that the standards for "democratization" in the SBZ would be the harshest in Eastern Europe.[37] De-Nazification, and the melange of

---

[37] Thus in measuring the democratization of civil administration, the SMAD took into account the party membership of the entire staff, including typists

propagandistic measures known as "anti-fascism," likewise assumed instrumental character. Only the SED could guarantee the extirpation of
fascism, and thus any policy which opposed SED rule was by definition fascist.[38]

De-Nazification proved well-suited to repressing political opposition. Here, too, the SMAD guaranteed the SED pride of place among
the communist parties constructing socialism in Europe. In no other
country outside the motherland of socialism itself did Soviet security
forces become so pervasively involved in terrorizing and silencing political opposition. German communists could wash their hands of com-
plicity in this method of securing power: they could avow ignorance
of arrests, or inability to have prisoners of the Soviets released.[39] The
terror quickly spread beyond former NSDAP members, to engulf opponents from other parties, including former social democrats.[40]

---

and janitors! See the example from 1948 of the Deutsche Verwaltung für
Volksbildung in Norman Naimark, *The Russians in Germany: A History of the
Soviet Zone of Occupation* (Cambridge, MA: Harvard University Press, 1995),
p. 290. Such rigor would not apply in other "people's democracies" until the
early 1950s, if ever.

[38] Meuschel, *Legitimation*, pp. 109–16.

[39] Karl Wilhelm Fricke, "Politische Verfolgung in der SBZ," in Alexander Fischer ed., *Studien zur Geschichte der SBZ/DDR* (Berlin: Duncker und Hum-
blot, 1993), p. 187.

[40] In mid-1947 Erich W. Gniffke, a former social democrat in the SED leadership until his flight in 1948, investigated the arrests of former social democrats
by the NKVD. He discovered that hundreds had been arrested; many were
interned at Buchenwald. Other pressing tasks caused him to discontinue this
project, to the great relief of his long-time friend, Otto Grotewohl. Grotewohl
evidently feared antagonizing the Soviet secret police. Erich W. Gniffke, *Jahre
mit Ulbricht* (Cologne: Verlag Wissenschaft und Politik, 1966), pp. 260–2. In
July 1947 Grotewohl denied knowledge of arrests of former social democrats
at a meeting of the SED Party leadership. Emma Sachse, herself a former
social democrat, reported to the assembly of a trip she had made to West
Germany: "We know what kinds of lies are told in West Germany. No matter how ridiculous, these lies find an audience [...] For example, it is claimed
that 800 Social Democrats and 200 Communists are interned in Buchenwald
(Grotewohl: the reports speak of many concentration camps). The newspaper explicitly mentioned Buchenwald. Last Sunday, when I was speaking in
Nuremberg, a comrade passed a Social Democratic newspaper to me with a
headline announcing: East German Soviet Republic. It claimed that a conference of SED functionaries had taken place in Dresden on June 12, and decided to ask the Party leadership to make a formal request of the Soviet Military
Administration for the Eastern Zone to be admitted to the Soviet Union as a

Soviet understandings of what constituted fascist or anti-Soviet remarks and behavior therefore promoted the reemergence of a sterile
political landscape in East Germany very soon after the War. Despite
purported desire to refrain from alienating Western allies, the SMAD
heavily intervened in the elections which took place in 1946. At this
early date the SED was not lagging behind counterparts in Romania or
Poland in disenfranchisement of the electorate, and was well ahead of
Hungarian and Czechoslovak communists, who were participating in
relatively open elections even in 1947.

Kuczynski and other SED scholars are correct in recalling that
their Party did not suffer the same "monster show trials" that visited
other East European communist parties. Despite the removal or isolation of a few top functionaries, the SED leadership did not consume
itself in terror.[41] Yet East German society did witness bloody mass terror no less costly than in Poland or Czechoslovakia. In all three states,
about two percent of the population became victims of terror, and
about one-tenth of that number died as a result.[42]

Upon closer examination, one finds that purges of the late 1940s
and early 1950s in East Germany did not differ greatly from those in
surrounding countries. Like its sister parties, the SED also expelled
hundreds of thousands of members, many of them former social democrats. If the SED distinguished itself, it was in the induction of new
members to replace the old. While the Polish and Czech parties were
diminishing in size during the Stalinist period, by 11.7 percent and 16.2
percent respectively, numbers of SED members remained constant, at
about 1.2 million members.[43] The SED remained a mass party, while
becoming a cadre party: it was hence a unique *mass cadre Party*. One
would therefore expect it to be the most pervasive and disciplined force
for political and social transformation in Eastern Europe.

---

seventeenth republic. (Amusement. Exclamation: the flags have already been
sewn!)" "Stenographische Niederschrift über die 12. Tagung des Parteivor-
standes der Sozialistischen Einheitspartei Deutschlands vom 1. bis 3. Juli 1947
im 'Zentrales Haus der Einheit' zu Berlin," Stiftung Archiv der Parteien und
Massenorganisationen im Bundesarchiv (SAPMO-BA) ZPA IV 2/1/11/1ff.

[41] Hodos, *Schauprozesse*, pp. 176–98.

[42] Jan Foitzik, "Die stalinistischen 'Säuberungen' in den ostmitteleuropäischen
kommunistischen Parteien. Ein vergleichender Überblick," *Zeitschrift für Geschichtswissenschaft*, Vol. 8 (1992): 739.

[43] *Ibid.*, pp. 741, 744–5.

East Germany's relatively slow economic transformation does not figure prominently in scholarly analysis of that society's slow progress toward socialism, but was probably foremost in the mind of Colonel Tiul'panov in 1948. East Germany entered and departed the Stalinist period with the relatively smallest nationalized economy:

Share of Collectivized Arable Land[44]

	1950	1953
Bulgaria	44%	62%
Hungary	19%	37%
Romania	12%	21%
East Germany	1%	8%
Czechoslovakia	25%	48%
Poland	12%	17%
Yugoslavia	18%	24%

Share of State, Municipal, and Cooperative Enterprises[45]

Bulgaria (number of enterprises)	1948 ...	95%
Czechoslovakia (employment)	1948 ...	96%
Hungary (gross output)	1949 ...	81%
Poland (gross output)	1950 ...	92%
Romania (gross output)	1948 ...	95%
Yugoslavia (gross output)	1948 ...	100%
East Germany (gross output)	1950 ...	76%
East Germany (employment)	1951 ...	72%

---

[44] Ivan Volgyes, *Politics in Eastern Europe* (Chicago: Dorsey Press, 1986), p. 76. Only after the building of the Berlin Wall would East German agriculture become fully collectivized. In Poland, the limited collectivization achieved would be undone after 1956.

[45] Wlodzimierz Brus, "Postwar Reconstruction and Socio-Economic Transformation," in M.C. Kaser and E.A. Radice, eds., *The Economic History of Eastern Europe 1919–1975* (Oxford: Clarendon 1986), p. 600. The figures for East Germany are taken from Staritz, *Geschichte der DDR*, p. 40 and J.P. Nettl, *Die deutsche Sowjetzone bis heute* (Frankfurt am Main: Verlag der Frankfurter Hefte, 1953), p. 268. The East German figures combine totals for nationalized (VEB) and Soviet-run (SAG) enterprises.

One should not overstate the importance of the economic lag, however. Agriculture played a smaller role in the East German economy than in any other East European state. Therefore, the impact of the failure to collectivize on the economy as a whole was relatively slight. More to the point, German and Soviet communists' early control of all political decision making meant that the SED could effect rapid changes in the economy when it desired. In 1960 the SED would collectivize agriculture when the Polish and Hungarian parties felt a need to be more circumspect; and in the early 1970s East German communists closed down remaining private business (mostly in services) just as the Hungarians and others were seeking ways to increase the private sector. Perhaps it was precisely the gradual pace in nationalization that permitted the state in the GDR to control the economy so completely by the 1970s.

The Paradoxical Fifties:
New Course vs. *Parteidisziplin*

The apparent paradox of East German development intensifies in the 1950s. Viewed upon an East European background, one would assume that the East German leadership had the greatest incentive to reform. The East German population was the only population in Eastern Europe which could vote against its regime. It did so with its feet. Either the SED reformed, or it lost population. Moreover, it faced pressure to reform from Moscow. In 1953, Stalin's successors demanded of East Germany, as of other East Europeans states, a New Course. Yet the East German leadership was perhaps the most resistant to reform, and moved to consolidate its control of East German society. It continued to repel population, and was finally driven to the most humiliating measure imaginable in order to survive: to build a wall through Berlin.

What caused the failure of the New Course, and this obvious admission of political bankruptcy? Scholars' attention has focused on Walter Ulbricht, and his relations with the Soviet government. Ulbricht's continued hold on power tended to make significant policy change less likely. The first great challenge of his time in office, namely 17 June 1953, actually bolstered Ulbricht's position, because it made East German stability a Soviet priority. Ulbricht skillfully used supposed connections of would-be SED reformers (Herrnstadt, Zaisser) to Soviet security boss Beria in order to crush them. The ascendance of Khrushchev over Malenkov in 1955 permitted Ulbricht a temporary retrenchment, because it signaled a return to more conservative policies within the Soviet Union. This conjuncture also allowed Mátyás Rákosi to oust Imre Nagy from the Hungarian leadership and return to more conservative policies in Hungary.

But Khrushchev did not intend restalinization either in the Soviet Union or in Eastern Europe, and soon the SED leadership would again come under pressure to reform. Once again, however, the need to repress a popular uprising would save it. The "counterrevolutionary putsch"—as the Hungarian uprising was described by East German historians up until 1989—permitted Walter Ulbricht to secure his position against challenges from security chief Ernst Wollweber, and Party personnel director Karl Schirdewan.

These explanations are only partially satisfactory, however. They concentrate almost entirely upon international relations, ignoring the instrument Ulbricht used to ground his power: the SED apparatus. Why was this apparatus itself not a more effective lever in pressing for reform in the 1950s, when its members had more incentive for supporting reform than any other communists in the East Bloc? They after all needed only to look across the street to West Berlin to see that the tales of destitution under capitalism had little factual basis. Many had relatives in West Germany who kept them well informed of the rising living standards there.[46] The riddle becomes greater when one recalls that would-be reformer Schirdewan, with his responsibilities for cadre matters, could for years staff this apparatus with people themselves presumably open to reform.[47] The story of "dissenters" within the SED—like Harich, Janka, Just, Loest, Zwerenz, Behrens, Kuczynski—are well

---

[46] Of course the SED leadership had early on recognized the dangers of West–East contacts, and instituted ever more severe measures to curb them, in the end creating a category of citizens that could have no contacts with persons from the western countries, the "*Geheimnisträger.*"

[47] Karl Wilhelm Fricke for example opines that Schirdewan and Wollweber supported reform precisely because their Party positions permitted them precise knowledge of the mood of the East German population. *Opposition und Widerstand in der DDR: Ein politischer Report* (Cologne: Verlag Wissenschaft und Politik, 1984), p. 114.

known; these men claim to have represented broadly shared desires for reform within the Party.

Within the leadership itself, such desires never cohered into a political challenge to Walter Ulbricht, however. His opponents never put forth alternative visions of rule, and they never overcame their divisions. Many of these men were mortal enemies. The hope of the late 1950s, Karl Schirdewan, for instance had supposedly demanded the physical destruction of the hope of the early 1950s, Rudolf Herrnstadt. Ostensible reformer Fred Oelssner had held the speech in the SED Central Committee that demanded the purge of Herrnstadt and Zaisser.[48]

The powerful were divided in all but one regard: support for Walter Ulbricht. He punished the few that went furthest in their criticism, and the rest fell in line, no matter what their "internal doubts." Throughout the 1950s one supposed "liberal" after another, whether Oelssner, Paul Wandel, Otto Grotewohl, Bruno Leuschner, Hermann Rau consistently found themselves supporting Ulbricht, *apparently against their will*. Schirdewan recalled that "Otto Grotewohl did not find the strength to speak out against the majority position of the Politburo: 'anything but a discussion of our mistakes' (*nur keine Fehlerdiskussion*)." Or Herbert Warnke:

> Herbert Warnke was not among the people who opposed me during disputes with the Ulbricht group in the Politburo. Rather he approved of my activities—though in a very careful manner. Warnke was outraged when Ulbricht, with the help of Honecker, began to eliminate me politically. He told me himself: "Karl, I am not going along with this any more. They are getting ready to attack you. This time Ulbricht wants to finish you off." But when I could have used his help in the Politburo, Warnke hesitated.[49]

Rudolf Herrnstadt was surprised to learn that Max Reimann had moved to exclude him from the Party. After all, the two had "worked together well and often." He therefore approached Reimann in the

---

[48] Rudolf Herrnstadt, *Das Herrnstadt-Dokument* (Berlin, 1990), pp. 167–8, 218.
[49] Karl Schirdewan, *Aufstand gegen Ulbricht: Im Kampf um politische Kurskorrektur, gegen stalinistische, dogmatische Politik* (Berlin, 1994), pp. 100, 114.

corridor and confessed, "I never would have thought possible that you would make a motion for my exclusion from the Party." To which Reimann explained "helplessly: 'I—must—believe—Walter.'" Herrnstadt's commentary on this betrayal is perhaps even more revealing of the discipline which pervaded the apparatus: "He was right"; Herrnstadt even "sympathized" with the motion, for, as he admitted to Reimann, it "was completely logical."[50] What strikes the reader in all these accounts is the loneliness of ostensible dissenters. With few exceptions (for example Jürgen Kuczynski) former "comrades" dutifully broke off all contacts with the ostracized, preferring to cross the street rather than be confronted with the dilemma of greeting them.

Perhaps more important than the atomization of Ulbricht's rivals was their authoritarian political culture and the shallowness of their reform agendas. Schirdewan's and Herrnstadt's ideas fell far short of the revisionism of Imre Nagy or the leaders of the Prague Spring. Even today, Schirdewan describes a man like Kurt Hager (later famous as "Tapeten-Kurt") as a would-be reformer. Wolfgang Leonhard remembered Herrnstadt, for whom he had worked in Moscow, as "autocratic."[51] Even the most radical reform proposals from within the SED—Uwe-Jens Heuer, Michael Brie, Rudolf Bahro—were remarkable for their failure to question SED hegemony.[52] Walter Ulbricht—and Erich Honecker—seemed the logical expression of these men's political imagination. Given their internal divisions and lack of coherent visions for reform, they fell back upon internalized Party discipline. Every one of the major purge victims remained inwardly true to the Party, and if permitted, continued to work for it. Franz Dahlem for example returned to work in a subordinate role in the higher education apparatus. In his memoirs Rudolf Herrnstadt still expressed loyalty to Ulbricht as Party leader.[53]

Unreflective discipline was remarkable among intellectuals as well. Elsewhere in Eastern Europe writers and intellectuals produced destabilizing dissent. Their counterparts in the GDR, like the SED

---

[50] *Das Herrnstadt-Dokument*, p. 168.
[51] *Die Revolution entlässt ihre Kinder*, Vol. 2 (Leipzig, 1990), p. 346.
[52] See for example Michael Brie/Rainer Land "Aspekte der Krise–Wege der Lösung," *Einheit*, Vol. 12, (1989): 1084–9; Rudolf Bahro, *Die Alternative: Zur Kritik des real existierenden Sozialismus* (Cologne, 1977), esp. pp. 415–6.
[53] Herrnstadt, *Das Herrnstadt-Dokument*, esp. pp. 81, 106.

leadership, failed to cohere either politically or intellectually. Here too, there was no honor among the comrades. Though they had enlisted his help in rescuing Georg Lukács from Budapest, Johannes R. Becher and Anna Seghers refused to come to the aid of arrested editor, Walter Janka. Janka later described their lack of courage in prose that became a sensation during the peaceful East German revolution of 1989:

> The writers in attendance, from Anna Seghers and Willi Bredel to Bodo Uhse did not take part in the screaming. They remained silent. Their faces were pale [...] The face of Heli Weigel, the widow of Brecht, who had shown Janka her sympathy by winking at him, had become ashen. She stared into space, full of consternation. The failure of even one of the friends of Lukacs who had come to the trial to protest the untrue allegations was for Janka the worst disappointment during the trial.

Alleged co-conspirator Wolfgang Harich enthusiastically denounced Janka.[54] Writer Erich Loest also reports that his supposed friend and collaborator "Lehmann" denounced him with gusto in their 1957 trial.[55] It was Ulbricht who gave Herrnstadt/Zaisser or Janka/Just a cohesive form: by persecuting them jointly.

Lacking cohesive visions of reform, intellectuals too fell back upon Party discipline. People like Harich, Janka, Loest, and later Havemann preferred to risk Stasi imprisonment than abandon the GDR.[56] "Independent" intellectuals like Walter Janka and Christa Wolf may have

---

[54] Walter Janka, *Schwierigkeiten mit der Wahrheit* (Hamburg: Rowohlt, 1989), pp. 90–4. For a denial, see Wolfgang Harich, *Keine Schwierigkeiten mit der Wahrheit* (Berlin: Dietz, 1993). To Janka's lament one might reply: if no one remained to defend him, that was because he and others like him had not spoken out sooner against injustice. True opposition left East Germany, one way or another. First it was the Christian democrats and liberals, and then the social democrats. In the 1950s came the turn of "revisionist" communists. Ironically, several of the victims of attacks on revisionism (F. Behrens, R. Havemann, Gerhard Harig, Willi Lehmann, Franz Wohlgemuth) had themselves been leading "Scharfmacher" in the late 1940s and early 1950s.

[55] Erich Loest, *Durch die Erde ein Riss: Ein Lebenslauf* (Leipzig: Linden-Verlag, 1990), pp. 320–1.

[56] Many East German oppositionist intellectuals hesitated going to the West because in their view a neo-fascist regime was emerging there. Furthermore, as communists they feared discrimination. See for example hesitations expressed by Alfred Kantorowicz in his memoir *Deutsches Tagebuch*, Vol. 2 (Munich, 1961); or Loest, *Durch die Erde*, p. 307.

written critical manuscripts, but they carefully withheld them from publication until 1989.[57]

If anything, the Party rank and file felt more disaffected than the intellectual and political aristocracy; yet it too failed to produce cohesive demands for reform. Walter Ulbricht's disingenuous destalinization in 1956 had given rise to murmurs of discontent. Aside from failing to review his own adulation of Stalin, Ulbricht even dared ridicule Communists who had accepted Stalinist dogma in good faith. The requirements made of SED members for prevarication became painful. To avoid confrontation with new realities of abundance in the West was one thing. One might limit travel there, or conscientiously switch off western news broadcasts. But confrontation with the dead Soviet leader was unavoidable. He had been close to many communists' hearts. The SED faithful in Thuringian Sondershausen wondered: "what are we supposed to do with the portraits of Stalin that we had to buy and hang up in our living rooms (*daheim in der guten Stube hängen haben*)?"[58]

When one examines the behavior of the SED base, one finds little activity to complement desires for a changed political style. Instead, one encounters the phenomenon of *vorauseilender Gehorsam*. Particularly in times when the Party line became difficult to anticipate, well-disciplined rank and file maintained "vigilance." Nowhere is this fact more apparent than in the problem of the open border. After 1953 the SED leadership commissioned reports from various tentacles of its bureaucracy on the reasons direly needed specialists were leaving East Germany. They issued directives to lower level functionaries to refrain from utterances and measures which might alienate the "bourgeois intelligentsia." Nevertheless, the lower tiers of the SED apparatus continued to intimidate, enrage, and repulse highly skilled experts. In May

---

[57] In Poland, Czechoslovakia, and Hungary, the events of 1968 pushed the leading dissidents out of and away from the ruling communist parties. These were recognized as unreformable. Leading GDR "dissidents" like Christa Wolf, Jürgen Kuczynski, Stefan Hermlin, and Robert Havemann remained communists, however. This East German peculiarity is recognized (but not explained) in Tony Judt, "The Dilemmas of Dissidence. The Politics of Opposition in East-Central Europe," in Ferenc Feher and Andrew Arato eds., *Crisis and Reform in Eastern Europe* (New Brunswick: Transaction, 1991), p. 255.

[58] Cited in Stefan Wolle and Armin Mitter, *Untergang auf Raten: Unbekannte Kapitel der DDR-Geschichte* (Munich: Bertelsmann, 1993), p. 196.

1958 an assistant professor at Leipzig's agricultural faculty received a letter from the assistant dean for graduate studies, informing him that he was being released from his duties because of ideological shortcomings. Supposedly, the assistant professor had expressed his political "attitude" by "referring to the policies of our government as 'dialectical acrobatics.'" Beyond this, he "ignored the advice of his colleagues and thus demonstrated his unwillingness to go the right way." Upon receiving this letter, he immediately "committed *Republikflucht*" and "within a few hours was recognized as a 'so-called' political refugee." The report concludes that "one would have to assume that the comrades in Leipzig have learned from this, but this year there are further such cases of *Republikflucht*."[59] But officials did not learn. Two years later a chief physician (*Oberarzt*) from Schwerin who applied to visit his sick father in West Germany was told by the People's Police: "You had better wait until he dies. You won't get permission twice."[60] He too left East Germany for good.

Even when people who had "betrayed" the GDR returned, grass roots party organizations insisted that they be punished. Party organizations at universities refused to allow students who returned from West Germany to continue their studies because these students had supposedly revealed themselves as unworthy.[61] In late 1959 a Prof. Hanke of the Technical College in Ilmenau failed to return from a trip to West Germany. Many of his colleagues were outraged at this behavior. Though his faculty's dean "made efforts to point out Hanke's good sides," a Prof. Döpel could not control his anger, and declared that he was:

---

[59] "Analyse der Republikflucht," August 8, 1959. SAPMO-BA, ZPA IV 2/9.04/669 (unnumbered). Reproduced in J. Connelly, "Zur 'Republikflucht' von DDR-Wissenschaftlern in den Fünfziger Jahren," *Zeitschrift für Geschichtswissenschaft*, Vol. 4, (1994): 341.

[60] "Ideologische Probleme und Argumente unter den Angehörigen der Intelligenz," October 29, 1960. SAPMO-BA, ZPA IV 2/9.04/669 (unnumbered).

[61] See the "Bericht an das Sekretariat des Zentralkomitees über die Republikflucht von Wissenschaftlern und Studenten an unseren Universitäten und der Deutschen Akademie der Wissenschaften im 1. Halbjahr 1955," March 19, 1955. SAPMO-BA, ZPA IV 2/9.04/669 (unnumbered). Reproduced in Connelly, "Zur 'Republikflucht'," p. 336.

Ashamed to belong to the faculty to which until recently Hanke also belonged. If the Academic Senate waits four weeks before making a statement about the *Republikflucht* of Megla and Hanke, then the population draws the conclusion that the College is an Institute for *Republikflucht*. I have not worn my academic robes, and will not wear them, until the Academic Senate realizes how it has been sullied (*beschmutzt*) by Hanke, and how Hanke has harmed us both materially and ideally. Unless we, the Academic Senate, investigate these cases in the most rigorous manner possible, and draw conclusions [...] then we cannot speak of a socialistic education at our College.[62]

In August 1961 the SED leadership finally ordered construction of a wall around West Berlin in order to stop the exodus of specialists. Several months later it ceased receiving detailed reports on the grievances of the "technical intelligentsia." Thus would end "pressure from above" for liberalization; "pressure from below" would not commence until shortly before the border's reopening in 1989. And then it came from outside the Party.

How does one explain the unique discipline of the SED, and the apparently schizophrenic behavior of its members?[63] The East European context suggests several answers. Specialists on the GDR uniformly emphasize the importance of "anti-fascism" in the SED's attempts at self-legitimation. Given the peculiarly drastic forms taken by German fascism, anti-fascism was bound to possess unusual force in unifying the Party cadre. It may also have inspired communists in Romania or Hungary, but anti-fascism was bound to attract the greatest commitment in the land from which fascism had wrought the greatest devastation.[64]

Fascism had pervasively affected German society; as Walter Ulbricht recognized, even the German working class had supported

---

[62] Last quarterly report for 1959, by Pergamenter, in SAPMO-BA ZPA IV 2/904/669 (unnumbered).

[63] GDR reality was certainly the most likely in East Europe to produce schizophrenic behavior. GDR citizens knew the most about the West, yet they were most loyal to the system of the East—more loyal than even the population of the Soviet Union. For reflections on schizophrenia in communist Eastern Europe, see Eva Hoffman, *Exit into History: A Journey Through the New Eastern Europe* (New York: Penguin, 1993), pp. 204–5.

[64] On this logic, see Meuschel, *Legitmation*, p. 154.

Hitler. Therefore German anti-fascism could not be diluted by nationalism, as could for example Hungarian anti-fascism. Many Hungarian intellectuals had a common cause with demonstrating Hungarian workers in the fall of 1956. GDR counterparts, on the other hand, saw the masses of 17 June 1953 as the resurgent, uncontrolled fascist enemy, rather than as a potential ally in a struggle for national liberation.[65] GDR anti-fascism worked to reinforce loyalty and make SED rank and file deaf to questions about GDR reality. If there was one thing they felt sure of, it was that the GDR was not fascist. With the gradual replacement of older cadres, "anti-fascist" became a word increasingly devoid of meaning. By 1989 it had become virtually synonymous with Party loyalty. Many in the SED continued believing, yet their belief had become eroded of substance. They hardly resisted the revolutionaries of 1989.

The East European background makes apparent that Party discipline possessed a power within East Germany independent of conscious ideological commitment. In the GDR discipline was a value in itself.[66] Nowhere else in Eastern Europe could a communist party make disciplined loyalty to the state organization so central a component of official identity; in fact the SED used "discipline" and other traditional "German" values to contrast East Germans from their Slavic neighbors.[67] These values were not historically new. When the SED

---

[65] Hans Mayer wrote the essay "Der 17. Juni—und die Rosenbergs" directly after the events. The demonstrators were "wirkliche Arbeiter, darüber soll man sich nicht täuschen—mit sog. 'sozialdemokratischen' Losungen gegen unsere Staatsmacht aufmarschiert. Aber ihre 'sozialdemokratischen' Losungen hatten sie aus faschistischen Händen empfangen und in einer faschistisch gelenkten Bewegung vorangtragen. Und damit waren es eben faschistische Losungen... Wir in Deutschland kennen doch die Weise, den Text, und die Herren Verfasser. Damals, 1933 oder 1938, präsentierte sich der Mord im Braunhemd. Heute im Wildwestkostüm." SAPMO-BA ZPA ZK d. SED IV 2/9.04/426/97-99.

[66] On the role of "Disziplin und Autoritätshörigkeit" in reproducing a "herkömmliche unpolitische Haltung," see Meuschel, *Legitimation*, p. 19.

[67] An East German author's collective writing on tradition in 1986 identified "Disziplin, Ordnung, Verantwortungsbewusstsein, Kollektivität, und Solidarität als feste Gewohnheiten und 'Tugenden' der Arbeitenden..." These were produced in the conditions of "industrial production." According to GDR economic historian Waltraud Falk—whom the authors cite—"'Es ist auch von grosser Bedeutung für das Verhältnis der Arbeiterklasse zur Arbeit

played the national card in its latter years, that card was Prussian blue. If a Marxist-Leninist organization was structured like the military, then the model for the SED was the Prussian army.[68]

As elsewhere in Eastern Europe, with the partial exception of Poland, this sense of discipline was not challenged by traditions of individual rights.[69] The open border even permitted a gradual removal of "liberal" (also from the SED) democratic strands of German political culture. Unlike anywhere else in Eastern Europe, people with a commitment to liberal democracy could freely leave East Germany for over fifteen years. Educated classes, in particular students, had put up the strongest resistance to the SED in the early years of the regime, and educated classes were overrepresented in the refugee populations.[70] The SED leadership was aware of the border's double function: harmful when skilled labor escaped, but beneficial when it permitted the draining away of potential resistance. In 1949, Anton Ackermann spoke to leading functionaries about the "serious problem" of "emigration of intellectuals," but admitted to distinctions: "When a reactionary philosopher or historian leaves the Eastern Zone, this makes us happy. But it's different with physicians, mathematicians, physicists, biologists or technicians, whom we need and cannot replace."[71]

überhaupt, ob der Sozialismus in einem entwickelten Industrieland oder in einem Agrarland aufgebaut wird.'" Citing Erich Honecker, the authors also speak of traditions of "Qualitätsarbeit deutscher Industrie- und Handwerksbetriebe." Autorenkollektiv, *Die SED und das kulturelle Erbe* (Berlin, 1986), pp. 455–7. They did not need to point out that only in the Czech Lands and the GDR had socialism been constructed in a developed industrial country.

[68] See Horst Kühne, "Legitimer Erbe aller progressiven militärischen Traditionen des deutschen Volkes," *Einheit*, Vol. 2, (1981).

[69] On democratic traditions in Polish political culture, see Andrzej Walicki, *Philosophy and Romantic Nationalism: The Case of Poland* (Oxford: Clarendon Press, 1982), pp. 11–30.

[70] In 1961 3.4% of the population of the male population of West Germany was college educated. Of the male refugees from East Germany, the percentage was 7.2 percent. Helge Heidemeyer, *Flucht und Zuwanderung aus der SBZ/DDR 1945/1949–1961* (Düsseldorf: Droste, 1994), p. 50.

[71] "Stenographische Niederschrift des Referats des Genossen Anton Ackermann auf der Arbeitstagung ber die Frage der Auswahl und Zulassung zum Hochschulstudium," May 6, 1949. SAPMO-BA ZPA IV 2/904/464 (unnumbered). Several scholars have also recognized that the regime may have encouraged some sorts of *Republikflucht*. Dietrich Staritz argues that the regime

One might argue that the mass flights of the 1950s helped settle a problem of overpopulation. By 1961 the territory of the GDR was approaching the population density of 1939.[72] East-Elbian Germany had long been a place of at least seasonal migration. Intended or not, the emigration of the 1950s meant that the GDR, alone in Eastern Europe, had been permitted to simply dispense with its bourgeoisie, rather than make accommodations for it, or attempt to transform it. The open border to the West also helped unify the SED. Those Party members dissatisfied with SED policies and with Party discipline could leave East Germany.

Also remarkable on an East European backdrop were the SED's efforts to politically transform the non-bourgeois classes. The SED possessed a most profound recognition of the potentials of the educational system for creating a loyal elite. In the late 1940s and early 1950s the Party leadership created sophisticated mechanisms for drawing underprivileged and talented youth into higher education. Large cohorts were channeled into worker-peasant faculties (ABF). In the early 1950s entering classes of ABF students were about 40 percent the size of the college freshman populations, before they decreased to one quarter in 1954.[73] East German "worker-peasant" cadres arguably possessed the best academic preparation of any in East Central Europe; Czech and Polish counterparts gave two and one years instruction respectively, East German worker-peasant faculties gave three years. East German

---

welcomed the flight of many farmers in the early 1950s, since they left it with land to form agricultural collectives. *Geschichte der DDR*, p. 92. Phillip Longworth has argued that "for a time the regime had found the losses tolerable, since they rid the country of the most disaffected elements." *The Making of Eastern Europe*, p. 22.

[72] In 1939, the territory of the GDR had a population of 16,745,000 (154 persons/km²); in 1948 its population reached 19,066,000 (176 persons/km²). By 1961, the population had dropped to 17,079,000 (158 persons/km²). Karl C. Thalheim, *Die wirtschaftliche Entwicklung der beiden Staaten in Deutschland* (Berlin Landeszentrale für politische Bildungsarbeit, 1978), p. 16.

[73] During the early 1950s entering university classes included about 10 percent ABF graduates in Poland, and between 4–6 percent in the Czech Lands. *Archiwum Akt Nowych* (AAN), KCPZPR 237/XVI/120/43; MSW 17/91–93; *Statisticka; ročenka Republiky Československé 1957* (Prague, 1957), p. 214. For GDR statistics: *Statistisches Jahrbuch der Deutschen Demokratischen Republik 1960/61* (Berlin: Deutscher Zentralverlag, 1961), pp. 132–3.

worker-peasant cadres were well-trained and highly organized political-ly.[74] The state gave them everything, and they paid back with loyalty; their lives had become evidence for the soundness of their beliefs. They became the most politically supportive elite in Eastern Europe. Intellectuals, and especially university communities, were conspicuous by their absence from the revolutionary events of autumn 1989.

Conclusion

East Germany differed in several important ways from other East European societies in its transition to socialism during the Stalinist period. It moved more slowly in nationalizing the economy, and it failed to produce the bloody sorts of inner-party purges witnessed in other places. Yet if by "Stalinism" one means pervasiveness of control, then one must describe the GDR as increasingly Stalinist: or ironically neo-Stalinist, with control increasing as terror was absorbed and sublimated into patterns of everyday life, akin to a self-censorship extending far beyond political statements and taken deeply into performed routines—in public life, in state-socialist economy and culture, and increasingly realms once thought of as "private"—a word with increasingly less relevance, even in the "society of niches" (*Nischengesellschaft*). The inhabitant of a "niche" (*Nischenbewohner*) was not a citizen but rather a socialist subject.[75]

This is a scenario with cause and effect: a society shaped decisively, if not in every last detail, by the centralized Party bureaucracy. The precise environment in which the SED developed its peculiar logic is not sufficiently understood. If anything, the foregoing discussion points to a need to analyze the Party as a whole, from top to bottom, in its formative years. It was this Party that made East Germany—a region formerly known as Central Germany—politically Eastern European. Precisely by

---

[74] Polish students of the 1950s were likewise drawn from worker-peasant milieus, but they did not join the Party. Czech students joined the Party, but were not drawn from worker-peasant milieus. See: John Connelly, *Captive University: The Sovietization of Higher Education in East Germany, the Czech Lands, and Poland* (Chapel Hill: University of North Carolina Press, 2000).

[75] On the idea of *Nischengesellschaft*, see Günter Gaus, *Wo Deutschland liegt: eine Ortsbestimmung* (Munich: DTV, 1986).

its divergence from the "people's democracies" in the early years, the SED succeeded in placing the Soviet Zone of Occupation and the GDR in an East European context. Only the SED made use of social democrats to bolster its core of functionaries from the start, only it had the benefit of careful, pervasive, and constant "assistance" of Soviet advisors. The SED managed, with Soviet help, to assert early domination over all politically relevant organizations: political parties, trade unions, government agencies. East German society was subjected to a most thorough political transformation in the early post-war years. Culturally, de-Nazification and the open border permitted East Germany the greatest transfer of elites in Eastern Europe. Rather than contributing to reform, the open border permitted the leadership to leak the steam of dissent westward.

The SED began to reveal its character during the crises of the post-Stalin era. Despite Bloc-wide de-Stalinization, the SED leadership and grass roots firmly rejected liberalization. Purported anti-Stalinists like Herrnstadt or Schirdewan never developed probing analyses of the system that had produced them.[76] Unlike Poland, Hungary, or Czechoslovakia, East Germany never knew a sustained period of liberalization, either in the economy or in culture. Unlike every other East European leadership save the Bulgarian, the SED leadership never underwent a substitution of cadres. The men who made policy in the 1950s were still largely in power in the 1980s, and with the exception of several years' carefully controlled economic experimentation, they never diverged from the course entered in the Stalinist period. A disciplined rank and file loyally followed. Never did it produce pressure for non-totalitarian approaches to politics.

How does one then bridge the apparent gap between certain "lags" in early GDR development—softer purges, gradual economic development—and the *durchherrschte* (pervasively ruled) society of the 1980s, a place with a surveillance system so pervasive as to earn the GDR the title "neo-Stalinist"?[77] On the one hand is a society that was successively

---

[76] This view contrasts with that offered in Martin Jänicke, *Der dritte Weg: Die antistalinistische Opposition gegen Ulbricht seit 1953* (Cologne: Neuer Deutscher Verlag, 1964).

[77] The word *durchherrscht* ("ruled pervasively") is from Jürgen Kocka, "Eine durchherrschte Gesellschaft," in Hartmut Kaelble, Jürgen Kocka, and Hartmut Zwahr eds., *Sozialgeschichte der DDR* (Stuttgart: Klett-Cotta, 1994), pp. 547–53.

emptied of elements likely to oppose dictatorial rule—one might say that the political culture of German communism had claimed, then purged the territory of East Germany.[78] On the other is a Leninist organization which emerged from a union of communists and social democrats, which though constantly purged, also constantly grew. Those who opposed Ulbricht have called themselves an "anti-Stalinist" opposition. In their revulsion to the rule of one man, they may have been that. But true opposition had long left East Germany by the time these men's turn came to be purged. The substance of their "reform" consisted in a "return to Leninist norms of Party life." This platform also provides a tentative explanation of the paradox of East German communism: regardless of the multiple breaks of Building Socialism, the New Course, or the challenges of the Twentieth Party Congress, the SED was never less than a Leninist Party. Perhaps the paradox of East German communism is not a paradox at all: it was not mild Stalinism which made the GDR different from the rest, but rather the most gradual and careful construction of Leninism, on the solidest foundations of tradition that Europe has ever known.

---

[78] This culture has complex origins: partly going back to the KPD of the 1930s, to training gained in the Soviet Union by top leaders and former prisoners of war; to social democratic practices predating World War I; and most importantly, to the early post-war years, when the SED was transformed from a mass party, to a cadre party, and then to a mass cadre party.

ANTONI Z. KAMINSKI and
BARTŁOMIEJ KAMINSKI

Road to "People's Poland": Stalin's Conquest Revisited[1]

"Much to the dismay of both Churchill and Roosevelt, Stalin was intent [already in December, 1941—AZK, BK] on defining the new geopolitical contours of the Continent after Hitler's eventual defeat. His armies had barely held their own on the outskirts of Moscow, but their leader was already looking ahead to a new European order that would satisfy his territorial ambitions." (Andrew Nagorski, *The Greatest Battle*, New York: Simon and Schuster, 2007, p. 272)

"The presence of the Red Army on the Polish soil was as natural a result of the course of war as was the presence of the American and British army in France or Netherlands. If France and Netherlands became free and independent countries whereas Poland was enslaved, this did not result from the purely military circumstances but from Soviet imperialist designs…" (Leszek Kolakowski, "Yalta & the Fate of Poland: An Exchange," *The New York Review of Books*, Vol. 33, No. 13, August 14, 1986)

"This war is not like wars in the past: whoever occupies a territory can impose his [own] social system. Everyone imposes his social system as far as he can go. It could not be any other way." (Stalin's remark to Tito quoted in André Fontaine, "Yalta, from failure to myth," *Le Monde*, February 5, 1985)

"What a magic ballot box!!! You vote Mikolajczyk and Gomulka comes out!" (Popular quip on the first parliamentary elections in People's Poland in 1947)

---

[1] Paper presented at the conference "Stalinism Revisited: The Establishment of Communist Regimes in Eastern Europe," organized by the Cultural Institute of Romania and Woodrow Wilson Center, held in Washington, D.C., November 29–30, 2007. The authors are grateful to Vladimir Tismaneanu, who inspired this research project, and to other participants of the conference, who provided useful comments.

Introduction

The 60th anniversary of the Communist Information Bureau (Cominform), coinciding also with the anniversary of the outbreak of the Cold War and the end of the communist takeover of Central and Eastern Europe, is a good opportunity to revisit the Soviet takeover of Poland, which became People's Poland, and which ceased to exist in 1989.

History has already delivered its final verdict on many previously controversial issues. The critics who claimed that communism was not a viable politico-economic order capable of overcoming capitalism turned out to be right. The Soviet Union lost the Cold War thanks to the system that Stalin built. With the benefit of hindsight, one can argue that the emergence of the Soviet bloc has provided a powerful impulse to a complete overhaul of traditional European politics. The Cold War facilitated the emergence of collective security arrangements (NATO) and structures supporting economic and political cooperation rather than competition (EU). These structures emerged largely in response to the Soviet threat. In consequence, with the demise of the Soviet Bloc, its Central European members were not left in a void but could operate in a friendly environment. For Poland, geography, for the first time since the early eighteenth century, ceased to be a curse.

But the price paid by Poland (as well as by some other countries, in particular, the Baltic states) for the opportunity to be part of today's friendly pan-European environment was particularly high. Poland lost the right to self-determination and was coerced to adopt an alien political-economic system. Despite participating in the anti-fascist Alliance and contributing to the military effort with the fourth largest force against the Germans in Western Europe, Poland was one of the biggest losers of World War II. Much of its infrastructure—including that in newly acquired, more developed Western territories—was largely destroyed. Her territory was diminished by about one-fifth of its pre-war size. As a result of the Holocaust, combat operations, deportations to Germany and the Soviet Union, exile, and mass executions carried out by both Germans and Soviets, Poland lost almost one-third of its pre-war population, or 12 million people. Beside an almost total extermination of Poland's Jewish population, the losses were particularly high among her "best and brightest," and her pre-war elites were practically wiped out.

Poland's road to People's Poland was also unique in several other respects. First and foremost, it began with the Soviet annexation of the Eastern part of Poland in 1939, disrupted in 1941 for two years by the German occupation. Second, it took place at the level of international high politics: during its initial phase, it was shaped by the collusion between Hitler and Stalin. During the next phase following the German invasion of the Soviet Union, it had been a recurrent theme of diplomatic dialogue between the Big Three, Stalin, Roosevelt, and Churchill. The solution, i.e., the emergence of People's Poland also sealed the fate of other European countries "liberated" by the Soviet Union. Third, despite betrayal of Poland by its American and British allies and their gift of at least a modicum of legitimacy to the communists by not recognizing Poland's new western borders, the communist takeover was possible exclusively because of the presence of the Red Army on the Polish soil; communists were a marginal force in Polish pre-war politics. Last but not least, the resistance of Polish society to the communist takeover had never evaporated and the communists had to somehow accommodate to these pressures: a program of full collectivization of the agricultural sector was abandoned and, in response to the 1956 upheaval, the authorities had to scrap their "successes" and "de-collectivized" a number of farms.

During World War II, the Polish society created a huge, functionally differentiated, underground network involving in different ways millions of people—an underground civil society with an underground state, and an underground market economy. The betrayal by Western allies had shaken the confidence in the West, but still, even under conditions of terror and intense communist propaganda, the society retained ties and networks allowing it to defend itself against the encroachments of the communist state. It is also plausible, that many communists of intelligentsia background did not follow orders from Moscow with the conviction necessary to make implementation effective.

Although seriously weakened, the Catholic Church could still command significant loyalty, particularly in the countryside. Similarly, intense opposition against collectivization hindered the whole process to the extent that to the very end of the communist system, over eighty percent of the arable land remained in private hands. A small relaxation of political terror resulted in the huge Poznan workers' demonstrations and in the Polish October. The events in Poland triggered similar processes in Hungary, and the communist world witnessed, even if only for just a few months, a positive feedback mechanism between the anti-communist protests in both countries.

With the benefit of hindsight, it seems that, as result of the incomplete imposition of Stalin's system, People's Poland represented the greatest challenge to the stability within the Soviet bloc. The sequence of upheavals climaxing in the Solidarity movement in 1980–81 contributed to the erosion of the Soviet control over Central Europe and the demise of the Soviet bloc. While this is of little consolation to those whose lives were destroyed by Stalin's conquest of Poland, their sacrifice turned out not to be in vain.

The remainder of this paper is organized as follows. Section 2 briefly outlines the developments that led to the fourth partitioning of Poland. Section 3 discusses how the communist future of post-war Poland was sealed during World War II, and Section 4 seeks to explain why Frank Delano Roosevelt (FDR) was so accommodating to Stalin's demands. Section 5 takes a closer look at how Stalin aptly and ruthlessly exploited every opportunity to make the Soviet takeover of Poland easier. In Section 6, we discuss the Soviet takeover following the Soviet occupation of Poland. Section 7 summarizes unique features of Stalin's conquest of Poland.

Phase One of Stalin's Conquest: Collusion with Hitler

The Soviet takeover of Poland was made possible by the "external" circumstances created by World War II and aptly exploited by Stalin. Stalin's persistence in pressing Roosevelt and Churchill to recognize the Soviet Western borders along the Curzon Line and turn Poland into a vassal state, paid off. These territories were seized by the Soviet Union after it decided to fulfill its Ribbentrop–Molotov Pact commitments to join the Germans in their aggression against Poland. After World War II, Poland was not formally annexed to the Soviet Union, but almost half of its pre-war territory became part of the USSR, including two of her major cultural and educational centers—Vilnius and Lwów (Lviv). Poland, transformed into People's Poland, continued its existence as the state recognized by international law, although its domestic and external policies were controlled by the Soviet Union.

The Soviet takeover of Poland can be seen as unfolding in two phases: the first phase was marked by the outbreak of World War II in 1939 and the second by the German attack on the Soviet Union in 1941. The first phase began with the Hitler–Stalin pact bringing together two totalitarian powers, the Soviet Union and Germany, Poland's Eastern and Western neighbors. Both were bent on changing the Versailles *status quo*. Both saw the disappearance of sovereign Poland as critical to this end. A week after the Hitler–Stalin pact was signed on August 23, 1939, Germany attacked Poland. France and Great Britain declared war on Germany but neither, to Stalin's surprise, started military operations. Poland alone, geographically squeezed between two giants, could not have survived their collusion. Stalin waited 17 days to invade the Eastern part of Poland. Three weeks later the Polish Army, encircled from both west and east, was defeated.[2] Five weeks into World War II Poland was partitioned for the fourth time in its history. The circumstances were reminiscent of earlier partitions in at least one respect: Poland was too weak to survive the existence of empires at its borders with the Russian empire seeking to expand westward and Germany seeking to expand eastward.

The shared goal of overhauling the political order established by the Versailles Treaty brought Nazi Germany and the Soviet Union together.[3] Hitler's rejection of the Versailles system created a unique opportunity for Stalin to restore to the Soviet Union the territories of the Tsarist Russia "lost" after the Bolshevik *coup d'état* in October 1917.

---

[2] It may strike one as a short period, but it took the German Army around six weeks to take over Belgium, Holland, and France in 1940. None of them had to defend against the combined forces of the Soviet Union and Germany.

[3] This should not suggest that Weimar Republic accepted its Eastern borders. German policymakers "were careful at Locarno... to accept only their Western frontiers as final but not their Eastern. They were also careful to follow up the Locarno agreement with a neutrality treaty with the USSR... They thus maintained a relationship, begun at Rapallo in 1922, that was seen by one of its authors, General von Seeckt, the commander of the army up to 1926, as a means for bringing about the partition of Poland, and by the others as at least allowing Germany to play off the Western powers against the Soviet Union to Germany's advantage." A.W. DePorte, *Europe between the Super-powers: The Enduring Balance* (New Haven: Yale University Press, 1986), p. 33.

As John Erickson showed in his seminal book *The Soviet High Command* (1962, p. 432), Stalin sought rapprochement with Hitler already in the mid 1930s, long before Hitler acquiesced to a deal with the Soviet Union. Irrespective of their particular territorial ambitions, for both Hitler and Stalin, Poland—described in both German and Soviet propaganda as a "bastard of Versailles" and "seasonal state"—had to be erased from the political map. The 1939 German–Soviet Non-Aggression Pact, also known as the Ribbentrop–Molotov or, more appropriately, the Hitler–Stalin Pact, set the groundwork for accomplishing this goal. The Secret Additional Protocol of the Hitler–Stalin Pact envisaged partitioning of the territory of Poland between Germany and the Soviet Union. It left open, however, the possibility of "… the maintenance of an independent Polish State and [stated that] how such a state should be bounded can only be definitely determined in the course of further political developments." (Article II).

The German attack on the Soviet Union in July 1941 opened the second phase in the road to People's Poland. It was marked by the defeat of Germany in 1945 and climaxed in the imposition of Stalin's system on Poland by 1948, when the anti-Soviet underground was effectively wiped out. So was the multiparty system of Poland and whatever was left of private capitalism. Hence, around four years after the end of World War, the stage was set to impose Stalinism in Poland.

Tacit Cooperation of FDR in Founding People's Poland

Thanks to Germany's attack on the Soviet Union, "the course of further political developments" gave Stalin much more than the Secret Protocol had ever promised. Instead of sharing the control over Poland with Germany, Stalin gained control over territories granted in the Secret Protocol to Germany and expanded its direct influence well beyond the Curzon line. Even more importantly, the Teheran and Yalta conferences had provided international legitimacy to the provisions of the Secret Protocol. "The shock of the German invasion of Russia in 1941 did not deter Stalin from wanting ultimately to reclaim the land he had acquired under the notorious Nazi–Soviet pact of 1939. This territory included not only a sizable chunk of Poland, but later also a 'frontier security' area encompassing Estonia, Latvia, Lithuania, Finland's Karelian isthmus, the Romanian province of Bessarabia, and Bukovina."[4]

But Stalin's gains were not only territorial. While these clearly mattered a great deal to him, much more important was that the conditions that he set in his wartime plans for Poland's existence were more than fulfilled. Leaving aside the Soviet annexation of the territories occupied after joining Hitler in the attack on Poland on September 17, 1939, Stalin wanted Poland to become a bridge state between the Soviet Union and Eastern Germany—the Soviet occupation zone which later became the GDR (German Democratic Republic)—with a political regime compliant to the Soviet government. The shift in the Soviet alliances forced by the German attack was critical to accomplish this goal, which went well beyond the provisions outlined in the Secret Protocol of the Hitler–Stalin pact, which merely allowed for shared partitioning.

The decisive battle for Poland's future took place during the war: with the presence of the Soviet Army on the Polish soil, the Communist takeover was then a foregone conclusion. In consequence, the fate of Poland, as a communist satellite of the Soviet Union, was sealed not after but during World War II. With the Soviet Army firmly in control of Poland, the Potsdam conference (June–July 1945) merely confirmed earlier agreements negotiated between FDR and Stalin during the Teheran (December 1943) and Yalta (February 1945) summits. Each Soviet victory against Germany worsened prospects for Poland's right to self-determination, as Stalin was increasingly in a position to extract concessions from FDR and Churchill. Both of them were surprisingly obliging and treated Poland as a hostage to unfolding fortune in war theaters.

While Stalin's ultimate goal was to transform Poland into People's Poland (i.e., a "bridge state" to the USSR's new acquisitions in the West with a Soviet-style political regime fully compliant to the Soviet government), his strategy changed reflecting realities of the war with Germany. The communist takeover of Poland proceeded in several

---

[4] Stanley E. Smith, *Winston Churchill and Eastern Europe. Part 2: Poland and Germany–The Balancing Act.* Downloaded from http://www.winstonchurchill.org/i4a/pages/index.cfm?pageid=90 on September 15, 2007.

phases. At the international stage, it was Stalin and Molotov who negotiated the fate of Poland. They paid attention not to antagonize their
western partners too early by revealing their real objectives.[5] For instance, under the pressure of the rapid advance of German forces into
the Soviet Union in summer of 1941 and the desperate need of US
military supplies, the Soviet government recognized the Polish government-in-exile and signed agreements on August 17, 1941, releasing all
Polish POWs from the Gulag and establishing the Polish Army on the
Soviet soil subordinate to the Polish government-in-exile.[6] At least 50
thousand people were released by the Soviet authorities.

As the Soviet military situation kept improving, diplomatic relations with the government-in-exile lost its relevance and ultimately led
to their termination. Stalin used any pretext to break up diplomatic
relations with the Polish government-in-exile as well as to get rid of
the Army controlled by the Polish government once they interfered
with his plans of subjugating Poland. In response to Poland's request
to have the International Red Cross investigate the Katyn mass graves,
found by the Germans in March 1943,[7] the Soviet Union broke off
diplomatic relations, and accused the Polish government of collabo-

---

[5] Wojciech Materski, *Dyplomacja Polski 'lubelskiej': lipiec 1944-marzec 1947* [Di-
plomacy of "lublin" Poland: July 1944–March 1947] (Warsaw: ISP PAN &
OW RYTM, 2007).

[6] General Wladyslaw Anders, released from the Lubyanka prison in Moscow on
August 4, 1941, became its Commander-in-Chief.

[7] It was confirmed that the graves contained the corpses of Polish officers missing since early 1940, or around 18 months before the Germans gained control of this territory. The Soviets, who were responsible for this massacre,
denied it. The US and Great Britain preferred to look the other way. Even
before the release of the documents by Mikhail Gorbachev show the involvement of the NKVD (excerpt from the minutes No. 13 of the Politburo of the
Central Committee meeting Resolution 144–March 5, 1940 regarding the
matter submitted by the NKVD USSR), it was clear that Germans were not
responsible for it. Consider the following: first, the families and the Polish
government-in-exile could not trace the whereabouts of around twenty thousand people since early 1940; second, while families had been getting letters
from the POWs before March 1940, all correspondence ceased after that date;
third, during excavations some diaries were found—all of them ended in April
1940; and, fourth, the Katyn massacre was not mentioned among atrocities
committed by Germans during the Nuremberg trials.

ration with the Nazis in their anti-Alliance propaganda.[8] The mere presence of an Army controlled by the Polish government would complicate Stalin's plans of gaining total control over Poland. Thus, the decision of sending it to fight elsewhere in Middle East, North Africa and Western Europe.

Yet, even before breaking diplomatic relations with the Polish government-in-exile and sending its army to Iran, the issue of Poland's eastern border was not resolved. Stalin insisted on the recognition of the provisions of the Hitler–Stalin secret protocol allowing for the annexation of Baltic States and almost half of Poland's territory. He was adamant about it. He raised the issue of the Soviet–Polish frontier in a meeting with Anthony Eden, the British Foreign Secretary, already in December, 1941, which coincided with the climax of the battle for Moscow with German troops still only a couple of miles from Kremlin.[9] During the meeting, Stalin presented Eden with the drafts of two treaties for the wartime alliance and another one on postwar arrangements and "... jolted his guests by proposing a secret protocol to the second treaty, which would spell out the future of European borders... There was a recent precedent for such secret protocols on the redrawing of borders: the Molotov–Ribbentrop pact."[10] While Anthony Eden did not accept the redrawing of Poland's borders at that time, Stalin got what he wanted two years later in December 1943 at the Teheran conference of the Big Three.

Indeed, with the Red Army on the offensive and lend-lease program in full swing, Stalin could safely change his strategic goal, shifting from the second best option: "Poland fully subordinated to the Soviet foreign policy but retaining the right not to become communist" to the

---

[8] While one may debate whether the Polish government should or should not press the issue of investigating the Katyn massacre, the crux of the matter is that diplomatic relations with the Polish government served little purpose to Stalin. To the contrary, they would make the conquest of Poland much more difficult.

[9] Malcolm Mackintosh, "Stalin's Policies towards Eastern Europe, 1939–1948: The General Picture," in Thomas T. Hammond ed., *The Anatomy of Communist Takeovers* (New Haven: Yale University Press, 1971). Quotation from Cordell Hull, *The Memoirs of Cordell Hull* (New York: MacMillan Company, 1948), Vol. II, pp. 1, 166–7.

[10] Andrew Nagorski, *The Greatest Battle: Stalin Hitler and Moscow* (New York: Simon and Schuster, 2007), p. 277.

best option: "People's Poland." He made rapid progress in carrying out his designs in two stages: in the first, he gained Western approval of the Soviet annexation of eastern Poland. Ironically, it was not Stalin but Churchill who proposed that Poland's borders be based on the Curzon line and the Oder–Neisse Rivers. It is also rather telling that both Churchill and FDR regarded Stalin's territorial claims not exceeding the former Tsarist boundaries as perfectly legitimate.[11] In Teheran, FDR ceded to Stalin all territories east of the Curzon Line.[12] The only concession that FDR appears to have won was that Stalin agreed that FDR—to avoid antagonizing Polish Americans—would not announce it publicly until after the forthcoming elections in the US.[13]

On 10 January 1944, the Soviet government publicly proclaimed the Curzon Line as its border with Poland. Hence, the frontier between Poland and the Soviet Union, roughly drawn in the Secret Protocol of the Molotov–Ribbentrop Pact, had once again become the reality sanctioned by the international community. Stalin thus erased the provisions of the Riga Treaty setting the borders between the Soviet Union and Poland that followed the Soviet defeat in the Polish–Soviet War in 1919–20.

By the time of the next Big Three summit at Yalta (February 1945), Poland was already under Soviet control. With the Soviet Army firmly in control of territories spreading all the way from Moscow to Berlin and taking into account—to paraphrase Leszek Kolakowski—Stalin's "imperialist designs," its future status as an "associated territory" of the Soviet Union was a foregone conclusion, even though Stalin subscribed to a Declaration on Liberated Europe, promising free elections in all liberated territories. The conference legitimized Soviet territorial gains and designated (temporarily) the Polish western border, albeit

---

[11] They might not have been aware that Lwow and Eastern Galicia had never belonged to the Russian Empire.

[12] It is ironic that on 11 July, 1920, during the Polish–Soviet War, British Foreign Secretary Lord Curzon proposed to the Soviet government a ceasefire along the line that he suggested in 1919. The Soviets, who at that time were rapidly advancing, rejected Lord Curzon's proposal. In September 1939 the Soviet Union annexed not only all territories east of the Curzon Line but also Białystok and Eastern Galicia.

[13] A former US diplomat Charles G. Stefan notes that "domestic politics—the six to seven million Polish-American voters—would, during an election year, prevent him from saying anything in public on this issue" (Stefan, 1997).

with a caveat. FDR insisted on curtailing Poland's western territory to the Eastern rather than Western Neisse River, this would keep German control over Wroclaw. Stalin did not give in to FDR's demands thus scoring important points for Polish communists in their propaganda against the West.

Considering that Roosevelt so quickly agreed to the Soviet annexation of around 40 percent of Poland's territory, it is not clear why they were so adamantly opposed to including a narrow strip of land between western and eastern Neisse Rivers. Churchill's remark voiced at Yalta that "It would be a pity to stuff the Polish goose so full of German food that it gets indigestion"[14] cannot be taken seriously especially since Germans were supposed to leave these territories. They were forced to do so and around two million Poles from territories annexed by the Soviet Union moved in. With Poland's western borders in limbo till the People's Poland–German Federal Republic Treaty of 1970, the issue of non-recognition was used by the communist propaganda to legitimize their power as a guarantee of preserving territorial integrity and the well-being of recent settlers from the East. It was also used to demonstrate the duplicity of Anglo-American policy towards Poland during World War II.

Why Was FDR So Accommodating?

One may ponder over the question why Stalin's plan to seize Poland met so little resistance from the Western Allies. Why did FDR and Churchill agree so easily to Stalin's demands that—according to an opinion—"were grossly out of proportion to what was needed to keep the USSR in the war"[15]? Why did we—to paraphrase the title of a book *I Saw Poland Betrayed* written by the first US ambassador to People's Poland, Arthur Bliss-Lane—see Poland betrayed? After all, Poland's

---

[14] Stanley Smith, *Winston Churchill and Eastern Europe. Part 1: The Polish Government*. Downloaded from http://www.winstonchurchill.org/i4a/pages/index.cfm?pageid=89 of Churchill Centre on October 14, 2007.

[15] Walter Jajko, "The Warsaw Rising: A View on the Betrayal After 60 Years," comments presented a private screening of *CNN Presents: Warsaw Rising: The Forgotten Soldiers of World War II*, The Institute of World Politics, Washington, D.C., June 3, 2004.

government was part of the anti-Axis coalition and participated actively in the war against the Germans until their surrender in May 1945. In the West, Polish forces fought alongside the Allies in the land, the air, and the seas. During World War II, the Polish army on both the Western and the Eastern front, counted over 700,000 men and women, making it the fourth largest army in the Alliance.[16] Poles played a very important role in cracking secret German codes and the Polish intelligence network covering not only Poland, Germany and the rest of occupied Europe but also Algiers and Turkey, closely cooperated with allies and made significant contributions. According to the British sources, Secret Intelligence Services "... received around 45 thousand reports from Europe in 1940–45 with almost half of them supplied by the Polish intelligence services."[17] As John Colville, personal secretary to Winston Churchill during World War II noted: "Probably the best all-round players in the [intelligence—AZK, BK] game were the Poles."[18]

While answering a question why FDR was so accommodating to Stalin's demands would go well beyond the modest format of this paper, some general observations are relevant for our discussion. Before making them, one should note that all decisions concerning Central Europe were made jointly by FDR and Stalin with Stalin calling the

---

[16] Jan Ciechanowski, "Rozważania o położeniu Polski i Polaków podczas drugiej wojny światowej" [Reflections about Poland and Poles during the second world war] in Polsko-brytyjska współpraca wywiadowcza podczas II wojny światowej: Ustalenia polsko-brytyjskiej komisji historycznej [Polish-British intelligence cooperation during World War II: Findings of the Polish-British Historical Commission], Vol 1 (Warsaw: NDAP, 2004), p. 87.

[17] Adam Daniel Rotfeld, "Wkład polskiego wywiadu do zwycięstwa nad III Rzeszą" [The contribution of Poland's intelligence services to victory over Third Reich] in Polska w niepewnym świecie [Poland in an uncertain world] (Warsaw: Polish Institute of International Affairs, 2006), p. 330.

[18] John Colville, Strange Inheritance (Salisbury: Michael Russell, 1983), p. 167, quoted in Andrzej Suchcitz and Jan Ciechanowski, "Literatura na temat działalności polskiego wywiadu w czasie II wojny światowej" [Literature on activities of the Polish intelligence during World War II] in Polsko-brytyjska współpraca wywiadowcza podczas II wojny światowej: Ustalenia polsko-brytyjskiej komisji historycznej [Polish–British intelligence cooperation during World War II: Findings of the Polish–British Historical Commission], Vol 1 (Warsaw: NDAP, 2004), p. 61, who also give a full account of the Polish contribution to the "Enigma-Ultra project," intelligence on the V1-V2 program.

shots. As the war unfolded, the importance of the Soviet Union had grown and that of Great Britain had been marginalized.[19] The Big Two, rather than the Big Three were making all the critical decisions, foreshadowing a post-war bipolar world. The fate of Poland was completely extraneous to Roosevelt's vision of the kind of a world order that should emerge after World War II. Roosevelt's vision of the post war world order was based on four powers that were to police their respective spheres of influence: the United States, the USSR, Great Britain, and China.[20] This had two implications: first, Stalin could claim on such grounds the right to "police" Poland; and, more importantly, by displaying reluctance to FDR's grand vision, he was in a good position to extract concessions. And he did. Stalin not only obtained legitimization of control of Poland at Yalta but also won FDR's approval of UN membership for the Soviet Ukrainian and Belorussian republics.

Poland was critical to Stalin's imperialist designs, while—as noted above—her fate was of no particular relevance to Roosevelt's grand vision of the post-war world and the Soviet Union's participation in it. By the same token, the geopolitical value of Poland was different to FDR and Stalin. It was close to zero for the former, while huge to the latter. Without Poland, the Soviet Union would not be a full-fledged European and world power and its reach into Western Europe would have been greatly curtailed. So would have been Stalin's freedom to maneuver in other parts of Central and Eastern Europe.

Another reason for Stalin's ability to extract concessions from his Western Allies was that FDR wanted to finish the war as quickly as possible at the least cost in US lives, while human lives did not figure in Stalin's political calculations. For Stalin, Soviet soldiers were an

---

[19] Consider that Roosevelt bought into Stalin's charges of Anglo-Saxon conspiracy and refused to meet Churchill in private during the summits in Teheran and Yalta. He also refused to approve of Churchill's suggestion to launch an invasion through the Balkans rather than France. It is rather telling that when FDR died in April 1945, Churchill decided against attending the funeral of his once very close friend. Some argue that Churchill hoped that the new president, Harry Truman, would then come to see Churchill in Britain (Meacham, 2004). This suggests that the Anglo-American relations must have reached a very low point if the presence at FDR's funeral was subject to such petty considerations.

[20] See Henry Kissinger, *Diplomacy* (New York: Simon & Schuster, 1994), Ch. 16.

expendable resource. While both Churchill and FDR sought to minimize the loss in human lives in conducting the war, Stalin sought to
make sure that his political goals be achieved no matter their human
costs. Adam Ulam noted that:

> A German counteroffensive in the Ardennes caught the Americans
> by surprise. There was a momentary fear of a serious military deba-
> cle, and Churchill and Roosevelt found themselves pleading for the
> Russians to unleash their offensive in the east... The Russians duly
> opened their offensive in January. Rundstedt's thrust by that time was
> clearly revealed as a diversion rather than a major offensive, of which
> the Germans were no longer capable. But the Russians could now im-
> ply that they saved the allies from a major defeat. Such was the pre-
> lude to Yalta.[21]

Stalin would not have asked for military help to save lives of Soviet
soldiers—he treated them as bargaining chips. Whereas FDR did ask
Stalin to enter the war against Japan, when the Japanese were already
ready to surrender. The democratic and totalitarian rationality clearly
differed. For instance, General Eisenhower declared Berlin not to be
a military objective and, instead, continued the advance of US troops
into Czechoslovakia. Eisenhower rejected the formula that war was
the use of force to achieve a political objective; otherwise it would be
a pointless slaughter.[22] In contrast, Stalin did not mind a "pointless
slaughter" brought about by the Berlin operation. FDR might have
occasionally confused realism with idealism: Stalin did not. For Stalin, like later for Khrushchev, the modus of negotiations was: "what is
mine is mine; what is yours is negotiable."[23] And what was his was his
because the Soviet Army was there. Furthermore, he skillfully played
semantics: for instance, there was an understanding reached that the
post-war Polish government should consist of "democratic Poles": but

---

[21] Adam Ulam, *Expansion and Coexistence. Soviet Foreign Policy 1917–1973*, 2nd
ed. (New York: Holt, Rinehart and Winston, Inc., 1974), p. 367.

[22] Walter Jajko, "The Warsaw Rising."

[23] President John F. Kennedy's comment on Khrushchev's statement that
"...the status quo could only be viewed in a 'dynamic' form, because history,
from time immemorial, had written into its programme the final triumph of
socialism." (André Fontaine, "Yalta, from failure to myth," *Le Monde*, February 5, 1985)

for Stalin the only "democratic Poles" were the communists while for FDR and Churchill the group included Polish politicians in exile.[24]

Last but not least, public opinion in the West was very favorably disposed towards Stalin and communism as an intellectually attractive social experiment. So was FDR's State Department as well as some prestigious newspapers in which Stalin, to his utmost displeasure, was portrayed as "Good Uncle Joe." The Soviet Union had a powerful lobby in Washington, which enhanced his bargaining position in negotiations with FDR.

In consequence, despite his dependence on the US-financed Lend-Lease program, Stalin had the upper hand in his negotiations with FDR. He was quite successful in creating a situation in which his new Allies, in particular Roosevelt, wooed him to ensure that the Soviet Union would remain in coalition at almost any price rather than the other way around. It was Stalin who had a final say in setting the sites, dates and agenda of the Big Three Summits in Teheran, Yalta, and Potsdam. It was Stalin who delayed the first meeting of the Big Three, which eventually took place in Teheran in late 1943, for more than two years, despite urgent calls from FDR. It was an ailing President Roosevelt who had to travel there. It was Roosevelt who turned down Churchill's invitation to stay at the British Embassy in Teheran. Instead, he stayed at the Soviet Embassy apparently persuaded that "he could convince old Joe to go our way."[25] If "our way" was to keep the Soviet Union engaged in fighting the Germans; to have them invade Japan a couple of days before its final surrender; to make it a member of the United Nations and its Security Council; and to have two Soviet republics—Belarus and Ukraine—as members of the United Nations, then FDR achieved his objectives. But in the process he agreed to Stalin's empire in Poland and other countries of Central and Eastern Europe.

Poland might have retained its sovereignty and prewar territories only if Western armies defeated Germany before the Soviet Army

---

[24] Adam Ulam, *Expansion and Coexistence.*

[25] The quote comes from FDR's son, James Roosevelt (in James Roosevelt with Bill Libby, *My Parents: A Differing View*, Chicago: Playboy Press, 1976, p. 167), who also wrote that FDR never gave up this conviction despite the fact that FDR thought that "Uncle Joe is smarter and tougher than I thought" (p. 203).

reached Poland's eastern borders, although this can not be taken for granted. The Soviet Union not only survived the German attack, but it also acquired in the course of war huge leverage, which allowed Stalin to decide the fate of countries that the Red Army seized while moving westward to Berlin. In contrast to FDR, Stalin did not believe in post-war cooperation in large part because—as George F. Kennan (1947) put it in his famous "X" article—"of the innate antagonism between capitalism and Socialism"—he was convinced of—"the inevitability of its [capitalism's] destruction." We cannot know for sure whether Stalin genuinely believed that capitalism was bent on destroying communism or that capitalism could perish without the Soviet intervention. But what we know with a high degree of certainty is that he trusted no one and sought total control through any available means. An alliance with "capitalist" powers was a marriage of convenience. Once Hitler was defeated, the capitalist powers would be portrayed as major foes that, in turn, would justify internal repressions, terror and "proletariat" dictatorship. That Stalin stopped the Soviet Army at the lines drawn jointly by Allies and that he did not move westward once the US Army was rapidly demobilized after the end of war in Japan; neither is proof of his willingness to cooperate with the West. One suspects that US nuclear monopoly might be one of the main reasons.

To sum up, the bottom line is that Stalin was calling the shots once the Soviet Army went on offensive. He needed Western Allies only to provide him with military supplies whose importance had been on the decline as the Soviet military industries moved to Central Asia started to operate. He did not want to end the war as quickly as possible but to finish it on his terms with the Soviet foot firmly in the heart of Europe. On the other hand, cooperation with the Soviet Union was critical to FDR's vision of post-war world political order. It seems that this is why (a) he offered the Soviet Union, on top of the permanent membership of UN Security Council, two extra memberships in the UN Assembly with voting rights for Belarus and Ukraine; and (b) why he invited the Red Army to seize Japanese territories in the waning days of the war. Although FDR might have thought that the Soviet sphere of influence would not have to be communist, the bottom line is that a communist Central and Eastern Europe did not go against his vision of the post-war world political order.

Preparing the Groundwork for Takeover: Getting Rid of Potential Future Opposition

Whether he would be in a position "to impose his own social system"—to borrow Stalin's phrase from his remarks to Yugoslav leader Josip Broz Tito—on Poland or not, Stalin, nonetheless, did everything that was in his power to make the task as likely to succeed as possible. Once the war theater moved to Polish territories granted to Germany under the Hitler–Stalin pact, the imposition of the Stalinist system began. It did not happen overnight, but proceeded gradually, slice by slice, with the final outcome predetermined by the presence of the Soviet Army and Soviet advisors *de facto* controlling all levers of the newly established state coercion and distributive apparatus.

Stalin capitalized on developments during World War II to clear the way for totally subordinating Poland's future polity to his rule. Getting rid of potential foes including mass executions was Stalin's favorite practice that he had used ruthlessly to establish—as Brzeziński succinctly describes it—"a system of terror that left no individual secure, not even Stalin's closest comrades."[26] This practice was replicated in Poland, with the Germans only "helping" the terror. In fact, no other country in Europe experienced so much cruelty and hostility as Poland did during the German occupation. Nazis ranked the Poles as the second lowest racial group in Europe next to the Jews and the Gypsies—all considered non-human and destined for extermination. Germans bear the direct responsibility for killing over six million Polish citizens—three million Christians and three million Jews. By this count alone, Poland lost around 17 percent of its citizens.

The Soviet Union contributed further to reducing Poland's population by around two million. Following the Soviet attack on September 17, 1939 and subsequent occupation of Eastern Poland, Stalin systematically used every opportunity to physically eliminate Poles but, in particular, the Polish intelligentsia regarded by him as a potential opposition to his plans. For instance, his 1940 order of mass executions of around 25 thousand of Polish officers and other POWs captured in

---

[26] Zbigniew Brzeziński, *The Grand Failure. The Birth and Death of Communism in the Twentieth Century* (New York: Charles Scribner's Sons, 1989), p. 23.

Poland's occupied territories served this purpose. The Soviet occupation following invasion in September 1939 was ruthless and cruel. Although many scholars believe that conditions in the Soviet zone "...were only marginally less harsh than under the Germans,"[27] it seems that in many ways it might have been even more difficult. Millions were deported to Siberia and Soviet Central Asia in 1939–40. Tens of thousands of Polish soldiers never got there as they were executed *en route*. While around 40 thousand deported Polish soldiers and a similar number of civilians managed to get out thanks to the formation of the first Polish Army,[28] many more either joined the communist-led Polish Army established later or perished in Siberia. In total, more than two million Polish citizens were imprisoned or deported to the Gulag by 1945.

The pre-war political class, albeit considerably decimated during World War II and the Underground State (controlled by the government in exile, in London) had to be wiped out in order to create space for an alternative, Soviet-controlled government. From this perspective, the decision to start the Warsaw Rising on August 1, 1944, just before the Soviet entry into Warsaw, and Stalin's decision to wait until the Germans had crushed the Rising make sense; it ultimately played into Stalin's hand. The Command of the Home Army knew about the fate of their colleagues, who, acting in cooperation with the Red Army, liberated Vilnius and Lwow and were subsequently killed or imprisoned by the same Red Army. But as a legitimate representative of the

---

[27] I.C.B. Dear and M.R.D. Foot., eds. *The Oxford Companion to the Second World War* (Oxford: Oxford University Press, 1995), p. 894, as quoted in Piotr Wrobel, *The Devil's Playground: Poland in World War II* (The Canadian Foundation for Polish Studies of the Polish Institute of Arts & Sciences, Price-Patterson Ltd, 2004, available at http://www.warsawrising.com/paper/wrobel1.htm)

[28] The Soviet Union and the Polish government in exile had agreed to form a Polish army under command of General Anders, who was imprisoned by the Soviets in 1939. By 25 October 1941 this Army had 41,000 men, including 2,630 officers. According to the official Soviet version, General Anders refused to fight on the Soviet–German front because of the border dispute between the Soviet Union and Poland, and the Polish army had to be sent elsewhere to fight. However, the point is that the presence of the Army formally controlled by the government-in-exile was not convenient, to say the least, to the Soviets.

Polish State, the Commander of the Home Army had no other choice but to start the battle counting on the fact that in due time the Soviets would come to their assistance. For the very same reason Stalin decided to halt the advance of the Red Army and watched as Germans slaughtered an estimated 250 thousand Polish people and then systematically leveled large swathes of Warsaw.

For this discussion, neither the wisdom of starting the Warsaw Rising nor the debate on whether the Soviet offensive ran out of steam and needed to bring closer logistic support is of any relevance. Three historical facts stand out that point to Stalin's resolve to use any opportunity—and the Warsaw Rising offered such an opportunity—to annihilate the Home Army. First, the Soviets complained to their Western allies about the Home Army not participating actively in fighting the Germans and in July 1944, the Soviet radio broadcasts repeatedly urged the people of Warsaw to start the Warsaw Rising. Second, Stalin refused British and American requests to use Soviet airfields to supply Warsaw by air. Third, as mentioned above, the units of the Home Army that joined the Soviet Army, which in early January 1944 crossed Poland's 1921 Eastern borders, were subsequently disarmed and its soldiers interned.[29]

Moscow considered the Warsaw Rising as anti-Soviet, simply because it was a demonstration of the nation's determination to fight the Germans. As such, it undermined the Soviet propaganda in the West portraying the Home Army and the Polish Underground State as Nazi collaborators. It was also the last act of the legitimate Polish government to assert itself as the true representative of the Polish people in the face of the Soviet Army. It was the only authority, which could, at least morally, oppose the replacement of one occupation by another. There are moments when, to quote Winston Churchill, "...you will have to fight with all the odds against you and only a precarious chance of survival. There may even be a worse case. You have to fight when

---

[29] For a full account of the NKVD fight against the Home Army, see Andrzej Paczkowski, "Poland, the 'Enemy Nation'," in *Black Book of Communism. Crimes, Terror, Repression* (Harvard University Press, London, 1999), pp. 372–5. Before the outbreak of the Warsaw Rising, that is between January and July 1994, around 25,000 soldiers, including 300 Home Army officers, were arrested, disarmed, and interned.

there is no hope of victory, because it is better to perish than live as slaves."[30]

That was what the Warsaw Rising was about. Norman Davies, in an interview for the Polish television in 1994, remarked that the fate of communism in Poland was heavily influenced by the fact that communists came to power over the dead bodies of soldiers of the Rising. This created a deficit of legitimacy the communist party could never overcome.

But, the Warsaw Rising, or more exactly the destruction of lives of young Poles by Germans, served Stalin's plans to facilitate consolidation of power by the newly established Provisional Government in July 1944, which was, needless to say, fully controlled by him. Furthermore, the failure of the Warsaw Rising also dealt a deadly blow to the Underground State. As Jajko succinctly summarized it:

> Stalin knew that the Underground State was an existing alternative government, organized throughout all of Polish society that would prevent his Sovietization of Poland. Stalin knew too that the Home Army was the force that would insist on Polish independence even unto war against the Soviet Union. Stalin's facilitation of the German suppression of the Warsaw Rising prevented the armed opposition to the Sovietization of Poland.[31]

The executions of Polish prisoners in the so-called Katyn massacre, the killings of soldiers of Home Army in "liberated" Polish territories, the decision to stop the Soviet Army's advance over Vistula before the Warsaw Rising was crushed, and refusing to allow British and American planes with supplies to land in Soviet controlled airports for refueling and help Warsaw Rising had one common denominator: the physical elimination of the people that might be opposed to his plan of imposing his [Stalin's] own social system.

Huge losses in human capital inflicted directly or indirectly by its successive occupiers—Germany and the Soviet Union—immensely weakened Poland's capacity to resist the external imposition of an alien politico-economic order. Poland experienced the highest casualty rate among the European states: its population had shrunk from 35 million

---

[30] Winston S. Churchill, *The Second World War*, Vol. 1, "The Gathering Storm." (London, 1960), p. 312.

[31] Jajko, *The Warsaw Rising*, p. 3.

before the war in 1939 to 23 million in 1945. Among these 12 million were those who remained in Polish territories annexed by the Soviet Union; those killed by the Germans and Soviets; those deported or in exile in the West or imprisoned in the Soviet Union; and those whose status was and remains unknown.[32]

But the reason that Poland's population losses were an asset for Stalin, relates less to the numbers involved but the quality of the vanished human capital. Both Germans and the Soviets sought to eliminate the pre-war political and intellectual elite in order to foil the rebirth of a sovereign Polish state. "The brightest and the best" from Poland's intellectual, political, and military class, were largely eliminated from the Polish scene. And those who survived the war were impoverished and marginalized. According to an estimate, Poland lost 40 percent of her university professors, 45 percent of physicians and dentists, 57 percent of her lawyers, over 18 percent of her clergy, and more than 15 percent of her teachers during World War II.[33]

For the Soviet Union, military occupation of Poland presented no difficulties. The country was destroyed and its population exhausted by the Nazi occupation. Moreover, the huge Polish underground was faced with a tragic choice: it had to deal with two enemies who themselves were involved in a deadly struggle. But at the same time, they both fought the Home Army everywhere they could. Under the circumstances, Polish authorities decided to act as allies of the Red Army and as hosts when it entered the prewar territory of Poland. As a matter of fact, no other solution was possible. Stalin's propaganda in the West presented the Home Army and the Polish Underground State as Nazi collaborators. His purpose was obvious: to make it easier for London to retreat on its obligations to Poland and for Washington to deny having any obligations at all. Thus, soldiers of the Home Army, who fought shoulder to shoulder with Soviet soldiers in liberating Vilnius, Lwow, or other lands of the prewar Poland were arrested, some summarily executed while others were sent to Siberian concentration camps. Dozens of thousands of young people met this fate, and many of them perished in the Soviet North.

---

[32] Wrobel, *The Devil's Playground*.
[33] Dear and Foot, *op. cit.*, p. 894.

From German Occupation to Stalin's Takeover

The imposition of the Stalinist politico-economic regime encountered very strong internal resistance despite the decimation of the politically most active and sophisticated strata of the Polish society, the disappearance of the landowning class and the loss of respect for the pre-war political regime following its retreat—regarded by many Poles as betrayal—to Romania. The communists had little, if any, popular support. Memories of their close collaboration with the Bolsheviks during the invasion of Poland by the Red Army in 1919–20, including even the establishment of a provisional Communist government,[34] were too fresh. So were memories of successive partitions of Poland by Russia including the fourth one carried out by Hitler and Stalin in 1939. Furthermore, the militant atheism of communism clashed with Poles' deep attachment to the Catholic Church, so closely identified with the historic quest for independence. Communists were regarded as traitors and agents of a foreign hostile power. Moreover, Poles had had direct experience of the communist regime during the twenty-one months of Soviet occupation of Eastern Poland. This certainly did not predispose them favorably to the incoming post-war reality. Thus, political opinion was overwhelmingly against the creation of a Soviet-type system. Under these circumstances, a communist takeover might have been a difficult and time-consuming project.

Yet, this did not turn out to be the case. The communist takeover of Poland proceeded at a similar pace as in other countries "liberated" by the Soviet Army, despite the fact that it encountered military resistance. While the presence of the Soviet Army was a decisive factor, there were other reasons that made a takeover much faster and easier than one might have expected. The combination of war fatigue, which was exacerbated by the Warsaw Rising, with a sense of powerlessness after the betrayal of Poland by Western powers discouraged resistance. There was a sense of inevitability about the Soviet takeover: this prompted some to cooperate with the new power structures and led many to merely vent their unhappiness at a ballot. The latter had little

---

[34] Norman Davies, *White Eagle, Red Star: The Polish–Soviet War, 1919–1920* (New York: Pimlico, 1972).

significance as the results were always rigged. Furthermore, the Communists were very well organized: with the help of the Soviet army, they systematically neutralized or eliminated the Home Army together with whatever was left from the pre-war political parties. In their place, they established police units and administrative structures, setting the ground for the imposition of the system that Stalin had built.

Stalin's objective of imposing "his own social system" on Poland came increasingly within his grasp as the Soviet Army continued its offensive. The immediate task was to create a new political class that would make it easier to establish a communist regime. Stalin took several steps to build up political bodies, both in occupied Poland and the Soviet Union, opposed to the government in London even before he broke off diplomatic relations in April 1943. These included reviving the Communist Party of Poland, which was dissolved in 1938 upon Stalin's order and around 5,000 members of which were either executed or sent to the Gulag; establishing a Polish army fully integrated into the Soviet command structures and creating a government alternative to the government-in-exile.

The re-establishment of the Communist Party in Poland's territories occupied by Germans encountered significant problems, showing that the communist takeover from within, without the presence of the Red Army, stood no chance of success in Poland. The Polish Workers' Party (PWP) was established in January 1942 by the so-called "troika" of communist activists—Marceli Nowotko, Paweł Finder, and Bolesław Mołojec—parachuted into Poland from Moscow a month earlier in December 1941. All members of the PWP troika were murdered or arrested in mysterious circumstances and for reasons that have not been fully elucidated. It is clear, however, that it happened as a result of internal squabbling and deep divisions. According to various accounts, Marceli Nowotko was probably shot by Mołojec's brother, who, in turn, was killed. It appears that several members of the Party leadership including Władysław Gomułka were involved. Paweł Finder, in turn, was arrested by Gestapo: it is not clear who turned him in.[35] During the German occupation the PWP was a very small organization with membership of around eight thousand a year later in January 1943.

---

[35] *Nowa Encyklopedia Powszechna PWN* [New universal encyclopedia of PWN] (Warsaw: Wydawnictwo Naukowe PWN, 2004).

The PWP did not have much success in recruiting new members until the Red Army ended the German occupation. Its membership dramatically increased after the end of World War II in 1945. Yet, it then amounted to only 210 thousand, less than one percent of Poland's population at the time (Figure 1–24). Two years later in January 1947, during the first parliamentary elections, its membership rose to 550 thousand people still well short of membership of the United Peasant Party, which was already decimated by repressions opposition party.

Figure 1: *Membership in Polish Workers' Party in thousands and in percent of total population in 1942–49*

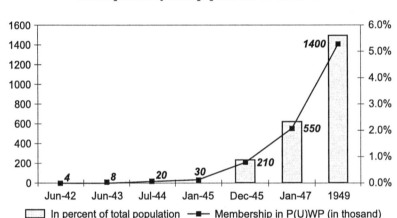

Source: Lotarski (1971) and the website accessed on September 21, 2007 at http://www.polskaludowa.com/dokumenty/pzpr/legitymacja_PZPR.htm.

The process of building state structures, including military force, alternative to the Polish government-in-exile began in earnest in 1943. The Polish I Corps—drawn from Poles who did not succeed in joining the First Polish Army—was established. In 1944 the I Corps was incorporated into the Polish People's Army, which by the end of war numbered 200 thousand soldiers and officers. The task of establishing a foundation of the future Communist government was first assigned to the Union of Polish Patriots headed by Wanda Wasilewska, Stalin's protégé and confidante. Stalin's decision to create the Union in March 1943 coincided with the severance of diplomatic relations with the Polish government-in-exile. The Union was formally established three months later in June 1943. Not surprisingly, the "Polish Patriots" agreed with Soviet demands that the government-in-exile refused to accept, including ceding of eastern territories to the Soviet Union and establishing a "progressive" social system. So did the State National Council established upon Stalin's orders on December 31, 1943 (See Table 1). The date again coincided with the Red Army's entry into German-occupied territories (recognized by Stalin as Poland's) again showing that the presence of the Red Army was the most important reason for the success in imposing the Soviet-style system on Poland.

Table 1: *Establishment of the communist rule in Poland: critical dates*

January 1942	Re-establishment of the Polish Workers' Party, i.e., Communist Party dissolved by Communist International (Comintern) in 1938 in Polish territories under German occupation.
April 1943	The Soviet government breaks off diplomatic relations with Poland's government-in-exile.
June 1943	Union of Polish Patriots (first Communist proto-government) established in the Soviet Union. It recognizes the Curzon line and promises establishing a "progressive social system."
December 1943	Soviet Army crosses the Curzon line.
January 1944	Polish Workers' Party establishes State National Council (since 1945 served as a provisional parliament) as "supreme governing body" under the Soviet occupation.
July 1944	State National Council establishes Polish Committee of National Liberation (in Moscow), which is a provisional government, headed by Osóbka-Morawski (Polish Socialist Party), comprising representatives of the Union of Polish Patriots and the State National Committee.
July 22, 1944	Manifesto of July 22 announces programs of socio-economic reforms including land reform; alliance with the Soviet Union; and establishes jurisdiction of the Red Army over Poland's territory.
April 1945	Treaty of friendship, mutual assistance and post-war relations signed with the Soviet Union.

June 1945	State National Council establishes the Provisional Government of National Unity (dissolved in 1947) with E. Osóbka-Morawski (Polish Socialist Party) as prime minister and W. Gomulka (Polish Workers' Party) and S. Mikołajczyk (United Peasant Party).
July 1945	The United States recognizes the Provisional Government of National Unity.
June 1946	"Three Times Yes" Referendum held in Poland.
January 1947	Elections to the Parliament: the opposition (Polish Peasant Party) removed.
October 1947	Stanisław Mikołajczyk (leader of the opposition) with several of his collaborators escapes from Poland.
December 1948	Unification Congress: Polish Workers' Party takes in Polish Socialist Party and becomes Polish United Workers' Party.

Although the Red Army fully controlled Poland's territory west of the Curzon line and the takeover could be carried out under its auspices, the general tactical lines adopted by Stalin contained two intertwined components: gradual eliminating the opposition, while observing ostensibly the "sticky points" of the Yalta conference,[36] and careful disguising of real intentions to disorient both local citizens and the Western powers. Hence, the communists promised land reform without mentioning the prospect of collectivization: the communist party did not bear adjective "communist" in its name; democratic institutions and procedures, albeit completely meaningless, were maintained.

Gradual change was also part of disguise or camouflage, a technique used by Lenin twenty-six years earlier. Communists employed it in Poland after 1944. The pattern was straightforward. As a point

---

[36] ".... the decisions of the Yalta conference included two "sticky" points. One was that the Provisional Government would be enlarged after representatives of the Big Three (Molotov plus the British and American ambassadors in Moscow) held conferences with representative Poles from London and Poland. In the second place, the Russians had promised to allow elections in Poland, where all "anti-fascist" parties would be allowed to compete. Stalin thought the elections might be held within a month." (Ulam, *op. cit.*, p. 378).

of departure, they sought to create a broad coalition of the left while eliminating the "right-wing" parties. The coalition government would be established with "cosmetic" ministerial portfolios offered to other parties with communists retaining control over key ministries such as ministry of public security or information. Then, they would eliminate competitors within the leftist camp, and finally impose a strict discipline within the party to eliminate internal "factions."

The pattern was clearly repeated in post-1944 Poland. The first move made by Polish Committee of National Liberation established on July 21, 1944 in Moscow was to co-opt "moderate" elements from the government-in-exile in London and assure their participation in the Provisional Government, which, of course, would not be headed by a communist. They were persuaded to return to Poland, and eventually join the communist-controlled government of "national unity." This was not easy, but—under combined British and American pressures— the prime minister of the government-in-exile, Stanisław Mikołajczyk, leader of the Polish Peasant Party, became the second deputy prime minister of the Provisional Government of National Unity.

The irony is that during Mikołajczyk's tenure as Deputy Prime Minister his government oversaw the campaign against the underground forces numbering around 35,000 people. The warfare was most ferocious in the November 1945 – July 1946 period coinciding with the "Three Times Yes" referendum. It is estimated that around 10,000 insurgents were either killed or imprisoned before the underground forces had been wiped out.[37] But this, a defense of soviet interests, did not change the perceived imperative of an exclusive communist takeover.

The next step on the road to assure the hegemony of communists was to neutralize the influence of Mikołajczyk's party, which required time. His party became the most important opposition force in the country sharing with the Polish Workers' Party commitment to land reform and nationalization of some sectors of the economy. Apparently alarmed by the results of free parliamentary elections carried in Hungary on November 5, 1945,[38] the communists decided to delay

---

[37] Susanne Lotarski, "The Communist Takeover in Poland," in Thomas T. Hammond ed., *The Anatomy of Communist Takeovers* (New Haven: Yale University Press, 1971) p. 362.

[38] The Independent Party of Smallholders, receiving 57 percent of the popular vote, was a clear winner with communists getting less than 20 percent.

the elections in Poland. Even communist electoral success in Yugoslavia, Albania and Bulgaria did not appease their anxiety. It is interesting
to note that Stalin urged Gomułka not to delay the elections for the
following reasons: people returning from England would vote against
communists; the opponents would organize better; and the economic
situation would deteriorate.[39] The extra time was used to establish a
"Democratic Bloc," which consisted of communists (Polish Workers'
Party), and two splinter groups from other parties: the Polish Socialist
Party and the Peasant Party. The communist leadership extended also
an invitation to the United Peasant Party (PSL) to join the Bloc on a
common electoral list. However, the offer was rejected. With a membership of half a million people, leadership consisting of well known
and respected politicians and an efficient organization covering the
country, the PSL had no reason to join the Bloc. On the contrary, its
raison d'être was to present itself as the leading opposition force to the
communist regime. It asked for the elimination of the Ministry of Public Security (the notorious political police) and Ministry of Information
and Propaganda and the liberation of all political prisoners. It came
out with a democratic program offering a clear alternative to the communist rule.

In February 1946, four rounds of talks were held between representatives of the Communist Party and the PSL during which the peasant politicians were under considerable pressure to join the Bloc. The
PSL was ready to agree only under the condition that 75 percent of
the slots on common electoral lists would go to the "representatives of
villages." This obviously was not unacceptable to the other side. Fear-
ing the defeat, Władysław Gomułka took advantage of a casual remark
made by Mikołajczyk about the possibility of a constitutional referendum. On April 5, 1946, the "Democratic Bloc" adopted the proposal
of a referendum. It consisted of three questions: Are you in favor of
eliminating the Senate? Do you approve of social reforms (most of all
the agricultural reform)? Do you support Poland's western frontier as
decided in Potsdam?

---

[39] See "Document No. 1: Gomulka's memorandum of a conversation with
Stalin," in Andrzej Werblan, "The Conversation between Wladyslaw Gomulka and Joseph Stalin on 14 November 1945," *Cold War International History Project Bulletin 11*, Woodrow Wilson Center, Washington, D.C., Winter
1998, p. 136.

This placed the PSL in a very difficult situation. First, the PSL had traditionally fought for land reform and had always been in favor of eliminating the Senate. Second, to oppose the new Western frontiers of Poland while the Eastern territories were already lost to the USSR would be suicidal. The PSL accepted the challenge and in order to distinguish itself from its competitor, it called upon its supporters to say "no" to the first question, i.e., to oppose elimination of the Senate. The referendum served the communists not only as a "training ground," but also as a way to delay parliamentary elections. As Andrzej Paczkowski noted: "The intention was among others to gain a better orientation in the geographical distribution of opposition's influence, to prepare administration for the control of results, and to mobilize and develop the apparatus of repression."[40]

As Stalin had predicted earlier, the difficult economic situation in the country as well as the manifest presence of the Soviet soldiers and their excesses did not favor the Bloc. But the powerful communist controlled machine of propaganda and repression was put in motion to subdue and terrorize into voting "Three Times Yes." Members of the PSL were removed from all positions of authority, and some local chapters of the Party were closed by the police under the pretext of collaboration with the "reactionary underground." The PSL daily newspaper was subject to increasingly frequent interventions, and its distribution was made more and more difficult. Thousands of members of the Party were subjected to "preventive arrests." These are just some of the irregularities that took place during the referendum.

According to Andrzej Paczkowski (1995), the communist leadership decided on 3 or 4 July to make public the completely "cooked" results showing an overwhelming victory of the Bloc. In fact, over three-quarters of the voters opposed the Bloc by answering "no" either to all questions or to the question whether the senate should be abolished.[41] That was a resounding defeat for the communists, but their power rested on other factors than mere popular support. After the

---

[40] Andrzej Paczkowski, *Pół wieku dziejów Polski, 1939–1989* [Half century of Poland's history, 1939–1989] (Warsaw: Wydawnictwo Naukowe PWN, 1995), p. 189.

[41] According to figures made public two weeks after over two thirds of the voters expressed support for the "Three Times Yes." See Paczkowski, *op. cit.*, pp. 192–3.

referendum, the Polish Workers' Party made another unsuccessful attempt to co-opt the PSL. But it was rejected. With the date set for the
parliamentary elections, the final act of the imposition of the Soviet-
style system began: preparations for the elections that communists *had
to* win. It seemed they were in a very strong position to obtain an easy
electoral victory, as the communist grip on the country continued to
grow stronger. The redistribution of wealth and rapid advancement of
young people from lower classes, uneducated and ready to do whatever
the new masters told them to do, helped build an effective apparatus
of terror, while the loss of hope for support from the West undermined
the morale of the opposition.

Furthermore, another unfortunate intervention from a former
Western ally in the struggle against Nazism, the USA, was a boost to
the Communists. On September 5, 1946, during his speech in Stuttgart, the American secretary of state, Mr. James Byrnes announced
that the Polish western frontier was to be decided in the "final treaty"
and that its final shape should not be taken for granted.[42] This gave
the communist camp an opportunity to start an anti-American campaign portraying Mikołajczyk and his party as "lackeys of American
imperialists."

Yet, the communists left nothing to chance: the "victory" of the
communist bloc was very carefully planned. Some leading politicians
from the PSL were arrested; "unknown" perpetrators murdered over
a hundred local PSL activists. As Lotarski writes, "The Party's cadres
were reduced through assassinations, arrests of Party leaders, dismissal
of local government officials belonging to the Party, and harassment
of Party adherents [...]. The terror [...] became particularly intense
just prior to the parliamentary elections in January, 1947."[43] All decisions concerning the membership of electoral commissions, names on
the party lists (opposition included) and electoral districts were made
by the leadership of the communist party. In ten out of fifty-two regions, authorities nullified the lists of PSL candidates on some invented grounds. Collective voting of organized groups, like soldiers, was

---

[42] Its full text was published in "Department of State Bulletin," 1946, No. 376,
pp. 496–501. Materski discusses political implications of this speech. Materski, *op. cit.*, p. 150.

[43] Lotarski, *op. cit.*, p. 357.

common. Last, but not least, written instructions were prepared for district electoral commissions on how to rig elections.

Contrary to expectations, the implementation of instructions was critical to the Bloc's electoral triumph. They were diligently followed resulting in a massive electoral fraud. PSL was officially reported to obtain a mere 10 percent of the total vote. Had it been anywhere close to a real number, PSL members would have to vote communist. The scope of electoral fraud can be only indirectly assessed. From information obtained by PSL activists about the results of elections in 1,300 out of 5,500 districts, PSL candidates won 69 percent of the vote. The official results hardly reflected the real numbers prompting a popular wisecrack: "what a magic ballot box: you vote Mikołajczyk and Gomułka comes out!"

The rigging of parliamentary elections was indeed massive: but the formal obligation *vis-à-vis* Stalin's Western Allies was met; Poland had popular elections. The PSL continued to be subjected to an all-out campaign launched by the communists who resorted to all means of terror available to them thanks to control of police and information. Stanislaw Mikołajczyk, warned of an imminent arrest, had to flee Poland and his party was broken. He managed to escape thanks to the help of US and British embassies, Mikołajczyk's arrest and trial in Poland would have been another embarrassment to both governments: after all they demanded that he resign as prime minister of the Polish government-in-exile and return to a Poland already occupied by the Red Army. Some of his colleagues succeeded in fleeing as well. Others spent years in jail, however,[44] an unknown number of young people disappeared without a trace, many of them executed without trial.

The process of establishing full hegemony was not finished until the next step was taken to subsume the Polish Socialist Party, despite its close cooperation with the communists. Its relative independence stood in the way of achieving full monopoly of power by the communists. Resorting to a combination of sticks and carrots, the Polish Socialist Party was forced to merge with the Polish Workers' Party in December, 1948, to create the Polish United Workers Party. Thus, political pluralism was

---

[44] At the beginning of 1950s, there were over forty thousand political prisoners in Poland (Paczkowski, *Pół wieku dziejów Polski*, p. 259).

dealt the final blow. In order to complete the process of setting up Stalin's system, whatever was left of economic freedoms following earlier nationalization of industry and banking had to be repressed. The late 1940s witnessed the elimination of small private firms and the introduction of central planning. As a result, both politics and economics lost their distinctive features as autonomous distinguishable spheres. Poland was thus saddled with Stalin's system for the next four decades, although its implementation was never completed.

In Lieu of Conclusions:
Unique Features of Transition to People's Poland

The Soviet takeover of Poland was unique in at least five respects. First, it spanned over a longer period of time than in other Central European countries as it occurred in two phases: the first phase took place in 1939 when the Soviet Union annexed 40 percent of Poland's territory and embarked upon massive deportations of Poles to the northern and eastern parts of the Soviet Union. The second phase took place in 1944–48 following the crossing of the Curzon line by the Soviet Army in January 1944. By 1948 political forces opposed to the Soviet rule were effectively eliminated and the stage was set for the imposition of the Soviet-style communism.

Second, Poland was the only member of the anti-German coalition that lost the right to self-determination after victory over Germany. She was forced to subject both her foreign and domestic policy to the Soviet empire's control. Throughout World War II, her government continued to exist both abroad and in occupied Poland. It went into exile, first to Paris and, after the Nazi invasion of France, to London. In Poland, an "underground state," with a legislative, executive, and judiciary powers, an underground administration, an educational system and an army (Home Army) loyal to the government-in-exile existed in Polish territories under German occupation. In 1945 the US, Great Britain, and France joined the Soviet Union in withdrawing its recognition of the government-in-exile and *de jure* sanctioning Stalin's conquest of Poland.

Third, Poles did manage to put up a very strong resistance to the imposition of the Soviet rule. But it happened in the context of having suffered the harshest and the longest Nazi occupation. In addition, the Poles leaving east of the Curzon line had also experienced the Soviet occupation, which was equally cruel, albeit shorter.

Fourth, because of its geographical location, gaining control over Poland was the key to the Soviet geopolitical position in Europe and, consequently, superpower status. Therefore, the option of "Finlandization," that is, the absence of sovereignty in foreign policy together with the right not to have a Stalinist system internally, was not feasible. Geography was not in favor of it. Even with a non-communist and dependent Poland, the Soviet reach into Europe would have been greatly curtailed. So would have been Stalin's freedom to maneuver in other parts of Central and Eastern Europe. Therefore, it comes as no surprise that Stalin thought that Poland was the biggest war reward.[45]

Fifth, the task of establishing People's Poland was not an easy one. Poland had been a member of the anti-German alliance since 1939, with a well organized underground administration, and a Home Army of 350,000 soldiers, not counting those who fought in the West or for whom joining the Polish troops under Soviet command was the only chance to escape from the Gulag Archipelago. Many Poles resisted militarily the imposition of communism. Moreover, before the Second World War, the communist support in Poland had been marginal, and their role in the anti-Nazi underground was insignificant. Stalin promised his Western Allies to respect the rules of democracy in Poland and to organize free elections immediately after the liberation. Stalin felt unable to renege on this promise, while at the same he could not comply with it. In consequence, he had to compromise and fell well short of imposing all components of the system that he built for the Soviet Union in the 1930s.

In sum, it seems that the initial conditions of implementing a communist regime played an important role in determining its future. The strategic purpose from the point of view of local communists was to gain full control of the country. If successful, they created problems for the metropolis, as they did not need Moscow's support to remain

---

[45] According to Stanislaw Szwalbe, member of a delegation of the Polish Lublin, headed by Boleslaw Bierut, that held talks in Moscow in 1945, Joseph Stalin said in his address that *"Polsza eto samyj bolszij trofiej vojny"* (Poland is our biggest trophy of the war). Source: late Professor Edward Lipinski in a conversation with Antoni Kaminski.

in power; lack of success created the problem of political instability which absorbed the attention of the metropolis. A good example of the first case is Tito's Yugoslavia, of the second—Poland, where people revolted against communism three times on a grand scale (1956, 1970, 1980), and twice on a smaller scale (1968, 1976). Thus, from Moscow's standpoint, there was an optimum level of dependence of a satellite country: an excessive level of independence as well as an excess of dependence always spelled trouble.

Part Three

STALINISM
AND
HISTORIOGRAPHY

JÁNOS RAINER

Revisiting Hungarian Stalinism

The concept of Stalinism is no longer a subject of wide debate in Hungary. There is still a lot of interest in the Stalinist period of Hungarian history, but less than there was, say, during the change of system, 15 or 20 years ago. Though Stalinism and its period form a common subject of discussion, the discourse takes a declarative, rather than interrogative form. Stalinism is understood and evaluated differently in Hungary today than 15 or 20 years ago, and differently again from 30 or even 50 years ago, when the concept first appeared in Hungarian parlance.

I will begin by clarifying the meaning of two concepts in the context of this study: of Stalinism and of *Hungarian* Stalinism. This calls for brief consideration of the history of this concept in Hungary. Then I will present three periods in the historiography of Hungarian Stalinism. The third part sets out to pinpoint the main historical problems raised by Hungarian Stalinism. It is intended also to respond to the question of what features are specific to Hungarian Stalinism. What is the aim and sense of *revisiting* Hungarian Stalinism? Does revisiting also imply revising, and is such a revision necessary and feasible? For my part, I would like to contribute to the consideration of one problem by offering an outline of the political history of how the Soviet-type system was introduced.

A Historical Outline of the Concept

The concept of Stalinism appeared in Hungary quite early and under curious circumstances. It was used by Imre Nagy, Hungary's prime minister in 1953–55. Nagy was among the first to attempt to correct the Stalinist system and to introduce reforms that went further than just corrections. The experiment failed; Nagy was dismissed and later expelled from the communist party. He then lived in internal exile in Budapest and tried to respond to the charges against him in scholarly studies. (His manuscripts circulated among a small group of intellectual friends.)[1] His September 1955 text entitled "A Few Timely Questions Regarding the Application of Marxism-Leninism" sought on the one hand to interpret Stalinism as a political philosophy. Since Lenin's death, Nagy wrote, further development of the Marxist-Leninist *method* had been prevented by "drastic regulations, denunciations and methods of power." On the other hand, Nagy defined "socialism" as the implementation of the Soviet model. This model became exclusive and was copied mechanically because "the Stalinist monopoly of Marxism-Leninism led to domination of the explanation of Marx's and Lenin's teachings and of the workers' parties' politics by views that acknowledged the ways, forms and methods used to build socialism in the Soviet Union as the sole correct way to apply the principles of scientific socialism." Stalinism denies the grounds for existence of any intermediate forms between capitalism and socialism, including one of Nagy's favorite old concepts, the "democratic species of proletarian dictatorship." The transition ought to build on national characteristics: "Our social, economic, and cultural relations, from which we set about the building of socialism, stand very close in many respects to those of the Western capitalist countries." Thus the transition could have come from "more considered, slower, and less painful and burdensome advance," while the Soviet way became "a historical mistake affecting the destiny of socialism."

Nagy went on to write a longer study at the end of 1955: "Timely Moral/Ethical Questions in Hungarian Public Life." There he described the system that was the outcome of *Stalinite policy* as a "degeneration of power." Power was "not imbued with the spirit of socialism and democratism, but with the spirit of minority dictatorship, of Bonapartism." The country might emerge from the resulting crisis, wrote Nagy,

---

[1] Imre Nagy, *On Communism* (New York: Praeger, 1957). The other quotations are also from here, from pp. 3–10, 43–65 *passim*. Instead of the 1957 translation a new one was used, based on Nagy's original text. Thanks to the translator, Brian McLean.

by "eliminating Stalinist policy and leading the country back to the June way."[2]

In his defence that Nagy wrote in Snagov, Romania, after the 1956 Hungarian Revolution he likewise equated Stalinism with the political system that emerged from Stalinite policy. He defined it as "a system of terror against the people that rests on personal or clique dictatorship,"[3] against which, in 1956, the communist reformers had moved in defense of true socialism. The basis of Nagy's critique was moral outrage; it did not lead to final abandonment of Marxism-Leninism, though he was close to doing so by criticizing the role of the party: "The party under our conditions has assumed rule, gained power as the party of the working class, not as the illegal party of the repressed proletarians... [and so] a new type of party is needed."[4] Nagy's critique does not necessarily extend to Stalinism as a political system or its entire practice. It largely remains within a regional framework—criticizing, in other words, the mechanical application of the Soviet (Stalinist) *pattern*. "Peoples and countries are only prepared to accept socialism as well if it ensures them or brings them national independence, sovereignty, and equality of rights. The essence of the Hungarian tragedy is that the concepts of socialism and of national independence have come into conflict."[5] Thus Nagy could keep the prospect of a still undefined (democratic or people's-democratic) socialism open, a hope in historical philosophical terms. To this end, in Snagov, Nagy also raised the concept of a so-called people's-democratic transition to socialism to a theoretical plane. To this he added in 1957 the lesson of '56:

> There is no doubt that the Hungarian Revolution would have triumphed... if the revolution had achieved its social and national goals; if a new road of transition from capitalism to socialism had come about; if a new type of democratic development in the direction of socialism appeared, which displayed essential differences from today's identical type of people's democracies; and if the concepts socialism, democracy, independence, sovereignty, etc.—the whole socialist

---

[2] This was Nagy's term for the corrective course pursued after June 1953.

[3] Imre Nagy, *Snagovi jegyzetek: Gondolatok, emlékezések: 1956–1957* [Snagov notes: Ideas and memories, 1956–1957] (Budapest: Gondolat Kiadó/Nagy Imre Alapítvány, 2006), p. 133.

[4] *Ibid.*, p. 147.

[5] *Ibid.*, p. 127.

terminology shorn of Stalinism—had returned to their original, true Marxist content and essence.[6]

The essence of the old, abandoned, but, at the same time, new transition was first, national independence of each country embarking on the socialist road. Second, a multiparty system of state and society, but with hegemony for the Marxist parties. Third, "the revolutionary spontaneity of the broad masses of people" or the importance of local revolutionary committees and workers' councils. The working class, according to Nagy, sought, through the workers' councils, to "ensure institutionally actual state power for itself... [so that] power should not be exercised on its behalf by a clique and its bureaucratic apparatus, in the name of the working class."[7]

Imre Nagy's ideas arose from the analysis of political practice. He relied in this on the so-called Blum Theses devised by Georg Lukács at the end of the 1920s, which started out from Hungarian conditions in recommending a democratic stage in the transition from capitalism to socialism. Lukács himself made an active contribution to the critique of Stalinism in 1956. But Lukács did not practice political criticism. As he remarked in an interview at the end of his life, he undertook (or would have undertaken) to offer an "ideology" for the reform of Stalinism.[8] During the philosophy debate in late spring of 1956 in the Petőfi Circle, the forum of the reform-communist intelligentsia, Lukács criticized Stalinism for impeding the steady development of Marxist philosophy and science by reducing them to static, immutable dogmas.[9] Lukács defined Stalinism as a *method*, contrasting it with true Marxism, for which he had hopes of a renaissance. He contrasted the described method of authoritarian dogmatism with the method of free research

---

[6] *Ibid.*, p. 126–7.

[7] *Ibid.*, 157.

[8] György Lukács, *Megélt gondolkodás: Életrajz magnószalagon* [Experienced Thought: A Biography on Tapes] (Budapest, 1989).

[9] "György Lukács felszólalása és zárszava a Petőfi Kör 1956. jún. 15-i filozófiai vitáján" [Contribution and concluding words of Georg Lukács at the philosophy debate of the Petőfi Circle, June 15, 1956]. In András B. Hegedüs and János M. Rainer eds., *A Petőfi Kör vitái—hiteles jegyzőkönyvek alapján* [The Petőfi Circle debates—based on original minutes] Vol. II (Budapest: Kelenföld Kiadó/ELTE, 1989) pp. 67–74, 92–4.

and debate based on recognition of reality and constant criticism. The excited audience at the Petőfi Circle interpreted his words as political criticism, of course, and Lukács, who had been heavily criticized at the end of the 1940s, was rehabilitated, which was undoubtedly a political act. But Lukács did not present an ideology to the anti-Stalinist communists of the 1950s. And the reason was not, as he explained in an interview, that Nagy had not approached him for that purpose (or any other). Lukács was even more cautious than Nagy, but at the same time more optimistic. He steered clear of offering a political ideology because that would have entailed analysing and criticizing the Soviet-type system as a whole. It would have involved sizing up the *history* of Stalinism, which he did not do. He stuck to the thesis of the homogeneity of the society produced by the Stalinist system. "The Marxists of the *thaw* felt that to preserve the class antagonisms of Soviet-type society could only help the conservative forces... The task—the Marxists of the thaw felt—was simply to find the means by which socialist goals could be realized. Stalinist policy in that interpretation appeared as a gigantic historical mistake."[10] In 1968, Lukács contrasted Stalinist bureaucratic socialism with true socialist democracy. In doing so, he did not cite the Hungarian workers' councils, but the direct democracy of the Soviets in 1917.[11] After the occupation of Czechoslovakia, he arrived, according to his memoirs, at a point of rating the entire experiment begun in 1917 as a failure.

Where Lukács never trod, some of his disciples would. But that entailed examining the lessons of '56. Efforts to integrate Lukács were made by the Kádár regime, as it broke with Stalinism in some respects and introduced a modified version of the Soviet system. But it marginalized Lukács's disciples and then "disowned" them, denying them publicity at home and squeezing them out of the country.

The first generation of Lukács's disciples, notably Ágnes Heller and Ferenc Fehér, adapted Hannah Arendt's concept of totalitarianism to their critique of Stalinism. Their subject of analysis was the Soviet

---

[10] Marc Rakovski (György Bence and János Kis), *A szovjet típusú társadalom marxista szemmel* [Soviet-type society through Marxist eyes] (Paris: Magyar Füzetek, 1983), pp. 189–90.

[11] György Lukács, *Demokratizálás ma és holnap* [Democratization today and tomorrow] (Budapest: Magvető, 1988). Published in English as *The Process of Democratization* (Albany: State University of New York Press, 1991).

system as a whole. When examining the legitimacy of the Soviet system, Heller pointed out the distinctions between Jacobin-Leninism (the terroristic/totalitarian Stalinist system), and post-Stalinism (non-terroristic totalitarian system), whose legitimacy rests on *tradition*.[12] Heller's analysis saw Stalinism as a historical stage of the Soviet-type political system. Stalinism evolved from the first stage and determined the second in many respects, but it is not identical with either.

The second generation of Lukács's disciples, principally György Bence and János Kis, set out in the 1970s to produce a Marxist (class-based) analysis of the Soviet-type societies. What Lukács had pointed to in the Petőfi Circle remained a problem for Bence and Kis in the mid-1970s. For want of a current conceptual apparatus to analyze existing socialism, they termed Stalinism as the "first," emerging stage of Soviet-type society. By that time they could start from the same point as the historiography of Stalinism would: from a completed story, whose effects nonetheless are highly topical. They did not define Stalinism, but the picture of the phenomenon is easily assembled from their analysis. Stalinism begins with the announcement of the great industrialization program and introduction of central economic planning. The function of Stalinism is to perform the Marxian "original accumulation," but, according to Bence and Kis, it is far from being the one and only inevitable way of doing so. On the contrary, the Stalinist system is what defined the specific complexion and "outcomes" of Soviet original accumulation.[13] The system relies on a bureaucratic ruling class that terminates the autonomy of all other formal organizations, keeps society in a state of perpetual motion, and probes deep into the spheres of private life. "The various waves of cleansing become functional, ensuring that all special interests are subordinate to the exclusive interest of accumulation."[14] At the same time, Stalinism was an ideology as well as a politico-economic system—Bence and Kis supported their thesis with an analysis of the peasantry debate with Bukharin—the ideology of a change whereby "the apparatus imposed its power by force on all the sectors of society that it had not controlled directly before."[15]

---

[12] Ágnes Heller, *A sztálini legitimáció és ami utána következik* [Stalinist legitimization and what follows it] (Paris: Magyar Füzetek 1981), pp. 8, 83–103.
[13] Rakovski, *op. cit.*, pp. 34–8.
[14] *Ibid.*, p. 39.
[15] *Ibid.*, p. 179.

7

At this point, the analysis of Bence and Kis shows some kinship with the section on Stalinism in György Konrád and Iván Szelényi's book. The conceptual framework of Konrád and Szelényi had room for Marx's class theory alongside Max Weber and Károly Polányi. Their book famously talks of the intelligentsia that attains the pinnacle of power as a class within the societies of East European rational redistribution. But in their view, power under Stalinism was exercised by only part of the intelligentsia: the elite of the party bureaucracy, with its feudal attributes. What Konrád and Szelényi meant by feudal was that intellectual expertise was not sufficient to obtain a controlling position, but also required previous merit earned in the labor movement, i.e., a privileged status.[16]

The Hungarian conceptual history of Stalinism does not need to be further discussed here. It is apparent that the concept entered Hungarian discourse quite early, not long after Stalin's death. The contributions to the discourse were unusual initially: they had direct political functions, employed the language of Marxism, began in the border zone between primary and secondary publicity, and gradually spread from there into the terrain of dissident opinion. The ideas of Nagy, Lukács, Heller, Bence, Kis, Konrád, and Szelényi could not appear in Hungarian until 1988–89, during the change in system. The Marxist description of Stalinism was closely related to its critical function. Its perceived goal was the possibility of a de-Stalinized (democratized, humanized) socialism. János Kornai, the Hungarian author, set about providing a systematic description based on the system paradigm of Stalinism just as this perspective and critical function was vanishing. His subtitle, *The Political Economy of Socialism*, signifies that the author uses the conceptual system of economics. Kornai terms the basic version of the Soviet (socialist) system *classical*. His starting point is the political system marked by the undivided power and dominant official

[16] György Konrád and Iván Szelényi, *Az értelmiség útja az osztályhatalomhoz* (Budapest: Gondolat, 1989). Published in English as *The Intellectuals on the Road to Class Power* (Brighton/New York, 1979). For a critical analysis of this, see Gábor Kovács, *Forradalom, életmód, hatalom, kultúra: A politikai gondolkodás jellemzői a hatvanas években* [Revolution, lifestyle, power, culture: Features of political thinking in the 1960s] in: János Rainer M., ed., "Hatvanas évek" Magyarországon ["Sixties" in Hungary] (Budapest: 1956-os Intézet, 2006), pp. 229–32.

ideology of the Marxist-Leninist party. From there it follows that state and semi-state property have a dominant position, and finally, from both of those, the excessive importance of bureaucratic coordination. Then all three derive a number of specific features from the management of the economy and its operating mechanism (plan bargaining, "rush," paternalism, soft budget constraint, forced growth, a chronic economy of shortage, etc.) Although Kornai did not consider the socialist (Soviet) system as a completely closed chapter, he did foresee the demise of the classical system: "In the coherence of the classical system lies its strength, but also its weakness. One might exaggerate slightly by saying it produces a fabric so closely woven that if one strand breaks, it all unravels sooner or later."[17]

Basic Historiographic Features

The authors cited in the last section used the concept of Stalinism in the sense of an ideology and/or a political system. This section deals mainly with the Hungarian historiography of the Stalinist political *system*. Of the literature on the ideological history, let me say only that a quite separate historical discourse developed on this in Hungary after the change of system. Authors who pursue the Marxian methodological tradition, accept the ideology of socialism, and are ready to rework its political program form a relatively closed group. Signals from other frames of reference hardly penetrate their works, and these authors hardly ever react to criticism (apart from a few summary dismissals). However, there has been a lively *internal* exchange of views on Stalinism as a phenomenon of world history, ideology, and system alike. The members of this group are mainly historians who have specialized in Russia, along with some philosophers, economists, and sociologists. They essentially uphold the heritage of Lukács and the Marxist renaissance. "The debate... takes place on three planes," writes Tamás Krausz, historian and Russian specialist, in his preface to a volume summing up the debate on *state social-ism*. "There is a political debate on whether it is at all possible in our

---

[17] János Kornai, *The Socialist System: The Political Economy of Socialism* (Princeton, NJ/Oxford: Princeton University Press/Oxford University Press, 1992), p. 383.

world to reconstruct a socialist tradition on which the groups interested can rely in their daily and more remote anti-capitalist struggles... It is a historical question whether the intelligentsia that is critical of capitalism and considers itself left wing can succeed in finding a point of reference between the interpretation of the past and of the present."[18] The third strand would have to do with social theory and serve to describe the concepts of the description of state socialism. Both the content of the list and the order of its points are revealing.

a. Hungary's first wave of strictly historical literature on Stalinism began appearing in the 1980s, for which the consent of the late Kádárite political leadership was required. One concern of the apparatus was for Hungary and its scholarship to appear acceptable to the world. It was also in its interest to cooperate with the quasi-reformer group of intelligentsia, which it saw as its main support in a threatening world. This group was concerned chiefly with the problem of '56, but unlike the dissidents, it would accept Stalinism as a substitute subject. The literature on Stalinism faced two main issues: access to primary sources, and arriving at a historical verdict and concept. Two radically different solutions were presented by two representative works of the first wave.

Bálint Szabó's work, *The "Fifties,"* was based on archives of the political leadership of the communist party, which nobody had seen before.[19] As the title shows, Szabó has produced a truly Kádárite work. He resolved the difficult problem of terminology by not naming the period of Hungarian Stalinism in *any* way. As for the days of the '56 Hungarian Revolution, he simply left them out of the story, which ends with effective measures by the Kádárite leadership to "correct errors." His account followed the chronology of political history. He used long quotations, so that the book was the first to shed light on the internal disputes among the communist party leadership. That aside, he followed the canon of the period by presenting the years after 1948 as a

---

[18] Tamás Krausz and Péter Szigeti eds. *Államszocializmus: Értelmezések—viták—tanulságok* (State socialism: Interpretations–debates–lessons (Budapest: L'Harmattan–Eszmélet Alapítvány, 2007), pp. 8–9.

[19] Bálint Szabó, *Az "ötvenes évek": Elmélet és politika a szocialista épités első időszakában Magyarországon, 1948–1957* [The "Fifties": Theory and policy of socialist building in the first period in Hungary, 1948–1957] (Budapest: Kossuth, 1986).

period of building socialism, whose achievements were "darkened" by the mistakes of Mátyás Rákosi and his clique.

No party archives were opened before the economic historians Iván Pető and Sándor Szakács, but they were able to use the vast documentation of the economic apparatus. Their monumental summary of economic history from 1945 went up to the 1968 reform, but remained a skeleton: the second volume, on the period from the reform until the mid-1980s, never came out.[20] Pető and Szakács were pioneers in avoiding any kind of ideological framework. Since they were dealing not only with economic policy, but with the performance of the real economy, they chose the language of descriptive economics. They termed the period of Stalinism that of "directive planning" and emphasized that the autonomy of the economy began to be severely limited in 1945. The economy was being coordinated increasingly by a bureaucracy controlled by politics. The economic project of the communist party resembled ever more closely the first five-year plan in the Soviet Union. Anything further to be said about Stalinism had to be reserved for the *samizdat* publication. (One of the authors, Pető, was a prolific writer of illegal publications.)

b. The second period in the historiography of Hungarian Stalinism began at the end of the 1980s and lasted about a decade.[21] Scholarly and public discourse about Stalinism was liberated, becoming in fact one of

---

[20] Iván Pető and Sándor Szakács, *A hazai gazdaság négy évtizedének története 1945–1985* [The four-decade history of the domestic economy, 1945–1985], Vol. I (Budapest: Közgazdasági és Jogi Könyvkiadó, 1985).

[21] On changes in Hungarian historiography after 1989, see several studies by Gábor Gyáni, including *Történetírásunk az ezredfordulón* [Our history writing at the turn of the millennium], in *Történészdiskurzusok* [Historians' discourses] (Budapest: L'Harmattan, 2002), pp. 35–55. Most recently there has been his book, *Relatív történelem* [Relative history] (Budapest: Typotex, 2007), especially pp. 285–97. More recent contributions have included Balázs Trencsényi and Péter Apor, *Fine-tuning the Polyphonic Past: Hungarian Historical Writing in the 1990s*, in Sorin Antohi, Balázs Trencsényi, and Péter Apor eds. *Narratives Unbound: Historical Studies in Post-Communist Eastern Europe* (Budapest–New York: Central European University Press, 2007), pp. 1–99; Sándor Horváth, "A mindennapi szocializmus és a jelenkortörténet: Nézőpontok a szocialista korszak kutatásához" [Everyday socialism and contemporary history: Criteria for research into the socialist period], *Századvég*, New series, Vol. 40, No. 2 (2006).

the most popular historical subjects. But not in its own right—rather it was written and spoken of as the antecedent of the '56 Revolution. No comprehensive monograph on Hungarian Stalinism appeared, and after a few initial attempts, there was no *historical* debate about it either. However, this second phase brought one or two works that analyzed the beginning and end of the period well.

Early in 1989, the Hungarian Communist Government set up a commission of historians and jurists to unearth the "illegalities of the Fifties." It was some time after the first democratic elections when the historians' group issued its report.[22] The text is nothing more than a largely unstructured mass of data, with practically no conceptual framework at all. But the report still set the thematic framework for discourse on Hungarian Stalinism for a long time to come. This meant initially a history of the *wrongs* and *torments* suffered by society.

As for interpretation, Marxism-Leninism died almost at once in 1989, or shrank into a subculture. "Objectivity" was emphasized by some historians, mainly those who had dealt with contemporary history in the 1980s. The broader profession did the same. The most common view of history went rather like this: "Enough of explanations, let's hear the facts!" This reflected the mistaken belief that all kinds of interpretation operate in the way the communist one did. The appropriate genre for it was a descriptive historical chronicle, light on interpretation and concentrated largely on the communist-led political center of power. Alongside this, a vast memoir literature accumulated and there was a renaissance of source publications.

The late 1990s brought a succession of national historical summaries, mainly for educational purposes. But there is no point looking for any analytical framework, for instance, in a comprehensive work by major contemporary historians at ELTE University in Budapest, the country's largest. They saw it as their task to sum up the facts.[23] The only evaluative remark they make on the period of Stalinism is that it resulted from foreign military occupation.

---

[22] Valéria Révai ed., *Törvénytelen szocializmus: A Tényfeltáró Bizottság jelentése* [Illegal socialism: Report of the Fact-finding Commission] (Budapest: Zrínyi/ Új Magyarország, 1991).

[23] Jenő Gergely and Lajos Izsák, *A huszadik század története: Magyar századok* [History of twentieth century: Hungarian centuries] (Budapest: Pannonica, 2000).

STALINISM REVISITED

A far more significant summary of Hungary's twentieth-century history came from a colleague of theirs, Ignác Romsics, one of the best-known figures in contemporary Hungarian history writing. His monograph is by far the highest-standard work of the second period. It shifts the emphasis from politics towards social and cultural history. Yet Romsics views Stalinism within a paradigm that describes it as a basically political system. He treats it as one of the totalitarian systems. As he views it, the integral "development" of Hungarian history was broken in 1945, or at the latest at the end of the 1940s. Stalinism is a total system introduced under Soviet pressure after a Soviet pattern. Stalin and his Hungarian agents were aiming at a Soviet-type transformation from the outset in 1945. Things changed somewhat due to '56—totalitarian dictatorship was tamed under János Kádár into a basically authoritarian system.[24] That does not mean that any kind of communist project can be reformed. Though Romsics does not cite it explicitly, he was influenced basically by the Kornai model and logic.

Historiography that views Stalinism through the totalitarian paradigm generally sees it as a product of the Cold War.[25] By the time the concept began to be used in Hungarian historiography in the 1980s, it had been subject to serious challenges in the West for several decades. It was also used widely in the thinking of the Eastern European opposition.[26] The totalitarian paradigm became the most widespread in the second period of Hungarian contemporary historiography after the change of system. The resulting narratives were very varied. At one extreme was Romsics's high-standard monograph, but at the other, "works" in which totalitarianism was just a rhetorical element used in

---

[24] Ignác Romsics, *Magyarország története a XX. században* (Budapest: Osiris, 1999). Published in English as *Hungary in the Twentieth Century* (Budapest: Corvina, 1999).

[25] Sheila Fitzpatrick ed., *Stalinism: New Directions* (London: Routledge, 2000), pp. 1–14. In Hungarian, see Eszter Bartha, *A sztálinizmus a régi és az új historiográfiában: a jelenség meghatározásának elméleti és módszertani problémái* [Stalinism in the old and new historiography: theoretical and methodological problems of defining the problem], in Tamás Krausz ed., *A sztálinizmus hétköznapjai* [Everyday Stalinism] (Budapest: Nemzeti Tankönyvkiadó, 2003), pp. 15–39.

[26] On the new wave of the totalitarian concepts in Eastern Europe, see Jacques Rupnik, "Totalitarianism revisited," in John Keane ed., *Civil Society and the State* (New York/London: Verso, 1988), pp. 263–89.

a discourse of unreflective and undifferentiated anti-communism that cannot be placed in any category of scholarly history writing. As one younger historian put it, the latter had simply changed the communist salvation story into one of anti-communist conspiracy.[27]

Only one line of the totalitarian paradigm/neutral factology appeared in the 1990s. The best example is the work of the Hungarian historian Iván T. Berend, and it may not be by chance that he wrote in the United States, not Hungary. Berend looks at Stalinism in an East European context and represents an old concept conceived before the theory of totalitarianism—that of modernization.[28] In his works before 1989, Berend followed Gerschenkron in arguing consistently that the state was the modernizer of the economy in this region. That process he saw as continuing after 1945. Stalinism was simply a form of a continuing integral historical formation. The communist program for transforming society was a response to real problems, and the project itself the object of constant reform and transformation. Of course the Hungarian adaptation of Stalinism *also* imposed serious burdens and involved excesses that were superfluous to it.

c. The 2000s brought a change of outlook, subject-matter and generation in the historiography of Hungarian Stalinism while the trends of the second period continued. There appeared a new group of young people brought up mainly as social historians, whose works differ fundamentally from those hitherto.[29] A big influence early in their careers

---

[27] Tamás Kende, "Kik azok a kommunisták?" [Who are those communists?] *Beszélő*, December, 2003.

[28] Iván T. Berend, *Central and Eastern Europe 1944–1993: Detour from the Periphery to the Periphery* (Cambridge: Cambridge University Press, 1996).

[29] Pál Germuska, *Indusztria bűvöletében: Fejlesztéspolitika és a szocialista városok* [Industry's spell: Development policy and socialist towns] (Budapest: 1956-os Intézet, 2004); Sándor Horváth, *A kapu és a határ: Mindennapi Sztálinváros* [Gate and border: Daily Sztálinváros] (Budapest: MTA Történettudományi Intézete, 2004); György Majtényi, *A tudomány lajtorjája: Társadalmi mobilitás és új értelmiség Magyarországon a II. világháború után* [The science ladder: Social mobility and the new intelligentsia in Hungary after World War II] (Budapest: Gondolat/Magyar Országos Levéltár, 2006); Eszter Zsófia Tóth, *"Puszi Kádár Jánosnak": Munkásnők élete a Kádár-korszakban mikrotörténeti megközelítésben* ["Kiss to János Kádár." Life of working women in the Kádár period—a micro-historical approach] (Budapest: Napvilág, 2007).

and on the approach they adopted was Gábor Gyáni, the Hungarian interpreter of post-modern historiography. These young historians deal with the history of daily life especially of the lower class (workers male and female, first-generation members of the intelligentsia, etc.) They are fond of using the methods of micro-history and historical anthropology. They pay great attention to recollected history, dealing to a great extent with interviews and other personal documents. They deliberately integrate the findings of other disciplines, from sociology to literature. They are deliberate in theoretical terms, reacting sensitively and rapidly to developments in international scholarly discourse. They keep their distance both from the history of politics and from historicizing political discourse.

From the outset, the new generation rejected the totalitarian model. They also questioned the significance of factographic chronicling, and rejected histories of suffering and grievance based on normative moral imperatives. They turned for their concept of Stalinism primarily to the German trend of *Alltagsgeschichte* and to the historical works of Sheila Fitzpatrick and Stephen Kotkin.[30] In his book on daily life of Sztálinváros, the Hungarian Magnitogorsk founded in 1951, Sándor Horváth took Kotkin's book as his direct source. Kotkin's theory of Stalinism as a civilization has had a great influence on the new generation of Hungarian historians, although only one chapter of the *Magnetic Mountain* has appeared in Hungarian. The new approaches, methodologies and parlances have spread to traditional research fields such as political history (turning from the politics of the communist party leadership to that of local branches and membership recruitment),[31] and brought renewal to political biography.[32]

---

[30] Stephen Kotkin, *Magnetic Mountain: Stalinism as a Civilization.* (Berkeley/Los Angeles/London: University of California Press, 1995); Sheila Fitzpatrick, *Everyday Stalinism: Ordinary life in extraordinary times: Soviet Russia in the 1930s* (New York: Oxford University Press, 1999).

[31] Kende, *op. cit.*

[32] György Kövér, *Losonczy Géza* (Budapest: 1956-os Intézet, 1998).

Hungarian Stalinism: Its Introduction

In 1999, Sheila Fitzpatrick defined *everyday* Stalinism as follows: "I use it here as a shorthand for the complex of institutions, structures and rituals that made up the habitat of *Homo Sovieticus* in the Stalin era. Communist party rule, Marxist-Leninist ideology, rampant bureaucracy, leader cults, state control over production and distribution, social engineering, affirmative action on behalf of workers, stigmatization of "class enemies," police surveillance, terror, and the various informal personalistic arrangements whereby people at every level sought to protect themselves and obtain scarce goods were all parts of Stalinist habitat."[33] I think this fruitful approach offers the most chances of distinguishing local variants of Stalinism (in this case the Hungarian variant). The Soviet variety of *Homo Stalinicus* obviously differed from the Hungarian one—in language, traditions, thinking, compliance, strategies, and tactics. This approach leaves a very large number of new questions pending about the Hungarian version of Stalinism, as many as there are aspects of daily life.

Yet I am not choosing this route as my starting point, but the system model of János Kornai. According to this, Hungarian Stalinism does not exhibit many differences from the structural point of view, at least not in the period of *high Stalinism*, which lasted in Hungary only from 1948 to 1963, or possibly only to the first correction attempt in 1953. The distinctions become clear if the *historical* development of the system is examined. Stalinism, whether understood as a political system or as a civilization, was the system and civilization of an empire. It was imbued, especially after World War II, by the great Russian imperial tradition (although it differed from it as well).[34] The Stalinism of the center of the empire could not be quite the same as that of its periphery. Hungary did not face some of the modernization tasks to which Stalinism in Russia was responding. But there were other tasks, such as dynamizing a social structure shot through in many respects

---

[33] Fitzpatrick, *op. cit.*, pp. 3–4.
[34] See Ákos Szilágyi, "Állam és birodalom" [State and empire], in Csaba Gombár and Hédi Volosin eds., *Nem élhetek birodalom nélkül* [I can't live without an empire] (Budapest: Helikon/Korridor, 2002), pp. 125–208.

with closed, rigid traditions, or broadening political participation. The question of *democratic* (i.e., not primarily technical), *cultural modernization* was also on the agenda in the more westernized region of Central Europe, differing in this respect from Russia. The communist project was only one possible and existing scenario for radical intervention—those of the Hungarian Populists, or even the social democrats or some groups of agrarians were not notably cautious either.

Hungarian Stalinism also differed in some ways from that of neighboring countries. One was the total national deficit. Introducing the Soviet system into Hungary at least left the formal criteria of statehood (in contrast with the Baltic states, for instance). Stalinism in Poland, Czechoslovakia, and Romania, though, went hand in hand with reconstituting statehood and/or restoring territorial losses. Hungarian national grievances and abasement were probably deeper than those elsewhere. Another probable Hungarian feature was the early and acute crisis involved. Likewise, the post-Stalinist corrective process was deeper and more radical in Hungary than elsewhere in Central Eastern Europe. The Hungarian corrective process led very early to alternatives for reform, and '56 remained a uniquely Hungarian phenomenon, though the crisis spread throughout the empire to every Soviet-type system.

Finally, Hungary was unusual in undergoing a long transition to Stalinism lasting several years. This ties in with a still undecided issue about Hungarian Stalinism: did the Soviet leadership originally want to Sovietize Hungary (or Czechoslovakia) at all? Was there a plan? Was the plan the opposite (i.e., not sovietizing those two countries)? Or was Stalin working "off the cuff"? That issue seems very simple, easily resolved by a single document found in some secret Kremlin archive, except that no such document has yet been found. But there is more to it. Advocates of preconceived Sovietization and a Great Plan argue that Stalinism had nothing to do with the previous course of Hungarian history and broke with all integral development—it was an imposed system in every sense. But those who doubt the existence of a Great Plan or point to cases of local communist autonomy, usually recognize that Stalinism—as a road to modernization or adaptation of the everyday frames of a civilization—was a real response to real challenges, though that interpretation does not deny that Stalinism was imposed by force.

There is also a historiography of how Hungarian Stalinism was introduced. Charles Gati's monograph of the mid-1980s summarized the position resting on the post-revisionist history of the Cold War and a differentiated view of Stalinism.[35] Gati argued that Stalin treated the region conquered in World War II in a different manner. He wanted to Sovietize certain countries and treat others as reserves. His thinking and Soviet policy were marked less by revolutionary intentions than by a sober and cautious review of imperial security interests. Gati also argued that the number of advocates of radical social change in Hungary was highly significant, encompassing half of the population in 1945.

László Borhi's work synthesizes the findings and debates of the 1990s,[36] and builds on the findings of the archive revolution. Borhi, like John Lewis Gaddis, tends to emphasize the role of revolutionary expansionism in Soviet foreign policy. To this he adds the aspect initial of the exploitative victorious state and then of the exploitative colonialist state. According to Borhi, Soviet economic penetration promoted political expansion; Sovietization was not a reactive step in Hungary or Czechoslovakia (for instance, a reaction to the announcement of the Marshall Plan). It was certainly the aim in the first place, even if there was no valid region-wide plan. But Borhi also points out that the local communist leadership appeared more dynamic than Moscow in 1945–47.

Although we still do not know enough about the past Soviet intentions toward Hungary, based on the archival evidence from the 1990s two popular judgments have to be modified. According to the first one Hungary's fate had been decided the moment the Red Army reached Hungarian soil, or even before. The second conviction holds that the Hungarian Communists acted only as Stalin's "agents," fulfilling his great "Plan" of total Sovietization of Eastern Europe including Hungary. The Soviet system was not introduced by one radical change in Hungary after World War II. On the contrary it was the result of a series of changes which came about one after the other.

a. The "plan." Ivan Maisky, deputy commissar for foreign affairs, raised four priorities of Soviet foreign policy in his 1944 *Desirable Principles of a Future World*: security for the Soviet Union (a 30–50 year period of

---

[35] Charles Gati, *Hungary in the Soviet Bloc* (Durham, NC: Duke University Press, 1986).

[36] László Borhi, *Hungary in the Cold War 1945–1956* (Budapest–New York: Central European University Press, 2004).

peace), expansion of the empire (i.e., consolidation of the Soviet territories obtained before and during the war), maintenance of the anti-
fascist coalition for the future, and imposing some kind of democratic
transition in the former enemy countries. As for the last he envisaged
doing it "in the spirit of the popular front and on the basis of broad
democracy... in order to build up true democratic regimes, necessary
measures should be taken with the assistance of other countries, that
is, in the first place, the Soviet Union, the United Kingdom and the
United States. One should not shrink from this intervention into the
internal affairs of other states, because only democratic systems can
guarantee effectively long-term peace."[37]

b. The first Hungarian people's democracy. Hungary was of no primary
importance to the Soviets. As Maisky says, "The Soviet Union is not
concerned with the existence of a strong Hungary," and unlike in Romania's case, there was no hint of particular, i.e., politico-military relations to be developed between the Soviet Union and Hungary. Yet
the provisional Hungarian legislature and government were formed under direct and continuous Soviet surveillance.[38] So Hungary became
a "people's democracy," like defeated Romania and Bulgaria, and formally victorious Poland.

The term "people's democracy" suggests a political structure in
accordance both with the Soviet intention to create a sphere of security in Eastern Europe and with the contents of the Yalta Declaration.
The first obligation was satisfied by the overwhelming majority of local
communists in Parliament and government, and in crucial positions in
the police and public administration (together with the Soviet-domi-
nated Allied Control Commissions, of course.) "Representativeness,"
i.e. at least formal participation in all democratic forces of the provisional "pseudo-coalitions," settled the second obligation. The situation
in Hungary between December 21, 1944 (the convening of the Provisional Assembly) and November 4, 1945 (the parliamentary elections)
by no means corresponded with this scheme.

---

[37] See *Istochnik*, Vol. 4 (1995).

[38] Murashko Islamov and Volokitina Noskova eds. *Vostochnaia Evropa v dokumentakh rossiiskikh arkhivov 1944–1953*, tom I, Sibirskii khronograf (Mos-
cow/Novosibirsk, 1997). Docs. Nos. 23, 25, 29, 33, and 34.

c. From "people's democracy" to democracy: the first change. The parliamentary elections November 4, 1945 brought about a new political situation. While the different political parties in Romania, Bulgaria, Poland and Yugoslavia participated in the elections in unions or blocs, in Hungary real elections took place. Although the parties of the Provisional Assembly had declared in advance their intention to govern together whatever the results would be, the new coalition reflected the real proportion of votes.

In December 1944, before the Hungarian communist leaders returned home, they had been offered quite significant independence by Stalin himself. However in 1945, as Rákosi sent frequent messages to Moscow requesting advice and getting hardly any reply, it turned out that this independence might even be too much. The situation can be explained by Hungary's specific status on the western periphery of the Soviet sphere of interest, a bit too far from the focus of Moscow's attention.[39] Consequently, the Hungarian Communist Party wanted to follow the trend and create a common election bloc, but as it had an almost blind faith in the success of the workers' parties it sought to ally itself only with the social democrats, which Rákosi thought would be enough to secure a parliamentary majority. The Soviet proposal for a wider bloc came only three weeks before the elections—and right after the "united front of the Hungarian Communist Party and the social democrats had been defeated in the municipal elections in Budapest."[40] The self-confident communists maneuvered themselves into a serious failure in the parliamentary elections and the Soviets showed clear aversion to the Hungarian party. A comprehensive 1947 report on its policy found that "in this respect the HCP abandoned the general political line which had prevailed in Yugoslavia, Bulgaria, Romania and Finland, where an electoral bloc of the democratic parties had been set up. That kind of bloc suited the interests of the Soviet Union well and up to the Budapest municipal elections it existed formally in Hungary, too... The HCP obviously tried to resolve the Hungarian question independently of the Soviet Union's general political line and sometimes it did not

---

[39] Gati, *op. cit.*

[40] Ferenc Nagy, *The Struggle Behind the Iron Curtain* (New York: MacMillan, 1948). See also *Vostochnaia Evropa...*, Nos. 98 and 100.

seem to understand this policy."[41] Hungary in early 1946 was still not considered by the Russians to be a "new, people's democracy."[42]

d. From democracy to "people's democracy": the second change. After the election failure, the Hungarian communist leadership came to the conclusion that its primary task was to alter the results (i.e., the vast majority of the Western-oriented democratic Smallholders' Party) by any means, first of all by adopting extra-parliamentary measures. As Rákosi put it in 1947, they made plans for splitting the Smallholders' Party right after the elections. He also intended to discriminate against political opponents by restricting the suffrage.[43] This time, Moscow did not want to keep this fervor under control. On the contrary, the Soviets gave active support to the communists several times. For example, Stalin intervened through the Allied Control Commission, just as negotiations on the formation of the government in November 1945 began, to offset the electoral victory of the smallholders.[44]

The second change can be divided into two stages. The first was the slow transition that started in January 1946, with the establishment of the communist-led Supreme Council of Economic Affairs. It was followed by a mass campaign against the smallholders, thanks to which their group in Parliamentary was shorn of more than 20 members (in March 1946), and by the dissolution of civil and religious associations in July 1946. At the end of 1946, the communist-dominated security police unveiled a quite insignificant alleged conspiracy in which a handful of politicians and bureaucrats of the old regime were said to be involved. Since the group had some contacts with the smallholders, it was like a Christmas gift for the communist leadership—an opportunity to shift from low gear into full throttle. Due to alleged participation

---

[41] *Ibid.*, p. 610.

[42] Boris Ponomarev, "Demokraticheskie preobrazhovanie v osvobozhdennykh stranakh Evropi," *Bolshevik*, Vol. 22, No. 6, March 12, 1946. On Hungarian Communist Party mistakes, see also Moshetov's report to Stalin, RTsKh-IDNI, f. 17. op. 128. d. 1090; and *Vostochnaya Evropa...*, No. 268.

[43] *PIL* (Archive of the Institute for Political History, Budapest) 274. f. 7/123. o. e. Notes of Mátyás Rákosi on the Hungarian Communist Party's first three years. See also *PIL* 274. f. 2/33. o. e. Rákosi's report on Hungarian Communist Party Central Committee session, November 22, 1945.

[44] *Vostochnaia Evropa...*, Nos. 105, 107, 111, and 113.

in the "conspiracy," six members of Parliament, one minister, and the general secretary of the Smallholders Party, Béla Kovács, were arrested, the last by the Soviet military police. Rákosi wanted to go further immediately and sent several messages to Stalin about a far-reaching conspiracy headed by the smallholder prime minister, Ferenc Nagy (with the Western powers in the background). At the end of April, Molotov, warned by the Truman Doctrine, put an end to the zealous Rákosi dream of a great show trial. But he was given the green light again by Stalin when communist ministers were expelled from the French and Italian governments at the beginning of May 1947. Soviet MGB organizations fabricated compromising material about the Hungarian prime minister, who had been vacationing in Switzerland since the beginning of March. Instead of returning home (to certain arrest), Ferenc Nagy chose resignation and exile (on May 30, 1947).

e. "People's democracy" in the Soviet bloc: the third change. So far Soviet policy toward Hungary and other East-Central European countries had fluctuated between caution and decisiveness. The Soviets were prompted to choose conflict with the West by the publication of the Marshall Plan, especially its clear intention to pursue West European integration. While Moscow thought it natural that they should control their sphere of security, the formation of another sphere based on democratic principles seemed unacceptable to them.[45] The first Soviet reaction was to force the Czechoslovak and Polish governments to refuse to participate in the Marshall Plan. There were also radical changes in Soviet intentions to establish some kind of organizational form of cooperation among the communist parties.[46]

By September 1947, when the Cominform meeting started in Szklarska Poręba, the Hungarian Communist Party was assessing its own position very carefully. According to József Révai, "It has not been

---

[45] M.M. Narinskii, "SSSR i plan Marshalla. Po materialam Arkhiva prezidenta RF," *Novaia i noveishaia istoriia,* Vol. 2 (1993), 11–9.

[46] See Grant M. Adibekov, *Kominform i poslovoyonnaya Evropa: Rossiya Molo daya* (Moscow: 1994); Leonid Gibianskii, *Kak vozhnik Kominform, Novaia i noveishaia istoriia,* Vol. 4 (1993); Grant Adibekov, "How the first conference of the Cominform came about," in *The Cominform: Minutes of the Three Conferences 1947/1948/1949* (Milan: Fondazione Giangiacomo Feltrinelli, 1994), pp. 3–9.

decided yet whether there will be a people's democracy or a bourgeois one in Hungary, whether Hungary joins the new democracies or becomes a stronghold of Anglo-American imperialism."[47] Although Zhdanov was not dissatisfied with Révai's report, the Hungarian communists failed to obtain Moscow's approval. In the August 1947 parliamentary elections, only a united front of the four independent coalition parties took part (including the purged smallholders), not a bloc. Despite grave electoral improprieties, the front received slightly more than 60 percent of the votes cast. The Democratic Opposition (the Christian Democrats and the Hungarian Independence Party) got about 40 percent. The results were all the more embarrassing because Rákosi had sent a very optimistic forecast to Moscow two weeks before the elections, estimating that the opposition would poll "less than 15 percent."[48] "The Communist Party... made fatal mistakes in the 1947 electoral campaign, too. [It] overestimated its own power and underestimated that of the reactionary forces," according to a summary report on activity by the Hungarian Communist Party made for Stalin at the end of 1947 by the CPSU International Department.[49]

After Szklarska Poręba, the Hungarian communists decided to "mobilize the masses" instead of using "parliamentary methods." The blocs of parties would have to create mass organizations under communist leadership; they would exclude all other parties from the headquarters of the armed forces, to "limit strictly, and eventually destroy the economic power of the bourgeoisie."[50] In general, the Hungarian Communist Party "would have to change its political line as a whole."[51] And so it happened. Some weeks after the Cominform was founded, the Hungarian Independence Party was suppressed. Within the Central Committee apparatus, elaboration of new principles of socialist economic policy began, with a parallel process of agricultural collectivization. The seminal political event of the third change was the forced fragmentation of the Social Democratic Party and its subsequent absorption into the Hungarian Communist Party in June 1948. This was

---

[47] RTsKhIDNI, f. 77. op. 3. d. 92.
[48] Rákosi's report of August 13, 1947. In *Vostochnaya Evropa...*, No. 231.
[49] RTsKhIDNI, f. 17. op. 128. d. 1090.
[50] *PIL* 274.f . 3/112. o. e. HCP PC Oct. 9, 1947. Report on International Conference, September 22–7, 1947, pp. 35–6.
[51] *Ibid.*, p. 38.

only postponed so late because Stalin, interestingly, advised caution on the Hungarian Communist Party again in late 1947 and early 1948.[52]

f. Soviet system, Soviet bloc: the fourth change. For Moscow, the alignment of the East European countries' foreign policy and political system with Soviet satellite policy claims was not enough. Even minimal divergence from the pattern was considered a risk if there should be Cold War or actual conflict. So after the foundation of the Cominform, Stalin may have thought the time had come to put an end to all ideas and practices of "national ways to socialism" or "relatively peaceful transitions." In the spring of 1948, the International Department of CPSU(b) Central Committee prepared successive reports on the "anti-Marxist," "nationalist" deviations of East European communist parties. Some were more like indictments than evaluations, especially on the Yugoslav, Polish, and Czechoslovak parties.[53]

It has been assumed by the Russian scholars Noskova and Murashko that Stalin planned a big purge of the leaders of satellite parties in spring 1948.[54] If that was so, the Hungarians had reason to be anxious. The report of March 1948 on "The nationalist mistakes of the Hungarian Communist Party leadership and the bourgeois influence in the Hungarian Communist press" was not so tough in tone as those on the Czechs and the Poles, however, it did not sound very well that the Hungarian party leadership: "while displaying the party before the country and the people as a national one, often misses the right line and takes nationalist positions." Or another example: Rákosi, Révai, and Farkas "didn't take into account" the economic interests of the Soviet Union. The major part of the report concerned inadequate propaganda about the Soviet Union, especially mishandling in the press (the communist-run satirical journal *Pesti Izé* was accused of being pornographic from start to finish.)[55] Now it is possible to smile at this "analysis," but then it had a very serious objective: to remove all the

---

[52] *PIL* 274. f. 3/134. o. e. Hungarian Communist Party Political Committee, February 26, 1948. Rákosi's report, 10.

[53] *Vostochnaia Evropa...*, Nos. 267, 272, and 274.

[54] G.P. Murashko and A.F. Noskova, "A szovjet tényező Kelet-Európa országainak háború utáni fejlődésében" [The soviet factor in the development of Eastern European countries after the war], *Múltunk*, Vol. 2 (1996): 76.

[55] *Vostochnaia Evropa...*, pp. 802–6.

vestiges of democracy and pluralism remaining within the framework of the "people's democracy" (limited freedom of the press, relatively autonomous national culture, etc.). As the Soviet–Yugoslav conflict became increasingly tense, Moscow could have added the earlier mistakes of the Hungarian Communist Party leadership to this rather comradely criticism: tactical faults in two elections, Rákosi's over-zealous behavior in other cases, his strikingly warm relationship with the Yugoslavs, etc. But Rákosi also realized what was at stake and quickly went further. Right after the merger with the social democrats, nationalization of all religious schools was announced and, almost at the same time, a crusade against the Catholics, the most powerful Hungarian church. After the nationalization of industry in March 1948, the pressure was put on individual farmers (branded as *kulaks*). In the summer of that year, the national "pathfinders" of the Hungarian Communist Party (notably Imre Nagy) found themselves openly criticized for right-wing deviation. So the Hungarian party leadership demonstrated its ability to learn from the Yugoslav lesson and start reconstructing society according to the Soviet pattern. One year later, in 1949, came the Rajk show trial, as additional proof.

BOGDAN CRISTIAN IACOB

Avatars of the Romanian Academy and the Historical Front: 1948 versus 1955[1]

The starting point of the institutionalization and centralization of history production in Romania under communism is the year 1948. At the time, the Academy turned into an enormous institution with several sectors/sections covering all the recognized sciences, history included. This initial stage was part and parcel of the so-called "Sovietization" of Romania (also known in the literature as "High Stalinism"). The Academy was to become the pinnacle of a pyramidal system, an omnipotent institution which aimed to "bring science closer to life" (*nauka v zhizn'*). However, a second look at this institution's development throughout the communist period reveals a much more complicated picture. Several stages of re-organization generated alternative functionalities and roles for the Academy (implicitly, for its institutes of history-production as well). The Academy was one of the crucial arenas for the ups-and-downs of the continuity-change process under communism. It was among the first spaces for an upswing towards a "national turn."[2] Moreover, it was the hub of historical syntheses and of historians' aggregation.

---

[1] This paper was originally presented at the conference "Stalinism Revisited: The Establishment of Communist Regimes in Central and Eastern Europe and the Dynamics of the Soviet Bloc" (Washington, D.C., 29–30 November, 2007) under the title "Fighting for the Intellectual Sphere: Control, Manipulation and Cooption in the Restructuring of the Romanian Academy." I changed the title in order to express the particularization of some of the general remarks made during my presentation.

[2] By "national turn" I understand the process of gradual appropriation of the Nation as a master symbol by the regime. In my opinion, it started in the early 1960s and it completed in 1974. This phenomenon affected all sectors of the party-state and each and every walk of life.

The aim of the present paper is to provide an example for this ambivalent epistemic state of affairs in Romania under communism. The historical field will be my trial run. I will first analyze the blueprint upon which the Academy of the Romanian People's Republic (RPR) was built, while simultaneously attempting to give some hints about the Soviet interpretation of the idea of "planned science." I will then turn to the evolution of the RPR Academy focusing on both instances of institutional reform and on election years. I counterpose two crucial juncture points in the evolution of higher-education: 1948 and 1955. Both were peak moments of confirmation and restructuring of the regime's "knowledge elite." I argue that establishing a connection between personnel dynamics and organizational premises within scientific communities (in my case, historians) can provide at least two important results. First, it reveals the seeds of change into the direction of a "national turn" within the higher education system. Second, it offers a context that helps one better understand the premises for the academia's widespread regimentation by the regime.

Preliminary Observations on the Soviet Conception of "Planned Science"

The main model for the Soviet organization of scientific communities was the Kaiser Wilhelm *Gesellschaft* developed in Germany in 1911. There was, however, a distinctive institutional twist to it, a specific standpoint generated by the Bolshevik leadership on the relationship between science and education. This generated the particular structure of knowledge communities in the new Soviet state. The original Humboldtian idea behind the creation of a system of *Hilfs-Institute* led to a three-tier structure of higher education: the Academy, the University, and the research institutes. Within such a complex of science-production, the talented professors and/or academicians were free to pursue their research interests. The burden of University teaching was therefore significantly alleviated. State-supported centers of fundamental research were independent from the Academy; while the universities maintained their modern role of *Lehranstalten* [institutions of higher education]. The intention of the initiators of the Kaiser Wilhelm scheme, people such as Adolf Harnack or Rudolf von Valentini, was to safeguard science from the effects of mass education, simultaneously maintaining the Prussian Academy of Sciences as an honorary institution, freed from state bureaucracy and control.[3]

The Soviet leadership and party-affiliated scientists maintained the three-tier project, but decided to attach the most important research institutes to the Academy of Sciences, gradually subordinating (mainly from 1929 onwards) the entire structure to the state. At the same time, the "bourgeois" Universities with their research centers (*VUZy*) were completely disregarded as remnants of the *ancien regime*, nests of has-beens and of counterrevolution. Often, until the mid-1930s, they had to permanently deal with the possibility of immediate disbandment.[4]

There were two main reasons behind such organizational setting. The first was the fact that the Bolsheviks conceptualized a "planned science" (the main "culprit" was Bukharin) that would put itself to use for their project of modernization. Moreover, they wished to rapidly create new elites ("Red Professors and Academicians"), which were to replace the has-beens that endangered the purity of the new society. Between 1921 and 1929, the Academy of Sciences gradually became a "safe heaven" for the latter category, a place where they could pursue their research more or less undisturbed by Soviet power. They were, nevertheless, used as "bourgeois specialists" in the training of the new elite of the Soviet state. While the universities became fully exposed from early on to the phenomenon of socialist mass education, the Academy personnel were involved into developmental projects by means of planned research. This way, an "ideal type" separation was generated between research and pedagogy.[5]

---

[3] Loren R. Graham, "The Formation of Soviet Research Institutes: A Combination of Revolutionary Innovation and International Borrowing," *Social Studies of Science*, Vol. 5, No. 3 (August 1975): 303–29.

[4] Especially during the civil war and the proletarization push of what Fitzpatrick coined the "cultural revolution" of 1928–31.

[5] Some of the most important studies of the evolution of the Soviet Academy of Science are: Loren R. Graham, *The Soviet Academy of Sciences and the Communist Party, 1927–1932* (Princeton, NJ: Princeton University Press, 1967); Alexander Vucinich, *Empire of Knowledge: the Academy of Sciences of the USSR (1917–1970)* (Berkeley: University of California Press, 1984); Vera Tolz, *Russian Academicians and the Revolution: Combining Professionalism and Politics* (New York: St. Martin's Press, 1997); Ethan Pollock, *Stalin and the Soviet Science Wars* (Princeton/Oxford: Princeton University Press, 2006).

The second factor which produced the specific profile and functions of the Soviet Academy of Sciences, later to become the institutional model for the new socialist states, was the Bolshevik leadership policy of "merging the national elite with a central planning authority." According to Michael David-Fox, "the new political power needed all the resources that could be drawn from the sanctions and legitimacy (in scientific and even in other matters) residing in the scientific elite."[6] The pyramidal, state-controlled and supported, structure of the Academy was the communist answer to the imperative of "putting science to work for the people." The Academy became a front on the struggle for communist Enlightenment. In the words of a Romanian academician in 1948, it renounced its "mere" formal "honorary and scholarly function, moving away from what it was in the past, a retired gentlemen's club nostalgic about the past, who were just having a pleasant rendezvous on a weekly basis."[7]

Nikolai Bukharin listed, at the First All-Union Conference of the Planning of Scientific-Research Work (April 1931), five directions upon which this structure was to come about. The aspects of science most likely to be subjected to planning were: (a) the determination of the share of the country's budgetary resources which should be devoted to science; (b) the *subjects* of scientific research; (c) the *support* of scientific-research institutions; (d) the geographical placement of scientific-research institutes; and (e) the determination of the supply of personnel, or "cadres," in relation to their number, distribution, qualification, and actual activity within specific projects.[8] [my emphasis] The two interconnected fundamental premises behind Bukharin's (and

---

[6] "On the Origins and Demise of the Communist Academic Regime," in Michael David-Fox and György Péteri eds., *Academia in Upheaval: Origins, Transfers, and Transformations of the Communist Academic Regime in Russia and East Central Europe* (Westport, CT: Bergin&Garey, 2000), p. 13.

[7] Speech given by Traian Săvulescu during the May 20, 1948 debate at the Romanian Academy on the 11-point draft of reform he presented in the name of the Scientific Section. This project was to become the basis upon which the Academy of the Popular Republic of Romania was created. See Dan Berindei, *Istoria Academiei Române (1866–2006)* (Bucharest: Editura Academiei Române, 2006), pp. 310–6.

[8] For a complete description of Bukharin's speech and of his ideas of planning scientific activity and knowledge see Loren R. Graham, "Bukharin and the Planning of Science," *Russian Review*, Vol. 23, No. 2 (April 1964): 135–48.

the Bolshevik) planning the scientific field were: (a) the dyad "practi-cality-party mindedness"(Michael David-Fox); and (b) the "complete absence of any desire to extend knowledge as an end in itself"(Loren Graham). The "planning of science" generated a symbiotic relationship between the academic community, political ideals, and the projects of the communist power. On the one hand, the scientific-field in general, and the Academy in particular, lost its autonomy. On the other, the interest of the communist states to provide the funds for research and project-development led to an unprecedented level of investment into knowledge production. For example, for the Romanian case, Frederick Kellogg provides the following evaluation: "the new socialist govern-ment nurtured the attempts to reinterpret the history of Romanians. It was an era [communist period] of multiple innovations, so numer-ous that we will brand it as the Mercury Age."[9] This new "communion of interests between the political and academic elites," in time, coun-ter-balanced the periodical purges and the ideological encirclement of scholarly communities.

General Problems Raised by the Transformation of the Romanian Academy

The period between the transformation of the Academy and the XIth Congress of the Romanian Communist Party (1974) represents, in my opinion, a cycle during which the institutional transfers from the Soviet Union gradually became deeply intertwined with a recuperation of the local Academy's traditions of science organization. By 1976, a hybrid organizational framework was in place with a distribution of respon-sibilities and benefits sharply different from the 1948 starting point. The Academy regained an honorary role, one however based now on prestige rather than on the actual coordination of the planning of science. At the same time, the University's productive and symbolic functions were rejuvenated, as compared to late 1940s or early 1950s. By the beginning of the third decade of "state socialism," the research institutes were already drifting toward the latter's area of influence.

[9] Frederick Kellogg, *A History of Romanian Historical Writing* (Bakersfield, CA: Charles Schlacks, Jr., Pu., 1990), p. 83.

Simultaneously, new institutions of party-state supervision and coordination appeared: the Council for Socialist Culture and Education[10] and the National Council for Science and Technology.

The "Sovietization" of the Romanian Academy became official by the June 9, 1948 law. It became the Academy of the RPR. It was reorganized into 6 sections and 25 subsections. The law gave priority to the natural and applied sciences, placing the socio-human sciences last in rank of importance. In the first two decades of the communist regime, the Academy and its scientific network grew considerably, from 7 research facilities with nearly 400 scientific collaborators in 1948 to 56 institutes or centers with about 2,500 employees in 1966. At the time of this initial re-shuffling, the Historical Section added other specialties, and became the Section of Historical Sciences, Philosophical Sciences, and Economic and Legal Sciences. It bore this title until 1965, when it reverted to the name of Historical Section. In 1949, the Section began to direct subordinate research institutes, such as those of history and those of archaeology in Bucharest, Iasi and Cluj, to which the Institute of South Eastern European Studies was later added. In time, several institutes of research in social sciences and the humanities where the relative weight of the historical sciences was greater, such as, for example, those in Sibiu, Târgu Mureş and Craiova, also came under its direction.

The hegemony of the Romanian Academy suffered a serious blow when in 1969 a decision of the Council of Ministers removed twelve institutes and centers of medical research (in Bucharest, Cluj, Iaşi, Timişoara, and Târgu Mureş) from the system of the Academy and placed them under the direction of the Academy of Medical Sciences. After 1970, a newly founded Academy of Social and Political Sciences swallowed all of the Academy's institutes of socio-human sciences. In 1974, the modifications of the Academy's code of bylaws put it under the direction of the National Council for Science and Technology. In the course of the same year, the Academy was stripped of all of its remaining institutes in Bucharest and other major cities—institutes of mathematics, statistics, geography, linguistics, literary history, folklore, the Astronomical Observatory, and others. These were redistributed to

---

[10] Vladimir Tismaneanu *et al.*, *Comisia prezindenţială pentru analiza dictaturii comuniste din România—Raport final* (Bucureşi: Humanitas, 2007), pp. 403–8.

the ministries of education and culture. However, in what concerns the community of historians, the Academy still retained a crucial institution that contained an important incentive element. I am referring here to the Committee of the Romanian Historians, which regulated the relationship between Romanian and foreign historians and it administered the Romanian historians' participation at international congresses. This body was continuing a pre-communist practice and structure. It was reorganized under communism in the proximity of the 1955 Rome International Congress of Historical Sciences, which registered the first "outing" of Romanian historians after the communist takeover.

In 1948, numerous acting, associate and honorary members were expelled from the Academy, since they were deemed unfit for the new cultural orientations and hostile to the communist regime. The Academy, restructured by the new regime, had 66 members nominated by presidential decree and dispersed among six scientific sections. From amongst the former members of the Academy, nineteen had been kept as acting members and fifteen as honorary members; most were specialists in theoretical and applied sciences. The transformation of the Academy was done through the marginalization of the members of the section for historical, juridical, economic studies and philosophy with the help of the prominent academicians from the scientific section. The debates within the "old" Academy about the necessity of reform correspondent to the new socio-political conditions in the country coincided with the public campaigns against some of its members. They were targets of incessant negative media coverage (of communist or of other "progressist" political coloring). It did not help, of course, that some of them were indeed, to various degrees, compromised by their political loyalties or administrative positions either during the late 1930s and/or the Second World War.

The pattern of reform and takeover bears similarities with the events that took place in the Soviet Union in late 1920s and the first half of the 1930s. There the first targets of Bolshevik authorities' and its newspapers were the Permanent Historical-Archeographical Commission [PIAK], the Pushkin House, and the library.[11] The Soviet

---

[11] For the complete description of the 1927–30 events, see Aleksey E. Levin, "Expedient Catastrophe: A Reconsideration of the 1929 Crisis at the Soviet Academy of Science," *Slavic Review*, Vol. 47, No. 2 (Summer, 1988): 261–79.

academicians came under the scrutiny of the Fignater Commission, subordinated to the Leningrad Regional Workers' and Peasants' Inspectorate (RKI). The latter was supposed to identify the "wreckers" and the anti-Soviet elements among the institution's membership and employees. The aims of the press campaign and of the control bodies were: (i) to annihilate the existing autonomy of the Academy, (ii) to identify the counterrevolutionary elements, (iii) to promote Red-membership, and (iv) to integrate the activities and role of the Academy within the general campaign of planned transformation of the society and the economy. Reaching such objectives became imperative particularly after Stalin's November 1929 article in which he stated that "a great break on all the fronts of Socialist construction" had taken place—the beginning of the First Five-Year Plan. By 1934, the Academy of Sciences was transferred to Moscow from Leningrad and was placed under the direct jurisdiction of the Council of People's Commissars. Different institutes for scientific research, which had been organized earlier by the Soviet government, were incorporated into the Academy. In 1936, the research institutes of the Communist Academy were also added to the Academy of Sciences. It became thus the leading scientific institution in all spheres of knowledge.[12]

To return to the Romanian case, indeed the Achilles' heel for members of the Academy and university professors (some of them holding both positions) was their involvement in governmental structures from 1938 to 1944. This weakness of the Romanian academic communities in the second half of the 1940s provided the pretext both for reform and purge. In the newspaper *Contemporanul* (October 14th, 1947), V. Enăchescu argued that "the great names of Romanian higher education formed two categories: 'sentenced war criminals,' such as prof. A Marcu, and 'war criminals not tried yet,' such as Ion Petrovici, Ghe Brătianu, Sextil Puşcariu."[13] Furthermore, Matei Socor, in his communist-inspired campaign for a purge of the higher-education

---

[12] George C. Guins, "The Academy of Sciences of the USSR," *Russian Review*, Vol. 12, No. 4 (October 1953): 270–1.

[13] Maria Someşan and Mircea Iosifescu "Modificarea structurii Universităţii în anii consolidării sistemului communist," p. 469, in Romulus Rusan ed., *Analele Sighet 6, Anul 1948—Instituţionalizarea Comunismului* (Bucharest: Fundaţia Academia Civică, 1988), pp. 445–80.

system, makes a thorough, though indiscriminate, description of the faults plaguing the academic community at the time: "all those who participated in Romanian–German associations, in cultural exchanges and at friendship concerts/events, in creating a *false* atmosphere of alliance and of 'brotherhood in arms' should be held responsible... Can they still hide behind the pretext of mere cultural activity?... They bear equal, if not greater, responsibility as those who killed in prisons." V. Condrea was adding a nail to the coffin when listing in an article what he labeled as "the Iron Guardist rectors and deans still active within the Romanian university system."[14]

The press campaign targeted both the University and the Academy, calling for the purification of research-education structures of has-beens (i.e., "collaborationists," "counterrevolutionaries," and representatives of the *ancién regime* on the "cultural front"). Ultimately, the extensive transformation of the scientific field was justified by means of substitution. Labels such as "enemy of the people" became synonymous with "collaborators with the enemy," "war criminal," "anti-democratic element," or "anti-Soviet attitude." Authors such as Someşan and Iosifescu emphasize the *ambiguity of categories* and *the transfer of meaning* contained in the post-1944 anti-collaborationism laws. If the first decree mentioned the "purification of public administration" (nos. 1486, 1944) making reference to those who were active in the fascist-type organizations in the country, and its second version (Law no. 594, 1944), promoted by the minister of justice, L. Pătrăşcanu, incriminated "those who paved the way for the fascist dictatorship," the last version (Law no. 217/1945) extended the array of indictment to "all those who adopted an antidemocratic attitude."[15] The collaboration of some academicians and professors with the royal dictatorship, with the Antonescu regime, with the German representatives, or with the Iron Guard was emphasized by the Sovietophile press and in the politics of the Democratic Parties Bloc (later the National Democratic Front) in counter-distinction with the campaigns

---

[14] Matei Socor and V. Condrea in *România Liberă*, September 10 and 12, 1944, *Ibid.*, pp. 451–2. For a thorough analysis of the epoch's *kulturkampf*, see Ana Selejan, *Trădarea intelectualilor: Reeducare şi prigoană* (Bucharest: Cartea Românească, 2005).

[15] In Someşan and Isofescu, *op. cit.*, p. 454.

for post-war democracy, antifascism, and reform of the Romanian nation-state.[16]

This procedure of merging political faults, academic integrity, and counter-proposals for reform (from non-communist areas of the public space) makes it, even nowadays, very difficult to analyze the profile of the 1940s Romanian cultural-scientific landscape. The lack of discrimination at the time, when judging various personalities was counter-balanced, after 1989, by a similar ascendence of qualification in their all-out rehabilitation. The irony is that many of these individuals were already pretty much rehabilitated by the communist regime itself, by the end of 1970s. A commonsensical observation would be that people such as Nichifor Crainic, Constantin C. Giurescu, Gheorghe Brătianu, P.P. Panaitescu, V. Marcu, Scarlat Lambrino, Al. Lapedatu, Petre Negulescu, Florian Ştefănescu-Goangă, Teofil Sauciuc-Săveanu, etc. would have been at least "arraigned" (to use a contemporary term) if not indicted for collaborationism or extreme-right beliefs/actions (some of them). Of course, they would not die in jail, as often happened, but a purge of the Romanian educational system would most likely have taken place in post-war Romania, regardless of the political regime. Considering the political dynamics of higher-education in Romania from mid-1920s onwards, one cannot but wonder if "the drama of the Romanian Academy and universities" (the established coinage in Romanian research) was not also partially self-inflicted.

An additional problem was the lack of non-communist initiatives of reform of higher-education and of its institutions. Moreover, many members showed a glaring lack of sense for the times and for the necessity of retreat from previous, now compromised, political positions.

---

[16] A similar argument is developed by Bradley Adams for the case of Czecho-slovakia, *"The Struggle for the Soul of the Nation": Czech Culture and the Rise of Communism* (New York/Oxford: Rowman & Littlefield Publishers Inc., Harvard Cold War Book Series, 2004). See also Norman Naimark and Leonid Gibianskii, *The Establishment of Communist Regimes in Eastern Europe, 1944–1949* (Boulder, CO: Westview Press, 1997). For a rather brief but still informative analysis of the involvement of historians and academicians in the politics of culture during the royal dictatorship and during Antonescu regime (also in the context of the Second World War), see Florin Müller, *Metamorfoze ale Politicului Românesc 1938–1944* (Bucharest: Editura Universităţii Bucharest, 2005) and Mioara Anton, *Propaganda şi Război 1941–1944* (Bucharest: Tritonic, 2007).

Grigore T. Popa, the dean of the Medicine Department of Bucharest University, brought forth, in a meeting of the Senate (October 1946), a petition in which he attempted to pinpoint the fallacies of Law no. 658 that annulled the autonomy of the institution. His speech, however, contained a statement telling for the lack of serious reassessment of pre-1945 past: "our universities do not deserve the veto given by Law no. 658. From the point of view of a big-picture analysis, the Romanian universities, in their arguably short existence and under circumstances of scarcity of support, did manage to position themselves honourably among the other universities of the world."[17] A similarly candid position was taken by Dimitrie Gusti, who upon his return from a trip abroad (United States, France and Palestine), filed a report, *Vers une conception réaliste et scientifique de la paix*, in which he argues that during his voyage he noticed a widespread preoccupation to extend on a global-level the "science of the nation." In other words, he was calling for the creation of an international institute focused on "the knowledge of the nation."[18]

Both examples indicate the lack of a counter-reform, of "politically correct" proposals coming from the non-communist influenced section of the Romanian academia. The two academicians, Popa and Gusti, show an incapacity to grasp the fact that the Academy and the University were not, at least initially, attacked on basis of the value of the scholarship produced, but from political positions. And for Popa, dean of a department which was one of the centers of the Iron Guard movement at the level of the student body, to simply ignore this fact indeed raises some eyebrows. Popa himself was black-listed by the Iron Guard in 1940. In 1944, he was among the signatories of the 1944 protest memorandum by a group of intellectuals requesting the end of Romania's involvement in the war and the denunciation of its alliance with Nazi Germany. The pro-communist social-democrat the Minister of Public Education, Ştefan Voitec, personally nominated Popa for his dean position. The latter did,

---

[17] Maria Someşan and Mircea Iosifescu, *op. cit.*, pp. 461–4.
[18] Zub, *Orizont Închis: Istorografia română sub dictatură* (Iaşi: Institutul European, 2000), pp. 39. Zub lists other three drafts of a reform of the Academy (of sectors or of the entire institution) authored by Anibal Teodorescu, Ion I. Nistor, and Radu Rosetti, but only the latter seems to attempt to adjust to the new political realities of the times. Zub however does not make any mention of retroactive evaluation in these documents.

however, refuse to become a fellow comrade, as he resigned from *AL-RUS*[19] and severely criticized the communist government.[20]

Gusti's proposal, on the other hand, comes dangerously close to the ideas promoted in the works of some historians during the war's (counter) propaganda about the Romanians in Transylvania, Bessarabia, Bucovina, or Transnistria.[21] Such activities, by 1946, were already causes for indictment.[22] Another proposal of reform came from S. Mehedinți in his lecture *The geographic method in natural and social sciences*, in which he argues in favour of "a national pedagogy, for which purpose the Academy was about to be transformed into an ethnopedagogical institution, a Senate of the Romanian intelligentsia."[23] Considering that one of the gravest of accusations was "great-nation chauvinism," advocating ethnocentrism was hardly a compromise solution. The Academy's group of "had-beens" (*foști*) antinomically positioned themselves in relation to both the idea of reform and the new political power. They, therefore, remained vulnerable to and inadvertently encouraged the undifferentiated political accusations that later turned

---

[19] The Romanian Association for Strengthening the Relationship with the USSR. For an introductory account about this organization, see Adrian Cioroianu, *Pe umerii lui Marx: O introducere in istoria comunismului românesc* (Bucharest: Curtea Veche Publishing, 2005), pp. 106–48.

[20] See *Subteranele memoriei: Pagini din rezistența culturii 1944–1954* (Bucharest: Editura Universal Dalsi, 2005), pp. 369–71.

[21] For example, Mihai Antonescu created in 1942 the Peace Bureau, an institutional structure within the Ministry of National Propaganda that had a *historical section*. Some of the famed names of the historical profession worked in or with the Peace Bureau or the MNP. See Mioara Anton, *op. cit.*, pp. 103–10 and Petre Out and Aurel Pentelescu, *Gheorghe I. Brătianu: Istorie și politică* (Bucharest: Grupul Editorial Corint, 2003).

[22] This point of view has additional weight if one reads Gusti's 1947 initiative in connection with the May 1941 project of Academy reform promoted by him along with Mihai Ciucă, P.P. Negulescu, Liviu Rebreanu, Radu R. Rosetti. They wished to adjust the institution to the post-1940 circumstances (Vienna diktat and the non-aggression pact) along the lines of "an intensified promotion of national culture in order to strengthen the spiritual frontiers of the nation, as compensation for the provisional mutilation of the national state." See Cristina Păiușan, "Epurările din Academia Română," pp. 538–44 in Romulus Rusan ed., *Analele Sighet 6, Anul 1948—Instituționalizarea Comunismului* (Bucharest: Fundația Academia Civică, 1988), pp. 539–40; and Dan Berindei, *op. cit.*, pp. 214–5.

[23] Al. Zub, *op. cit.*, p. 52.

into sentences and ultimately led to the tragic end of many of these personalities of the Romanian cultural-academic space.

The Stages of the Academy's Transformation and the Push for Cultural Revolution

The socialist reform of the Academy was performed in several stages. The ultimate transformation of 1948 is just the tip of the iceberg. It was rather the result of the policy adopted against the professorship of the Universities and against those academicians who also held positions in various political parties or had undertaken governmental activity before August 1944. Historians, jurists and literati were most affected because they formed a distinct occupational category with heavy pre-war and war political involvement. Constantin Iordachi argues that one of the specific problems of the historical field in the Central and Eastern Europe was the association between being a historian and "doing" politics.[24] This category of "historian-politician" played an important role in behavior of the communist power toward those historians members of the Academy (and toward their respective university departments). And it also explains a great deal of the rehabilitation process during the "national turn" from the late 1950s onwards.

The first step toward the creation of a communist controlled Academy was Law no. 217 (1945). It was aimed at purging public administration of those employees "who, by their own will, had participated in any way to promote a public opinion favorable to fascist or Hitlerist purposes," or those "who pursed activities, of any form, focused on establishing or strengthening dictatorship," or "who, through the manner of fulfilling their duties or by means of publicity and propaganda have taken an antidemocratic attitude."[25] This law affected people such

---

[24] In Constantin Iordachi, "Entangled Histories: Re-writing the History of Central and Southeastern Europe from a Relational Perspective," *European Studies/Etudes Européennes/Europaichen Studien*, Vol. 4 (29 April 2004), the Council of Europe; and *Enlargement Research Bulletin* (June 2004). Republished in *Regio*, Yearbook 2004, pp. 113–47.

[25] Maria Someșan, *Universitate și Politică în deceniile 4–6 ale secolului XX—episoade și documente* (București: Editura Universității din Bucharest, 2004), pp. 268–70; and Someșan and Iosifescu, *op. cit.*

as Eugen Chirnoagă, Radu Meitani, P.P. Panaitescu, Radu Paul, Victor Jinga, Iuliu Haţieganu, O. Ghimbu. The Commission-in-Charge of the purge of the education system was made up of S. Stoilov, Al. Rosetii and P.P. Stănescu, future pillars of respectability for the new Academy.

The second stage was the so-called "the rationalization of higher education." This phase was managed by another commission made up of Traian Săvulescu, Miron Nicolescu, C. Tegădeanu, Constantin Daicoviciu, and P. Constantinescu-Iaşi (as president of the Professors' Trade Union). Upon this commission's recommendation, Ştefan Voitec issued on 2 October 1947 a decree with retroactive applicability that declared over 80 professors retired, who were implicitly being taken out of the system. A third practice was that of simply disbanding departments or University positions. A decision on October 4 stated that by September 1 over 300 positions were eliminated from the nomenclature of the university structures in Romania.[26] In some special cases, however, the person holding the professorship was yet again signalled out (*se comprimă persoana*): e.g., Ghe Brătianu, Dragoş Protopopescu, Gr. T. Popa. Maria Someşan estimates that the consequence of these legal decisions within the higher-education system was the decimation of the old guard. According to this author, of the pre-1945 academia only 3.5 percent were still teaching philosophy, only 23 percent philology, 35 percent law, and only approximately 16 percent history. All in all, by 1948 the position of many of the Academy's members was seriously weakened, if not already gravely endangered, both politically and professionally. Some of them were already under home arrest or in detention camps, while others were soon to join them in the Romanian Gulag system.

The first and most obvious outcome of the above described campaign was, according to the Academy's president, Andrei Rădulescu, that "in accordance with the principle adopted by the Academy, those members who had been already previously sentenced cannot anymore be part of our institution."[27] Therefore, at the May–June 1948 meeting

---

[26] Also see Alexandru Zub, "Despre anul istoriografic 1948 în România: impactul stalinist," in Romulus Rusan ed., *op. cit.*, pp. 553–564 and Al Zub, *op. cit.*, pp. 17–58.

[27] Florin Muller, *Politikă şi istoriografie in Romania 1948–1964* (Cluj-Napoca: Editura Neremia Napocae, 2003) p. 108.

only 40 acting and 40 associate members were present to analyze the 11-point draft program presented, in the name of the Scientific Section, by Traian Săvulescu (already a minister in the new communist government by that time). This document proposed the creation of an Academy representative of the new "popular democracy." His main opponents, as mentioned previously, were part of the History and Literature sections: Dimitrie Gusti, Al. Lapedatu, Ion Petrovici, C. Rădulescu-Motru, Ion Nistor, etc. The main argument of the Scientific Section was that the Academy needed to go through a revolutionary transformation in order to gain the ability of functioning according to the ethos of the present. C. Parhon also specified that in case of a veto of the draft, the members who brought it forward would resign and create a new, "truly democratic" Academy. It never got to this point, for despite opposition and heartening speeches, such as that of G.T. Popa, the votes went in the direction of reform. Accordingly, on 9 June 1948, the old Academy was disbanded and a new statute was promulgated by the president of the Council of Ministers, P. Groza, by the Minister of Justice, Avram Bunaciu, C. Parhon, and Emil Popa. The inaugural meeting of the Academy of the Popular Republic of Romania took place on 18 October 1948. It was presided over by C. Parhon in the presence of Gheorghiu-Dej and P. Groza, among others. At this first public event of the new Academy, around 100 former members were not present, as they had not been mentioned on the membership list. Many of them were already in jail or unemployed and had been socially marginalized by communist regime.

Traian Săvulescu's opening addresses during the inaugural session offers a clear definition of the new institution's role. He stated that

> the Academy will no more be just a forum of prestige confirmation, a club for people distanced from the realities of social life. It will regain its place at the forefront of the mass of toilers and thus it will elevate the country's working people, for it is to become a site of resilient and permanent activity. In contrast to prior conceptions that made it an amorphous scientific body, our Academy will foster a planned science, conforming to the overall developmental targets for the country's economic and the people's cultural progress.[28]

---

[28] Traian Săvulescu, "Ştiinţa, literatura, arta şi slujitorii ei în RPR," *Analele Academiei Republicii Populare Române, 1948–1949*, pp. 102–24.

Furthermore, in a lecture on history and literature (November 1948), P. Constantinescu-Iaşi was already setting the RPR Academy's goals in these two fields: "the entire cultural patrimony of our past and the Romanian historical research have to be reconsidered altogether along the lines of the most advanced system of theoretical thought [Marxist-Leninism]."[29] The immediate consequence of such an aim was the publication of the *Index of the banned books* (May 1, 1948), a 522-page long volume, listing over 8,000 titles.

These speeches expressed the two axes upon which higher education was and would be transformed. First, the Academy had to fall into line with the new conception about the practicality of science. Second, the institution was to pursue its activity within a particular ideological system of reference. Its new profile and functions are best described by Vasilescu-Karpen's statement that "the Academy's autonomy will exist in accordance to the norms of 'popular democracy'."[30] Subsequently, the Academy's reform, along with that of the entire institutional corpus of the Romanian higher education, became part and parcel of the cultural revolution instrumentalized by the communist regime. In 1948, M. Roller argued that despite early successes, decision-makers would nevertheless have to increase their class vigilance.[31] Furthermore, C. Parhon announced the creation of a "third front" in the battle for "building the groundwork of socialism": "last year's decision of the Academy's Presidium prescribing the proper directions for scientific activity in our country were aimed at up-rooting cosmopolitanism, objectivism, remnants of bourgeois ideology, all the weeds and debris that prevent the blossoming of some researchers' scientific work."[32]

The new Statute of the Academy clearly advocated for the creation of a "progressive" knowledge elite. The institution was meant to

---

[29] P. Constantinescu-Iaşi, "Probleme de istorie şi literatură," *op. cit.*, pp. 148.

[30] Petru Popescu-Gogan, Claudia Ilie-Voiculescu, "Desfiinţarea Academiei Române şi înfiinţarea Academiei R.P. Române," in Romulus Rusan ed., *op. cit.*, pp. 487–505.

[31] Mihail Roller, *Pe drumul revoluţiei noastre culturale* (Bucharest: Editura Scânteia, 1949), p. 18.

[32] Parhon's introductory article to the first edition of *Studies and Research on Endocrinology*, Vol. 1, No. 1 (June 1950).

identify and promote all individuals showing cultural and scientific worthiness, who also have a moral behavior and a politically demo- cratic mindset. It will insure that all necessary conditions will be met so that their flourishing activity in their fields of study would also be used for the benefit of the people. Thus, for this purpose, the Acad- emy will coordinate the activity of all institutes and centers of research through the country.[33]

There was, therefore, an ambivalent character to the organization and aims of the new governing body of the Romanian higher education. On the one hand, its birth-pangs brought about a set of *negative* practices: the old-guard was purged and the traditional academic ethos was re- jected by the new leadership. This exclusionary aspect was, at the time, riding the wave of overall communization of Romanian society and of its institutions. On the other hand, though, as the statute shows, the new rules and goals had a *positive potential* in a context of the acknowl- edgement of the ideological framework set up by the party-state.

The period of 1948 to 1952 in the history of the Academy and of the historical field can be easily characterized as one of "revolutionary breakthrough" brought about by "High Stalinism." However, starting with 1953 the institutions already showed signs of assimilative tenden- cies. One notices an incipient process of negotiation and bargaining between the academia and the political authorities. This will represent the preparatory phase for the "national turn" within historical produc- tion. Following Al. Zub's argument, I believe that the communist im- pact upon the Romanian writing of history was a permanent struggle for equilibrium between *persecutio* and *creatio*. In his own words, *con- tinuity is no less interesting than the breach* [my emphasis].[34] Such bick- ering was possible because of the negative-positive/exclusion-inclusion simultaneities that, as Michael David-Fox argues, are intrinsic to the "the Bolshevik cultural project."[35] The party destroyed the structures

---

[33] Dorina Rusu, *op. cit.*, p. 323.

[34] Alexndru Zub, "Romania's Sovitization: historiographical implication," in Al. Zub and Flavius Solomon, eds. *Sovietization in Romania and Czechoslova- kia—History, Analogies, Consequences* (Iasi: Polirom, 2003), pp. 11–7.

[35] Michael David-Fox, "What is Cultural Revolution?," *Russian Review*, Vol. 58, No. 2 (April 1999): 181–201. His article was an evaluation of the litera- ture on the "cultural revolution" after Sheila Fitzpatrick's. It provoked a brief exchange with Fitzpatrick: Sheila Fitzpatrick, "Cultural Revolution Revis-

that characterized the former state organization, but it also brought about environments of ambiguity because it was impossible to expect the creation of an entire state or society anew. This grey zone allowed for compromise and synthesis. Under circumstances of change in party line, this brought about a nascent reorientation toward the past, toward tradition and its representatives—a counterpart or compensation for continuous repression.

The Party did create alternative structures, such as the "Ştefan Gheorghiu" University (1947), the "A.A. Jdanov" Higher School of Social Studies (1948), the Party History Institute (1951), or the system of vocational education (fast-track education of the working-class, an initiative drawing inspiration from the Soviet *rabfak* model). This however, by 1955, only led to a *division of labor* within the historical field. The Academy would become the highest forum expressing such dynamics within the regime's knowledge elite. It would become an environment within which a re-enchantment with the past would be performed, in parallel and even antedating the party-line ideological shifts.

The Seeds for Change in the Academy and on the Historical Front

The year 1955 is significant for the historical field, and in perspective, for the "national turn." First of all, because of the process of change it brought about within the Academy's membership. In 1948, the elections of new members took place. Among those honored with a place within the now famed institutional pinnacle of the new socialist organization of science and education were, as full acting members: P. Constantinescu-Iaşi, Iorgu Iordan, Constantin Balmuş, Mihail Ralea, Mihail Roller, and Camil Petrescu. The following people were also elected as associate members: Emil Condurachi, Constantin Daicoviciu, Andrei Oţetea, David Prodan, Geo Bogza, and Dumitru Panaitescu-Perpessicius (they would be joined by Gheorghe Ştefan). The individuals from the two lists were elected into the newly created

---

ited," *Russian Review*, Vol. 58, No. 2 (1999): 202–9; and Michael David-Fox, "Mentalité or cultural system," *Russian Review*, Vol. 58, No. 2 (April 1999): 210–1.

Section for history, philosophy, economy and law. Most of them were historians, some of them literati—all of them played crucial roles in the regime's politics of culture and in its attitude to the writing of history in Romania. From 1948 these academics would be "the barons of culture" roughly until 1954. The elections of 1955 were the moment of a limited relaxation. Emil Condurachi, Constantin Daicoviciu, Andrei Oţetea, David Prodan became acting members (joined by Ion Nestor and Virgil Vătăşianu as associate members) along with Geo Bogza, Dumitru Panaitescu-Perpessicius, Tudor Arghezi, Cezar Petrescu, Zaharia Stancu, Tudor Vianu, etc. In all fairness, 1955 is also the year when high-ranked party representatives became members of the Academy: Alexandru Bârlădeanu, Ion Gheorghe-Maurer, and Lothar Rădăceanu.

The historians who were included in this wave of promotions had black spots in their biographies. Ion Nestor was a founding member of the Romanian–German Association (1942), probably the translator of *Mein Kampf* into Romanian, and was a subaltern of C.C. Giurescu at the Ministry of Propaganda during the war.[36] David Prodan, was vulnerable to accusations of factionalism (which indeed were raised in 1953, when he was accused of "right-wing deviation").[37] Daicoviciu was dean at the Bucharest University during the Antonescu regime and one of the closest pupils of Ghe. Brătianu. Vătăşianu was the former Secretary of the Romanian School of Roma. Condurachi used to be a prominent member of the same institution and also spent a significant period of time at the correspondent school in France. All of these historians experienced early in their careers plenty of exposure to Western scholarship and historical schools (Leipzig, Rome, Munich, Berlin, Paris, etc.). They hardly seemed to be the model of anti-cosmopolitanism, of Soviet educated or favorable professors, or of the "builders of socialism" for that matter. They did form, however, under the leadership of Andrei Oţetea, the personnel and institutional bedrock favorable for a "national turn" in the historical field in parallel and in connection with the political transformation taking place at

---

[36] Ioan Opriş, *Istoricii şi Securitatea* (Bucharest: Editura Enciclopedică, 2004), pp. 21–37.
[37] David Prodan, *Memorii* (Bucharest: Coperta, 1993), pp. 66–70.

the party level.[38] When analyzing these personnel changes one has to also keep in mind that starting with 1950, the position of president of the RPR. Academy was inserted into the nomenclature of the Central Committee (CC) of the Romanian Workers Party (RWP). The person holding this position was nominated by the party and validated by the politburo. As one author writes, "the nominations of new members of the Academy were approved at the highest levels of the party. The Academy's acting and associate members entered the nomenclature of the CC of the RWP based upon the nominations made by the CC's Propaganda and Agitation Section, which put these names forward to the Secretariat."[39] Therefore, it can be argued that the promotion of a different type of academician was indeed signaling a change in the party line on the scientific (i.e., historical) front.

One author characterizes the triumvirate of Oţetea, Daicoviciu, and Condurachi in the following manner:

> they represent some of the most devoted historians [to the cause of national historiography]. They succeeded in obtaining decision-making positions within the academia and in Romanian society. In holding the highest academic, university and political ranks, they controlled and guided for decades the university and academic post-war milieu. Also using their long-term connections with political leaders—such as Petru Groza, Constantinescu-Iaşi, Tudor Bugnariu, Miron Constantinescu, and even Gheorghiu-Dej—they brought about benefits for the historical profession.[40]

---

[38] For complete biographical details of the members of this first wave of what I will later brand as *smenovekhovtsy* historians, see: Ştefan Ştefănescu *et al.*, *Enciclopedia Istoriografiei Româneşti* (Bucharest: Editura Ştiinţifică şi Enciclopedică, 1978); Florin Müller, *Politică şi istoriografie în România 1948–1964* (Cluj-Napoca: Editura Neremia Napocae, 2003); Florica Dobre ed. (Consilul Naţional pentru Studierea Arhivelor Securităţii), *Membri CC ai PCR* (Bucharest: Editura Enciclopedică, 2004); Ioan Opriş, *op. cit.* and volume II (Bucharest: Editura Enciclopedică, 2007); Florin Constantiniu, *De la Răutu şi Roller la Muşat şi Ardeleanu* (Bucharest: Editura Enciclopedică, 2007).

[39] Nicoleta Ionescu Gură, *Stalinizarea României. Republica Populară Română: 1948–1950. Transformări instituţionale* (Bucharest: Editura ALL, 2005), pp. 454–64.

[40] Ioan Opriş, *op. cit.*, p. 16.

Another excellent indication of the new times to come was an informative note to the secret police, made on October 1956, about historian M. Berza. It reads: "in Romania there is no place for *politicians of science* anymore, but only for true eminence. This is what he [Berza] claims [the informant comments] to have been personally told by the minister Murgulescu, when he was handed-over the decree of re-entitlement as full-time professor."[41]

The two most representative figures for the category of "politicians of science" were Mihail Roller and Contantinescu-Iaşi. The first fits into the category of *praktiki*, personifying the cultural-scientific orthodoxy in the historical field, thus becoming a factor of reference in judging the ideological deviation of those who fell under his jurisdiction (institutional or symbolic).[42] The second was more of a *historian-censor*,[43] who was involved in the purge commissions and in the drafting of the *Index of Banned Books*. Constantinescu-Iaşi did attempt three times[44] to take a public position in reference to political conformity with professional norms, but he never produced a textbook like Roller. The latter set the standard of historical writing from 1947 until 1955. He led the group of authors who wrote the high school textbook *Istoria R.P.R.*, which cre-

---

[41] Ioan Opriş, *op. cit.*, p. 555.

[42] In Sheila Fitzpatrick, "Culture and politics under Stalin: a reappraisal," *Slavic Review*, Vol. 35, No. 2 (June 1976): 213–31.

[43] One possible comparative case that could be relevant for a better understanding of the *historian-censor* category is that of Anna Pankratova. She was one of the pace setters for Soviet historiography under Stalin (see her contribution at the *Twenty-five years of Historical Scholarship in the USSR*), but she also adopted recurrently maverick attitudes and approaches within the Soviet historical field under Stalin and in the years following his death. See: Konstantin F. Shteppa, *Russian Historians and the Soviet State* (New Brunswick/New Jersey: Rutgers University Press, 1957); Roger D. Markwick, *Rewriting History in Soviet Russia—The politics of revisionist historiography, 1954–1974*, foreword by Donald J. Raleigh (New York: Palgrave Macmillian, 2001); Reginald E. Zelnik ed., *Perils of Pankratova: Some stories from the annals of Soviet historiography* (Seattle: Herbert J. Ellison Center for Russian, Eastern European, and Central Asian Studies, University of Washington, 2005).

[44] The first is the already mentioned 1948 Academy address, the second is the 1955 *Realizările istoriografiei române între anii 1945–1955*, and the third is "Valenţele educative ale istoriei," *Studii şi articole de istorie*, Vol. 17 (1972).

ated a new historiographical paradigm (*rollerism*[45]). Its preface stated that "this history is structurally different from all the previous histories because of the scientific notion and method upon which it relies"—dialectical and historical materialism. In other words, "the textbook converted into the acknowledged culture the cultural arbitrariness presupposed by the very existence of the 'people's democracy' regime."[46] Roller was deputy-chief of the Propaganda Section of the RWP and vice-president of the RPR Academy (1949–54). In 1955, he was demoted to the position of vice-president of the Institute of Party History. M. Roller's activity as a party historian was severely criticized during the 9–13 June 1958 plenary session of the RWP. Roller gradually lost influence. He did not survive, both politically and physically, the change in party-line.

Constantinescu-Iaşi, however, was more of a symbolic figure for the party. During the inter-war period he was the main character in a public trial on charges of "agitation in favor of communism." The international, local communist, and Sovietophile newspapers mobilized some sectors of public opinion in his favor. The Constantinescu-Iaşi trial was one of the few moments of public visibility of communists at the time.[47] The key positions he occupied from 1948 until the mid-1970s allowed him to affect decision-making at the highest levels of party leadership.[48] His most authoritative writings were on the histo-

---

[45] For more details in English about *rollerism*, see Dennis Deletant, "Rewriting the Past: Trends in Contemporary Romanian Historiography," *Ethnic and Racial Studies*, Vol. 14, No. 1 (January 1991): 64–85; Keith Hitchins, "Historiography of the Countries of Eastern Europe: Romania," *American Historical Review*, Vol. 97 (1992): 1064–83; Serban Papacostea, "Captive Clio: Romanian Historiography under Communist Rule," *European History Quarterly*, Vol. 26, No. 2 (1996): 181–208; Constantin Iordachi, *op. cit.*; Vladimir Tismaneanu, *Stalinism for all Seasons—A Political History of Romanian Communism* (Berkeley/Los Angeles/London: University of California Press, 2003).

[46] Andi Mihalache, *Istorie şi practice discursive în România "democrat-populară"* (Bucharest: Editura Albatros, 2003), pp. 76–8.

[47] For details about Constantinescu-Iaşi's political biography, see Vladimir Tismăneanu, *op. cit.*; Stelian Tănase, *Clienţii lu' tanti Varvara—istorii clandestine* (Bucharest: Humanitas, 2005); Adrian Cioroianu, *op. cit.*

[48] He was the president of the Society for historical science (from 1948 onwards) and of the Union of the scientific societies of the Romanian professors, the director of the National Committee of Sciences (1955–74), president of the historical section from 1948–55, and vice-president of the RPR Academy (1948–55).

ry of the party and of the socialist movement in Romania. The rather ambivalent nature of Constantineascu-Iaşi's activity was strengthened by his participation in the Commission of rehabilitation from 1965, a mirror-image of his prior involvement of in the 1947 purge commission. Of course, the latter focused on the higher education system, while the former aimed at "investigating" the abuses of the Gheorghiu-Dej leadership of party members. But both, through their institutional and personnel consequences, led to different re-writings of histories. Constantinescu-Iaşi's presence in both moments certainly raises a question mark on the possibility that he was a source of historiographical orthodoxy like in M. Roller's case (who produced *both* censorship and dogma).

Constantinescu-Iaşi assumed a less visible and a more honorary role after 1955. In his yearly report at the Academy, he argued that Romanian historiography *only* from that point on could truly produce socialist history. What had been written before was still tainted by bourgeois influence. For Constantinescu-Iaşi, the 1948 to 1955 period was that "of our cultural revolution as we go." If one reads his statements in the context of the new elections, they seem like a validation for the new elite within the historical field, one ready to write, using Marxist-Leninist theses, a reconsidered and reformed national historiography. From the point of view of the paradigmatic struggles within history-production, Constantinescu-Iaşi did remain a highly influential representative of the internationalist camp with a view to Romanian modern and contemporary history.

Under the circumstances of Mihail Roller's forced retirement of (1956),[49] the new group that caught the limelight in the Section of Historical Sciences, Philosophical Sciences, Economic and Legal Sciences was made up of a very specific type of historian-academician. They accepted the new socialist state and its developmental goals, thoroughly integrated in the party-state institutions, but, at the same time, had been educated and/or mentored within the pre-communist paradigms with little, superficial or "right-wing deviationist" training in dialectical materialism. I believe that the term which best characterizes one group of these

---

[49] In 1955, he was not included in the Romanian delegation at the Historians' Congress in Rome. Upon his death, his obituary from the journal *Studii* (No. 3, 1958) was not signed.

historians (Nestor, Vătăşianu, Daicoviciu, Condurachi, Berza, Dionisie Pippidi, etc.) is that of *smenovekhovtsy*. The category describes those nationalist intellectuals who accepted to work for the communist regime because they envisaged it as a valid incarnation of the nation-building principle.[50] The second crucial category was that of *poputchik* (fellow traveler) and it applies to academicians such as Andrei Oţetea, Iorgu Iordan, or Emil Petrovici. These four categories—*praktiki, historian-censor, smenovekhovtsy,* and *poputchik*—indicate the various possibilities of personnel aggregation and of interest groups within the structures of history-production of the socialist state. Such pluralism under the umbrella of the party-line set the stage for the institutional reform and conceptual shift in the Romanian historical field between 1963 and 1974.

The changes of personnel within the RPR Academy, at the level of the historical and literature subsections, were accompanied by three significant documents which put forth the directions of development in the following years. On 2 July 1955 a new Statute for the Academy was issued and approved. Article no. 3 of this document stated that "the Academy pursues research by its own initiative, at the request of the government, of various other institutions or state enterprises." Another novelty was article no. 8, which contained the decision to create autonomous subsections for history, linguistic and literary studies, and the arts—all of them though constituting the Section of history, language/literature, and art.[51] On 21 February 1956, a *Hotărârea* (decision) was adopted at the end of the general session of the Academy. It emphasized the need for an increase in the role of the institution's sections, which, it was said, "greatly overlook their responsibilities of guidance, coordination and particularly those of permanent control of the activity of the units they are made of." The same document called for "the strengthening of the social sciences institutes, especially of the

---

[50] For more details about the *Smena vekh* group: Mikhail Agursky, *The Third Rome: National Bolshevism in the USSR* (Boulder: Westview Press, 1987); Robert C. Tucker, *Stalin in Power—The Revolution from Above 1928–1941* (New York/London: W.W. Norton & Company, 1990), pp. 35–8; Robert C. Williams, "'Changing Landmarks' in Russian Berlin, 1922–1924," *Slavic Review*, Vol. 27, No. 4 (December 1968): 581–93; Terry Martin, *The Affirmative Action Empire—Nations and Nationalism in the Soviet Union, 1923–1939* (Ithaca/London: Cornell University Press, 2001), pp. 9–15.
[51] Dorina Rusu, *op. cit.,* p. 339.

Academy's Philosophy and Economy Institutes, with qualified cadres and by providing the practical conditions for the flourishing of their activity." Moreover, *Hotărârea* signaled a change of scientific reference at the level of the Academy by arguing for "expanding the publication exchange with foreign scientific bodies and for a de-centralization of such interaction."[52] The two decisions (*Statutul* and *Hotărârea*) indicate a new organizational propensity toward the sections' autonomy in establishing research objectives, plans of action, and scientific projects.

It is also interesting to point out that *Hotărârea* was drafted 5 years prior to the two 1961 UNESCO conventions that regulated the exchange of publications among international scientific and education institutions. Furthermore, 1955 was a turning point in book production in Romania. It was the first year when the ratio of original (national) production to translations (mainly from Russian) was be in favor of the former. At the same time, within the Party History Institute, the number of defended doctorates with topics from modern and contemporary history of the country surpassed the number of doctorates from abroad (mainly USSR).[53]

Another piece in the puzzle of the 1955–56 turnaround in the historical field was a report signed by A. Oțetea, and Constantin Daicoviciu (drafted along with Barbu Câmpina, Georges Haupt and Vasile Maciu) entitled *În legătură cu unele fenomene care frânează activitatea itoricilor români* [Report on the issues hindering the activity of Romanian historians]. This document was created at Pavel Țugui's request, head of the Section on Culture and Science of the Central Committee, who presented it to the RWP leadership.[54] It was the first party-

---

[52] *Ibid.*, p. 343.

[53] Marian Pruteanu, *Memoria comunismului: Fondul ISISP din Biblioteca Centrală Universitară din Bucharest* (http://www.bcub.ro/continut/unibib/memoria_comunismului.php).

[54] Țugui is another puzzling party censor who was involved in the new institutional and conceptual transformations between 1955 and 1960. He was an alternate member of the Central Committee of the RWP until June 1960, head of the literature and art sector of the Propaganda and Agitation Section, deputy minister of culture (1953–55), head of the Culture and Science Section of the C.C. of RWP (until 1960), and member of the scientific council of the Party History Institute (from 1958 onwards). In Florica Dobre, *op. cit.*, p. 593. For a version of the historians' report, see Ion Țugui, *Istoria și limba română în vremea lui Gheorghiu-Dej* (Bucharest: Editura I. Cristoiu, 1999), pp. 43–54.

encouraged attack against *rollerism*. For the first time, this paradigm was publicly chastised for being antinational, antipatriotic, and a danger to "the people's most sacred rights," its history and language.

Conclusions

The first conclusion about the events of 1955–56 is twofold. On the one side, there is, both institutionally and methodologically, a certain degree of return to tradition (an upsurge of *positive*, inclusionary cultural revolution). On the other, national historiography singled out its enemy, that is, the left-deviation of *rollerism* (the post-1947 paradigm in the historical field). Therefore, one can notice a slow but definite shift of professional systems of reference. The second conclusion is related to the impetus suggested by the *Statute* and *Hotărârea* toward a subordination of the Academy's sections and subsections (the historical one being among of them). A remarkable moment of changing-of-the-guard and of thematic shift was the writing, in late 1950s, of the treatise *Istoria României*. These were the first signs of a process of decentralizing "the planning of science," which would prepare the ground for the new organization of the historical field in the 1960s. And third, these steps toward re-institutionalization, the demise of *rollerism*, and the clarification of the Party History Institute statutes generated a dual (both ambivalent and contradictory) configuration of the historical field. It was based upon the division of labor that was developing between the so-called "national" and "party" historians.

While keeping in mind the serious setback caused by the 1958-1961 purges among Romanian intellectuals, by 1956, only 6 years removed from the disbanding of the "old" Academy, historians had managed to regain epistemic recognition and obtain a voice within the ideologically driven discourse of the Nation. The overall narrative of those years and of the ones that followed (including present memoirs and scholarly literature) created a heroic plot. The *nation* was snatched from the jaws of the Stalinist school of falsification (*rollerism*) and historical studies resurged as true science at its service. However, at the core of the institutional and personnel process I sketched in the present article, starting from the Academy's 1948 transformation up until the elections of 1955, lies the reality of gradually balancing repression and exclusion with recognition and co-option. In the long run, the Romanian history-production became a prisoner of this carrot-stick game, the prize of which was the symbolic capital and preeminence over the community's imagination. The party-line inexorably took on national tenets and, by 1974, it already had another official historiographical paradigm synthesized in *Platforma Program* (the RCP XIth Congress). The initial repression of the years of "High Stalinism" was not the only cause for the lack of a thematically and methodologically pluralistic historical field. Critical alternatives to the regime's orthodoxy did not develop because the respective epistemic communities never functioned outside the discursive space defined by the regime.[55] Most historians, regardless of the category they fell into, accepted the party's representational monopoly in exchange for the validation of their epistemic position.

---

[55] Christian Joppke makes a similar point when explaining the scarcity of open opposition and of dissent on the part of East German intellectuals to the SED's discourse monopoly over founding conceptual landmarks such as "socialist democracy" or "anti-fascism." See Christian Joppke, "Intellectuals, Nationalism, and the Exit from Communism: The Case of East Germany," *Comparative Studies in Society and History*, Vol. 37, No. 2 (April 1995): 213–41; and *East German Dissidents and the Revolution of 1989: Social movement in a Leninist regime* (London: Macmillan, 1995).

EKATERINA NIKOVA

Bulgarian Stalinism Revisited

Any attempt to set the chronological boundaries of Bulgarian Stalinism puts us in the middle of two continuing debates. The first one is the great controversy about who unraveled the wartime alliance and when, subsequently starting the Cold War and provoking the division of Europe. An implicit subplot to this story is whether Stalin had a master plan to Bolshevize Eastern Europe and if so what place Bulgaria held in it.[1] The second one is the domestic Bulgarian debate about the nature of the autochthonous developments in 1944–47 and their correlation to endogenous and exogenous factors driving these developments.

The pre-1989 Bulgarian historiography tended to present the period as a struggle between the progressive forces and the reactionary counter-revolutionary bourgeoisie. A voluminous literature studied meticulously "the historical prerequisites for the socialist revolution" and the "correlation between the external and the internal factor," stressing the importance of the latter. The role of the communist party (then called Bulgarian Workers' Party) and the scope of the communist-led anti-fascist resistance were grossly exaggerated. The role of the Soviet Union was acknowledged with gratitude, but it was gradually reduced to that of "an active support."[2] The period was characterized as the defeat of the bourgeois opposition, the establishment and consolidation of

---

[1] For an analysis of recent scholarship, see Melvyn P. Leffler, "The Cold War: What 'Do We Now Know?'" *The American Historical Review*, Vol. 104, No. 2 (April 1999); Eduard Mark, *Revolution by Degrees: Stalin's National-Front Strategy for Europe, 1941–1947*, Woodrow Wilson International Center for Scholars Cold War International History Project, Working Paper No. 31, Washington, D.C., February 2001.

[2] *Kratka istoriia na Bulgaria*, "Nauka i izkustvo," Sofia, 1983, p. 416.

the peoples' democracy and the defense of national sovereignty.[3] The period was treated rather parenthetically in official Bulgarian historiography as an unpleasant and embarrassing incident. In general, it was believed that the communist takeover in Bulgaria was accomplished without significant resistance and that Bulgarian Stalinism was milder than elsewhere in the region. Explanations were sought and found in the traditional leftism of one of Europe's most egalitarian countries, in the relative strength of the Bulgarian communist party, but first and foremost, in the historical friendship with Russia—"Grand Father Ivan" who fought the Russian–Turkish war in 1877–78 and liberated Bulgaria from the Ottoman Empire.

Like elsewhere in Eastern Europe, the term "Stalinism" is new for Bulgarian scholarship. In Bulgaria, too, Stalin's name inspired such awe and reverence that long after his death it was avoided. Besides, being directly associated with crimes, camps, brutality, and paranoia was ideologically dangerous. In 1967 philosopher Assen Ignatov was castigated for using using the anti-Marxist notion "Stalinism" in an article published in an Austrian journal on the intellectuals' role in socialism.

If "Stalinism" is used to characterize the period instead of the habitual euphemisms, then its lower chronological boundary should be moved to include the years 1944–47. As it will be argued further, Stalinism in the Bulgarian case started from day one. If "high/pure" Stalinism has been usually dated from 1947–48 to 1953, the upper boundary is also rather debatable. De-Stalinization was slow and hesitant in 1953–56. In April 1956 the Bulgarian Communist Party held a special plenum—the legendary April Plenum, a landmark event in the Party's history which exposed the "deformities and deviations" of the "cult of personality" of Bulgaria's "little Stalin" Vulko Chervenkov. A special commission investigated the most notorious cases of abuse of power, of which the most prominent was the spectacular legal murder of Traicho Kostov, the third man in the Party's *nomenklatura*. A number of detainees were liberated from camps and prisons, the important party functionaries among them were rehabilitated, and the party solemnly took a new line, which for the next thirty-three years was called "the April Line." Todor Zhivkov—a rather grey, second echelon figure,

---

[3] Voin Bozhinov, *Zashtitata na natzionalnata nezavisimost na Bulgaria, 1944–1947* (Sofia: Izdatelstvo na Bulgarskata akademiia na naukite, 1962).

who had been by no means an innocent bystander in the event—was chosen personally by Khrushchev to be the main figure of the Plenum. By distancing himself decisively from his predecessor, Zhivkov became the uncontested leader of the Party for the next three decades. According to the official line Stalinism was rejected in 1956 and replaced by *Zhivkovism*, which lasted until November 1989.

Whatever young Zhivkov's intentions might have been, he could not go very far. The Hungarian Revolution put an end to the Bulgarian timid thaw. Discussions and criticism in the party and society were abruptly interrupted, camps were re-opened for the "usual suspects" (being closed as late as 1962), and thousands of students were preemptively expelled from the universities. The Party restored its iron grip on Bulgarian society.

In the late 1970s several carefully selected historians were given the opportunity to work in the Party Archives on carefully selected topics from this period. Accordingly, they were able to shed light on the period and its basic personalities, remaining however strictly within the official doctrine. The work of the renowned historian Mito Issusov should be mentioned first and foremost. His two seminal books on Traicho Kostov and Stalin's role in Bulgaria were published immediately after the fall of the communist regime, but they were well researched in Bulgarian and Soviet archives and had been partly known much earlier.[4] Much to the horror of the ideological Cerberuses, Professor Issusov liked to present his iconoclastic findings on Bulgarian Stalinism at the annual conferences of the young historians.

Revisiting Stalinism in the true sense of the word could happen only after 1989. In the early 1990s Bulgarian archives—the Central State Archive, the Archives of the Ministry of Foreign Affairs, and the Party—were declassified and restructured. Despite severe resistance and with a considerable delay, the Archives of the Ministry of Internal Affairs, including those of the State Security (DS), were made accessible too. In general, Bulgarian society has been slow to assess, critically, its recent past. The main reason is the unwillingness of the Socialist Party, which, under the conditions of the negotiated, peaceful,

---

[4] Mito Issusov, *Poslednata Godina na Traicho Kostov* (Sofia: Izdatelstvo Hristo Botev, 1990); and *Stalin I Bulgaria* (Sofia: University Publ. St Kliment Ohridski, 1991).

Bulgarian transition, has preserved strong positions and powerful levers to influence the issue. Currently, two opposing processes can be observed: the growing public and academic interest in the secrets of communist regime clashes with the tacit rehabilitation of events, people, or cultural traits of the communist regime. Amidst the fatigue and the apathy of the prolonged transition, condemnation of the communist regime is often stigmatized as "obsolete and primitive anti-Communism" and in "bad taste."[5]

Bulgarian scholars of the period have also been able to take advantage of the "archival revolution" in Russia of the early 1990s and their good working relations with their Soviet/Russian colleagues. A long-term scholarly project, "Russia and Bulgaria in the 20th Century—New Documents, New Ideas," materialized in several symposia and two excellent books covering the period's most dramatic issues.[6] Access to important Russian collections allows researchers to lift the curtain on the Soviet side of the story; archival material from the now accessible archives of important Soviet institutions like the Party, the Ministry of Foreign Affairs, etc. is added to materials and documents from the conferences of the Comintern and Cominform[7] and the fundamental editions of the *Nauchnii Centr po istorii stalinisma v Vostochnoi Evrope* at the Russian Academy of Sciences.[8]

In the last decade we have seen a true avalanche of important new books, memoirs of people from both sides of the barricades (the

---

[5] There are several new institutions working to set up a comprehensive database on Bulgarian communism collecting memoirs, interviews, archival material, and books: New Bulgarian University, http://www.nbu.bg/historyproject/index.htm; The Institute for Studies of the Recent Past, http://minaloto.org/; Center for Advanced Studies, Bulgarian Communism, Critical Studies, Bibliography, Sofia, http://www.red.cas.bg/id-36/home.html.

[6] *Bulgaria v sferata na suvetskite interesi (Bulgaro-ruski nauchni diskusis)*, Academichno Izdatelstvo "Prof. Marin Drinov," Sofia, 1998; *Bulgaria I Rusia prez XX vek. Bulgaro-ruski nauchni diskusii* (Sofia: Gutemberg, 2000).

[7] An Italian edition translated into English was published in Milan, 1994; the Russian one in Moscow, 1998.

[8] *Vostochnaya Evropa v dokumentah rossiiskih arhivov; Tome 1: 1944–1953.* (Moscow-Novosibirsk, 1997); *Tome 2: 1949–1953* (Moscow-Novosibirsk: ROSSPEN, 1998); *Sovetskii faktor v Vostochnoi Evrope; Tome 1: 1944–1953,* (Moscow: ROSSPEN, 1999); *Tome 2: 1949–1953* (Moscow: ROSSPEN, 2002).

political figures and the victims, sometimes they exchanged places), diaries (including those of Georgi Dimitrov), biographies, etc. Local district archives, where work has only started, are promising to be real golden mines. Not all the secrets of the period have been revealed, but we can say that the period of Bulgarian Stalinism is now pretty well illuminated.

New findings on Bulgarian Stalinism could put the period in its proper context—the Sovietization of Eastern Europe. Recent scholarship is trying to call things by their proper names and find the true measure of the various events and phenomena. Research is being done in several concentric circles. The first circle is that of the great powers' politics—the geopolitical and balance of power considerations of each of the Big Three of the Grand Alliance. Then comes the circle of research focused on the Soviet/Stalinist policy *vis-à-vis* Bulgaria that has to answer whether the Kremlin was promoting its legitimate security interests beyond the Soviet Union's territory or promoting a world proletariat revolution, or the two things at the same time. Closely connected is the circle of questions regarding the relations between the Bulgarian communists and Moscow, and the degree of Soviet involvement and responsibility for what was happening inside the country. At the very center of this scheme is the study of the internal political struggles—a study going beyond the visibility of the inter-party struggles and searching for what had really happened on the ground, in the country's towns and villages. At the time, just like in a Greek tragedy, many of the actors on the Bulgarian and East European political scene played their roles without knowing the script that the "Gods" had written. So far, for the short two decades of active research on Bulgarian Stalinism, despite serious achievements, scholarship has not been able yet to properly conceptualize the multi-facet processes and to incorporate the different narratives into a single, overarching one.

Like elsewhere in Eastern Europe, the opening of the archives and the freedom of expression was a huge chance for Bulgarian historians. New evidence led to the re-assessment of the old questions, but it also suggested new ones. It has certainly not freed us from the inherited highly stereotypical, "black and white" thinking of the Cold War era.

As to Bulgarian Stalinism, we are very far from claiming that "we now know." It can be assumed, most neutrally, that as early as the autumn of 1941 the Soviet leadership was preparing plans for post-war Europe and that Bulgaria had a place in them. Slavic, Orthodox, Russophile, the country which the tsars liked to see as a *zadunaiskaya guberniya* and which lay on the road to Russia's historical expansion to the Straits, was to be included in the USSR's sphere of interests. The messianism of pan-Slavism was blended with that of the international communist movement just like the world revolution turned into a *realpolitik* instrument for the achievement of a stronger and more secure Soviet Union.[9] Furthermore Bulgaria's strong communist party was one of the most loyal and active sections of the Comintern, led by the influential figure of Georgi Dimitrov, the organization's Secretary General and author of the tactic of the popular fronts. In Bulgaria, an ally of Nazi Germany, Moscow organized and tightly controlled a small but noteworthy resistance movement from 1942 on—a Fatherland Front uniting four anti-fascist parties. Rather unexpectedly, on 5 September, the Soviet government declared war on Bulgaria. Three hundred thousand Ukrainians from the Third Front occupied the country. According to the terms of the armistice agreement the United States and the United Kingdom gave full authority to its Soviet commander, Marshal F.I. Tolbukhin and the "general supervision" to the Soviet representative on the Allied Control Commission General S.S. Biryuzov.[10]

Within this broad framework however important questions remain unanswered. Did Stalin have consistent far-reaching plans to Sovietize Bulgaria? Was the people's democracy a stillborn child, a tactical and propaganda tool for Soviet domination or an alternative new road to democracy?[11] If Soviet instructions and instructors had been instrumental in the establishing the new regime, wasn't there any feedback, any role for the so-called domestic factor of the revolution. In

---

[9] For an extended analysis, see John Lewis Gaddis, *We Now Know: Rethinking the Cold War* (New York: Oxford University Press, 1997); Vladislav Zubok and Constantine Pleshakov, *Inside the Kremlin's Cold War: From Stalin to Khrushchev* (Cambridge, MA: Harvard University Press, 1996); Vojtech Mastny, *The Cold War and Soviet Insecurity: The Stalin Years* (New York/ Oxford: Oxford University Press, 1996).

[10] See Cyril E. Black, "The Start of the Cold War in Bulgaria: A Personal View," *The Review of Politics*, Vol. 41, No. 2. (April 1979).

[11] Regretfully, we could not read Vesselin Dimitrov's *Stalin's Cold War: Soviet Foreign Policy, Democracy and Communism in Bulgaria, 1941–1948*, due from Palgrave Macmillan in 2008. Judging from its bibliographical description, the book promises to clarify these important linkages.

connection with this point, G. Nikova speaks of a slight tension between the Russian and the Bulgarian historians working on this problem. According to the Bulgarians, the Russian authors and collections of documents tend to emphasize the role of the domestic factor, omitting at the same time crucial actions and documents of the Soviet side.[12]

The new reading of the Stalinist period has brought to light a surprising amount of forgotten persons, events, jargon, newspapers, even jokes and nicknames—a whole layer of historical memory which was still alive under the ashes of prohibition and oppression. If there was one particular surprise for the Bulgarian society in confronting the new facts of the Stalinist period, it was the scale of the repressions and murders committed in 1944–53. One small episode illustrates this. In the spring of 1990 the newly born anti-communist opposition (UDF), advised by a well-meaning famous French advertising guru, used in its otherwise cheerful and colorful electoral campaign a map of Bulgaria, dotted with the communist labor camps, marked by skulls. The Bulgarians, however, were not ready for this truth; the shock and the disbelief caused by this map were so great, that as later analyses showed, the map cost the UDF at least 10 percent of the votes and the victory in the final run. In the next years the full extent of the communist terror was made clear—whether through tragic personal accounts or the dry language of the militia reports. The historical memory of the ruthlessness of the regime was easily re-activated. A decade later it is difficult to imagine how Bulgarian society was made to believe that the communist takeover was met with mass enthusiasm and only negligible resistance.

Numbers are notoriously unreliable, yet the picture of these years is horrifying. The waves of terror came one after the other, as if following the well-known Hannah Arendt's scheme of the Great Terror during the Bolshevik revolution. In early September, during the first ten days of the communist takeover 25,000–30,000 people were killed or disappeared. Some of them were police and army officers, mayors and clerks responsible for the persecution of the anti-fascist resistance; but the majority were mayors, lawyers, journalists, teachers,

---

[12] See Gospodinka Nikova, "Nai-novata bulgarska istoria v ogledaloto na ruskata istoriografia," *Istoricheski Pregled,* Vols. 1–2 (2005).

clergymen, or just well off, outstanding figures in their own town or village. There were spontaneous acts of revenge and class hatred, yet the scale cannot be ascribed only to a "revolutionary fury." Punishment of fascists and collaborators occurred all over occupied Europe. During these "extra-judicial" score-settlings some 10,000 people were killed in France and another 15,000 were killed in Italy.[13] The number of the victims in Bulgaria was approximately equal to the total number of the French and Italian victims. But France and Italy are not only much bigger countries, they also had experienced real occupation with real collaborators, fascists and traitors. In Bulgaria these first purges (the Russian word *chistka* was quickly adopted) had a different meaning: under the slogan of punishing the fascist elements, the mass murders were aimed mostly at the annihilation of all eventual potential class enemies. This was a well-guided "spontaneity." A telegram signed "Central Committee" and dated 13 September 1944, informs Dimitrov (in Russian!): "In the first days of the Revolution we squared accounts with the most malicious enemies, fallen into our hands... The fight is not over. Armed members of the Party and the Comsomol will form striking commands for particularly important assignments." Two weeks later, on October 1 the Central Committee reported: "Despite the discontent of our feeble allies at our revolutionary liquidation of the fascist *agentura*, we decided that the purge will go on for one more week. After that the purge will continue by lawful means."[14] Eyewitnesses testified that direct instruction came directly from Moscow from Dimitrov and Kolarov and that the special services of the Red Army came with ready lists of names.[15]

By October it was time to put an end to the "unauthorized" killings and to start the legal ones. Under pressure from General Biryuzov, a Decree was passed which established the People's Court for the trial of all those accused of "monarcho-fascism," war crimes, and collaboration. The People's Court was set up under the Statutory Ordinance on the Trial of the Culprits for the Involvement of Bulgaria in the War against the Allied Powers and for the Related Crimes; it operated

---

[13] Tony Judt, *Postwar* (London: Penguin Books, 2005), p. 42.

[14] http://www.geocities.com/decommunization/Documents/T1.htm.

[15] Georgi Gunev, *Kum brega na svobodata ili za Nikola Petkov i negovoto vreme* (Sofia: Informatzionno obsluzhvane AD, 1992), p. 24.

between November 1944 and April 1945.[16] The defendants were the Regents and the Tsar's advisors, cabinet ministers of all governments and all members of the parliament from the years 1941–44, senior state and military officials. The People's Court tried 135 cases against 11,122 defendants, of whom 2,730 were sentenced to death, 1,516 were pronounced not guilty, and the rest were given different prison terms.[17] Here again, proportionally to the population these numbers were unprecedented in European practice.[18] Moreover, this happened in a country where there had been no fascist movement, which never sent troops to the Eastern front, and saved its 50,000 Jewish population. Very few of the defendants had really committed war crimes; most of them were just political opponents. The Court and the "spontaneous" purges managed to decapitate the pre-war political, economic, and cultural elites and virtually destroyed the old center and right of Bulgarian politics.[19]

Then came the turn of the opposition within the Fatherland Front; by March, Stalin was losing patience: a second Fatherland Front cabinet was formed without the representatives of the opposition. "The elections are over and your opposition can go to hell"—he told Dimitrov. In June 1946 the first of the many trials began against the social democrat Pastuhov and the Agrarian leader G.M. Dimitrov (*in*

---

[16] Dinyu Sharlanov and Polya Meshkova, *Bulgarskata gilotina: Tainite mehanizmi na Narodnia sud* (Sofia: Agentzia Demokratzia, 1994); Peter Semerdjiev, *Narodniat sud v Bulgaria, 1944–1945* (Sophia: Makedonia Press, 1997); Dinyu Sharlanov, Lyubomir Ognyanov, and Plamen Tzvetkov, "Bulgaria pod komunistichesko robstvo: Prestuplenia, suprotiva i represii," in *Cherna kniga na komunizma, 2. chast. Istoria i pamet za komunizma v Evrope,* Po idea i pod redaktziata na Stéphane Courtois, (Sofia: Prozoretz, 2004).

[17] By sheer chance Dimitar Peshev, the MP who initiated the campaign in defense of the Bulgarian Jews was sentenced to "just" 15 years of forced labor. With an exceptional professional mastery his Jewish attorney Yossif Yasharov saved his life. The other MPs were less lucky: 20 out of the 43 of them who had signed the letter of protest against the plan of genocide were sentenced to death, six to life imprisonment, eight received prison sentences of 15 years, four were sentenced to a term of 5 years imprisonment, and one to a year in prison. See M. Bar-Zohar, *Beyond Hitler's Grasp: The Heroic Rescue of Bulgaria's Jews* (Holbrook: Adams Media Corporation, 1998).

[18] See Tony Judt, *op. cit.*, pp. 44–62.

[19] R.J. Crampton, *The Balkans Since the Second World War* (London: Pearson Education, 2002), p. 57.

absentia). The army was spared until 1946; later mass purges among the officers were carried out under fabricated accusations of military conspiracies (*Neutral Officer* and *Military Union*). Thousands of the victims' family members were expelled from their city homes and interned to distant villages, many sent to camps.[20]

Bulgaria was one of the first East European countries to organize labor camps (Work Education Centers—TVO) for "the politically dangerous people": as early as 20 December 1944 a special ordinance-law was adopted signed by ministers of all parties and the regents (many of them unsuspecting of their future fate). In violation of the 1879 Turnovo Constitution it gave exclusive rights to the Interior Ministry to incarcerate people without charge or trial. The exact numbers of people passed in 1944–62 through the camp system of 88 camps and labor "boarding houses" is still difficult to pinpoint; it varies from 25,000 to 184,000.[21] The "democratization" of the Bulgarian Orthodox Church then followed. In 1948, after years of severe persecutions of clergymen, the government curtailed religious freedoms by forcing Orthodox clergy into a Union of Bulgarian Priests, taking control of Muslim religious institutions, and in 1949 dissolving Bulgarian branches of Roman Catholic and Protestant churches.

The Bulgarian Agrarian National Union (BANU) presented the most serious challenge to the Bulgarian Stalinists' hegemony. Solidly entrenched in an egalitarian peasant society, the great Agrarian party with its long history, ideology, and leaders was by far the country's most numerous and organized political force and a formidable opponent.[22] In this respect, the political situation of Bulgaria stood out.

---

[20] Penka Stoyanova and Emil Iliev, *Politicheski opasni litza: Vudvoriavania, trudova mobilizatzia, izselvania v Bulgaria sled 1944* (Sofia: Universitetsko izdatelstvo Sv. Kliment Ohridski, 1991); Hristo Hristov, *Sekretnoto delo za lagerite* (Sofia: 'Ivan Vazov', 2000); Hristo Devedjiev, *Stalinization of Bulgarian Society 1949–1953* (Philadelphia: Dorrance & Co, 1975).

[21] Dinyu Sharlanov, Lyubomir Ognyanov, and Plamen Tzvetkov, *op.cit.*, pp. 307–8.

[22] On BANU, see Nissan Oren, *Revolution Administered: Agrarianism and Communism in Bulgaria* (Baltimore and London: The Johns Hopkins University Press, 1973); John D. Bell, *Peasants in Power: Alexander Stamboliski and the Bulgarian Agrarian National Union, 1899–1923* (Princeton: Princeton University Press, 1975); and Joseph Rothschild, *East Central Europe between the Two World Wars* (Seattle and London: University of Washington Press, 1974).

After Bulgaria's defeat in WWI, the Agrarians managed to contain the rising revolutionary tide; in the early twenties they had ruled the country for three years; and in the late thirties after severe blows they were able to re-gain their important role in Bulgarian politics. After WWII, with the restoration of the party system, they were the party that grew most rapidly; by the end of 1944 their membership amounted to 750 thousand, plus another 230 thousand members of the Youth Organization. In the meantime, the Bulgarian communists (13,000 on the eve of the takeover) reached 250 thousand. N. Oren noticed another anomaly: unlike the other East European communist parties, which had reached their maximum strength during and after the war, the Bulgarian communists with their wartime record incomparable to the Yugoslav, Greek, or Albanian record, were weaker in 1944 than in the twenties.[23] In opposition since the summer of 1945, and led by a man with enormous personal courage, Nikola Petkov, BANU fought bravely against the spreading lawlessness, for democracy, freedom of speech, and for its own autonomy. There is no doubt that, had the terms of the game been equal, the Agrarians would have prevailed.[24] During the Union's short life (from 7 September 1945 to 26 August 1947), the Communist Party in Bulgaria faced an audacious and vocal opposition. Its press—the newspaper *Narodno Zemedelsko Zname* together with the Social Democrats' *Svoboden Narod*—spoke with a clear and loud voice.

In the 1946 elections for the Grand National Assembly, despite mass terror, murder of activists, and falsifications, the opposition won 1.2 million votes, 28 percent of the overall MP seats. Political opposition against the communists crystallized around two mass left wing parties, which in itself is a singular development in postwar Eastern Europe. This opposition kept on fighting against all odds hoping that with the Peace Treaty and the withdrawal of the Red Army, their chances would grow. What actually happened was exactly the opposite—the day the U.S. Congress ratified the treaty, Nikola Petkov was arrested in the National Assembly, accused of planning an anti-government coup and a military conspiracy, tortured and sentenced to death.[25] The rank and

---

[23] Nissan Oren, *op. cit.*, p. 82.
[24] *Ibid.*
[25] Georgi Gunev, *op. cit.*, 105–47.

file of the two Fatherland Front parties joined the "bourgeois opposition" in the Bulgarian Gulag.

The crushing of the BANU "Nikola Petkov" marked the beginning of Bulgaria's "high" Stalinism. The peculiarity of the Bulgarian case was that the bulk of the repressions had already taken place. The small political, cultural and economic elite that this peasant nation had been growing for the sixty-six years of its independent existence was practically wiped out: physically annihilated or intimidated into oblivion. The whole thin layer of urban culture disappeared, stamped as "rotten bourgeois." Even more important was the breaking of the backbone of the peasantry comprising 80 percent of the population. The *tabula rasa* for the total Sovietization of the country was prepared in 1944–47.

There was only one obstacle left to the final atomization of Bulgarian society and it was the Party itself. Terror turned to the enemy within, the "enemy with the Party card." The trial of Traicho Kostov— the deputy prime-minister and the most prominent "domestic" communist—was a chapter of Stalin's show trials (Koči Dzodze, Rudolf Slansky, László Rajk) all aimed at crushing any intra-party opposition to the new line. Kostov was charged with ideological deviations, treason, anti-Sovietism, and collaboration with Tito against Stalin.[26] His execution in December 1949 was followed by the trials of hundreds of high placed and highly educated communist specialists in the economy, banking, military, the State Security, including the arrest and torture of the legendary partisan heroes, now generals in the People's Army.[27]

Like elsewhere in Eastern Europe, Stalin, who personally disliked Kostov, taught a final lesson of obedience—if somebody with the position and reputation of Kostov could be proven guilty overnight, nobody was immune. The purges in the Communist party registered another sad Bulgarian record: by June 1950 every fifth member of the Bulgarian Communist Party (BCP)—nearly 100 thousand people—had been expelled, accused of various deviations like nationalism, a bourgeois past, Titoism, Kostovism, or Trotskyism (presumably they knew

---

[26] Mito Issusov, *Poslednata godina na Traicho Kostov.*

[27] Their late memoirs produced a shock among the Party believers. Slavcho Trunski, *Nevuzmozhnata istina* (Sofia: Slavika RM, 1994); Dencho Znepolski, *Posmurtna izpoved* (Sofia: "Hristo Botev," 1997).

who Trotsky was).[28] Curiously, in the camps and the other places of detention many high ranking communists shared suffering and humiliation with their "class enemies," victims of earlier purges. Typically for the BCP, it was not divided so much between Moscovites and domestic communists—since the 1920s a great number of them had passed through emigration and the Comintern schools. The tensions in the party were rather generational and career-based. The Bulgarian communists saw how in the course of six months the three most prominent figures of the Bulgarian Communist Party had died (under suspicious circumstances?)—Georgi Dimitrov in June 1949, Traicho Kostov in December 1949, and Vassil Kolarov in January 1950. The purges delivered a heavy blow to the Party. They produced an atmosphere of fear and insecurity, they shook its entire hierarchy, and the Party lost its revolutionary spirit and turned into an obedient and faithful bureaucratic structure. It had been purged of all potential subversive or simply disloyal elements and sank into a mediocrity that would characterize it for the next 20 years until it grew its own intelligentsia. A new set of cadres was promoted—young, ignorant, inexperienced, insecure, easily manipulative, and loyal to the USSR and the party line, which in this case was one and the same.

Revisiting the Bulgarian case of Stalinism puts the whole argument about the people's democracies in a new light.[29] In the well-recorded Stalin–Dimitrov communication we see a fatherly Stalin who is warmly advising the Bulgarian comrades: "The Soviet form is not the only one leading to socialism; there can be other alternatives like a democratic republic even under certain circumstances—a constitutional monarchy." Further on:

> ...the tasks ahead are so immense, so much beyond the powers of one single party, that you need not a Soviet regime, but a democracy with freely elected parliament... Preserve the coalition of four parties... do

---

[28] L. Ognyanov ed., *Borbi I chistki v BKP 1948–1953*, in *Arhivite govoriat*, Tome 17, Sofia, 2001. This a collection of 270 documents from the former Central Party Archive.

[29] People's democracy—a myth or reality? See T.V. Volokitinia, G.P. Murashko, and A.F. Noskova, *Narodnaya Demokratiya: Mif ili Real'noct': Obshchectvenno-politicheskiye Protzessi v Voctochnoi Evrope, 1944–1948* (Moscow: Nauka, 1993).

not create problems [...] you need an opposition—you are not a class-less society like ours ...legalize it so that you can keep an eye on it, the parliamentary track might be slower but surer.

Your constitution—he preached—should be more right-wing than the Yugoslav one [...] you need a Labor party in order to unite your party with the other parties of the working people's like the Agrarians... A People's Party or the workers and peasants—that will be much more acceptable and appropriate for your case ...you'll get a broader base and a convenient disguise for the today's period...[30]

If in 1945 Stalin criticized the Bulgarians for political maximalism, sectarianism, and dogmatism, by the summer of 1946 he changed the tone—they were reproached for political passivity, lack of principles, and delaying the revolutionary transformations.[31]

Theorizing, in fact, mattered much less than practice. At the time of this friendly correspondence the Bulgarian communists were con-tinuing a deliberate policy of mass terror and brutal elimination of all adversaries of the regime. Like elsewhere in Eastern Europe from day one, they insisted on controlling the ministries of justice and interior. At a very early stage the two most important centers of power became the People's Militia and the Party's Central Committee.[32] An edito-rial of the oppositional *Narodno zemedelsko zname* called this a double bookkeeping: on the one hand solemn declarations of the desire to es-tablish peace and order, on the other—a *carte blanche* for continuing the terror and the murders.[33]

The literature on the period is divided. There are a great number of personal stories and scholarly research on the victims, stressing their tragedy. There is also a growing literature on the political struggles of the period. The problem is that these two bodies of literature rarely refer to each other. Even in well-researched work the repressions are mentioned only hastily and parenthetically. Thus Mito Issusov flatly states that Stalin had nothing to do with the purges, that their motives

---

[30] Georgi Dimitrov, *Dnevnik: March 1933–February 1949* (Sofia: Ik Iztok Za-pad, 1998), various entries.

[31] Mito Issusov, *Stalin i Bulgaria*, p. 46.

[32] Roumen Daskalov, quoted in *Kultura*, 13 December 2007.

[33] *Narodno zemedelsko zname*, 3 January 1947, as quoted in *Narodna demokratzia ili diktatura. Hristomatia po istoria na Bulgaria 1944–1948* (Sofia: Literaturen forum, 1992), p. 98.

were domestic and followed the line of constant tensions, feuds, and a civil war from 1918 on.[34]

Now that we know the scope and the inhumanity of the violence, it is difficult to accept the period of 1944–47 as a "democratic intermezzo." Terror was not a collateral phenomenon; it represented the very essence of what was happening. The Bulgarian case shows that Stalin never lost his long-term perspective; if Stalinism meant a full monopoly of power, then this had been the aim of the Soviets and their Bulgarian comrades from the very first day of the communist takeover. The question is why or whether Bulgaria needed a terror of such proportions. The answer is not easy. It had occurred after all in a country which had managed to stay away from the great cataclysms of the war, especially if compared to its devastated Balkan neighbors. According to the Soviet writer, then wartime correspondent, Konstantin Paustovskii, when the Red Army stepped on Bulgarian territory, the soldiers experienced a cultural shock; they saw a prosperous and quiet agricultural country, crowds of friendly people offering them bread and grapes. This country had a lawful government, not compromised in collaboration with the Nazi and well disposed towards the Allied Forces. Its institutions, army, administration, elites, and intelligentsia were intact. This was a nation which had collectively wept and mourned its Tsar Boris who died unexpectedly in August 1943.[35] Even the much-appraised Ninth of September coup happened without a single bullet being shot and without a single drop of blood.

Bulgaria was not an idyll. Its parliamentary democracy was easily nullified; its political class was often corrupt, authoritarian, and venal. The resistance movement, which according to newly revised data consisted of 8,000 partisans and 20,000 supporters, was severely persecuted. According to the official Museum of the Revolutionary Movement all the victims of repressions in the period 1923–44 amounted to 5,639 people; almost half of them perished in the wars against fascism including in the Spanish Civil war and WWII. The wartime marshal

---

[34] Mito Issusov, *Stalin i Bulgaria*, p. 171.

[35] On the day of the Tsar's funeral, Adolf Beckerle, the German minister to Sofia, wrote in his diary about the mass and sincere mourning and his amazement of the coherence of a nation in the middle of a war.

courts of Tsarstvo Bulgaria passed 1,590 death sentences, 199 of them were executed. [36]

These numbers refute the thesis of the overzealous party historians, who created, retrospectively, the myth of a persistent latent civil war. The orgy of violence which grasped the country in the immediate aftermath of the communist takeover and went later on in tidal waves was unmatched by anything else in the nation's history. Nor does this scope of violence fit in Jan Gross's social history approach—to see the war as a revolution.[37] When the horrified leader of the Agrarians, Nikola Petkov, ran to Traicho Kostov and asked him to stop the killings, Kostov shrugged his shoulders: "This is a revolutionary situation!" Petkov was sincerely surprised: "What revolution? I don't see any barricades!"[38]

Here is one of the possible explanations for the unprecedented scope of violence in Bulgaria—a revolutionary situation *had* to be created. Very much in line with Hannah Arendt's distinction between the societal tasks of the Nazis and Stalin, in order to turn a revolutionary dictatorship into a totalitarian rule the Bulgarian Stalinists had to create artificially this same atomized society that the war had created or prepared in the rest of Eastern Europe. The French-Bulgarian philosopher Tzvetan Todorov, who felt obliged after the success of his *Facing the Extreme: Moral Life in the Concentration Camps* to also publish *Voices from the GULAG: Life and Death in Communist Bulgaria* pertinently remarked: "Once terror has been installed—that is, once the people know that the threat of death or repression is not mere verbiage—society changed dramatically."[39] The memory of the terror, that is *fear*, lived on until the very end of communism and paralyzed people's will and mind.

If Stalinism as a political practice was introduced in Bulgaria immediately after the communist takeover of 9 September 1944, it developed into a full-blown system after a conference of communist party leaders

---

[36] Dinyu Sharlanov, Lyubomir Ognyanov and Plamen Tzvetkov, *op.cit.*, p. 306.

[37] Jan Gross, "War as Revolution," in Norman Naimark and Leonid Gibianskii eds., *The Establishment of Communist Regimes in Eastern Europe, 1944–1949* (Boulder, CO: Westview Press, 1997).

[38] Georgi Gunev, *op.cit.*, p. 60.

[39] Tzvetan Todorov, *Voices from the GULAG: Life and Death in Communist Bulgaria* (University Park, Pennsylvania The Pennsylvania State University Press, 1999), p. 7.

in Szklarska Poremba in September 1947. The period of high Stalinism is connected with the name of Vulko Chervenkov. Stalin made the right choice—a trusted *protégé*, Dimitrov's relative, trained at the KGB school, Chervenkov would complete the conversion of the BCP into a one-man dictatorship. A comic replica of his Soviet mentor, the "little Bulgarian Stalin," as he was called, combined top government and party positions, the control over the State Security plus the monopoly of the information channels with Moscow.[40] In no other East European state had there been such a concentration of power in the hands of one person, or such an over-centralized and fully controlled state apparatus.[41]

After the Tito–Stalin break, the Bulgarian Workers Party (communist) congress of June 1948 expressed the party's staunch loyalty, subservience, and total obedience to the USSR, the All-Union Communist Party (bolseviks), and personally, to comrade Stalin. There was also the obligatory element of self-persecution for not realizing quickly enough the inevitability of the intensification of class struggle, for the lack of revolutionary vigilance and a solemn vow to purge ranks from hostile enemy forces.[42] Following the universal pattern, at its Fifth Congress (1948), the BCP adopted Stalin's thesis that the people's democracy was a variant of the dictatorship of the proletariat and the blueprint for the construction of the Socialist society through industrialization, reconstruction of the village and socialist cultural revolution.

Bulgaria strictly adhered to the Stalinist model of party and state structures, of virtually merging the judicial with the executive and the legislative branches under the absolute dominance of the Party, with its formal parliamentarism, formal rights and freedoms, cadres organization (*nomenklatura*), etc.[43] Naturally, elections in 1949 were won by 97.59 percent and those in 1953 by 99.8 percent.

---

[40] Iliana Marcheva, *Todor Zhivkov—putiat kum vlastta: Politika i ikonomika v Bulgaria 1953–1964* (Sofia: Institut po istoria, BAN, 2000).

[41] Lyubomir Ognianov, *Durzhavno-politicheskata sistema na Bulgaria 1944–1948* (Sofia: Standart DD, 2006); Stalinizmut v politicheskiya zhivot na Bulgaria (1948–1956), unpublished manuscript, 2007.

[42] See *BKP v rezolutzii i reshenia na kongresite i plenumite na TzK*, Tome III, (Sofia: Partizdat, 1954).

[43] For more details, see Iliana Marcheva, *op. cit.*; Evgenia Kalinova and Iskra Baeva, *Bulgarskite prehodi* (Sofia: Paradigma, 2002).

Collectivization, which in Bulgaria started as early as 1945, was given a strong push. In spite of intense peasant resistance,[44] the collectivization drive continued intermittently until the process was virtually complete in 1958 and the Party Congress could proudly report that Bulgaria was the second country after the USSR, where socialism had triumphed in the village. Mass Sovietization started early and probably went further than anywhere else in the region. In Slavic and Russophile Bulgaria, Sovietization looked wholehearted and zealous. The genuine Russophilia of the Bulgarians was overblown to grotesque proportions and fortified by the myth of the "double liberation." There were numerous delegations traveling to and from the Soviet Union to exchange their experience in the building of socialism, a dense network of Bulgarian–Soviet Friendship societies, huge circulation of Soviet books, films, and magazines. Monuments were raised to the Red Army; the country's third city (Varna), the biggest dam, and highest mountain peak were named after Stalin, Stalinist baroque decorated the new center of Sofia.[45] Based upon the myth of the "double liberation," the Soviet–Bulgarian friendship—"eternal and indestructible"—became the strongest mantra of the regime.

Soviet specialist/advisors came in large numbers and were assigned to every central Bulgarian level—the Council of ministers, ministries, the army, the judiciary, the economy, etc., where they started directly imposing the Soviet model.[46] The advisors represented a whole subsystem of governance, subordinated directly to Moscow. And if in the field of economy the Soviet specialists' role was considered mostly ben-

---

[44] Most indicatively, the first comprehensive study of Bulgarian collectivization appeared as late as in 1995. Vladimir Migev, *Kolectivizatziata na bulgarskoto selo (1948–1958)* (Sofia: Universitetsko izdatelstvo "Stopanstvo," 1995).

[45] Vladimir Migev, "Suvetskiiat opit, suvetskiiat primer v Bulgaria," in *Bulgaria i Rusia prez XX vek. Bulgaro-ruski nauchni diskusii*; in the same, Sashka Milanova, "Suvetskoto vliianie vurhu politicheskiia zhivot na Bulgaria"; and Roumiana Bogdanova, "Moskva i 'nationalnite' putista kum socialism."

[46] Al'bina Noskova, "Vozniknovenie sistemi sovetskih sovetnikov v stranax Vostochnoi Evropi: (1949–1953)," in *Bulgaria v sferata na suvetskite interesi*; in the same, Lubomir Ognyanov "Suvetskoto vliianie vurhu organizatziata i deinostta na organite na sudebnata vlast v Bulgaria (1949–1956)"; Tat'ana Volokitina, "Moskva i politicheskie repressii v Vostochnoi Evrope v kontze 40-h godov: (Po dokumentam rossiskih arhivov)"; and Gospodinka Nikova, "Politicheskite protzesi v Bulgaria 1949–1953."

eficial, especially after the destruction of the old regime's cadres, there was one sphere where the advisors left most sinister traces. Soviet advisors were instrumental in the political trials, staged in political circles of Moscow and Sofia and the organs of State security. They brought Vyshinski's experience from the purge trials in the USSR, including special interrogation techniques, and combined successfully, in the words of a colleague, *Yezhovstina* with *Zhdahovstina*. The institution of the Soviet advisors is a typical white spot in the studies of the period; most of the studies remain descriptive and will be detailed only after the opening of the respective Soviet archives.

De-Stalinization in Bulgaria demonstrated several peculiarities too. It was slow, reluctant and limited. In 1953–56 there was a certain relaxation of the terror, some 10,000 political detainees had been released, and several of the most notorious Soviet advisors were sent back to Moscow. There was also certain ease in the collectivization drive and a shift in the economic planning away from heavy industry toward consumer goods. Vulko Chervenkov's fate however was sealed when at the 20th Congress of the CPSU its new leader Nikita Khrushchev denounced Chervenkov's patron Stalin and Stalin's cult of personality. Not quite aware what was happening, Chervenkov himself wrote the Party report on the necessity of de-Stalinization and exposing mistakes and deformities. But the Soviet leader had already other plans; he already signaled out the new secretary—Todor Zhivkov. At the April 1956 Plenum of the BCP, he read the main report. We know now that every point of this report had been carefully coordinated with the Soviet leadership and that during the plenum itself Zhivkov phoned Moscow at least three times. Chervenkov was proclaimed to be the only bearer and the main culprit for the mistakes (not yet crimes!) of Bulgarian Stalinism. He was branded for his cult of personality and for almost all existing problems—from lawlessness to agriculture. But the measures and decisions of this so acclaimed plenum were modest. Chervenkov was reduced to the rank of deputy prime minister and remained member of the Politbüro. When the Plenum's protocols were finally made public in 2002, it became clear why they had been kept secret for such a long time.[47] The record was in sharp contradiction

---

[47] *Aprilski plenum na TzK na BKP. Pulen stenografski protocol. TzK na BKP,* Sofia, 2002.

to the official legend; there was nothing heroic, changes were dictated from Moscow, they began and ended from above. In his memoirs
Zhivkov wrote: "The April Plenum was basically neo-Stalinist. There
could be no question of a change under the circumstances in the socialist community and the world. I was young; I had no experience or
authority. Most of the people in Politburo were connected with the
previous policy and wanted it to go on."[48] The Bulgarian 1956—writes
Iskra Baeva—demonstrated what was specific about the country: the
changes started and finished from above, without any participation of
society.[49]

Revisiting Stalinism helps us to better understand Bulgarian communism and Bulgarian "real socialism." Most of their basic features
can be traced back to the years 1944–56 and consequently explained.
The ruthless "social cleansing" of that period had prepared the ground
for the uncontested rule of the communist party and for the personal
regime of its Secretary General Todor Zhivkov. By the standards of
Eastern Europe his regime was considered moderate—more corrupt
and manipulative than openly oppressive. By skillful maneuverings (his
favorite word which he wrongly pronounced), Zhivkov managed to
manipulate the party, the intelligentsia, and society and parry all potential threats. His secret trick was one of total subjection and unconditional loyalty to Moscow. A favorite of Khrushchev, he was quick to
woo all his successors and fell from power only after he failed to woo
Gorbachev. The Soviet connection was the basic source of the legitimacy and the stability of Zhivkov's thirty-five year long rule. In his own
words: "Bulgaria and the Soviet Union will act as a single body, breathing with the same lungs and nourished by the same blood stream."[50]
Soviet resources and markets were the main factors for Bulgaria's accelerated growth. Soviet support was indispensable for Bulgaria's position in the Balkans and in the world.

Domestically, Zhivkov's regime, as present scholarship has increasingly revealed, was highly voluntaristic, verging on adventurism.
Bulgarian development was characterized by megalomaniac projects

---

[48] Todor Zhivkov, *Sreshtu niakoi luzhi*, (Bourgas: Delfin Press, 1993).

[49] Iskra Baeva, *Iztochna Evropa sled Stalin: 1953–1956* (Sofia: Universitetsko
izdatelstvo "Sv. Kliment Ohridski," 1995), p. 294. On the Plenum, see pp.
250–94.

[50] *Rabotnichesko Delo*, 20 September 1973.

like the hyper industrialization or Europe's most concentrated agriculture and huge blunders like the renaming of the one million Bulgarian Muslims in 1984–89. Why was all this possible? A recent biographer of Zhivkov gives a simple answer: because he *could*.[51] Zhivkov had been an active participant (in a different quality) in the events of the Stalinist period and had correctly read its lessons.

---

[51] Iskra Baeva, *Todor Zhivkov: Biografia* (Sofia: IK Kama, 2006).

DORIN DOBRINCU

Historicizing a Disputed Theme: Anti-Communist Armed Resistance in Romania[1]

The wars waged by small irregular groups against regular military forces or even big armies, of the "classical" type, have been known since Antiquity. But the term "guerrilla war" entered the military vocabulary with the Napoleonic invasion to Spain, at the beginning of the 19th century, when the Spanish irregular forces played an important part in Napoleon's defeat. The term "guerrilla" means "small war" or "irregular war" waged by unprofessional civil-soldiers, who transform into fighters when their country is invaded by a foreign power.[2] Therefore, if a war is carried on with regular armies, it is considered to be the "great" (classical) war, while guerrilla warfare is the "small war," the unconventional one, a "harassing war," which brings together "functions and practices of fight, where the cunning, the cheating, the surprise and the secret intercross and support each other."[3]

---

[1] The title of the paper delivered on 29 November 2007, in Washington, within the symposium "Stalinism Revisited—The Establishment of Communist Regimes in East-Central Europe and the Dynamics of the Soviet Bloc", was "The Anti-Communist Armed Resistance in Romania in Comparative Perspective." Considering the fact that the topic of the anti-communist armed resistance in Romania is very little known in the English language historiography, we though it might be useful to insist more upon the development of the phenomenon, offering in the final section the so necessary comparative perspective.

[2] Virgil Ney, "Guerrilla Warfare and Modern Strategy," in *Modern Guerrilla Warfare: Fighting Communist Guerrilla Movement, 1941–1961*, Franklin Mark Osanka ed., introduction by Samuel P. Huntington (New York: The Free Press of Glencoe, 1963), p. 25.

[3] Alain Dewerpe, *Spionul: Antropologia secretului de stat contemporan*, transl. from French by Dan C. Mihǎilescu (Bucharest: Editura Nemira, 1998), p. 61.

The "guerrilla war," the "unconventional war," the "irregular war," the "internal war," the "maquis" (a term for the French Resistance only), the "paramilitary operations," etc., are all concepts that compelled recognition during World War II and continued during the Cold War. They started to be attentively investigated after World War II[4] giving birth to a rich military and political literature. But in the second half of the 20th century, in certain political and military circles, they substantiate the idea that the guerrilla war, the partisan war, is not just a liberation war, but one against colonialism and capitalism. Actually, this was only about the left wing partisan war, particularly the communist one.[5] There was no place left for the anti-communists' partisan war, as they were all together and automatically associated with fascists. The anti-communist Resistance in Eastern Europe was not known in the West, except at a quite superficial, even false, level. On the other hand, because of the hostile public environment in countries like France, where the intellectuals had been blinded by communism after World War II, it was not possible to know any better. As a result of these generalized reductionisms, the idea that being an anti-communist corresponds to being a fascist spread.[6] Jean-Paul Sartre's statement became famous: "All anti-communists are dogs." For an intellectual of his importance—holding a place in the foreground of the international intellectual stage for so long—being an anti-communist was nothing more and nothing less than a moral crime.[7] After World War II, this kind of intellectual opinion maker played an essential part in the formation of a negative perspective on anti-communists all over the world, especially in Eastern Europe.

In the present paper, we shall dwell on the anti-communist armed resistance in Romania. We have in view the temporal and spatial

---

[4] Samuel P. Huntington, "Guerrilla Warfare in theory and policy," introduction to F.M. Osanka ed., *Modern Guerrilla Warfare*, p. xv.

[5] *Guerilă, rezistenţă, război popular: Culegere de texte din literatura social-politică şi militară străină* (Bucharest: Editura Militară, 1972).

[6] François Furet, *Trecutul unei iluzii: Eseu despre ideea comunistă în secolul XX*, transl. from French by Emanoil Marcu şi Vlad Russo (Bucharest: Editura Humanitas, 1996), pp. 373–5, 396.

[7] Raymond Aron, *Spectatorul angajat*, interview with Jean-Louis Missika and Dominique Wolton, transl. from French by Miruna Tătaru-Cazaban (Bucharest: Editura Nemira, 1999), p. 165. See also Monica Lovinescu, "O paranteză cât o existenţă," *Secolul*, Vol. 20, Nos. 10–12 (1997), No. 1–3 (1998): 173.

development of the resistance, the characteristics of the phenomenon and, and for a better understanding, we opted, in the final part, for a comparative perspective.

The Discovery of a Historiographical Subject: Anti-Communist Armed Resistance in Romania

The anti-communist armed resistance in Romania, or the "resistance in the mountains," has represented, for decades, a subject that was dwelt on only ideologically, by the actors on both sides of the barricade. It has been looked upon from two totally opposite perspectives: either as a form of heroic opposition against the Soviets and the regime installed in Romania at the end of World War II, or as an "expression of the last convulsions of the bourgeois-landlord rule." The members of the anti-communist resistance have always considered themselves anti-communist fighters or partisans organized in a "group." On the other hand, the Securitate used to give the partisans the name of "bandits" or "terrorists," respectively "band" and "terrorist band."[8]

Until 1989, in Romania, the texts on this theme were rare and made only to order. A few historians in the service of the regime of Bucharest, but of quite a low professional qualification, mentioned the subject only briefly, with conclusions in accordance with the ideological orthodoxy of the moment. The official theses of the communist regime regarding the anti-communist armed resistance were expounded in different propaganda works.[9]

---

[8] For instance, although confronted with death, Ioan Novac, from the Ion Gavrilă group, which operated in the Făgăraş Mountains' north side, wrote at the end of an inquiry on 19 April 1957: "Instead of the word 'band' in the declaration, I think it would have been necessary to use the term 'group,' as by 'band' we rather understand an association of bandits, of criminals" (Ion Gavrilă-Ogoranu ed., *Brazii se frâng, dar nu se îndoiesc*, Vol. IV (Făgăraş: Editura Mesagerul de Făgăraş, s.a. 2004), p. 328, document from Arhivele Consiliului Naţional pentru Studierea Arhivelor Securităţii, fond "Informativ," dos. 770, Vol. 61, f. 400).

[9] See Mihai Fătu and Ion Spălăţelu, *Garda de Fier: Organizaţie teroristă de tip fascist*, ediţia a II-a, revăzută şi adăugită (Bucharest : Editura Politică, 1980), chapter 22, "Ultimele zvîrcoliri," pp. 364–85; general-maior Luigi Martiş, general-maior Constantin Mleşniţă, colonel Ion Şerbănescu, and colonel Ilie

In the Romanian exiles' academic writings, the anti-communist
armed resistance was barely mentioned, obviously because of the inac-
cessibility of the sources. The existence of the phenomenon had already
been pointed out in 1964, by Ghiţă Ionescu, in his synthesis of the Romanian communist history,[10] who placed the term, here and there, between inverted commas. The Romanian political analyst noticed that,
because of the systematic repression, "there was no real possibility for
an organized resistance." Inaccuracies were not completely missing, for
instance, the statement that in 1946–47 there was an attempt to unify
the "Sumanele Negre" (*suman*: a kind of long, coarse peasant coat; *the
Black Coats*), partisan groups were mainly composed of isolated and
intransigent elements of the Iron Guard.[11] This was probably the moment when in the Western circles (including the historiographic ones)
the idea appeared that the anti-communist armed opposition and the
Romanian legionary resistance were synonymous.[12] In reality, the latter
was only a segment, an important one, indeed, of the former. In 1984,
a history of the Romanian Communist Party was published in Den-
mark, signed by Victor Frunză.[13] The author underlined the fact that
"the resistance in the mountains, in the period 1948–1952 (?) [Victor
Frunză's question mark, D.D.] is the chapter that the official historiography absolutely hushed up." Although he did not have access to

Coman, *În slujba patriei socialiste: File din istoria trupelor de securitate*, Ministe-
rul de Interne, Comandamentul Trupelor de Securitate, Serviciul Editorial
şi Cinematografic, 1980, chapter I, "Contribuţia unităţilor militare ale Mi-
nisterului de Interne la transformările revoluţionare din anii revoluţiei demo-
crat-populare," pp. 17–28; and especially chapter II, "Crearea trupelor de
Securitate: Participarea lor la lupta pentru apărarea cuceririlor revoluţionare
şi a construcţiei bazelor socialismului (1948–1958)," pp. 29–65.

[10] Ghiţă Ionescu, *Communism in Romania, 1944–1962*, (Oxford: Oxford University Press, 1964).

[11] See *Ibid.*, Romanian edition, 1994, pp. 162–3.

[12] See, for example, Andrzej Paczkowski and Karel Bartosek, "Cealaltă Europă
victimă a comunismului," in Stéphane Courtois, Nicolas Werth, Jean-Louis
Panné, Andrzej Paczkowski, Karel Bartosek, and Jean-Louis Margolin ed.,
Cartea neagră a comunismului: Crime, teroare, represiune (Bucharest: Editura Humanitas, Fundaţia Academia Civică, 1998), p. 367.

[13] Victor Frunză, *Istoria Partidului Comunist Român* (Aarhus, Editura Nord,
1984); see also the 2nd edition, under the title *Istoria stalinismului în România*
(Bucharest, Editura Humanitas, 1990), chapter "Rezistenţă şi represiune,"
pp. 383–7.

documentary sources, the Romanian dissident exiled in northern Europe grasped the exact reason of the communist regime's silence: "By hushing up and ignoring them, those resistance groups were suggested to be isolated, not supported by the masses."[14] Vlad Georgescu too, in his synthesized history of Romania, mentioned the phenomenon of the anti-communist armed resistance. Referring to the years 1944–48, the famous historian only observed that then "were defeated the few attempts of military resistance."[15]

Immediately after 1989, in Romania, the public interest in the anti-communist armed resistance flourished, a fact underlined in the articles and interviews with the survivors published in cultural journals, in journals about anti-communist memories, in the daily or periodical press, and in radio and television broadcasts. The public interest in this subject has remained high. The editorial flux on subjects of recent history has become stunning over the last years. In this respect, the anti-communist armed resistance probably shares the first position with the history of the Romanian communist gulag and the history of the Securitate. Naturally, as always happens with subjects intensely investigated by different researchers, the results are unequal, the valuable papers neighbouring works that do nothing else but indicate the growing interest for the theme.[16]

---

[14] See *Ibid.*, 2nd edition, 1990, p. 386.

[15] Vlad Georgescu, *Istoria românilor de la origini până în zilele noastre*, 3rd edition (Bucharest: Editura Humanitas, 1992), p. 258.

[16] There is a rich bibliography on the subject of the anti-communist armed resistance in Romania. Hoping that, even if brief, the bibliographic suggestions are useful, we try to provide here an overview.

Volumes of documents: *Cartea Albă a Securității*, Vol. I, *23 August 1944–30 August 1948*, s.l. (Bucharest: Serviciul Român de Informații, 1997); Vol. II, *August 1948–Iulie 1958*, s.l. (1994); Vol. III, *1958–1968*, (1995); Vol. IV, *Perioada 1968–1978*, s.l. (1995); *Cu unanimitate de voturi: Sentințe politice adunate și comentate* by Marius Lupu, Cornel Nicoară, and Gheorghe Onișoru (Bucharest, Fundația Academia Civică, 1997); Ioana-Raluca Voicu-Arnăuțoiu ed., *Luptătorii din munți: Toma Arnăuțoiu. Grupul de la Nucșoara. Documente ale anchetei, procesului, detenției* (Bucharest, Editura Vremea, 1997); Radu Ciuceanu, Octavian Roske, and Cristian Troncotă eds., *Începuturile Mișcării de Rezistență în România*, Vol. I, *11 aprilie 1945–31 mai 1946* (Bucharest, Institutul Național pentru Studiul Totalitarismului, 1998); Vol. II, *1 iunie–18 noiembrie 1946*, (2001); Adrian Brișcă and Radu Ciuceanu eds., *Rezistența armată din Bucovina. 1944–1950*, Vol. I (Bucharest, Institutul Național pentru Studiul

Totalitarismului, 1998); Adrian Brişcă ed., *Rezistenţa armată din Bucovina*, Vol. II, *1 octombrie 1950–10 iunie 1952* (Bucharest: Institutul Naţional pentru Studiul Totalitarismului, 2000); Miodrag Milin ed., *Rezistenţa anticomunistă din Munţii Banatului în documente* (Bucharest: Fundaţia Academia Civică, 2000); Radu Ciuceanu ed., *Mişcarea Naţională de Rezistenţă din Oltenia*, Vol. I, *1947–1949* (Bucharest: Institutul Naţional pentru Studiul Totalitarismului, 2001); Vol. II, *1949–1952*, (2003); Vol. III, *1953–1980*, (2004); Nicolae Chipurici and Tudor Răţoi eds., *Rezistenţa anticomunistă din sud-vestul României. Opresiune şi rezistenţă. Documente*, Vol. I–III (Craiova: Editura MJM, 2004–2007); Ion Gavrilă-Ogoranu ed., *Brazii se frâng, dar nu se îndoiesc*, Vol. IV, (Făgăraş: Editura Mesagerul de Făgăraş, s.a. 2004); Adrian Brişcă ed., *Rezistenţa armată din Banat*, Vol. I, *1945–1949* (Bucharest: Institutul Naţional pentru Studiul Totalitarismului, 2004); Constantin Ionaşcu, *Rezistenţa anticomunistă din Dobrogea* (Constanţa: Editura "Ex Ponto," 2000); Marian Cojoc ed., *Rezistenţa armată din Dobrogea, 1945–1960* (Bucharest, Institutul Naţional pentru Studiul Totalitarismului, 2004); Camelia Ivan Duică ed., *Rezistenţa anticomunistă din Maramureş. Gruparea Popşa, 1948–1949* (Bucharest: Institutul Naţional pentru Studiul Totalitarismului, 2005); Marius Oprea ed., *Banalitatea răului: O istorie a Securităţii în documente. 1949–1989*, foreword by Dennis Deletant (Iaşi, Editura Polirom, 2002); Florica Dobre, Florian Banu, Camelia Duică, Silviu B. Moldovan, Elis Neagoe, and Liviu Ţăranu eds., *"Bande, bandiţi şi eroi": Grupurile de rezistenţă şi Securitatea (1948–1968). Documente*, foreword by Florian Banu şi Silviu B. Moldovan (Bucharest: Editura Enciclopedică, 2003).

Memoirs: Filon Verca, *Paraşutaţi în România vândută: Mişcarea de rezistenţă. 1944–1948* (Timişoara: Editura Gordian, 1993); Adriana Georgescu, *La început a fost sfârşitul: Dictatura roşie la Bucharest*, Ediţie îngrijită de Micaela Ghiţescu, Prefaţă de Monica Lovinescu (Bucharest: Editura Humanitas, 1992); Ion Gavrilă-Ogoranu, *Brazii se frâng, dar nu se îndoiesc: Din rezistenţa anticomunistă în Munţii Făgăraş*, Vol. I (Timişoara: Editura Marinesa, 1993), Vol. II (1995); Ioan Victor Pica, *Libertatea are chipul lui Dumnezeu*, Prefaţă de Mihai Sin, s.l. (Cluj-Napoca: Editura Arhipelag, 1993); Nicolae Ciolacu, *Haiducii Dobrogei (rezistenţa armată anticomunistă din Munţii Babadagului, Dobrogea)* (Hallandale, Florida: Colecţia "Omul Nou," 1995); Ion Ioanid, *Închisoarea noastră cea de toate zilele*, Vol. I, *1949, 1952–1954* (Bucharest: Editura Humanitas, 1999); Vol. II, *1954–1957* (2000); Ion Antohe, *Răstigniri în România după Ialta* (Bucharest: Editura Albatros, 1995).

Oral history interviews: Ştefan Bellu, *Pădurea răzvrătită. Mărturii ale rezistenţei anticomuniste* (Baia Mare: Editura Gutinul, 1993); *Povestea Elisabetei Rizea din Nucşoara. Mărturia lui Cornel Drăgoi*, culese şi editate de Irina Nicolau şi Theodor Niţu, prefaţă de Gabriel Liiceanu (Bucharest: Editura Humanitas, 1993); Dumitru Andreca, *Drumuri în întuneric (Destine mehedinţene; 1945–1964): Transcrieri după înregistrări audio efectuate în anii 1994 şi 1998* (Bucharest: Fundaţia Academia Civică, 1998); *Calvarul deţinuţilor anticomunişti botoşăneni*, eyewitness of the survivors registered by

Dumitru Ignat (Botoşani: Inspectoratul pentru cultură al judeţului Botoşani, 1997); Constantin Hrehor, *Muntele mărturisitor: Anii rezistenţei/anii suferinţei* (Iaşi: Editura Timpul, 2002) (Editura Apologeticum, 2004); Cornel Jurju and Cosmin Budeancă, *"Suferinţa nu se dă la fraţi..." Mărturia Lucreţiei Jurj despre rezistenţa anticomunistă din Apuseni (1948–1958)*, foreword by Doru Radosav (Cluj-Napoca: Editura Dacia, 2002); *Rezistenţa armată anticomunistă din România. Grupul "Teodor Şuşman" (1948–1958). Mărturii*, Denisa Bodeanu and Cosmin Budeancă eds., foreword by: Cornel Jurju and Cosmin Budeancă (Cluj-Napoca: Editura Argonaut, 2004); *Rezistenţa anticomunistă din România. Grupul "Capotă-Dejeu" (1947–1957)—Mărturii*, Denisa Bodeanu and Cosmin Budeancă eds., foreword by: Cornel Jurju and Denisa Bodeanu (Cluj-Napoca: Editura Argonaut, 2006); Miodrag Milin ed., *Rezistenţa anticomunistă din Munţii Banatului (Zona Domaşnea-Teregova): Interviuri şi evocări* (Timişoara: Editura Marineasa, Editura Presa Universitară Română, 1998); by the same author, *Rezistenţa anticomunistă din Munţii Banatului (Zona Mehadia-Iablaniţa-Breazova). Interviuri şi evocări* (Timişoara: Editura Marineasa, 2000).

Several collective or individual works deal with the anti-communist armed resistance in certain areas from the standpoint of oral history: Doru Radosav, Almira Ţentea, Cornel Jurju, Valentin Orga, Florin Cioşan, and Cosmin Budeancă, *Rezistenţa anticomunistă din Apuseni: Grupurile: "Teodor Şuşman," "Capotă-Dejeu," "Cruce şi Spadă." Studii de istorie orală* (Cluj-Napoca: Editura Argonaut, 2003); Aurora Liiceanu, *Rănile memoriei. Nucşoara şi rezistenţa din munţi* (Iaşi: Editura Polirom, 2003).

A synthetical treating of the phenomenon was attempted, both in book form, see Cicerone Ioniţoiu, *Rezistenţa armată anticomunistă din Munţii României. 1946–1958,* 2nd edition (Bucharest: Editura Gândirea românească, 1993); and in popular articles, see Eugen Şahan, "Aspecte din rezistenţa românească împotriva sovietizării în perioada martie 1944–1962," *Analele Sighet,* Vol. 2 (1995): 213–78; and Adrian Brişcă, "Rezistenţa armată anticomunistă din România," *Arhivele Totalitarismului,* Vols. 22–3, Nos. 1–2 (1999): 42–67, or of academic essays, see Georges Diener, *L'autre communisme en Roumanie: Résistance populaire et maquis, 1945–1965,* préface de Catherine Durandin (Paris: L'Harmattan, 2001); *Mişcarea armată de rezistenţă anticomunistă din România, 1944–1962* (Bucharest: Editura Kullusys, 2003).

Quite a few contributions on the anti-communist armed resistance were published in academic journals in Romania (*Anuarul Institutului de Istorie "A.D. Xenopol," Xenopoliana, Analele Ştiinţifice ale Universităţii "Al. I. Cuza" din Iaşi-Istorie, Revista de Istorie Socială, Anuarul Institutului Român de Istorie Recentă, AIO—Anuarul Institutului de Istorie Orală, Arhivele Totalitarismului, Anuarul Institutului de Istorie "George Bariţ" din Cluj-Napoca, Studii CNSAS, Arhivele Securităţii,* etc.), in journals meant to preserve memory (*Memoria, Din documentele rezistenţei*) or in collections of the same kind (*Analele Sighet*).

Several doctoral theses, some of them finalized, dealt with the anti-communist armed resistance.

Armed Resistance in Romania:
Temporal and Spatial Perspectives

The phenomenon under consideration sprang up in Romania at the end of World War II, as a form of fighting the Soviets and it fairly soon acquired an explicit anti-communist character. Different authors have proposed different periodizations of the development of the anti-communist armed resistance in Romania: 1944–58,[17] 1944–62,[18] 1945–62[19] or 1946–58.[20] As far as we are concerned, we believe that we can speak about this phenomenon as belonging to the period 1944 to the beginning of the 1960s, with the greatest intensity at the beginning of the 1950s. Though we cannot speak of a rigid delimitation, one could identify two phases of the resistance: 1944–47 and 1948—the beginning of the 1960s. In the first phase, the State was not yet completely controlled by the communists—though they had managed to assume a major role in the government after 6 March 1945—and there still were forces that opposed the government's becoming all "red." The second phase developed under the conditions of the totalitarian State, which was taking all the necessary steps to control the territory and the population, among other things by perfecting its repressive instruments, rendering the anti-communists' situation tougher and tougher.

The resistance started in the spring of 1944, with the entrance of the Soviet troops in north-eastern Romania, as a result of the Uman-

---

[17] Cristian Troncotă, "Procesul Mişcării Naţionale de Rezistenţă. 1946," *Arhivele Totalitarismului*, No. 3 (1995): 120.

[18] Eugen Şahan, "Aspecte din rezistenţa românească împotriva sovietizării în perioada martie 1944–1962," *Analele Sighet*, Vol. 2 (1995): 213–94; Adrian Brişcă, "Rezistenţa armată anticomunistă din România," *Arhivele Totalitarismului*, Vols. 22–3, Nos. 1–2 (1999): 42–67; *Mişcarea armată de rezistenţă anticomunistă din România, 1944–1962* (Bucharest: Editura Kullusys, 2003). This chronological delimitation is taken by Doru Radosav too, "Rezistenţa anticomunistă armată din România între istorie şi memorie," in Ruxandra Cesereanu ed., *Comunism şi represiune în România. Istoria tematică a unui fratricid naţional* (Iaşi: Editura Polirom, 2006), pp. 82–107.

[19] Dennis Deletant, *România sub regimul comunist*, translated into Romanian by Delia Răzdolescu (Bucharest: Fundaţia Academia Civică, 1997), p. 78.

[20] Cicerone Ioniţoiu, *Rezistenţa armată anticomunistă din Munţii României. 1946–1958*, 2nd edition, (Bucharest: Editura Gândirea românească, 1993).

Botoşani operation. Because of the abuses by the Soviet soldiers, as well as of the generalized practice of the requisitions by the Red Army, and because of the evacuation of the local population from the area of the front to the area behind it, numerous inhabitants at the foot of Obcinile Bucovinei took refuge in the woods, between the battle lines. To defend against the attacks of Russian patrols and to benefit from the help of the military regular forces in Bucovina, the locals formed several groups of partisans under the leadership of Vladimir Macoveiciuc, Ion Vatamaniuc, Vladimir Tironeac and Constantin Cenuşă. Each group consisted of about 15–20 members—farmers, "premilitaries" (the young people aged between 18–21, supposed to join an organized pre-military service in Romania, before the Second World War), the discharged, or the soldiers on leave. They were well armed and trained by German and Romanian instructors. The missions of the partisans of Bucovina aimed at sending the local population, who had taken refuge between the two fronts, to the area left under Romanian administration; at patrolling the woods; at reconnoitring and collecting information about the Soviet forces in the area, as well as at creating disruptions behind the Red Army. The occurrence of the coup d'état in Bucharest on 23 August 1944 brought about the end of the groups' activities. Some of the partisans of Bucovina managed to leave the German forces, while others were forced to withdraw towards the West. The Soviets—who were not used to forgive those who had dared to oppose them—submitted the Romanian partisans to repression; these were tried, sentenced and thrown into the immensity of the Gulag. Persistently pursued, some of the partisans continued the fight, being annihilated over the next years, while others (re)entered the resistance after 1948.[21]

The *coup d'état* of 23 August 1944 resulted in Romania's leaving the Axis—a disaster for Germany, who now tried to regain its lost position. The Germans relied, in the attempt to achieve their goals, on the Legionary Movement (which also had its own objectives, that is reconstructing its territorial structures and its return to power in Bucharest),

---

[21] Adrian Brişcă and Radu Ciuceanu eds., *Rezistenţa armată din Bucovina: 1944–1950*, Vol. I (Bucharest: INST, 1998); Dorin Dobrincu, "Bucovineni contra sovietici: Rezistenţa armată anticomunistă din Bucovina (martie–august 1944—iulie 1946)," in *AIO—Anuarul Institutului de Istorie Orală*, Vol. 5 (2004): 123–82.

but also on the German Ethnic Group. The Romanian traditional political circles hoped that they would have the West's support, that the
West would moderate the Soviets and even force them to leave Romania. If, in the context of the last months of war, a German counteroffensive had determined an Anglo-American intervention, this would
have only been beneficial to this country. But the Germans' and the
legionaries' plans, involving diverse forces (including guerrilla groups)
and contacts were doomed to failure. Romania was occupied by strong
Soviet powers, consisting of both Red Army troops and NKVD units.
Some of the commandants of the Romanian Army suspected of disloy-
alty were neutralized, while the leaders of the anti-Soviet action were
captured and found their end in the Gulag. In order to prevent such
actions from happening again, but also because this was part of the
logic of their own system, the Soviets took measures meant to weaken
the internal opposition in Romania. Germany's attempt to get Romania back under its control proved to be unachievable, and the pro-German resistance lost its reason to be because of the defeat in the trench
warfare of the very power that had inspired it.[22]

The installation of Petru Groza' government, on 6 March 1945,
signaled the country's return to dictatorship. The manifestation of political opposition became problematic, considering that the police control was every day clearer and prompter. As the positions adverse to
the government were repressed, numerous subversive groups arose,
having as their main purpose the anti-communist fight. Among them,
there were the organizations "Tinerimea liberă" (The Free Youth) and
"T." The former was led by Mircea Ştefanovici; it originated in the
left wing, but it soon adopted anti-communist positions, in the context of the repression the Groza government had started. The latter

---

[22] Perry Biddiscombe, "Proding the Russian Bear: Pro-German Resistance
in Romania, 1944–1945," *European History Quarterly*, Vol. 23, No 2 (April
1993): 193–232; Florin Constantiniu, "Prima încercare de scoatere a Ar-
matei Roşii din România," in *6 martie 1945: Începuturile comunizării României*,
Bucharest: Editura Enciclopedică (1995): 288–294; Günter Klein, "Incepu-
turile rezistenţei antisovietice în România (23 august 1944–6 martie 1945),"
in *6 martie 1945. Începuturile comunizării României* (Bucharest: Editura
Enciclopedică, 1995), pp. 295–311; Dorin Dobrincu, "Un '23 august invers'?
Tentativa de readucere a României în Axă (toamna 1944– primăvara 1945),"
Anuarul Institutului Roman de Istorie Recentă, Vol. 2, (2003): 221–90.

was initiated by Remus Țețu and eventually gathered members of the National-Liberal youth, as well as National-Peasant young people and Social Democrats, the platform being an explicitly liberal one. The contacts with the democratic political circles did not fail; even the re-sort to armed fighting was acceptable if the circumstances were favor-able, especially in case of a war between the Anglo-Americans and the Soviets. Discovered by the repressive services of the government, the two organizations were annihilated, and their members arrested, ques-tioned, tried and sentenced. In the trial that took place in September 1945 in Bucharest, the discrediting of the democrat parties was one of the goals, but this attempt was eventually a failure for the authorities, as they did not yet completely control the justice system or the press, and foreign representatives were present in court. However, this was a lesson that the communists, from a dominating position of power in the government, learnt, as one can see in the next period.[23]

The starting of the "royal strike" in the summer of 1945 clearly underlined the fact that the anti-communists' position was weak in their confrontation with a regime ready to use all legal or illegal means in order to impose and extend its control over the State institutions. In this context, anti-government organizations appeared, with more radi-cal platforms. The most important ones were the subversive organiza-tions "Haiducii lui Avram Iancu—Divizia Sumanelor Negre" (Avram Iancu's Outlaws—Sumanele Negre Division), the so-called "Mișcare Națională de Rezistență" (National Resistance Movement), "Graiul Sângelui" (The Blood's Voice), and the so-called "Grup Înarmat Si-naia" (Sinaia Armed Group). The organization "Haiducii lui Avram Iancu" was set up by a group of former members of the "Iuliu Maniu" Volunteer Battalion, headed by Gavril Olteanu, and proved to be very active from the propaganda perspective, practicing an anti-communist discourse from national, even chauvinistic positions. This harmed the organization's image, if we take into consideration the reproaches from certain democratic political circles, and the communists, who saw all

---

[23] Dan Cernovodeanu, "Una dintre primele mișcări de rezistență anticomunistă: Organizația 'T'," in *Arhivele Totalitarismului*, Vols. 24–5, Nos. 3–4 (1999): 211–8; Petre Țurlea, *Procesul organizației "T,"* (Bucharest: Editura Libra, 2000); Dorin Dobrincu, "În numele libertății: Organizațiile anticomuniste 'Tinerimea Liberă' și 'T'" (1945), *Xenopoliana*, Vol. 13, Nos. 1–4 (2005): 127–49.

nationalists as fascists, had further pretexts to repress the group. General Aurel Aldea, Admiral Horia Măcellariu, and other high officers and political men of different affiliations started the "Mişcarea Naţională de Rezistenţă" (National Resistance Movement, MNR), which tried to bring together the resistance groups in Romania, establishing contacts with the Opposition political groups, with the Royal Palace and the Missions of the United States of America and of Great Britain to Bucharest. MNR did not go beyond the phase of debates, of preliminary relationships, its potential for action being extremely limited. The organization "Graiului Sângelui" was founded by Ion Vulcănescu and confined itself to elaborating a series of documents regarding the present and the future of the State/nation. "Grupul Înarmat Sinaia"—the name was given by the Romanian repressive services—was made of militaries from the mountain corps of the area Sinaia-Predeal-Braşov, who had at their disposal weapons and ammunition deposited in the neighbouring mountains. The four groups we have mentioned had a pretty small number of active members, and the activity of "Haiducii lui Avram Iancu" and of "Graiul Sângelui" was limited to writing and spreading manifestos. The adherents to these groups hoped, together with the political opposition and an important segment of Romania's population, that the pro-Soviet regime in Bucharest would collapse if a conflict started between the free world and the power of Kremlin. Infiltrated by the information services of the Groza government, these organizations were kept under observation for a long time and then annihilated. After brutal inquiries, there came a trial (the sentence was given on 18 November 1946), mainly aiming, like the previous year, at compromising the political opposition.[24]

---

[24] Dorin Dobrincu, "Începuturile rezistenţei armate anticomuniste în România," *Anuarul Institutului de Istorie "A.D. Xenopol,"* Vol. 34 (1997): 127–33; Radu Ciuceanu, Octavian Roske, and Cristian Troncotă, eds. *Începuturile Mişcării de Rezistenţă în România,* vol. I, *11 aprilie 1945–31 mai 1946* (Bucharest : Institutul Naţional pentru Studiul Totalitarismului, 1998); vol. II, *1 iunie–18 noiembrie 1946,* (2001); Nicoleta Raluca Spiridon, "Preliminariile rezistenţei armate, 1944–1946," in *"Experimentul Piteşti": Comunicări prezentate la Simpozionul "Experimentul Piteşti-reeducarea prin tortură." Opresiunea ţărănimii române în timpul dictaturii comuniste,* 4th ed., Piteşti, 24–26 septembrie 2004, editor and coordinator Ilie Popa (Piteşti: Fundaţia Culturală Memoria, Filiala Argeş, 2005), pp. 401–18.

The annihilation of these anti-communist/anti-Soviet organizations, as well as of others, which were active in the period 1945–47, somehow marked the end of the first stage of subversive anti-communist resistance in Romania. The second phase, which started in 1948 and lasted more than a decade, was marked by the toughness of the armed confrontations and the ampleness of repression, as well as by the isolation of the partisan groups. The resistance of this period was mainly manifest in the mountain and wooded regions of Romania. Fourteen zones of resistance appeared, with different anti-communist groups: Bucovina, Moldova, Vrancea, North Transilvania, Central Transilvania, Apuseni Mountains, Crişana, Arad, Banat, Oltenia, Făgăraş Mountains—north flank, Făgăraş Mountains—south flank, Iezer Mountains, Muntenia, and Dobrogea. The climax of the armed resistance was reached at the end of the 1940s and the beginning of the 1950s. The last groups—inactive for several years—were liquidated in 1957–58, and the last isolated armed partisan fugitives were annihilated at the beginning of the 1960s.

The causes for the (re)appearance of the phenomenon of anti-communist armed resistance at the end of the 1940s in Bucovina were diverse, from the persecution of the former anti-Soviet partisans, those who opposed the new political realities in the country, to the radical economic measures of the regime, particularly the collectivisation of agriculture. Among the partisans who stood out at the end of the 1940s and in the 1950s, there were Constantin Cenuşă, Vasile Motrescu, Cozma Pătrăucean, Constantin Gherman, Gavril Vatamaniuc, Grigore Sandu, Gheorghe Vasilache, and others. They acted either as isolated fugitives, or by combining in groups or even organizations (e.g., "Gărzile Decebal"—Decebal's Guards), who had as a platform the fight against the "democrat-popular" regime. Most of the partisans from Bucovina had been on the fronts of the Second World War, especially in Russia, where they had gained useful combat experience. Like in the rest of the territory, the communist authorities did not tolerate manifestations of opposition, and even less an armed one, so that these opponents were annihilated too, some of them being shot down, others tried and sentenced to prison, together with their supporters. The last isolated partisan fugitive in this area, Gheorghe Munteanu, was caught in 1961.[25]

---

[25] Adrian Brişcă and Radu Ciuceanu, eds. *op. cit.*, vol. I; Adrian Brişcă ed., *Rezistenţa armată din Bucovina*, vol. II, *1 octombrie 1950–10 iunie 1952*, (Bu-

Even if, for the most part, Moldova did not offer favorable conditions to a partisan movement, many anti-communist organizations and
groups appeared here too, both in the rural and in the urban zone;
most of them were subversive groups, but there were some armed ones
too, involved in guerrilla actions. Important groups proved to be those
headed by Vasile Cămăruță and Vasile Corduneanu, the organization
"Frontul Patriei" (National Front) and "Centrul de rezistență" (Resistance Center) from Uturea. Most of them were small groups, counting a few members, but there were bigger ones as well. All of them
had supporters in the region, without whom their survival would have
been problematic, if not impossible. Several organizations had political
platforms, more or less articulate, while others were rather confused in
their opposition to the communization. Most of them were actually just
circumstantial/temporary associations of political fugitives.[26]

charest: Institutul Național pentru Studiul Totalitarismului, 2000); Constantin
Hrehor, *Muntele mărturisitor: Anii rezistenței/anii suferinței* (Iași: Editura Timpul, 2002); Dorin Dobrincu, "Sfidarea Securității în Bucovina. Grupul de
rezistență armată anticomunistă Gavril Vatamaniuc (1949–1958)," *Revista
de Istorie Socială*, Vols. 8–9 (2003–2004): 363–412; *Idem*, "Nesupunere în
Bucovina: Grupurile de rezistență armată anticomunistă Cenușă–Motrescu,
Pătrăucean-Gherman și Cenușă-Pătrăucean (1948–1951)," *Anuarul Institutului de Istorie "A.D. Xenopol,"* Vol. 42 (2005): 451–81; *Idem*, "Rezistența
armată anticomunistă din Bucovina: 'Gărzile Decebal' și grupul Grigore
Sandu (1949)," *Memoria*, Vols. 51–2, Nos. 2–3 (2005): 33–48; *Idem*, "Grupuri 'minore' din rezistența anticomunistă bucovineană (1948–1961)," *Cod-
rul Cosminului*, No. 12 (2006): 179–94; Marian Olaru, *Bucovineni împotriva
comunismului: frații Vasile și George Motrescu*, prefață de Dimitrie Vatamaniuc,
postfață de Vasile I. Schipor (Suceava: Editura Universității, 2006); Liviu
Țăranu and Theodor Bărbulescu eds., *Jurnale din rezistența anticomunistă:
Vasile Motrescu, Mircea Dobre, 1952–1953*, foreword by Ion Gavrilă-Ogoranu
(Bucharest: Editura Nemira, 2006), pp. 23–211.
[26] Neculai Popa, *Represiune și rezistență în ținutul Neamțului* (Bucharest: Editura Vremea, 2000); Cezar Zugravu ed., *O istorie a rezistenței și a represiunii,
1945–1989* (Iași: Editura Tipo Moldova, 2002); Dorin Dobrincu, "Fapte
uitate: Iașul și rezistența anticomunistă (1946–1950)," *Anuarul Institutului
de Istorie "A.D. Xenopol,"* Vol. 41 (2004): 389–412; *Idem*, "Un 'front' puțin
cunoscut: rezistența armată anticomunistă din nordul Moldovei (1948–1954),"
Analele Științifice ale Universității Al. I. Cuza din Iași, serie nouă, Istorie, tom L
(2004): 219–51; *Idem*, "Formațiuni din rezistența armată anticomunistă în
sudul Moldovei (1945–1958), *AIO—Anuarul Institutului de Istorie Orală*,
Vol. 6 (2005): 163–92.

In the district Curbura Carpaților, more precisely in the county of
Vrancea, at the beginning of the communist regime there were two active important partisan groups. The Ion Paragină group arose in 1948,
in the Panciu zone, as a result of some legionaries' initiative, but pretty
soon national-peasant party members, national-liberals, or people with
no political affiliation enrolled. The members of the group were University students, pupils, teachers, priests, tradesmen or farmers. The
partisans wrote manifestos and a battle guide (*The Outlaw's Manual*),
they gathered weapons, took military instruction, and established useful contacts in case a conflict would have started between the West and
the Soviets. Infiltrated by the Securitate, the group was annihilated in
October 1949.[27] The inhabitants of the historical region of Vrancea,
desperate at the end of the 1940s, as their main resources—mountains
and woods—had been confiscated ("nationalized"), were subjected to
harsh taxes, and they were attacked daily on their still archaic ways of
social organization. They were also waiting—like all Romanians and
Eastern Europeans—for the situation to change, for help to come from
somewhere, even if it came with the price of a new war; in other words,
they were waiting for "the Americans to come." The people of Vrancea
were simple people, mountain people with few contacts with the world,
but brave to madness, ready to follow anyone who had a project at all
coherent to remove the communist regime. In this context the organization "Vlad Țepeș II" appeared, started by Victor Lupșa, from the
county of Trei Scaune. The organization had nuclei in three counties—
Putna, Trei Scaune, and Râmnicu Sărat—including hundreds of persons, especially farmers, but also workers, civil servants, intellectuals,
discharged officers, and university students. A series of simultaneous

---

[27] Laura Stancu and Liviu Burlacu, "Organizația de rezistență 'Paragină' în
atenția Securității," in *Totalitarism și rezistență, teroare și represiune în România
comunistă* (Bucharest: Consiliul Național pentru Studierea Arhivelor
Securității, 2001), pp. 146–53; Laura Vlădoiu-Stancu, and Liviu Burlacu
eds., "Manualul haiducului—cod de instructaj al organizației de rezistență
'Paragină'," *Arhivele Securității*, Vol. 1 (2002): 219–27; Mihai Timaru,
Amintiri de la Gherla (Timișoara: Editura de Vest, 1993); *Idem, Destinul unui
ofițer: Amintiri* (Bucharest: Fundația Academia Civică, 2000); Dorin Dobrincu, "Rezistența armată anticomunistă din Vrancea: grupul Ion Paragină
(1948–1949)," in Cosmin Budeancă, Florentin Olteanu, and Iulia Pop eds.,
Rezistența anticomunistă—cercetare științifică și valorificare muzeală (Cluj-Napoca: Editura Argonaut, 2006), pp. 74–89.

actions in the three mentioned counties occured in the night of 23–24 July 1950. The insurgents only took over the control at Bârseşti, drawing out the rapid and brutal intervention of the Securitate in all the villages where they found nuclei of the organization. Encounters with the Securitate were also recorded, several rebels being killed, hundreds of people arrested, and their families ill-treated. The trials (there were 18 batches with over 300 defendants) ended with death sentences or many years in prison. Victor Lupşa surrendered after a few years, and was executed in 1956.[28]

In North Transilvania several anti-communist groups existed. Brothers Vasile and Ioan Popşa tried in 1949 to unify the resistance in Valea Izei, by initiating the subgroups of Ieud, Rozavlea, and Dragomireşti, in which tens of persons were involved; the groups were annihilated during the clashes of 1949–50. Another important group was formed by the unification of the groups headed by the forester Nicolae Pop called Achim (in 1944 he had saved several Jews that were about to be deported by the Hungarian Germans to the extermination camp of Auschwitz; he was subsequently awarded the medal "Righteous Among Nations," together with Maria Pop and Aristina Pop, Săileanu-to-be—by the Yad Vashem Memorial, in Israel) and the Greek Catholic priest Atanase Oniga. Active in the Ţibleşului Mountains, the Lăpuşului side, this group proved to be the most important one in North Transilvania. The Securitate did not manage to annihilate it completely until 1953. The last isolated partisans in North Transylvania were killed in 1956–58 (Gheorghe Paşca and Vasile Blidaru).[29]

---

[28] *Arhivele Serviciului Român de Informaţii*, fond P, dosar nr. 64409, vol. 1–25; "'În 1948 ne-au luat muntele...'. Răscoala ţărănească din Munţii Vrancei—23 iulie 1950. Destăinuirile participanţilor," recorded by Ruxandra Mihăilă, *Memoria*, Vol. I, No. 11 (1994): 35–45; Vol. II, No. 13 (1995): 102–5.

[29] Ştefan Bellu, *Pădurea răzvrătită: Mărturii ale rezistenţei anticomuniste* (Baia Mare: Editura Gutinul, 1993); Camelia Ivan Duică ed., *Rezistenţa anticomunistă din Maramureş: Gruparea Popşa, 1948–1949*, (Bucharest: INST, 2005); *Jurnale din rezistenţa anticomunistă: Vasile Motrescu, Mircea Dobre, 1952–1953*, Liviu Ţăranu and Theodor Bărbulescu eds., foreword by Ion Gavrilă-Ogoranu (Bucharest: Editura Nemira, 2006), pp. 213–49; chapter "Solidaritate şi salvare. Români printre cei 'Drepţi între Popoare'," subsection "Lista cetăţenilor români distinşi de Yad Vashem cu titul Drept între Popoare," in *Comisia Internaţională pentru Studierea Holocaustului în România, Raport final*, Preşedintele comisiei: Elie Wiesel, edited by Tuvia Friling, Radu Io-

In Central Transilvania several anti-communist groups operated. "Garda Albă" (White Guard) / "Liga Naţională Contra Comunismului" (National League Against Communism) / "Organizaţia de
rezistenţă a partizanilor din Munţii Rodnei" (Partisans' Resistance Organization in Rodna Mountains) (all three designations appear) was
founded by Leonida Bodiu, former officer of the Romanian Army; he
had been a Soviet prisoner, he then returned to Romania with the "Tudor Vladimirescu" Division, was taken prisoner by the Germans and
came back home after the war. The region in which the organization
was active included part of the Năsăud county, with important nuclei
in the communes of Parva, Rebra, and Rebrişoara, made up of rural
intellectuals, rich, middle, and poor peasants. Two important writers
had contacts with this group as well, Teohar Mihadaş and Constant
Tonegaru. The group was annihilated in January–February 1949. Several members, (including the leader) were executed without trial, as
repeatedly happened in Transilvania and in other regions as well. The
other arrested were tried and sentenced to many years in prison.[30] Another organization in this area was called "Partizanii Regelui Mihai—
Armata Secretă" (King Mihai's Partisans—Secret Weapon) / "Partizanii Majestăţii Sale Regele Mihai I" (Partisans of His Majesty, King
Mihai I), or "Garda Albă" (White Guard) / "Armata Albă" (White
Army); this was started in 1948 in Cluj, at the initiative of Alexandru
(or Vasile) Suciu, Gheorghe Mureşan, and Lazăr Bondor. It spread in

anid, and Mihail E. Ionescu (Iaşi: Editura Polirom, 2005), p. 313; Dorin
Dobrincu, "'Oamenii de pădure': Rezistenţa armată anticomunistă din nordul Transilvaniei (1945–1958), *Anuarul Institutului de Istorie "George Bariţ"
din Cluj-Napoca, Series historica*, Vol. 43 (2004): 317–71; *Idem*, "Formaţiuni
'minore' de rezistenţă anticomunistă şi fugari solitari din nordul Transilvaniei (1949–1958)," *Annales Universitatis Apulensis: Series Historica*, Vol. 10
No. 1 (2006): 133–46; *Idem*, "Biografii neconvenţionale în istoria Holocaustului şi Gulagului din România: 'Drepţi între popoare' şi luptători în
rezistenţa armată anticomunistă," in Ruxandra Cesereanu ed. *Caietele Echinox*, Vol. 13, Gulag şi Holocaust (Cluj-Napoca, 2007), pp. 168–75; Andreea
Dobeş, "Speranţă şi iluzie în anii '50· Aspecte privind rezistenţa armată
anticomunistă în Maramureş," *AIO—Anuarul Institutului de Istorie Orală*,
Vol. 5 (2004): 96–122.
30 Teohar Mihadaş, *Pe muntele Ebal* (Cluj: Editura Clusium, 1990); Viorel Bodiu, "Fratele meu, ostaş în divizia 'Tudor Vladimirescu', împuşcat ca antico-
munist pe Dealul Crucii," *Memoria*, No. 22 (1997), pp. 122–7.

the neighbouring localities, from Turda to Gherla, including the villages. Their goal was to fight the communist regime and to bring the king back to power. The group was destroyed in the spring of 1949, after the betrayal by one of the members. But some of the group members managed to flee, taking refuge in the woods and engaged in armed fighting. A group headed by the Greek Catholic Priest Eusebiu Cutcan, annihilated at the end of 1950, was particularly conspicuous.[31]

The Apuseni Mountains were one of the most important areas of anti-communist armed resistance. On the eastern side, in 1948, the "Frontul Apărării Naționale-Corpul de Haiduci" (National Defense Front-Outlaws' Corps) was formed under the leadership of major Nicolae Dabija and of the sub-engineer Traian Macovei. The partisans built a blockhouse in Muntele Mare, and support groups appeared in the localities at the foot of the mountains—as was the case of "Liga Apuseană a Moților" (Western League of the Apuseni Mountains Inhabitants). As well as a network offering information about the authorities' actions, Major Dabija developed a plan aiming at nothing less than starting an insurrection in 1949, when the war between the Soviets and the Americans was expected to begin. Their objectives were the occupation by force of the State institutions, of some weapon and ammunition deposits, as well as of some strategic districts in the country, especially of some mountain passes. Connections with Bucharest were arranged, and steps were made to establish contacts with western diplomatic circles from the capital. The Securitate managed to avert the starting of a significant anti-communist movement in the Apuseni Mountains: Nicolae Dabija's group was destroyed, many partisans died during the fights, and others were caught then or later. A trial that took place in Sibiu, in October 1949, ended in the sentencing to death of some of the arrested partisans, while others were executed in spite of intial prison sentences. Another group from the same eastern side of the Apuseni Mountains, in the area of the communes of Băişoara and Muntele Băişoarei, was headed by commander Diamandi Ionescu. The partisans were involved

---

[31] Liviu Malița and Ovidiu Pecican, "Urmăriți, prindeți, arestați pe individul Eusebiu Cutcan, fost preot...," interview with Eusebiu Cutcan, *Apostrof*, Nos. 5–7 (1990): 40–1; Dan Curean, "După 40 de ani Stoica Stoian rupe tăcerea," *Nu*, No. 56 (11–18 noiembrie 1991), p. 9; Valentin Naumescu, Gabriel Năsui, "Şi crucea şi spada simbolizează biruința," interview with Eusebiu Cutcan, *Echinox*, Nos. 10–11 (1991): 4.

in daring actions against the communist authorities (in August 1949 they occupied the commune of Muntele Băişoarei, removing for a short while the party and State administration), but after a brutal clash they were annihilated. Some of the fighters or their supporters were executed on the spot, others were tried and sentenced to death or to different periods of time in prison.[32] In the south-eastern slope of the Apuseni Mountains a group headed by Leon Şuşman and Simion Roşa operated for almost one decade a group who stood in (armed) expectation, rather than in an active, paramilitary mode.[33]

In Depresiunea Huedinului there were several anti-communist groups. One of them was "Echipa Cruce şi Spadă" (Cross and Sword Team), headed by Gheorghe Gheorghiu called Mărăşeşti and Gavrilă Forţu. Founded in 1948 in Bucharest, the organization "migrated" to the area of Huedin, where it had supporters. The Securitate's quick and determined intervention led to the destruction of the group, most of its members being caught, tried and sentenced (but none of them received a death sentence). The leaders and a few other partisans were executed and their corpses were displayed in public. Teodor Şuşman from the commune of Răchiţele, in the south of Depresiunea Huedin, was one of the numerous individuals persecuted by the communist regime on grounds of social origin, his prestige having been built on traditional values and of unconventional convictions. Together with his elder sons, Teodor Jr. and Visalon, he founded an armed group that operated for several years in the area of the Vlădeasa Mountains, on north side of the Apuseni Mountains. The group became, step by step, one of the most important groups of anti-communist armed resistance

---

[32] Ion Cârja, *Canalul morţii*, (Bucharest: Editura Cartea Românească, 1993), *passim*; Dorin Dobrincu, "'Frontul Apărării Naţionale: Corpul de Haiduci' în luptă contra regimului comunist în sud-estul Munţilor Apuseni (1948–1952)," *AIO—Anuarul Institutului de Istorie Orală*, Vol. 7 (2006) pp. 140–82; *Idem*, "Rezistenţa armată anticomunistă din partea sud-estică a Munţilor Apuseni. Grupul Diamandi Ionescu sau "Muntele Băişorii" (1948–1950)," *Memoria*, Vols. 58–9, Nos. 1–2 (2007).

[33] Elisabeta Neagoe, "Grupul de rezistenţă Leon Şuşman (1948–1957)," in *Mişcarea armată de rezistenţă anticomunistă din România, 1944–1962* (Bucharest: Editura Kullusys, 2003), pp. 45–71; Dorin Dobrincu, "Anticommunist Resistance Groups (Leon Şuşman, Simion Roşa, Leon Şuşman-Simion Roşa) in Central Transylvania—The Apuseni Mountains (1948–1957)," *Revue Roumaine d'Histoire*, Vol. 45, Nos. 1–4 (Janvier–Décembre 2006): 245–65.

in Romania, according to the Securitate's classifications. After years of confrontations with the Securitate, some of the partisans killed themselves (the leader and the two sons, on different dates), others were killed in combat (Mihai Jurj) or were seized, sentenced to death, and executed (Roman Oneţ) or sentenced to prison (Lucreţia Jurj), together with many of their supporters. In the same region of Huedin, there was a subversive organization known as "Frontul Naţional Creştin Iuliu Maniu" (Iuliu Maniu Christian National Front), "Gruparea de luptă pentru Libertate, Patrie şi Cruce" (Fight Group for Freedom, Nation and Cross), or the Iosif Capotă–Alexandru Dejeu Group. This group confined itself to spreading anti-communist manifestos.[34]

Crişana was one of the smaller hotbeds of resistance, but here too, there were several subversive organizations and armed groups: the Ştefan Popescu group, "G4" and "Vlad Ţepeş II" organizations. These had a heterogeneous political, social, and ethnic composition, some of them being led by former members of different political parties (National Peasant Party), others having no political affiliation. They were supported by both well-to-do and poor people, young (most of them) and old people, by Romanians, in the majority, but also by Hungarians (men and women).[35]

---

[34] Cornel Jurju and Cosmin Budeancă, *"Suferinţa nu se dă la fraţi…" Mărturia Lucreţiei Jurj despre rezistenţa anticomunistă din Apuseni (1948–1958)* (Cluj-Napoca: Editura Dacia, 2002); Doru Radosav, Almira Ţentea, Cornel Jurju, Valentin Orga, Florin Cioşan, and Cosmin Budeancă, *Rezistenţa anticomunistă din Apuseni. Grupurile: "Teodor Şuşman," "Capotă-Dejeu," "Cruce şi Spadă." Studii de istorie orală* (Cluj-Napoca: Editura Argonaut, 2003); Denisa Bodeanu and Cosmin Budeancă eds., *Rezistenţa armată anticomunistă din România. Grupul "Teodor Şuşman" (1948–1958). Mărturii*, introduced by Cornel Jurju and Cosmin Budeancă (Cluj-Napoca: Editura Argonaut, 2004); Oana Ionel and Dragoş Marcu, "Rezistenţa împotriva comunismului prin difuzarea de manifeste: Cazul Iosif Capotă," in *Mişcarea armată de rezistenţă anticomunistă din România, 1944–1962* (Bucharest: Editura Kullusys, 2003), pp. 111–32.

[35] Antonio Faur, *Ştefan Popescu—liderul grupului de rezistenţă anticomunistă din sudul Bihorului (1946–1950)* (Oradea: Editura Universităţii din Oradea, 2007); Gabriel Moisa, "Rezistenţa anticomunistă (din nord-vestul României)," in Ion Zainea (coord.), Corneliu Crăciun, Antonio Faur, Mihai Drecin, Gabriel Moisa, Augustin Ţârău, and Nicolae Mihu, *Democraţie occidentală şi democraţie populară: evoluţia spectrului politic în nord-vestul României (1944–1950)* (Oradea: Editura Universităţii din Oradea, 2004), pp. 169–238; Cornel Onaca, *Martori şi martiri: Din temniţele comuniste* (Oradea: Editura Imprimeriei de Vest, 2000).

In the area of Arad, the armed resistance was present especially on the Eastern side. Gligor Cantemir and Ioan Bogdan headed organizations that extended to the mountain area of Arad, in the period 1948–49; the Securitate soon liquidated them. Some of those who escaped arrests regathered into smaller groups, and they proved to be particularly active over the next years; considerable display of force was necessary to destroy them. This was the case of the Zaharia Berău-Ioan Luluşa–Pavel Dobrei group, and that of Ilie Sasu's group. The resistance groups in the area of Arad represented a real problem for the Militia and the Securitate at the period, as they were involved in armed clashes, that ended with victims on both sides. Eventually, they were infiltrated and annihilated as well.[36]

One of the regions where the phenomenon of armed resistance manifested itself intensely and for a long time was the region of Banat. Colonel Ion Uţă—who had extensive military, administrative, and political experience (he was a member of the National Peasant Party)—was one of the most important leaders of the resistance there. The people around him were, for the most part, peasants from the mountain villages of the county of Severin, but he also had contacts in the important cities of Banat. Hoping that the much expected East–West war would start, colonel Uţă initiated a plan meant to build a "National Bloc" that would include all the resistance groups in Banat and start a general anti-communist riot in the region. Informed in time, the repressive structures of the communist State intervened with force at the beginning of the year 1949; during the fights, several partisans were killed, including colonel Uţă. At the end of the 1940s, under the leadership of lawyer Spiru Blănaru, commander Petru Domăşneanu and notary public Gheorghe Ionescu, with different political affiliations (the first two were legionaries, while the last one was a national-liberal), several anti-

[36] Steliana Breazu, "Grupul de rezistenţă anticomunistă al lui Gligor Cantemir din Munţii Zarandului şi Munţii Codrului, pe Valea Crişului Alb," *Analele Sighet*, Vol. 2 (1995): 334–7; Gheorghe Poenaru, "O organizaţie de rezistenţă anticomunistă din judeţul Arad, în perioada 1948–1956," *Analele Sighet*, Vol. 1 (1995): 257–62; Corneliu Cornea, *Jurnalul detenţiei politice în judeţul Arad, 1945–1989*, prefaţă de Viorel Gheorghiţă, (Arad: Editura Mirador, 2000); Dorin Dobrincu, "Organizaţii şi grupuri de rezistenţă armată anticomunistă din zona Aradului (1948–1956)," *Acta Transylvanica: Anuarul Centrului de Istorie a Transilvaniei*, Vol. I (2004): 171–202.

communist groups were created in the same mountain area of the county of Severin. For certain periods, they united, but because of different political ideas, and because of the leaders' vanities, frictions appeared, which led to the disintegration of the groups. The groups headed by Blănaru and Ionescu in particular had major clashes with the numerous forces of the Securitate in the area. The Securitate eventually gained the upper hand over them, the leaders and most of members being seized. Engineer Aurel Vernichescu and lawyer Ioan Târziu, former members of the National Peasant Party, were, in the autumn–winter of 1948–49, the leaders of a resistance group that operated in the villages south and east of the city of Caransebeş. The "Organizaţia Naţională Creştină de Luptă Împotriva Comunismului, Partizanii României Mari" (National Christian Organization of the Fight Against Communism, Great Romania's Partisans)—also known as "Vulturul Negru" (Black Eagle) or "Bastionul Negru" (Black Bastion)—was founded at Timişoara in the autumn of 1948 on the initiative of Ion Tănase, private servant, and former member of the National Peasant Party. The group spread towards the Banat region, planning to start, on 18–19 March 1949, an anticommunist riot, by simultaneously attacking and occupying the public institutions, the headquarters of the Communist Party, etc., in the main cities and villages of the region. A cooperation contact was established between the two above-mentioned groups in February–March 1949. The Securitate, however, counteracted these anti-communists' actions, seizing the members and the supporters of the organization. The leaders and the important members of all of the above-mentioned organizations were gathered in as an exemplary batch, and tried at Timişoara, in June 1949, in a show-trial. Several death sentences were given and executed, and subsequently, other partisans were executed as well, even if they had been given prison sentences. Besides these, there were other subversive or armed groups in Banat. Moreover, there were isolated anti-communist fighters. The most famous case was Ion Banda's, referred to as the last anti-communist fighter in Banat, and in Romania, as he was only liquidated in 1962.[37]

---

[37] Miodrag Milin ed., *Rezistenţa anticomunistă din Munţii Banatului (Zona Domaşnea-Teregova): Interviuri şi evocări* (Timişoara: Editura Marineasa, Editura Presa Universitară Română, 1998); *Idem* (coord.), *Rezistenţa anticomunistă din Munţii Banatului (Zona Mehadia-Iablaniţa-Breazova): Interviuri şi evocări* (Timişoara: Editura Marineasa, 2000); *Idem* ed., *Rezistenţa*

The most important anti-communist groups in Oltenia were the "Carlaonţ-Ciuceanu" subversive organization, the "Arnota" group and "Mişcarea Română de Rezistenţă" (Resistance Romanian Movement). Their members had different political affiliations (they were peasant party members, liberal party members, legionaries, social-democrats) or were apolitical; they had different professions (former military officers (including high officers), teachers, elementary school teachers, university students, pupils, engineers, workers, and peasants). Some of these groups were involved in clashes with the Securitate, but they were violently annihilated, with victims on both sides of the barricade.[38]

---

anticomunistă din Munţii Banatului în documente (Bucharest: Fundaţia Academia Civică, 2000); Ileana Silvean, *Cărările speranţei: Destine ale rezistenţei anticomuniste din Banat*, Vols. 1, 3–4 (Timişoara: Editura Marineasa, 1998), 2002–2003; Adrian Brişcă, ed., *Rezistenţa armată din Banat*, Vol. 1, 1945–1949 (Bucharest: INST, 2004); Dorin Dobrincu, "Lupta deschisă cu regimul comunist în Banatul de munte: Grupurile de rezistenţă armată conduse de Spiru Blănaru, Petru Domăşneanu şi Gheorghe Ionescu (1948–1950)," *Acta Transylvanica: Anuarul Centrului de Istorie a Transilvaniei*, Vol. 2 (2005): 119–68; *Idem*, "Organizaţia Naţională Creştină de Luptă împotriva Comunismului, Partizanii României Mari şi planul de răsculare a Banatului (1948–1949)", *Analele Ştiinţifice ale Universităţii "Al. I. Cuza" din Iaşi*, serie nouă, Istorie, Vol. 51 (2005): 293–316; *Idem*, 'Rămăşiţele grupului Ion Uţă': formaţiunile de rezistenţă din Banat conduse de fraţii Duicu, Dumitru Mutaşcu şi Dumitru Işfănuţ (1949–1954)," *Annales Universitatis Apulensis*, Series Historica, Vol. 9, No. I (2005): 193–215; "Grupul bănăţean de rezistenţă Liviu Vuc-Ioan Beg (1948–1958)," *Memoria*, Vol. 54, No. 1 (2006): 52–61; *Idem*, "Formaţiunile 'minore'" de rezistenţă anticomunistă din Banat, 1947/1948–începutul anilor '60," *Anuarul Institutului de Istorie "A.D. Xenopol,"* Vols. 43–44, (2006–2007): 549–71.

[38] Dumitru Andreca, *Drumuri în întuneric (Destine mehedinţene: 1945–1964): Transcrieri după înregistrări audio efectuate în anii 1994 şi 1998* (Bucharest: Fundaţia Academia Civică, 1998); Cristina Păiuşan ed., "Grupul Mişcarea Română de Rezistenţă din Oltenia, 1949–1952," *Arhivele Totalitarismului*, Vols. 28–29, Nos. 3–4 (2000): 139–54; Aristide Ionescu, *Dacă vine ora H, pe cine putem conta?*, 3rd revised edition (Bucharest: Editura Ramida, 2001); Radu Ciuceanu ed., *Mişcarea Naţională de Rezistenţă din Oltenia*, Vol. I, *1947–1949* (Bucharest: Institutul Naţional pentru Studiul Totalitarismului, 2001); Vol. II, *1949–1952* (2003); Vol. III, *1953–1980* (2004); Monica Grigore, "Grupul Arnota, un episod al rezistenţei anticomuniste româneşti din nordul Olteniei," in *Mişcarea armată de rezistenţă anticomunistă din România, 1944–1962* (Bucharest: Editura Kullusys, 2003), pp. 99–110; Dorin Dobrincu, "'Arnota'—un grup de rezistenţă armată anticomunistă din Oltenia montană

The north side of the Făgăraş Mountains proved to be, from a historical point of view, one of the most important hotbeds of hostilities against the communist regime in Romania. Profiting from the geographical advantage—the Făgăraş Mountains were the most important massif in the Romanian Carpathians—many of the young people from the localities in the former county of Făgăraş, almost all of them members of the "Frăţii de Cruce" (Cross Brotherhood), the youth organization of the Legionary Movement, became involved after 1948–49/50 in open actions against the communist regime. These university students, high school pupils, workers, peasants, and foresters formed a group known as "Grupul carpatin făgărăşan" (Făgăraş Carpathian Group), "Grupul 73 Carpatin de eliberare naţională" (73 Carpathian Group for the National Liberation), or simply Gavrilă group (the Securitate used the expression "Gavrilă band"). The most famous leader was Ion Gavrilă. In the mountains, there were few partisans, not more than 11 or 14, but they adapted to the new conditions and proved to be extremely efficient in the guerrilla actions, even if important Securitate and Militia forces were mobilized against them, as well as a large number of informers. In an extremely hostile environment, the fighters from Făgăraş resisted several years, due to the important support of the locals. Securitate's persistence eventually yielded results, the last partisans being ambushed, captured, tried, sentenced, and executed at Jilava. Numerous supporters were tried as well and sentenced to different periods in prison. Among the partisans, the only one who escaped was the leader himself, Ion Gavrilă, who hid for more than 20 years; by the time of his capture in 1976 there were no criminal consequences any more.[39]

(1949), in Dumitru Ivănescu and Marius Chelcu eds., *Istorie şi societate în spaţiul est-carpatic (secolele XIII-XX): Omagiu profesorului Alexandru Zub* (Iaşi: Editura Junimea, 2005), pp. 431–51.

[39] Iuliu Crăcană, "Rezistenţa anticomunistă din Munţii Făgăraş între anii 1948–1955: Grupul Gavrilă," in *Mişcarea armată de rezistenţă anticomunistă din România, 1944–1962* (Bucharest: Editura Kullusys, 2003), pp. 9–44; Ion Gavrilă-Ogoranu, *Brazii se frâng, dar nu se îndoiesc: Din rezistenţa anticomunistă în Munţii Făgăraş*, Vols. 1–2 (Timişoara: Editura Marineasa, 1993, 1995) and Vol. 4, (Făgăraş: Editura Mesagerul de Făgăraş, f.a. [2004]); Ion Gavrilă-Ogoranu and Lucia Baki Nicoară eds., *Brazii se frâng, dar nu se îndoiesc: Rezistenţa anticomunistă în Munţii Făgăraşului*, Vol. 3, (Timişoara: Editura Marineasa, 1999); Ioan Victor Pica, *Libertatea are chipul lui Dumnezeu*, preface by Mihai Sin (Cluj-Napoca: Editura Arhipelag, 1993).

On the south slope of the Făgăraş Mountains and in the Iezer Mountains other important armed resistance groups were active. Geography played an important part again, as well as the population structure (energetic people, supporters of historical political parties). The initiators of the armed resistance in the area were a few career soldiers, discharged after the purges conducted by the Communist Party. Colonel Gheorghe Arsenescu, a competent officer who had participated in the fights on the Eastern front, and after the war had become an active member of the "Tătărescu" National Liberal Party, started, together with other locals, an anti-communist organization—and subsequently an armed group—installed, in 1948, near the commune of Dragoslavele; the group was annihilated by Securitate in the spring of 1949. Taking refuge in Bucharest in the winter of 1948–49, colonel Arsenescu established connections with different anti-communists, among whom the former lieutenant Toma Arnăuțoiu, coming from the commune of Nucşoara, the county of Muscel; Toma also had battle experience (he had even been hurt on the Western front), and he joined the National Peasant Party when he left the army. Fostering the conviction that the war between the Soviets and the Americans was imminent, the two officers developed an armed resistance organization in the Nucşoara zone. Named "Haiducii Muscelului" (Outlaws of Muscel)— the names of "Gruparea de partizani (haiduci) de pe râul Doamnei" (The Group of Partisans/Outlaws on Doamna River) "Rezistența Națională" (National Resistance), and "Partizanii Libertății" (Partisans of Freedom) were also used—this group had a paramilitary structure, including in particular, inhabitants of the village of Nucşoara. Several confrontations with the Securitate occurred; some of the group followed Gheorghe Arsenescu, others Toma Arnăuțoiu. The group headed by Arsenescu was quickly annihilated (autumn of 1949), only the leader managed to escape and hide in the area of Câmpulung for more than a decade. On the other hand, the Arnăuțoiu group created real problems for the Securitate for years. These partisans' survival was due to both their courage (some of them killed or injured Securitate, Militia officers, or Romanian Workers' Party members), and the loyalty of their supporters. Even if, at a certain moment, the partisans entered a quasi-total conspiracy, the political police continued the pursuit, and in 1958 managed to find and annihilate them. Numerous persons were grouped in batches, tried and sentenced to death (executed at Jilava,

including Toma Arnăuţoiu) or to many years in prison. Colonel Arsenescu was also captured in 1960, tried, sentenced to death, and executed, while his supporters were given heavy prison sentences.[40]

In Muntenia, several anti-communist armed groups stood out. The
Dumitru Apostol group was formed in 1948 and its members were legionaries. They were active in the Argeş Mountains, but were destroyed
in May 1949; the repression was excessively severe—people were killed
in battle or discretely executed. In the area of the locality of Lehliu,
in the middle of the field of Bărăgan, Major Constantin Hocic's group
operated, in the period 1950–52. Şerban-Drăgoi's and Şerban-Voican's
groups operated in the county of Muscel, but they also were annihilated
by the Securitate in the years 1951–52, and 1957, respectively.[41]

In Dobrogea, the anti-communist armed resistance was manifest
especially among the Macedo-Romanians; from among them came
the leaders (Gogu Puiu, brothers Nicolae and Dumitru Fudulea, Nicolae Ciolacu, etc.) and most of the members. As for their political

---

[40] Alexandru Marinescu, "Pagini din rezistenţa armată anticomunistă. Zona
Nucşoara-Făgăraş," *Memoria*, Vol. 7 (1992): 47–58; Irina Nicolau and The-
odor Niţu, *Povestea Elisabetei Rizea din Nucşoara. Mărturia lui Cornel Drăgoi*,
foreword by Gabriel Liiceanu (Bucharest: Editura Humanitas, 1993); Ion
Constantinescu-Mărăcineanu, "Un erou de legendă. Colonelul Gheorghe
Arsenescu," *Analele Sighet*, Vol. 8 (2000): 565–71; Ioana-Raluca Voicu-
Arnăuţoiu ed., *Luptătorii din munţi. Toma Arnăuţoiu. Grupul de la Nucşoara.
Documente ale anchetei, procesului, detenţiei* (Bucharest: Editura Vremea,
1997); Aurora Liiceanu, *Rănile memoriei: Nucşoara şi rezistenţa din munţi* (Iaşi:
Editura Polirom, 2003); Dorin Dobrincu, "The Anti-Communist Armed
Resistance on the Southern Slope of the Făgăraş Mountains and the Iezer
Mountains: The Groups Led by Colonel Gheorghe Arsenescu and Lieuten-
ant Toma Arnăuţoiu (1948–1960)," (I), *Revista Arhivelor*, Vol. 84, Nos. 3–4,
(2007): 249–72.

[41] *Arhivele Serviciului Român de Informaţii*, fond D, dosar nr. 2168, dosar nr.
2168, ff. 238, 283–5, 345; Răzvan Ciolcă and Claudia Căpăţână, "Dumitru
Apostol (1905–1950)," *Arhivele Totalitarismului*, Vol. 21, No. 4 (1998):
229–30; *Idem*, "Rezistenţa anticomunistă de pe Valea Topologului. Interviu
cu Dumitru Apostol," *Arhivele Totalitarismului*, Vols. 22–23, Nos. 1–2 (1999):
217–25; Vasile Novac and Gheorghe Nicolescu, "Grupul de rezistenţă Şerban-
Voican din Capu Piscului, Muscel. 1952–1958," *Arhivele Totalitarismului*, Vols.
15–16, Nos. 2–3 (1997): 138–57; Dorin Dobrincu, "Rezistenţa armată
anticomunistă din Muntenia. Grupurile Dumitru Apostol, Nicolae Diaco-
nescu, Constantin Hocic, Şerban-Drăgoi şi Şerban-Voican (1948–1957),"
Studii şi Materiale de Istorie Contemporană, Vol. 6 (2007): 67–83.

affiliation, the most important partisans had been legionaries, although peasant party members, liberals or even nominal members of the Communist Party and Working Youth Union were not lacking. From a social point of view, the major part were peasants, but also elementary school teachers, discharged or active militaries, churchmen, etc. The resistance in Dobrogea was at its peak in 1949–50; in the fights, several partisans were killed, captured, tried, sentenced to death or prison (many of them were executed in the so-called "trains of death"). The resistance in this area was completely annihilated in 1951–52.[42]

The resistance developed especially in the areas favourable to guerrilla warfare, particularly in the mountains, woods, in the places, therefore, difficult to access, which offered the possibility of camouflage for the anti-communist fighters. But anti-communist groups also existed in the hill areas, sometimes even in the lowlands and in the cities.

From a political point of view, the partisans were former members of the National Peasant Party, of the National Liberal Party, of the Legionary Movement, or even people who had enrolled in the Romanian Communist Party or in satellite parties or mass organizations it controlled, and who, at a certain moment in time started a conflict with the new regime and had to join clandestine groups in order to escape arrest. But on the whole, the members of the resistance groups and their supporters were not politically affiliated.[43]

---

[42] Nicolae Ciolacu, *Haiducii Dobrogei (rezistenţa armată anticomunistă din Munţii Babadagului, Dobrogea)*, Hallandale, Florida, Colecţia "Omul Nou," 1995; Olimpia Cotan and Taşcu Beca eds., *Rezistenţa: Mărturii, însemnări inedite, documente, note despre lupta de Rezistenţă Nord Dobrogeană, 1946–1964* (Constanţa: Editura Fundaţiei "Andrei Şaguna," 1995); Constantin Ionaşcu ed., *Rezistenţa anticomunistă din Dobrogea* (Constanţa: Editura "Ex Ponto," 2000); Silvia Angelescu, "'Născută din nevoile ţăranilor'. Rezistenţa anticomunistă din Dobrogea," *AIO: Anuarul Institutului de Istorie Orală*, Vol. 2 (2001): 293–310; Dorin Dobrincu, "Macedo-românii şi rezistenţa armată anticomunistă din Dobrogea (1948–1952)," in Leonidas Rados ed., *Interferenţe româno-elene (secolele XV–XX)*, foreword by Alexandru Zub (Iaşi: Fundaţia Academică "A.D. Xenopol," 2003), pp. 233–75; Marian Cojoc ed., *Rezistenţa armată din Dobrogea, 1945–1960* (Bucharest: Institutul Naţional pentru Studiul Totalitarismului, 2004).

[43] For instance, the Securitate managed to arrest, in the first months of 1949, 804 members of the partisan groups and resistance supporters, whose distribution on age, social category, and political affiliation criteria were, in our opinion, relevant; we therefore present them below.

The distribution by age was as follows: 1) 347 were 35–50 years old (43%); 2) 250 were 25–35 years old (31%); 3) 125 were 17–25 years old (16%); 4) 82 over 50 years old (10%).

The distribution by class was: 1) 360 were poor pesants (45%); 2) 180 middle pesants (22%); 3) 71 workers (9%); 4) 45 well-to-do peasants (6%); 5) 30 petty bourgeois(4%); 6) 25 university students (3%); 7) 17 civil servants–retired (2%); 8) 15 priests (2%); 9) 15 traders (2%); 10) 12 teachers (1%); 11) 11 craftsmen (1%); 12) 10 discharged militaries (1%); 13) 4 professionals (under 1%); 14) 3 military sub-officers (under 1%); 15) 3 school students (under 1%); 16) 2 notaries public (under 1%); 17) 1 without profession (under 1%).

According to political affiliation: 1) 448 were not politically enrolled (56%); 2) 88 were members of Maniu National Peasant Party (PNȚ)(11%); 3) 24 PNȚ sympathizers (3%); 4) 73 members of the Legionary Movement (9%); 5) 13 legionary sympathizers (2%); 6) 79 members of the Ploughmen Front (10%); 7) 42 from the Communist Party/Working Party (5%); 8) 12 from the Communist Youth Union / Working Youth Union (1%); 9) 15 from Brătianu National Liberal Party (2%); 10) 6 from the German Ethic Group (1%); 11) 2 Bejan National Liberal Party (under 1%); 12) 2 from PSDI (under 1%). (Arhivele Serviciului Român de Informații, fond "D," dos. 2168, f. 423. See also Dorin Dobrincu, "Rezistența armată anticomunistă la începutul 'republicii populare'," *Analele Sighet*, Vol. 6 (1998): 233–235). For a political perspective on the resistance, limited to the central and western Romania, see Liviu Pleşa, "Apartenența politică a grupurilor de rezistență din Ardeal (1948–1958)," in *Mişcarea armată de rezistență anticomunistă din România, 1944–1962* (Bucharest: Editura Kullusys, 2003), pp. 141–81.

The presence of the legionaries, in particular, in the anti-communist armed resistance raised a question mark among the researchers with liberal-democratic convictions, including the Western ones. The question that many analysts ask is: Can those who had a totalitarian orientation (the legionaries) and fought in the resistance, be placed next to the other anti-communist fighters? In other words, are the adepts of a totalitarianism that fights another totalitarian system fight for democracy or for the victory of their political creed, essentially anti-democratic? This is a justified question. Undoubtedly, the Romanian society of the 1940s, when the resistance started, was a polarised one. Today, in post-communist Romania, the political representation of the anti-communist armed resistance raises not only problems of historical nature, but also questions in the field of memory. Now at its beginnings in Romania, social history could help us better understand the different phenomena, most often simplistically or passionately dealt with. As we have seen, in a temporally limited segment of the resistance, the first months of the year 1949, the former members of the Communist Party / Working Party (or of the mass organizations the Party controlled) were much more than the legionaries and their sympathizers. Methodologically, we could not make an extrapolation on the resistance as a whole, but the number, for a precise interval, is sufficient to make us prudent in front of mythologizations, of the interested exaggerations, and the attempts to politically confiscate the resistance.

The partisans' leaders were most often people invested with an important symbolic standing in the regions of their activity, but not in the entire national territory. The armed Resistance in Romania did not have a command centre, although there were attempts to make one; instead the resistance groups tried to survive until a favourable context to remove the communist system appeared. While the Resistance in Bukovina in 1944 and that of the Legionaries in 1944–45 was a pro-Germanic one, the Resistance after 1945 was openly pro-Anglo-Saxon. The hope that some help would come from the West, especially from the United States of America (hence the extremely widespread myth "The Americans are coming!") played a certain part in fortifying the anti-communist partisans, as well as an important segment of the population.[44] Under Truman, the Americans developed a draft aimed at freeing the Soviet satellites in Eastern Europe from the Kremlin's

---

[44] For this interesting topic from a historical point of view, see Gheorghe Onişoru, *România în anii 1944–1948: Transformări economice şi realităţi sociale* (Bucharest: Funndaţia Academia Civică, 1998), pp. 132–45; Cornel Jurju, "Mitul 'venirii americanilor': Studiu de caz: rezistenţa anticomunistă de la Huedin," *AIO: Anuarul Institutului de Istorie Orală*, Vol 3, (2002): 173–92; Neagu Djuvara, *O scurtă istorie a românilor povestită celor tineri*, ediţia a III-a revăzută, (Bucharest: Edit. Humanitas, 2001), pp. 225–7; Bogdan Barbu, *Vin americanii! Prezenţa simbolică a Statelor Unite în România Războiului Rece: 1945–1971* (Bucharest: Editura Humanitas, 2006). The irony of history is that the Americans really came to Romania, but after 50 years (see the thematic issue "Vin americanii," *Dilema*, No. 105 (13–19 ianuarie 1995); Daniel Barbu, *Şapte teme de politică românească* (Bucharest: Editura Antet, 1997), pp. 180–81. Today Romania is a North Atlantic Treaty Organization and European Union member and an American air base is placed near Constanţa, the most important city-harbor of the country at the Black Sea.

According to some sources, the Romanians' expectations from the other countries, from the West in particular, have always been great, in their modern history. For instance, Rene de Weck, the author of the Legation of the Swiss Confederation to Bucharest during the World War II, wrote after the disaster suffered by the Romanian army at Stalingrad: "What shocks today in the Romanians' propositions [towards the Anglo-Saxon Allies, D.D.], either in the power or in the Opposition forces, is that nobody is capable to elaborate a national liberation policy. They are always waiting to be saved by external powers" (René de Weck, *Jurnal: Jurnalul unui diplomat elveţian în România: 1939–1945*, ed. transl. from French, Viorel Grecu and Claudia Chinezu [Bucharest: Editura Fundaţiei Culturale Române, 2000], p. XXXVI.

influence, but by measures with gradual effects, provoking no direct military confrontation with the Soviet troops.[45] But as this was not a fact that the Romanians (including the communist partisans) knew or could have known, many of them tried to fasten upon what was desirable, even if it had no real substance.

Not numerous, in groups varying from 2–3 to several tens of persons, the Romanian partisans had limited resources: light weapons, most of them left from World War II, improvised equipment, food and medicines offered by the locals. The partisans were helped by some of the locals in the mountain areas, especially by members of their families, relatives and people with the same political and, in some areas, the same religious convictions. Those who acted against the partisans were the Securitate, the political police, the Militia and the extended networks of informers, recruited from diverse socio-professional circles.

In a Securitate report drawn up in January 1959, in which both the subversive and the paramilitary groups were included, 1,196 "counter-revolutionary/subversive organizations and groups" were annihilated in the period after 23 August 1944–59. According to year, the distribution of these groups was the following: 1944: 1; 1945: 15; 1946: 5; 1947: 16; 1948: 119; 1949: 200; 1950: 89; 1951: 69; 1952: 74; 1953: 60; 1954: 50; 1955: 26; 1956: 42; 1957: 68; 1958: 182.[46] At the end of the 1940s, the clandestine opposition to the communist regime was, indeed, quite significant, but it subsequently decreased. At the same time, as the regime took control of the situation and its self-confidence grew significantly, the criteria for the identification of the "people's enemies" became more relaxed. The fact that the number of annihilated subversive organizations was again large, in 1957, and especially in 1958, was caused by the oppositional wave that appeared in Romania as an aftershock of the Hungarian revolution (1956), the communist regime resorting to terror in order to control the situation. But these figures were, most likely, exaggerated by the Securitate, who aimed, first of all, at emphasizing its merits in the fight against the "class enemy," and some of the "organizations" might have been nothing but

---

[45] Liviu C. Țîrău, *Între Washington și Moscova: Politicile de securitate națională ale SUA și URSS și impactul lor asupra României (1945–1965)* (Cluj-Napoca: Editura Tribuna, 2005), p. 15.

[46] *Arhivele Serviciului Român de Informații*, fond "D," dos. 7778, vol. 3, ff. 71–81, 112.

discussion groups that suffered the consequences of the severe laws of the time, while others might have even been invented by the Securitate officers, eager to get promoted at any price. Yet, if only half of these organizations had been part of the real Resistance, it underlines the statment that the phenomenon was widespread enough to keep the Securitate's attention.

The anti-communist fighters consciously risked their lives and freedom, opposing an extremely powerful enemy, ready to use any means to annihilate them. Many partisans died fighting, others were captured, tried, and sentenced to death (and executed), or sent to the Romanian Gulag; the same happened to their supporters. Moreover, numerous executions were registered, some of them in spite of the sentences given by the communist justice system.[47]

As we have seen above, in Romania, after the Second World War, there were numerous isolated initiatives to oppose the communization of the country, but a unification of them, under a national leadership, was not possible. The anti-Communist armed resistance in Romania was, on the whole, rather a fight for survival than a visionary one. The phenomenon partially resembled that of the pre-modern outlaw and less the modern guerrilla. The resistance was made of a multitude of small groups, spread all over Romania, which were not interconnected.

A Useful and Necessary Comparison: Anti-Communist Armed Resistance in Romania and Anti-Soviet/Anti-Communist Armed Resistance in Other Eastern European Countries

As we have already mentioned, the anti-communist armed resistance in Romania was rediscovered after the communist regime's collapse; it was one of the most frequently analyzed subjects for the "memory retrievers" and some of the historians, who, however, limited themselves to publishing documents or dealing with sequences, fragments of the entire phenomenon. That led to the absence of an overview image and

---

[47] Vladimir Tismăneanu, Dorin Dobrincu, and Cristian Vasile eds., *Comisia Prezidenţială pentru Analiza Dictaturii Comuniste din România, Raport Final*, revised edition (Bucharest: Editura Humanitas, 2007), pp. 679–80.

to unavoidable distortions.[48] The idea that the anti-communist armed resistance in Romania was a unique phenomenon emerged and became widespread, coming from both former partisans and activists.[49] The Sovietization of the territories occupied by the Red Army was a process that started immediately after the Second World War, and the resistance was manifest in many parts.[50] A look at the Eastern European region, under the Kremlin's control after 1944–45 (either directly

---

[48] There are numerous partisan approaches of the anti-communist armed resistance in Romania. On the one hand, the theses of the old Securitate and of the Communist Party were perpetuated by former officers of the political police or by party activists. But especially the contrary perspectives were asserted. The exaggeration, after 1989, of the importance and scope of the anti-communist armed resistance seems to have aimed at "washing out" the lost honor of many fellow citizens, particularly, by public intellectuals, journalists, historiography dilettantes. In fact, few Romanians participated in the resistance, while millions of people were PCR members, plus millions were members of other mass controlled organizations (see *Comisia Prezidenţială pentru Analiza Dictaturii Comuniste din România, Raport Final*, pp. 49–154, 176–98). The exaggerations in the writings of recent history are often related to other agendas than the historiographical one. This is an aspect that even the researchers, sometimes, take no notice of.

[49] There are many examples in this direction, but we shall only mention a few. An insignificant text, published at the beginning of the 1990s, in a journal for the retrieving of the communist victims' memory: "Among the countries in the Soviet orbit at the end of the Second World War, *Romania was the only one where communism confronted a strong armed resistance, which did not last a while, but a few years, more precisely, from the moment of the Soviet invasion, on 23 August 1944, to the years 1959–1960, when it was defeated.*" [underlined in the original, D.D.] "Figuri de luptători din Munţii Făgăraş—Versantul nordic," *Memoria*, Vol. 12 (1994): 102. Ion Gavrilă Ogoranu, former leader of a group of partisans: "[Anti-communist armed resistance in Romania] is a unique phenomenon in this area of Soviet occupation, this is be our emblem, Romania's, our page of dignity and glory and sufferance." Ion Gavrilă Ogoranu testimony, in "O viaţă de fugar," recorded by L.Ş., in *Monitorul de Cluj*, No. 276, 25 noiembrie 2005, p. 8. Monica Lovinescu, a critical voice from the civic positions of the communist regime in Romania: "Nationalism is for us (Romanians) barking, and criticism is replaced with raillery. We are haughty when we have no reason to be, and timorous when we could be proud (like in the case of the mountain resistance, the only one in the Europe occupied by the Red Army). We are most original. That is why the comparison with the satellitic neighbours, like us, is avoided." Monica Lovinescu, *Insula Şerpilor: Unde scurte*, Vol. 4 (Bucharest: Editura Humanitas, 1996), pp. 197–8.

[50] Liviu C. Ţîrău, *op. cit., passim*.

or by interceders) shows us that the anti-communist (and anti-Soviet, according to the situation) resistance was quite extensive—in Estonia, Latvia, Lithuania, in Poland and Ukraine, but also in Bessarabia— in some places even more than in Romania. Far from attacking the "uniqueness" so often claimed in certain circles in Romania, this statement is made in accordance with the facts that occurred in Eastern Europe some decades ago.

The anti-communist armed resistance had a few common causes for the whole region: the Soviet occupation, the rapid and brutal transformation of the State and of the society, the political and religious persecutions, but also the ethnic one in the territories directly occupied by the Soviets, and so on. A phenomenon with many controversial aspects, the anti-communist resistance must be historicized in order to reveal its true dimensions.

This comparative perspective helps us understand both the specificities of the anti-communist armed resistance in Romania and the resemblance of similar phenomena in Eastern Europe in the first decade after the war. The phenomenon of armed resistance appeared in the second half of the 1940s and the beginning of the 1950s in other countries in Eastern Europe under Soviet domination, being particularly significant in the Baltic countries, Ukraine, and Poland.[51]

---

[51] From the rich literature on the phenomenon of anti-Soviet and anti-communist resistance in different countries of Eastern Europe, we only mention a few works, that we have used for the final segment of our paper.

For the Baltic States: K.V. Tauras, *Guerilla Warfare on the Amber Coast* (New York: Voyages Press, 1961); A. Silde, *Resistance Movement in Latvia* (Stockholm: Latvian National Foundation, 1972); Juozas Daumantas, *Fighters for freedom: Lithuanian partisans versus the USSR (1944–1947)*, translated from the Lithuanian by E.J. Harrison (New York: Manyland Books, 1975); Thomas Remeikis, *Opposition to Soviet Rule in Lithuania. 1945–1980*, (Chicago, Illinois: Institute of Lithuanian Studies Press, 1980), pp. 39–64; *War after War: Armed anti-Soviet Resistance in Lithuania in 1944–1953*, Catalogue of the exhibition, Second edition, Vilnius, 2005; Andres Küng, *A Dream of Freedom: Four Decades of National Survival versus Rusian Imperialism in Estonia, Latvia and Lithuania. 1940–1980* (Cardiff–New York–Stockholm–Sydney–Toronto: Boreas Publishing House, 1981), *passim*; Mart Laar, *War in the Woods: Estonia's Struggle for Survival. 1944–1956*, translation by Tüna Ets, foreword by Tönu Parming (Washington, D.C.: The Compass Press, 1992); Anatol Lieven, *The Baltic Revolution: Estonia, Latvia, Lithuania and the Path to Independence* (New Haven and London: Yale University Press, 1994), p. 87–90.

First of all, we should take into consideration the different conditions in Romania, as well as those in Poland, on the one hand, and those in Western Ukraine and the Baltic states on the other. Romania was a country that the Soviets had occupied after 23 August/12 September 1944, formally independent after 1947 (the Peace Treaty of Paris); Poland was theoretically independent too, while Ukraine, the Socialist Soviet Republic of Moldova (most of it was the formerly the Romanian region of Bessarabia), and the Baltic states were included in the USSR, as union republics. As we mentioned before, the causes of anti-communist resistance were diverse in Eastern Europe. While

---

For Ukraine: John A. Armstrong, "The Chronicle of the Ukrainian Insurgent Army (UPA)," *Harvard Ukrainian Studies*, Vol. 14, No. 1–2 (June 1990): 171–5; *Idem, Ukrainian Nationalism*, third edition, (Englewood, CO: Ukrainian Academic Press, 1990), pp. 219–39; David R. Marples, *Stalinism in Ukraine in the 1940s* (New York: St. Martin's Press, 1992), pp. 97–160; P. Potichnyi and Y. Shtendera eds., *Political Thought of the Ukrainian Underground. 1943–1951* (New York: Columbia University Press, 1955); *The Ukrainian Insurgent Army in Fight for Freedom* (New York: United Comittee of the Ukrainian–American Organizations of New York, 1954); Y. Tys-Krokhmaliuk, *UPA Warfare in Ukraine: Strategical, Tactical and Organizational Problems of the Ukrainian Resistance in the World War II* (New York: Vantage Press, 1972).

For Poland: Richard F. Staar, *Poland. 1944–1962: The Sovietization of a Captive People* (New Orleans: Louisiana State University Press, 1962); John Coutouvidis and Jaime Reynolds, *Poland. 1939–1947* (Leicester: Leicester University Press, 1986); Krystina Kersten, *The Establishment of Communist Rule in Poland. 1943–1948*, translated and annotated by John Micgiel and Michael H. Bernhard, foreword by Jan T. Gross (Berkeley, Los Angeles, & Oxford: University of California Press, 1991); John Micgiel, "'Bandits and Reactionaries': The Suppression of the Opposition in Poland. 1944–1946," in Norman Naimark and Leónid Gibianski eds., *The Establishment of Communist Regimes in Eastern Europe. 1944–1949* (Boulder, CO: Westview Press, 1997), pp. 93–110.

For Bessarabia/Soviet Socialist Republic of Moldova: Elena Postică, *Rezistenţa antisovietică în Basarabia: 1944–1950* (Chişinău: Întreprinderea Editorial–Poligrafică "Ştiinţa," 1997); Ion Ţurcanu, *Moldova antisovietică: Aspecte din lupta basarabenilor împotriva ocupaţiei sovietice* (Chişinău: Editurile Prut Internaţional şi Ştiinţa, 2000); Comisia Prezidenţială pentru Analiza Dictaturii Comuniste din România, *Raport Final*, chapter "Represiunile comuniste în Moldova sovietică," section "Rezistenţa antisovietică," pp. 755–8.

For a general perspective, see Andrzej Paczkowski and Karel Bartosek, "Cealaltă Europă victimă a comunismului," in *loc. cit.*, pp. 337–427.

the Baltics, the western Ukrainians, some of the Polish, but also the Besserabians (most of them, of Romanian ethnic origin) had been arrested, deported *en masse,* and summarily executed by the Soviets in the period 1939–41, and then after 1944–45;[52] the Romanian citizens had no experience with all this until 1944–45.

In Romania only a small number of people, enrolled in the partisan groups just like in Besserabia. The situation was different in Ukraine and the Baltic states, where tens, even hundreds of thousands of people joined the groups, in a population incomparably smaller, especially in the case of the Baltics. Some of those who fought communism were apolitical or had democratic convictions, but an important number of the partisans had been members of nationalist, authoritarian, and even totalitarian political groups.

In western Ukraine and in the Baltic States, the anti-communist resistance had the characteristics of both a war for national independence, against a foreign occupier, and an ideological battle, with aspects resembling a civil war. In Romania and Poland, the resistance had an explicit anti-Soviet element, but in the field the fight was waged especially against the local communists.

The communists called the anti-communist and anti-Soviet fighters "bandits" and "terrorists" (everywhere), while the population mostly thought of them as "partisans," "outlaws," but also "men of the woods" in Romania, and "brothers of the woods" in the Baltic States. It is difficult today to describe the difference between guerrilla and non-guerrilla, considering the fact that many of the anti-communist groups were training for armed resistance, some of them being involved, one way or another, in the actions meant to support the partisans' military actions.

In Romania, Latvia, and Estonia, there was no unified command center of the resistance,[53] while in western Ukraine and in Lithuania

---

[52] Nicolas Werth, "Un stat împotriva poporului său," in Stéphane Courtois, Nicolas Werth, Jean-Louis Panné, Andrzej Paczkowski, Karel Bartosek, and Jean-Louis Margolin, *op. cit.,* pp. 192–224.

[53] Although some witnesses referred to the formation, in 1947, of a "unique command center" of the anti-communist resistance of Romania (Ion Gavrilă-Ogoranu, "Rezistența armată anticomunistă din munții României," *România liberă,* No. 1164, 27 ianuarie 1994, p. 2); *Idem,* "Rezistența armată anticomunistă din munții României," *Analele Sighet,* Vol. 1 (1995): 99;

there was one, at least for a long period of time. Even if in Romania there were some attempts to unify the resistance, they were not successful, each group acting by itself, fighting for its own survival and hoping that the domestic and international context would change and lead to the collapse of the communist regime.

The resistance was repressed pitilessly in all Eastern European countries. The organizations involved in the repression of the resistance movement were the NKVD, GKB and MVD in the Baltic States, Ukraine and Soviet Moldova, and the "national" Securitate in Romania or in Poland, but with support from the Soviets. In this vast operation against the resistance not only the common echelons of the Securitate and Militia were involved, but also a large number of troops from the same organizations, and in some cases troops from the regular army. Moreover, the political organizations that the communist party controlled offered logistic support and forces for the annihilation of the resistance. In order to collect information about the partisans, the repressive organizations attracted, through different methods (co-involvement, manipulation or, most of the time, blackmail) many persons, recruiting especially among those who came in direct contact with the anti-communists.

The communist regimes made constant efforts to isolate the partisans from their supporters, from the population in general. To this end, they also tried to compromise the resistance by making up groups of false partisans, who were wandering in the woods and mountains, sometimes even robbing civilians (particularly in the Baltic States). Besides, in order to deprive the partisans of the possibility to collect food supplies, to get information and so on, the authorities isolated the regions with a significant population of partisans. Moreover, whole countries were inaccessible to Westerners at the beginning of the communist period. For instance, in the Baltic States, foreign tourists were only allowed in the mid-1950s. The communist regimes also made use of deportation measures against the locals—as happened in the Baltic

---

Idem, Brazii se frâng, dar nu se îndoiesc, Vol. 4 (Făgăraş: Editura Mesagerul de Făgăraş, s.a., 2004), pp. 2–3; or even of the "Anti-communist Front," Radu Ciuceanu ed., "Cuvânt introductiv," in *Idem* ed., *Mişcarea Naţională de Rezistenţă din Oltenia*, Vol. I, *1947–1949* (Bucharest: Institutul Naţional pentru Studiul Totalitarismului, 2001), p. 32, comprising all the opposition forces, such a thing did not exist for real.

States, western Ukraine, south-eastern Poland, Romania—both as a punitive measure against the supporters and to deprive the partisans of the help they needed.

The authorities did not confine their actions to repressive measures in order to isolate the partisans from their supporters, they also tried to attract on their side as large a number of locals as possible: by co-opting them in party and communist youth organizations (Comsomol, Communist Youth/UTC, etc.) and by social measures, including the possibility to be socially promoted.

The partisans responded in some cases with violent measures as well, for instance by threatening or even executing NKVD, Securitate or Militia local collaborators. This was a spiral of violence, like in all cases of guerrilla actions and anti-guerrilla measures.[54] In the Baltic States, the partisans managed, in the first years after the war, to paralyse the functioning of the Soviet administration, but this was not possible any more after 1946 (Latvia and Estonia), 1949 (Lithuania), or 1948 (West Ukraine). In Romania, this never happened.

Nowhere in Eastern Europe, including Romania, were the anti-communist/anti-Soviets fighters captured by the authorities treated as war prisoners, but as criminals, as "bandits," as "terrorists." They were tortured, tried by military courts and severely sentenced, often to death or to many years in prison. This undoubtedly happened because guerrilla warfare is a type of war where the rules established by the modern conventions of war fall by the wayside, most of the times, in the field. Unlike what happened in other areas and other historical periods, for instance in the Second World War, when the actions against the partisans failed as a whole,[55] the actions organized by Moscow and its satellites against the eastern European anti-communist resistance were successful. The zones where resistance made itself visible were pacified, even if at the price of a generalized terror.

In the context of the large-scale repression that the communist regimes organized, the evolution of the international situation offered discouraging signals for the resistance; for instance, the fact that the

---

[54] Florin Diaconu, *Secolul războiului total. Războaie totale şi războaie clasice-limitate în secolul al XX-lea : caracteristici, surse, instrumente şi metode* (Bucharest: Institutul Diplоatic Român, 2007), p. 262.

[55] *Ibid.*, p. 266.

war in Korea (1950–53) did not extend to Europe, or the fact that the Hungarian Revolution of 1956 was defeated. Even if there were hopes that the West would intervene, the Eastern European anti-communist/anti-Soviet resistance did not rely on external help anywhere, but exclusively on the local population's support. The Eastern European partisans were disappointed when faced with the West's attitude; they felt abandoned in front of the occupying forces, considering that a segment of the population was decimated through executions, arrests and deportations, especially in the Baltic States and in western Ukraine. One of the explanations why, *grosso modo*, the anti-communist armed resistance was not successful was the very absence of external help, which was present in just a few places and quite insignificantly. As the last century demonstrated, the efficiency of partisan war under the circumstances of a confrontation with an extremely powerful foreign enemy also depends on the scope and rhythm of foreign help.[56]

Anti-communist armed resistance lasted until 1950 (Latvia), 1953 (Estonia), or 1955 (Lithuania), although there were isolated survivors until the beginning of the 1960s. In western Ukraine, resistance was annihilated at the beginning of the 1950s, as in Poland. As far as Romania is concerned, the organized groups were active until the mid-1950s; some of them survived until 1958, and the last fighters/isolated fugitives were annihilated at the beginning of the '60s.

A general conclusion arises from our analysis: the difficulty with which armed resistance groups were created and, above all, maintained, during the communist regimes. There are many explanations for that, but the most important ones of them are: the state-party's quasi-complete control over the territory, people and resources; the hash measures against their opponents, from arrests and deportations to executions, including arbitrary ones.

The political stake in the annihilation of the Resistance was particularly important. It was, first of all, a political fight, and only secondly a military one. The communists and the Soviets eventually won. Only if seen in the long run and from a symbolic standpoint, could one argue that the partisans got the upper hand.

---

[56] *Ibid.*, pp. 265–6.

Part Four

NATIONAL
OR
REVOLUTIONARY
BREAKTHROUGHS?

BRADLEY ABRAMS

Hope Died Last: The Czechoslovak Road to Stalinism

Having written quite extensively on the immediate post-war period in Czechoslovakia, I will be drawing upon many of those writings to discuss the path that Czechoslovakia took from liberation in 1945 to Stalinism in 1950 as two different, but deeply related phenomena. The first is relatively straight-forward and is in distinction to what usually takes center stage in discussions of the Sovietization of Eastern Europe: international aspects of, in my case, Czechoslovak developments. In what I will call the Czechoslovak Road to Socialism, I will focus on domestic events and briefly examine some of what I see as the most important turning points on the path that took the country from liberation to Communist dictatorship, in essence a domestic view of Czechoslovakia's road to Socialism. I will interweave into this a discussion of the fate of the, in quotations, "specific Czechoslovak Road to Socialism," the Communist Party's political offensive that began in the fall of 1946, tacitly promising a divergence from Soviet practices. Its ultimate failure, occurring in the months after the Communist Party successfully gained total power in the state, has clear international roots, and the story of this failure can be seen as the story of the Czechoslovak Road to Stalinism. Of course, there could be no Czechoslovak Road to Stalinism without a Czechoslovak Road to Socialism, since it prepared the ground domestically for the international pressures that led to the Stalinization of the state and society. Nonetheless, I wish to keep these two notionally separated, in order to foreground some of the Czechoslovak specificities of the times.

The structure of this essay is also important. I will start by discussing notions of socialism common in the first years after the end of the Second World War, including the "specific Czechoslovak Road to Socialism." Then I will touch briefly upon four important developments that had important domestic roots and/or consequences. The first is entirely domestic: the 1946 elections, which were important both for the state and for relations between Czechs and Slovaks. The second picks up on this and focuses on Czech–Slovak relations, including the trial of Jozef Tiso. The third, the Czechoslovak reception of the Marshall Plan, seems international, but I will be focusing on its important domestic implications. The final one, the Cominform meeting in Szklarská Poręba (September 1947) clearly allows me to talk about the East more generally, while staying with my theme of the road to socialism. I then conclude with the crisis of February 1948, which resulted in the Communist Party's assumption of total power and brought the Czechoslovak Road to Socialism to a close, although not resolving the fate of the "specific Czechoslovak Road Socialism."

In the second part of the essay, on the Czechoslovak Road to Stalinism, I will focus on two periods in which moderate and dogmatic elements within the Communist Party of Czechoslovakia (CPCz) competed for dominance, until the pressures of international developments assured the victory of the latter. The first, which lasted from the communists' assumption of total power in February of 1948 until the expulsion of Yugoslavia from the Cominform on 28 June, 1948, shows features of a continuation of the CPCz's strategy of forging a "specific Czechoslovak road to socialism." I will argue that it was the Bucharest meeting that signaled the beginning of the end of this, and constituted a major turning point on the road to Stalinism, a road that began at the time of the Marshall Plan fiasco. This road was completed in the second period, by the steps taken by the regime in the fall of 1948 and the spring of 1949, when the party adopted policies that completed the Stalinization of the state. Following this, I would like to offer some speculation on why there was no de-Stalinization drive in 1956, arguing that the events of 1953, in the immediate aftermath of Stalin's death, created the conditions for the maintenance of Stalinism until the onrush of the Prague Spring of 1968. In the conclusion, I'd like to evaluate the Communist Party's seizure of total power in February 1948, most commonly seen as the dominant turning point in early post-war Czechoslovakia, in the light of those of 1945 and late 1948, and wrap up with a few reflections on the fate of domestic impulses for radical social and political change in the first years after the Second World War.

About one thing there can be little doubt, thanks to a host of recent research, and that is the enthusiasm, especially among Czechs, for
radical social change in the wake of the war. The political import of this
was magnified by the decisions taken by, and the ideas of, the political
leaderships of even the major non-communist parties. Already during
the war the decision was taken by the government-in-exile to limit the
number of political parties permitted to contest elections, resulting in a
truncated political spectrum that was decidedly skewed to the left. For
the Czech lands, there were four permitted parties: the Communists,
the Social Democrats, the National Socialists and the People's Party.[1]
Perhaps surprisingly, President Edvard Beneš, the moral and political
leader of the bourgeois parties, argued that even this was too many
and that three would be sufficient: the Communist Party, the Social
Democratic Party, and some amalgam of center and center-right politicians.[2] In Slovakia, there were initially only two permitted parties: the
Communist Party of Slovakia (CPS) and the Democratic Party. This
lineup afforded many advantages to advocates of socialism, of whom
there were many. President Beneš' decrees, in addition to providing the
framework for the expulsion of Czechoslovakia's German and Hungarian communities, also fed the cause of socialism by nationalizing all
banks, insurance companies, and large industrial enterprises, meaning
that almost 60 percent of industrial output came from the state sector, and over 60 percent of the workforce was employed by the state.
Similarly, planning was introduced into the economy with the formulation of a two-year plan for 1946–48. Both of these economic measures
were accomplished with the support (albeit with reservations) of the
non-communist parties. These and other steps, including the beginnings of a large-scale land reform, were part of the striving for radical social reform that was summed up by President Beneš' description
of postwar Czechoslovakia as a "socializing democracy." The ultimate

---

[1] Despite the radical shrinking of the number of parties from which to choose,
57.5% of Czechs surveyed in 1946 found the number "sufficient" and 34.2%
thought that there were "too many," while only 5.6% believed the number
"too few." See Čeněk Adamec, Bohuš Pospíšil, and Milan Tesař eds., *What's
Your Opinion? A Year's Survey of Public Opinion in Czechoslovakia* (Prague:
Orbis, 1947), p. 13.

[2] On Beneš' wartime views, see Václav Pavlíček, *Politické strany po únoru*, Volume I (Praha: Svobodné slovo, 1966), p. 72.

content and destination of this "socializing" was never made clear, however, exposing a significant political ambiguity on the part of the non-communist forces.[3] These initial post-war measures proved quite popular, as just a few examples will show. In the 1946 surveys, admittedly only in the Czech lands, 63.9 percent agreed entirely with the Košice Program, the immediate postwar procalmation that created the National Front government and mandated the nationalizations and the complementary land reform, while a further twenty-eight agreed with reservations, making for over 90 percent support for the wholesale re-ordering of Czechoslovakia's political and economic systems. Similarly, 41 percent believed that the two-year plan would be entirely successful, and a further 36 percent at least partly so. The belief in, and popularity of, these concrete measures benefitted those who were seen as their embodiment—President Beneš and CPCz head Klement Gottwald—who ranked first and second, respectively, as the politicians who most enjoyed public confidence.[4]

While "socializing democracy" was on the agenda for the non-communists, the CPCz was formulating its own position. Party leaders described the moves of the first year after liberation as a "national and democratic revolution," and shifted seamlessly to the "specific Czecho-slovak road to socialism" in the fall of 1946. Though announced after Stalin had indicated his tolerance for such variety, the Czechoslovak Party was perhaps best equipped to take advantage of the opening.[5] It had carefully reinvented itself as national-patriotic and democratic, while also committed to social justice and social change. Moreover, the elements the party stressed as being components of its "specific Czechoslovak road" were precisely those that we have seen proved so popular: socialism, the National Front, the nationalizations, and the

---

[3] On non-communist ideas of socialism, see my *The Struggle for the Soul of the Nation: Czech Culture and the Rise of Communism*, The Harvard Cold War Studies book series (Lanham, MD: Rowman and Littlefield, 2004), pp. 199–233.

[4] Also, of the 30% of respondents who had changed their view of the Western Powers since the end of the war, 79% now viewed them less favorably. As with the West, so with Churchill: 38% had changed their opinion of him, 92.5% of which now viewed him less favorably than at the end of the war. Adamec *et al.*, pp. 14–5, 18–9.

[5] Stalin had laid out the possibility of different roads to socialism in a conversation with British Labour Party representatives in the summer of 1946.

two-year plan, as well as the aim of gaining a majority of electoral support for the party.[6] The larger picture from all this seems clear: both the Communists and the non-communists were committed to radical social change, and talked of "socialism" and "socializing democracy" without specifying what the socialism being sought would consist in, and the Czechoslovak public was broadly supportive of the changes being made in socialism's name.

This judgment is borne out by the results of the first post-war elections, held in May of 1946. In them, the CPCz—already the largest party in Czech history, with over 1,000,000 members, a title it still holds today—won a decisive victory, gaining 38 percent of the vote. Its tally was almost twice as large as that of its leading rival, and, together with its ally, the Social Democratic Party, secured a majority of the vote. There are two important features of the results that need to be kept in mind. First of all, in the Czech lands, almost four-fifths (79.5 percent) of the electorate gave their votes to expressly *socialist* parties, half of which went to the CPCz. Socialism was undoubtedly important and desirable to the Czech public. This does not mean that communism was, although the decidedly moderate stance the CPCz adopted certainly made it attractive to socialist voters. Secondly, the CPCz's sister party in Slovakia, the CPS, did more poorly, managing to gain only 31 percent of the vote, despite the fact that it faced only one serious opponent, the Democratic Party. The Democrats, a fractious coalition of Catholics and Protestants, resistance fighters and former supporters of the wartime Slovak state that had been allied to Nazi Germany, emerged the clear victors.

This brings me to my second point, having to do with Czech–Slovak relations. The electoral result certainly showed the differing strengths of socialism in the two halves of the country, and of the state's two communist parties, but the reactions to these results showed something more important. In the wake of the elections, the National Front government met three times in quick succession. The Communists came to these meetings hoping to weaken the power of the Democratic Party by dismantling Slovak regional governing institutions,

---

[6] For more detail on all of the issues surrounding the thorny issue of the communists' "specific Czechoslovak road to socialism," see Abrams, *The Struggle for the Soul of the Nation*, pp. 178–98.

institutions which had been granted considerable powers by the Košice Program of April 1945. Instead of meeting opposition from the Czech non-communists, Czech and Slovak Communists found that the Czech non-communists were more than willing to sharply curtail Slovak autonomy. Within weeks, agreement was reached to subordinate the Slovak authorities to their Prague counterparts, to allow the central government to suspend acts of the Slovak administration, and to limit Slovak self-administration in other important ways. Here it seems that the Czech non-communists regarded the Democratic Party as a "reactionary" threat to the socialist aims they shared with the communists and that, largely because of this, Slovakia itself constituted a political problem. This "problem" reared its head again in April of 1947, in connection with the question of granting clemency to the leader of the wartime Slovak state, the Roman Catholic priest Jozef Tiso, who had been sentenced to death. At that time, the Democratic Party argued that he should be given clemency, not least as a nod toward Slovak national and religious sensibilities and as an attempt to gain Slovaks' goodwill toward the reconstituted state. The communists argued for carrying out the death penalty, and achieved victory with the support of the Czech Social Democrats and National Socialists.[7] All these steps, to my mind, deeply harmed Czech–Slovak relations, and led to the ease with which the Communists could diminish the Democratic Party's influence and ultimately remove it from power in Slovakia in February of 1948.

Within months of the Tiso trial, in the summer of 1947, the question of Czechoslovak participation in the Marshall Plan came to center stage. This has widely and correctly been seen as a turning point, although perhaps for the wrong reasons. In the standard telling, the Czechoslovak government agreed to participate, and then the prominent leaders were called to Moscow, where Stalin browbeat them into changing their minds, leading Foreign Minister Jan Masaryk to comment ruefully, "I left for Moscow as a Czechoslovak minister, I returned as Stalin's lackey." It is true that the Czechoslovak government

---

[7] For a treatment of the maneuvering surrounding, and the political implications of, the Tiso trial, see Bradley Abrams, "The Politics of Retribution: The Trial of Jozef Tizo in the Czechoslovak Environment," in István Deák, Jan T. Gross, and Tony Judt, eds. *The Politics of Retribution in Europe: World War II and Its Aftermath* (Princeton: Princeton UP, 2000), pp. 252–89.

unanimously, i.e., including the CPCz's ministers, approved participation in the Paris organizing talks. It is also true that the Prime Minister Gottwald, Foreign Minister Masaryk, and the National Socialist Justice Minister Prokop Drtina, among others, met with an angry Stalin a few days later, although a delegation was scheduled to go to Moscow beforehand. It is also true that the Czechoslovak government rescinded its decision regarding participation. What this account omits, however, is that, after hearing from Gottwald prior to their meeting with Stalin that the Soviet leader was angry, Drtina and Masaryk agreed to hear Stalin's arguments and to explain to him why participation was important to Czechoslovakia. At the meeting, after Stalin had declared that the issue was a matter of Czechoslovak–Soviet friendship, the minutes of the meeting record that:

> Minister Masaryk emphasized that all political parties are agreed that Czechoslovakia may not undertake anything which would be against the interests of the Soviet Union. The delegation will promptly notify Prague that the Soviet government considers acceptance of the Anglo-French invitation to be an act directed against it, and Minister Masaryk does not doubt in the least that the Czechoslovak government will act accordingly without delay. But Minister Masaryk here requests that the Soviet Union help us in our delicate situation… Perhaps the matter can be fixed in such a manner that one would go to the conference on one day and leave it on the next.[8]

What is remarkable about this is that Masaryk, indeed the foreign minister of a sovereign state, made little show of defending an action taken unanimously by his state's government. Rather, he devoted his energies to finding a way to maintain the *appearance* that his state is acting with sovereignty, while reassuring Stalin that Soviet interests take precedence over Czechoslovak ones. In fact, the delegation, immediately after returning to its accommodations from the Kremlin, composed a telegram to Prague demanding an emergency cabinet session to immediately reverse the decision to participate. The cabinet did meet and

---

[8] The minutes of the meeting were printed as Appendix IV of Prokop Drtina, *Československo můj osud* (Prague: Melantrich, 1992), pp. 683–90. An English translation appears as "Stalin, Czechoslovakia, and the Marshall Plan: New Documentation from Czechoslovak Archives," introduced by Karel Kaplan, with an analysis by Vojtech Mastny, translated by John M. Deasy, *Bohemia*, Vol. 32 (1991): 134–44. The quotation is from this latter translation.

reversed the decision, again unanimously. The reversal shows that the Czechoslovak political elite was willing to sacrifice almost any initiative in order not to provoke the Kremlin. Given that, of all the Eastern European states on the road to communist dictatorship, Czechoslovakia had the most room for maneuver one has to ask how its representatives *used* that room. There is no evidence that there was a serious weighing of what Czechoslovakia concretely risked by not acceding to Stalin's wishes versus the harm that would come by not participating in the Marshall Plan. If Czechoslovak sovereignty was damaged by the whole episode, it was damaged by the Czechoslovak political elite itself. This is a large step down the road to socialism of a particular stripe, and can be seen as the first step in the outright Stalinizing of the state. But it should be reiterated that this is a case of self-Stalinizing on the part of the Czechoslovak government.[9]

My final example is one that decidedly looks East, the Cominform meeting in Szklarska Poręba a few months later, in September of 1947. The story of this should be familiar to all: representatives of nine European communist parties met, and the French and Italian parties were subjected to sharp criticism for their gradualist approaches and, in the French case, for being excluded from government. Less well known is that the penultimate draft of Zhdanov's memorandum to Stalin on the content of the planned meeting contained the point "criticism of mistakes made by certain Communist Parties (French, Italian, Czechoslovak and others)." This was only changed in the final memo to "criticism of mistakes made by certain communist parties, especially the mistakes of the French and Italian CPs." Although the CPCz received no direct criticism, the Communist Party of the Soviet Union was clearly disturbed by the CPCZ's failure to show even greater progress than it had enjoyed. A CPSU Foreign Political Department memorandum drawn up before the Cominform meeting indicted Gottwald's team for missing the opportunity to seize power while the Red Army was still on Czechoslovak soil, for not taking the nationalizations far enough (interestingly, the CPCz stepped in to water down the initial

---

[9] The material in these paragraphs draws upon Bradley F. Abrams, "The Marshall Plan and Czechoslovak Democracy: Elements of Interdependancy," in Martin Schain ed., *The Marshall Plan: Fifty Years After* (New York: Palgrave, 2001), pp. 93–116.

plan for nationalizations, presented by the Social Democratic Party), and for not adequately resolving the national question, which was seen as leading to the growth of "reaction" in Slovakia.[10] The most important result of the meeting, from our perspective, is that it sent a clear signal to the Czechoslovak communist leadership that the "national roads" policy was no longer one subscribed to by the Soviets. It is not surprising, then, that this is when there was a sharp reduction in action on the "specific Czechoslovak road to socialism." I say reduction in and not end to, because there were still several important figures within the party who continued to invoke it, and, more importantly, its main elements continued to occupy center stage in communist rhetoric, even if not expressly labeled the "Czechoslovak Road." For example, the Deputy Secretary General, Maria Švermová, continued to view the battle for a majority of the electorate in the elections scheduled for May of 1948 as the decisive one.[11]

The Czechoslovak Road did, of course, end in socialism. However, this story does not end in February of 1948. I am not going to go into detail about all of the various misjudgments that plagued the decision of the Czech National Socialist and People's parties and the Slovak Democratic Party to resign over the Communists' clear attempt to pack the police leaderships. Briefly, I do want to point out that they relied on a frail President Beneš not to accept their resignations and clearly did not think about any other way of resolving the crisis they had caused than through discussions and possibly early elections. Further, they did not ensure that a majority of ministers would resign, and they did not forewarn their local leaderships of the step they were taking, thus their supporters were never mobilized in the way that the Communists proved able to mobilize theirs.[12]

---

[10] See Grant Adibekov, "How the First Conference of the Cominform Came About," and Anna Di Biagio, "The Establishment of the Cominform," in Giuliano Prcacci *et al.*, eds. *The Cominform: Minutes of the Three Conferences 1947/1948/1949* (Milan: Fondazione Giangiacomo Feltrinelli, 1994), pp. 5 and 19–20, respectively.

[11] See Karel Kaplan, *The Rise of a Monopoly of Power in the Hands of the Communist Party of Czechoslovakia, 1948–1949*, Part I, The Experiences of Prague Spring 1968 Research Project, Study 2 (1979), p. 7.

[12] Several leading National Socialist leaders even left Prague for their weekend houses during the crisis.

The Communists seem to have been caught off guard by the resignations. As Klement Gottwald put it six weeks later: "At first, I couldn't believe it would be so easy. But then it turned out that this is just what happened—they handed in their resignations. I prayed that this stupidity over the resignations would go on and that they would not change their minds."[13] The response the CPCz was able to muster was impressive. Within days, hundreds of thousands of protesters were flooding the streets of Czech cities and towns, filling their squares to hear Gottwald's speeches to the nation. On 25 February a crowd of 250,000 pro-communist demonstrators in Prague, and hundreds of thousands elsewhere across the nation, waited for President Beneš to declare whether he would accept the Communists' solution for the crisis, which was a reconstructed National Front with only those from the non-communist parties whom the Communists considered reliable allowed to participate. In the opposing camp, a few thousand students marched past the Prague Castle, demonstrating no more than their support for the president.[14] In the face of all this, Beneš conceded defeat and the communist victory was complete. Just as in 1945, when the society was radically reconstructed in distinction to its prewar incarnation, "this break in continuity called out no widespread protest in the public."[15] In fact, Vilém Prečan was willing to go even further: "With a certain, but not great, amount of exaggeration it is possible to say that the wide layers of the Czech nation welcomed the power monopoly of the [Communist Party], if not with flying banners then at least without a general, visible or marked opposition."[16]

It is the speed of the non-communist collapse and the shock of achieving total power that, I believe, somewhat explains why Czecho-

---

[13] Cited in Karel Kaplan, *The Short March: The Communist Takeover of Czechoslovakia 1945–1948* (London: C. Hurst, 1987), p. 179.

[14] Karel Kaplan, *The Short March*, pp. 182 and 185.

[15] Eva Schmidt-Hartmann, "Das Konzept der 'politischen Kultur' in der Tschechoslowakei," in Hans Lemberg ed., *Sowjetisches Modell und nationale Prägung. Kontinuität und Wandel in Ostmitteleuropa nach dem zweiten Weltkrieg*, Historische und Landeskundliche Ostmitteleuropa-Studien 7 (Marburg/Lahn: J. G. Herder Institut, 1991), p. 195.

[16] Vilém Precan, "Politika a taktika KSČ 1945–1948," in his *V kradeném čase: Výběr ze studi', článků a úvah z let 1973–1993* (Prague: ÚSD, 1994), p. 116. Milan Kundera perceived February in much the same way: "And so it happened in February of 1948 the Communists took power not in bloodshed

slovakia's road to socialism ended in February of 1948, but the complete transformation of this road into the road to Stalinism was yet to come. The Communist Party, in a sense, was handed power: the anticommunists had deserted the government and seemingly taken only one step (consulting the president) to prepare themselves for the final confrontation. Rushed into power, the Communists apparently didn't know what to do. As one historian, quite unsympathetic to the Communists, has written, "In the immediate post-February period... the Party leaders appeared to have no definite notion of a great many specific features of socialism."[17] The shock of total power is only part of the reason why the Czechoslovak road to Stalinism was not coterminous with the Czechoslovak road to socialism, however. The other factor is what the dean of North American historians of Czechoslovakia, Gordon Skilling, called "the dualism of Czechoslovak communism."[18] The party's politics had traditionally been split between a moderate, parliamentary course, which defended national sovereignty and relied on social democratic traditions, and a more dogmatic aspect, which cleaved to the Soviet Union and properly Bolshevik traditions. This resulted, especially under conditions in which the party had truly become a mass party, in "schizophrenia in the party's behavior."[19] In the months after the party claimed power, this was particularly evident, as a marked feature of the period is what has been called "the communists' heterogeneity of ideas" about socialism.[20] This theoretical ambiguity, as the leading communist historian of the period noted, "emerged among many party functionaries and was gradually clarified within the international workers movement at the end of 1948 and the

---

and violence, but to the cheers of about half the population. And please note: the half that cheered was the more dynamic, the more intelligent, the better half." Milan Kundera, *The Book of Laughter and Forgetting*, translated by Michael Henry Heim (New York: Penguin, 1981), p. 8.

[17] Radomír Luža, "February 1948 and the Czechoslovak Road to Socialism," *East Central Europe*, Vol. 4 (1977): 54.

[18] See Chapter Two, entitled "The Dualism of Czechoslovak Communism from Gottwald to Novotný," of his *Czechoslovakia's Interrupted Revolution* (Princeton: Princeton UP, 1976).

[19] Barbara Wolfe Jancar, *Czechoslovakia and the Absolute Monopoly of Power* (New York: Praeger, 1971), p. 51.

[20] Karel Kaplan, *Utváření generální linie výstavby socialismu v Československu* (Prague: Academia, 1966), p. 140.

beginning of 1949."[21] As you will see from the remainder of this paper, I believe that some sections of the party certainly believed that Czechoslovak socialism would be distinctive, and that the condemnation of Yugoslavia in June of 1948 tipped the balance toward Stalinism.

The changes that took place in the immediate aftermath of the Communist Party gaining total power were not systematically implemented, and the most serious of these were done without the party's leadership. For example, as John Connelly has pointed out, there was a purge of the professoriate. This, however, was not carried out by the party itself, but by self-appointed "Action Committees" established as the crisis was unfolding. These activist students were not only fired by revolutionary zeal, but also by "intergenerational animosity."[22] Other, similar actions were undertaken by action committees in other spheres of social life, especially in local government and in the factories. To be sure, the non-communist parties had their leaderships replaced, many of their members jumped ship in the weeks after the crisis, and an estimated 30,000 people across the state were removed in the immediate wake of the February crisis. However, it must be recognized that "the purge affected only a small minority, [with] the much wider purge coming in 1949–50," and that, in many ways, this was just an extension of the purge of collaborators that had begun in 1945.[23] The Communists' success in becoming masters in the state also led to grandstanding among their intellectual supporters, as can be seen in the triumphalist and self-congratulatory speeches given at the Congress of National Culture, held in Prague on April 10–11.[24]

Additionally, there were strong elements of continuity. On the symbolic level, there was the fact that Foreign Minister Masaryk stayed

---

[21] Karel Kaplan, "Zakotvení výsledků únorového vítěztví," *Československý časopis historický*, Vol. 10 (1962): 154.

[22] John Connelly, *Captive University* (Chapel Hill & London: University of North Carolina Press, 2000), p. 129. As he points out, the party actually had to retroactively modify some of the more extreme decisions taken by the action committees. For more on the radicalism of Czech youth in the early post-war, see my *The Struggle for the Soul of the Nation*, pp. 148–51.

[23] Robert K. Evanson, "The Czechoslovak Road to Socialism in 1948," *East European Quarterly*, Vol. 19 (1985): 476.

[24] See the collected speeches in *Sjezd národní kultury, 1948* (Prague: Orbis, 1948).

at his post until his suspicious death on 10 March, and President Beneš remained in office until abdicating on 7 June.[25] Similarly, the pre-February parties continued to function, except for the Social Democratic Party, which was merged with the Communist Party on 27 June. Further, the National Front and the parliament continued their work, much as before February, although there were communists representing all the parties. Also in this early period the CPCz entered into negotiations with the Roman Catholic Church, attempting to settle such thorny issues as religious education and the disposition of Church land.[26] There are several other aspects of the immediate post-February course that could be discussed, but I would like to focus on two that I see as particularly revealing: the May 1948 elections and the constitution that came into effect in the same month.

The elections had been scheduled for 30 May well before the government crisis and the Communist Party was faced with the question of how to organize them. For six weeks after achieving a de facto monopoly of power, the top leadership maintained that they would be multiparty elections. The communists had believed before February that they would be able to gain a majority of the votes, and believed thereafter that they might gain 65 percent. On 15 March, the party leadership decided that it would fight to gain 75 percent of the vote. This was a clear continuation of the party's pre-February strategy, and "the Communists may have believed that its transfer [i.e., the Communist Party's monopoly of power, B.A.] could be legitimated ex post facto by an enlargement of the party's popular following."[27] The party continued in its attempt to secure the support of three-quarters of the population until 5 April, when it became evident that it would fall short of its goal by 5–10 percent. It was only at that time that the party

---

[25] Masaryk's death was termed a suicide, although this seems highly suspicious. On Beneš' wavering back and forth over the question of abdication, see Karel Kaplan, *Poslední rok prezidenta* (Prague: ÚSD, 1994).

[26] On this period, see Karel Kaplan, *Stát a církev v Československu v letech 1948–1953* (Prague: ÚSD, 1993), pp. 23–41. He sees the period of real negotiating lasting from March until late June of 1948.

[27] Zdenek L. Suda, *Zealots and Rebels: A History of the Communist Party of Czechoslovakia* (Stanford, CA: Hoover Institution Press, 1980), p. 223.

decided to field a united slate of candidates, with the distribution of parliamentary seats among the parties decided beforehand.[28]

A similar sense of continuity and moderation can be seen in the May Constitution. Edward Taborsky, who had served as Beneš' personal secretary for matters of international law, wrote extensively about it in his *Communism in Czechoslovakia, 1948–1960*. He called it "a unique specimen *sui generis* which had no equal within the Soviet-controlled orbit. It was an elaborate hybrid, a combination of western parliamentarianism with sovietism." Among the Western elements that he noted were the retention of the parliamentary system, the separation of powers, protection against arbitrary arrest, the renunciation of preliminary censorship "as a rule," the absence of any mention of anti-religious propaganda (such as was contained in the Soviet constitution), and the protection of private ownership of land up to fifty hectares and of small enterprises of up to fifty employees. To be sure, there were also present strong elements of communist constitutioncraft that should be familiar to us all. It enumerated the categories of means of production that were exclusively within national ownership and provided for a uniform economic plan, gave the local national committees a constitutional basis, included social rights alongside political rights, included a section on the duties of the citizen, and so on. Nonetheless, its hybrid quality shows particularly well the dual nature of Czechoslovak communism.[29]

From the preceding, it should be evident that in the first post-February months the CPCz had expanded upon, but not radically altered its pre-February course. I would argue that it was the expulsion of Yugoslavia at the June 1948 Cominform meeting and the invocation of Stalin's theory of the intensification of the class struggle during the building of socialism that pushed the Czechoslovak leadership forward. It is only after this meeting, and against the background of deepening shortages and rising black market prices in July and August, that the regime rapidly accelerated on its road to Stalinism. While the Czechoslovak leadership held off on attacks on Yugoslavia until February of

---

[28] Karel Kaplan, "Zakotvení výsledků únorového vítěztví," pp. 159–64. The CPCz-led slate received 89.3% of the vote, with the other ballots left blank in protest.

[29] Edward Taborsky, *Communism in Czechoslovakia, 1948–1960* (Princeton: Princeton UP, 1961), pp. 167–75.

1949, and Czechoslovak engineers even worked on a power plant in the country as late as May of that year, it seems, from the available evidence, that the Tito–Stalin split had serious policy consequences. This should not come as a surprise, given the narrow escape the CPCz had had at the 1947 Cominform meeting, and its moderation, relative to the USSR and the other Eastern European states, in the months after gaining total power. Already at a 28 June meeting of the CPCz Presidium, the leadership realized that changes would have to be made in light of the condemnation of separate roads to socialism.[30] This sense was made concrete when Stalin criticized the party's policies in a meeting with CPCz leader (and Beneš' successor as president) Klement Gottwald in meetings in Moscow in late September.

Perhaps the most instructive example of the change in policy comes from an examination of the party's attitude toward membership. The party had surpassed 1,000,000 members by March of 1946, and had roughly 1,500,000 by February of 1948. New members were added to the ranks of the Communists at a dizzying rate after February, without much concern for class status or previous political affiliation, as the party's moderate, social-democratic tradition continued. This "policy of inclusion"[31] added 1,049,585 between February and mid-July. By this time roughly one in three adult Czechoslovak citizens were party members. In the wake of the Cominform resolution on Yugoslavia, however, the leadership decided, on 11 July, to halt its massive recruitment drive.[32] This policy was taken to the next level only in the fall, after Gottwald's discussions with Stalin. The CPCz had 2,418,199 members in October of 1948 and clearly did not look like the cadre party that Leninist theory called for and the USSR had. So the leadership decided to reduce its number through the certification of all party members. By January of 1949, it had shed more than a quarter-million members, and by February of 1951 its membership had fallen to a still

---

[30] Noted in Robert K. Evanson, "The Czechoslovak Road to Socialism in 1948," p. 481.

[31] The phrase is from Robert Evanson's "The Czechoslovak Road to Socialism in 1948," p. 474.

[32] The figure on new recruits and the information about the halting of recruitment come from *Dějiny KSČ v datech* (Prague: Svoboda, 1984), p. 541.

large but more acceptable 1,489,234.[33] This represents a loss of some forty percent of the membership in under two and one-half years and signaled the ascent of the CPCz's more dogmatic traditions.

The beginning of the purge was not the only measure the regime took in the fall of 1948, however. Rapid change came in almost every sphere in the fall of 1948 and the first half of 1949, after Gottwald's meeting with Stalin, which pushed the CPCz even harder down the road to Stalinism. In the last three months of 1948, a law on forced labor camps was passed by the parliament (25 October),[34] the Five-Year Plan Act was promulgated (27 October), the government abolished the historic provinces of Bohemia, Moravia and Slovakia, replacing them with 19 administrative regions (3 December), and a Czechoslovak–Soviet trade agreement was signed, slating to increase trade between the two states by 45 percent, at the expense of Czechoslovak trade with the West (12 December). Additionally, the Cultural Council was formed in September, which began to institute preliminary censorship restrictions and, in October, the first list of banned books was composed.[35] Further, the Czechoslovak League of Youth (as it was known after the December merging of Czech and Slovak institutions) began checking the reliability of the universities' student bodies in November. By March of 1949, some 18 percent of Czech, and 6.5 percent of Slovak students were no longer permitted to study.[36] Finally, in the sphere of law, a Law on the Defense of the People's Democratic Republic, which lent itself to wide abuse, was passed (6 November) and a law providing for

---

[33] The figures are taken from Vratislav Busek and Nicholas Spulber, *Czechoslovakia* (New York: Praeger, 1957), p. 70.

[34] The law set the duration of punishment at anywhere from three months to two years for those who, "avoid[ed] work, or endanger[ed] the building of the people's democratic order or economic life." It further provided for those convicted to be liable for the loss of their living quarters, the nationalization of their businesses or other assets, and the loss of their trade licences. Hence, it is clear that it was aimed at the remaining small traders in the state. See Vlastislav Chalupa, *Rise and Development of a Totalitarian State* (Leiden: H.E. Stenfert Kroese, 1959), p. 169.

[35] For the development of censorship restrictions, see Karel Kaplan and Dušan Tomášek, *O cenzuře v Československu v letech 1945–1956* (Praha: ÚSD, 1994).

[36] These figures are taken from Vlastislav Chalupa, *Rise and Development of a Totalitarian State*, p. 153.

lay judges serving on court benches was passed (22 December). These were but the first steps of a legal "Two-Year Plan" that significantly altered the state's civil and criminal and penal codes.[37]

The run up to the CPCz's Ninth Congress, in May of 1949, was equally busy, as the party created its new line.[38] One month after the establishment of the Council for Mutual Economic Assistance (Comecon) in January, a law on economic planning was passed. Complementing this, the regime adopted the Unified Agricultural Collectives Act in February 1949, creating the legal framework for the collectivization of agriculture. These two measures extended the reformation of the economy along Soviet lines. Throughout the military, officers were purged, so that 28.7 percent of the Czechoslovak Army officer corps had been discharged by the end of 1949.[39] To train new ones the regime opened three military schools in late 1948 and early 1949, and an army reform bill in February 1949 introduced political officers into the ranks and restructured the armed forces such that they approximated the Soviet structures.[40] Finally, the communists changed their policy toward the Roman Catholic Church. After an intermezzo from July of 1948 to January of 1949, the regime and Church resumed negotiations, with the CPCz seeking a declaration of loyalty from the clergy.[41] When this was not forthcoming and negotiations stalled, the regime moved to cripple the church, passing laws requiring government sanction for all religious appointments, providing for clerical salaries to be paid by the state, closing ecclesiastical office to those convicted in civil court, and requiring a loyalty oath. While most priests had taken this oath by the end of January 1950, no bishops had by that time.[42] In my view, because of the steps taken in the year prior to it, we can safely call the state Stalinized by the time of the CPCz's Ninth Congress, in May of 1949.

---

[37] On this, see Vlastislav Chalupa, *Rise and Development of a Totalitarian State*, pp. 162–5.

[38] This is covered extensively in Karel Kaplan, *Utváření generální linie výstavby socialismu v Československu.*

[39] Kaplan, *Rise of a Monopoly of Power*, II, p. 29.

[40] On developments in the military, see Dana Adams Schmidt, *Anatomy of a Satellite* (Boston: Little, Brown, 1952), pp. 222–5; and Vlastislav Chalupa, *Rise and Development of a Totalitarian State*, pp. 176–8.

[41] On this period, see Karel Kaplan, *Stát a církev*, pp. 42–72.

[42] On the persecution of the Roman Catholic Church after the Ninth Congress, see Karel Kaplan, *Stát a církev*, pp. 73–162.

After the Ninth Congress, however, the party, state and social institutions experienced very little change before Stalin's death. All energies
in this era were consumed by the hunting down, trying, imprisoning,
and, fairly often, executing thousands of "enemies" of the regime.[43]
These persecutions began with the trials and executions of actual political opponents, like the "bourgeois elements" in the armed forces
(the judicial murder of Generals Karel Kutlvašr and Heliodore Pika in
early 1949) and Czech National Socialist Party leaders (culminating
in the execution of Milada Horáková in 1950). They then extended to
the imprisonment of potential enemies in the Roman Catholic Church
(Bishops Jan Vojtaššák, Michal Buzalka, and Peter Gojdič in January
1951) and insufficiently friendly friends in the now disbanded Social
Democratic Party.[44] These trials became cannibalistic when they entered the ranks of the communists themselves, in the attacks on Slovak
"bourgeois nationalists" (among them the future CPCz head Gustáv
Husák, already in 1950). By early 1951, communist officials, activists,
and eventually party leaders became the most common arrestees. Most
famously, these proceedings reached their peak with the November
1952 show trial of the deposed General Secretary of the CPCz, Rudolf
Slánský and thirteen other highly placed communist officials, among
them the former Foreign Minister, Vladimír Clementis. Of the fourteen, eleven were sentenced to death and executed.[45] While the apparent anti-Semitism of its trial is often noted (eleven of the fourteen defendants were Jewish), it should be pointed out that the charge of being
Titoist agents took precedence over that of being Zionist agents. The
salience of the anti-Titoist element was given partly by the Czechoslovak trial's relationship to the earlier trial of László Rajk in Hungary,
but may also have been prompted by delay between the Cominform's

---

[43] Roughly 300 death penalties were meted out, and roughly 180 of these were
carried out.

[44] On the Horáková trial, see Jiří Radotinský, *Rozsudek, který otřasl světem*
(Prague: ČTK-Pressfoto, 1990). On the whole subject of the purges of social
life and especially the trials and imprisonments of thousands of people, see
Vilém Hejl, *Zpráva o organizovaném násilí* (Prague: Univerzum, 1990).

[45] There are many studies of the Slánský trial and its background, including its
relationship to the Rajk trial. The two best in English are Karel Kaplan, *Report on the Murder of the General Secretary* (Columbus: Ohio State UP, 1990);
and Jiri Pelikan, *The Czechoslovak Political Trials 1950–1954* (Stanford: Stanford UP, 1971).

condemnation of Yugoslavia and the CPCz's significant shift in policy in the fall, after Gottwald's discussions with Stalin.

After the Slánský trial, the next major events occurred in the wake of Stalin's death on 5 March, 1953, and here my argument will turn towards a hypothesis about why there was no upheaval in 1956 in Czechoslovakia. Two events strongly affected Czechoslovak developments. The first was the death of the CPCz leader, Klement Gottwald. In a burst of historical irony, Gottwald caught a cold at Stalin's funeral, contracted pneumonia and died on 14 March. Then, ten weeks later, on 30 May, the government announced a currency reform, whose purpose was to deprive wealthier people of savings accumulated before 1948, while attempting to limit the blow on those whom, it was assumed, would have less money in the bank: workers and smaller farmers. This spawned a strike by workers who, because of the unavailability of consumer goods, had considerable savings, and there were riots in several cities, most notably Plzeň. The Plzeň events represented the first public mass demonstration in the Eastern Bloc, bringing 5,000 demonstrators to the city hall. Troops called to the scene refused to fire on them, and eventually the episode ended peacefully. These two, I believe go far towards explaining why Czechoslovakia's de-Stalinization crisis did not happen until late 1960. First of all, there was no Stalinist leader to be besieged by revisionist forces. Gottwald had died, so there was no individual leader at whose feet blame for Stalinist excesses could be laid, and the leadership was mostly the same as it had been as long ago as the CPCz's Bolshevization in 1929. Equally, with the execution of Slánský and Clementis the year before, there was no member of the leadership who had a strong enough base from which to launch such an attack. Even more important, in my view, was the economic factor. This was directly related to the government's toeing the line on the currency reform. Because the reforms lowered purchasing power, they led to a stockpiling of commodity reserves. This meant that over the following three years the regime could raise the standard of living gradually, keeping social tensions from reaching a boiling point. For three years after mid-1953, raising the living standard became the aim of the regime, and involved yearly wage rises, price drops, and rises in consumer production.[46]

---

[46] The information in this paragraph is taken from my own argumentation, augmented by the views of Karel Kaplan in his "Die Ereignisse des Jahres 1956

In looking at the whole period from 1945 to 1953, a few conclusions can be drawn. Most importantly, there were really two major struggles occurring simultaneously. The first was between the Communist Party and its opponents in other parties. This can be called the battle over the Czechoslovak Road to Socialism. This commenced already before the end of the Second World War, but intensified thereafter, with socialism emerging victorious in February of 1948. The other battle was occurring simultaneously *within* the Communist Party, between more moderate and national forces and those more susceptible to Stalinism and more slavish towards the Soviet Union. This battle intensified from the time of the Marshall Plan, reached its height after the Cominform resolution on Yugoslavia, and Stalinizing tendencies emerged triumphant after the September Gottwald–Stalin discussions. This was the trajectory of the Czechoslovak Road to Stalinism. In many ways, the important date is not the often cited February of 1948, but rather the two dates of May of 1945 and June of 1948. February of 1948 in many ways represented an significant extension—but still only an extension—of a transformation that was at its most powerfully radical at its inception in 1945. Nationalization, land reform, the planning system in the economy, these were not invented by the post-February communist regime, but rather deepened by it. In this sense, Czechoslovakia in May of 1948, four months after CPCz claimed total power, looks more like Czechoslovakia in January of 1948, just before the crisis, than Czechoslovakia in late 1945 looks like prewar Czechoslovakia. Similarly, Czechoslovakia at the time of the Ninth Congress, in May of 1949, looks more radically different from Czechoslovakia of May 1948, just before the expulsion of Yugoslavia from the Comintern, than the Czechoslovakia of May 1948 does *vis-à-vis* the Czechoslovakia of January 1948.

In conclusion, I'd like to turn to the first part of my title, "Hope Died Last." It seems to me that this is true for many, many communists and non-communists alike after 1945. For non-communist socialists in the Social Democratic Party and the National Socialist Party, their hope of carrying out radical changes that would create a socially

---

in der Tschechoslowakei," in Hans Henning Hahn and Heinrich Olschowsky eds., *Das Jahr 1956 in Ostmitteleuropa* (Berlin: Akademie Verlag, 1996), pp. 31–45.

just society while remaining faithful to Czechoslovakia's democratic heritage came to pieces. Their hopes died over the course of the period, with some losing faith in working alongside their communist counterparts early, before or as a direct result of the Marshall Plan fiasco, an increasing number during the fall of 1947, as the CPCz increased the pressure, and still others after February. For many communists, their hopes for building a particularly Czechoslovak brand of socialism were extinguished during the second half of 1948 as the increasing rigidity of the system led by the Soviet Union became apparent. The ending of the Czechoslovak road in Stalinism was deeply disillusioning for many of those on the more moderate end of Czechoslovak communism, and, for all but the most rabid of Czechoslovak Stalinists, the show trials of the late 1940s and early 1950s, culminating in the trial of Rudolf Slánský, signaled the end of their hopes. In this regard, as Norman Naimark has written, Stalinism was in fact counter-revolutionary.[47] The Stalinization of Eastern Europe, particularly in the case of Czechoslovakia, extinguished independent developments spurred by desires for radical social change in the wake of the war. In the case of Czechoslovakia, these hopes were rekindled in 1968, and the second crushing of hope for a specifically Czechoslovak brand of socialism marked the end of any belief in Marxism, even among communists themselves.

---

[47] Norman M. Naimark, "Revolution and Counterrevolution in Eastern Europe," in Christiane Lemke and Gary Marks eds., *The Crisis of Socialism in Europe* (Durham, NC: Duke UP, 1992), pp. 61–83.

CRISTIAN VASILE

Propaganda and Culture in Romania at the Beginning of the Communist Regime

In the aftermath of the communist takeover, high on the Romanian Communist Party's to-do-list was the creation of a Soviet-type culture. According to the official discourse, this new culture was going to be the creation of the working class. But it is no surprise that its genesis was attentively and exclusively monitored by the communist leadership. The agency designed for such purpose was the dreaded Propaganda and Agitation Department, an institution attached to the party's Central Committee.

The present paper has two parallel goals. It analyzes the activity of the Propaganda and Agitation Department during the Stalinist period (1948–53). And, it presents the changes within the Arts Unions, and other cultural and educational institutions. By the end of the article, I will attempt a few conclusions that serve as clues for a dilemma that has been haunting the Romanian post-communist cultural milieu. Namely, I will look into the questions of *why did so many Romanian intellectuals accept the terms of the communist propaganda?* And, more precisely, into *why did they not rebel, especially after 1953?*

I am predominantly relying upon archival materials issued by this Department. The documents were recently de-classified as a consequence of the research activities carried out in 2006 by the Presidential Commission for the Analysis of the Communist Dictatorship in Romania. Their declassification, however, was incomplete due to political reasons. The most obvious is the fact that Ion Iliescu, former president of Romania between 1990 and 1996, and again between 2000 and 2004, was head of the Propaganda Department in the 1960s. After the 1989 revolution he unsurprisingly avoided an honest assessment of both his communist past and the regime's censorship practices.[1] With the significant exception of a few privileged researchers,[2] study of the Propaganda and Agitation Department (PAD) documents was possible only after 1996–97. By then, the declassified archival material was only remotely relevant.

From the very beginning, one can easily argue that the two main consequences of the organization and functioning of the PAD were: the perversion of the discourse regarding the Arts; and the harassment of the intellectuals more or less reluctant to being cowed by the regime's politics of culture. One of the main goals of the Department's activity was the suppression of cultural diversity. The cadres of the PAD were determined to fight against any spontaneous intellectual movement, showing complete contempt for artistic freedom. The *guidance* of the Arts was in fact a synonym for political censorship.

In some Soviet-controlled countries of Central and Eastern Europe, such as East Germany, the agitprop networks succeeded in gaining ground and influenced the working class and even intellectual urban milieus.[3] In Romania, however, the communists had to overcome a rather refractory attitude among intellectuals toward their co-option attempts. Nevertheless, by the end of 1948, the PAD apparently succeeded in breaking down their resistance, hesitation, and unwillingness to get involved.

The responsibility for agitprop activities within the Romanian Communist Party (RCP), between 1945 and 1948, was entrusted to the Central Section of Political Education (the PAD predecessor).[4] It was, however, a rather incoherent and inconsistent organization. This situation was also determined by the fact that the RCP did not control

---

[1] Cristian Vasile, "Un martor important: Ion Iliescu şi scrierea istoriei României comuniste," *AIO: Anuarul Institutului de Istorie Orală*, Vol. 6 (2005): 391–2.

[2] Predominantly employees or former employees of the Romanian National Archives, an institution directly subordinated to the Interior Department, one of the most unreformed government sectors.

[3] I am adopting Richard Bodek's conclusions in his study about everyday life in interwar-era Berlin; see Richard Bodek, "The not—so—Golden Twenties: Everyday life and Communist Agitprop in Weimar-era Berlin," *Journal of Social History*, Vol. 30, No. 1 (Fall 1996).

[4] Arhivele Naţionale Istorice Centrale (Central Historical National Archives, Bucharest, hereafter: ANIC), Fund Central Committee of the Romanian Communist Party—Propaganda and Agitation Section, File no. 13/1947.

all the governmental sectors. Many local party organizations simply did not have agitprop departments due to a lack of qualified activists. A similar state of affairs confronted the Yugoslav Communists immediately after 1944.[5] An equivalent low degree of organization can be noticed in the case of the counterpart Department of the Soviet Bolshevik Communist Party in the first years after October 1917.[6]

However, the Central Section of Political Education (SCEP)[7] developed a network of regional sections throughout Romania's counties and districts. These political organizations granted their consent to the publishing of new journals and magazines within their area of competence, thus doubling and overlapping the state's censorship. The whole process was under the direct subordination of the Ministry of Information—a communist-controlled department. As a rule, each regional section had a commission, which checked and controlled all the activities regarding local literature and the arts, including public representations and other performances.

The SCEP cooperated in some respects with the Secret Police.[8] The communist leadership periodically convened conferences and meetings with the aim of training and disciplining, from an ideological point of view, the heads and the representatives of local agitprop units. During these proceedings, Iosif Chișinevschi and Leonte Răutu, the two leaders of RCP's propaganda,[9] defended the Marxist-Leninist orthodoxy. SCEP regional units had to fulfill several tasks based on the assignments delivered by the two heads of the Propaganda. The array of duties assigned to the delegates increased in 1947, primarily after Andrei A. Zhdanov's open pronouncement of the Two Camp theory (his 1947 Cominform speech) and after the triggering of the anti-

---

[5] Carol S. Lilly, "Problems of Persuasion: Communist Agitation and Propaganda in Post-War Yugoslavia, 1944–1948," *Slavic Review*, Vol. 53, No. 2 (Summer 1994): 408.

[6] Sheila Fitzpatrick, *The Commissariat of Enlightenment: Soviet Organization of Education and the Arts under Lunacharsky October 1917–1921* (Cambridge: Cambridge University Press, 1970), p. xiv.

[7] In Romanian: Secția Centrală de Educație Politică.

[8] ANIC, Fund Central Committee of the Romanian Communist Party—Propaganda and Agitation Section, File no. 13/1947, p. 51.

[9] Iosif Chișinevschi and Leonte Răutu were old cadres of the Romanian Interwar Agitprop. Vladimir Tismaneanu, *Stalinism for All Seasons: A Political History of the Romanian Communism* (Berkeley: University of California Press, 2003).

cosmopolitanism campaign. Beginning with the autumn of 1947, the SCEP significantly increased the level of its denunciatory pronouncements against the so-called Western ideological offensive. This turned into an excellent opportunity to put the country's communist militants on guard and to stress that the Section had to increase and expand its activities. It even threatened with suppression of the local Communist newspapers that had published "inadequate" articles, that is, materials containing ideological errors.

Around the same time, the communist press yielded to the orders to discredit Tudor Arghezi, Romania's most important living poet. He was subsequently accused of decadence.[10] It was definitely no coincidence that the decisive attack took place in early January 1948, during the discussions regarding the reorganization of the Romanian Writers' Society (SSR—*Societatea Scriitorilor Români*).[11] The congress of the procommunist Trade Unions of Artists, Writers and Journalists Organization, to which the SSR was subordinated, pleaded for a sort of standardized art and literature. The model, of course, was Soviet socialist realism, the only officially accepted method of artistic creation. Simultaneously, many non-communist and independent political and cultural magazines were closed down or undermined by the communist government. Thus, at the beginning of 1948 one can notice the disappearance of intellectual doubt and crystallization of a uniformity of opinions in Romanian mass-media. In fact, in Friedrich Hayek's terms, this was the end of truth in post-war Romania.

Although the role of propaganda became overwhelming, the RCP needed the intellectuals to fulfill the role of pawns in its legitimization strategy.[12] However, the Romanian writers and artists had to abide to the communist terms, particularly to the Party's *cultural guidance*. In

---

[10] Ana Selejan, *Trădarea intelectualilor: Reeducare şi prigoană* (Bucharest: Editura Cartea Românească, 2005), pp. 301–73; Sorin Toma, "Care este adevărul în cazul 'Arghezi'," in *Privind înapoi: Amintirile unui fost ziarist comunist. Redactor şef al "Scânteii" din 1947 până în 1960* (Bucharest: Editura Compania, 2004), pp. 328–31.

[11] Ion Ianoşi, "Uniunea Scriitorilor în sistemul culturii socialiste şi segmentul literar în tranziţia românească," in Adrian Miroiu ed., *Instituţii în tranziţie* (Bucharest: Editura Punct, 2002).

[12] See the analysis of Alina Tudor Pavelescu, "Une stratégie de légitimation politique: Le Parti Communiste Roumain et la reconfiguration du champ culturel," *Studii şi Materiale de Istorie Contemporană*, Vol. 3 (2004): 139–152.

the summer of 1952, during a political meeting aimed at imposing the party-line regarding cultural problems within the ranks of the creative Unions' members, Ofelia Manole (deputy head of the Romanian Agitprop), offered an explanation for the existence of the cultural guidance, and censorship in other terms. She stated that

> someone could ask us why we are fighting, why we, the communists, do not leave the people, the writers and artists alone, why one does not set them free. Because we reckon that your work is one of the most important jobs for the benefit of the toilers. The proletariat needs to have literary and artistic works, and we reckon that you are a part of the working class and you must stand by all workers during the struggle for building Socialism. The Arts are a strong weapon of the working class.[13]

The ideological pressure during the first communist decade was exerted especially through the agency of Ofelia Manole and Nicolae Moraru. The latter was an alleged specialist in aesthetics. He, however, was an impostor, very poorly educated, who acted as deputy of Leonte Răutu, the top leader of the Romanian Agitprop. After 1947, Nicolae Moraru closely supervised the forging of a new artistic elite of painters, actors, musicians, and writers with a so-called "healthy" social background.[14] Nicolae Moraru benefited from the use of the levers of control as a dignitary. On the basis of the positive evaluation he received for his activity within the PAD, he was later appointed Secretary General of the Ministry of the Arts and Information.[15]

In order to impose efficient "guidance" over Romanian culture, the PAD became a sort of political tamer. It determined both the reorganization and purge of the traditional artists and writers' associations. These associations were transformed after the Soviet model into ideologically conformist creative unions with obedient leaderships, whose

---

[13] Mihaela Cristea ed., *Reconstituiri necesare: Şedinţa din 27 iunie 1952 a Uniunilor de creaţie din România* [Neccessary acts of restoring cultural history: The Romanian Creative Unions' sitting from June 27, 1952], preface by Marius Oprea (Iaşi: Editura Polirom, 2005), p. 214.

[14] ANIC, Fund Central Committee of the Romanian Communist Party—Propaganda and Agitation Section, File no. 9/1947, f. 82.

[15] After 1948 Nicolae Moraru became professor at the Arts Institute in Bucharest.

sole function was to discipline the troublesome intellectuals. The creative unions' magazines and periodicals were controlled both by the unions' power structures and by the new state censorship—the General Department of Press and Prints. In its turn, this institution was under the supervision of the Propaganda and Agitation Department. Some Communists used to say that due to detailed personal files, the propagandists, instructors, and other party cadres of the PAD could read each and every artist like an open book.

The Department, through the activity of its different sectors, especially the Sector for Literature and Arts, sometimes sent the orders and instructions directly to the low-level subordinate bodies or Ministry of Arts' officials. This way, it neglected and avoided governmental control, namely Eduard Mezincescu (the Minister of Arts and Information), who represented the more moderate cultural line within the party. It is no surprise then that Mezincescu complained about the insufficient communication and exchange of information with Leonte Răutu and Iosif Chişinevschi. This administrative abnormality tacitly imposed the subordination of this state sector to the national party. "The way we keep in touch hinders the Ministry of Arts and Information, preveting it from developing its own initiatives," concluded Mezincescu.[16] One needs only to take Anatol Lunacharsky's case,[17] his Soviet homologue in Russia after October 1917, in order to get the full picture of Mezincescu's chronic lack of authority over the regime's politics of culture.

The Agitation and Propaganda Department became an important political actor. Probably referring to Orwell's Ministry of Truth, but using juridical terminology and taking into account the decision making process on cultural policies, some scholars compared the Romanian Agitprop with a sort of communist Supreme Court. In my opinion, the comparison of it with an abusive General Prosecution seems more fitting. Moreover, the leadership of the various artistic unions in place at the time can be equated with law courts or other lower judicial bodies. The PAD took on not only the functions of a Supreme Court, for it judged the refractory intellectuals and autocratically arbitrated the

---

[16] ANIC, Fund Central Committee of the Romanian Communist Party—Chancellery, file No. 127/1949, p. 4.

[17] Sheila Fitzpatrick, *The Commissariat of Enlightenment: Soviet organization of Education and the Arts under Lunacharsky October 1917–1921*, pp. 110 and sqq.

disputes between artists, writers, and publishing houses. But it was also assigned the task of selecting and distributing the cadres for cultural and ideological institutions, such as the Ministry of Arts and Information (later known as the *Committee for Arts*, after the Soviet model), the Ministry of Education, the Romanian Academy, the General Department of Press and Prints, and creative unions.[18]

Another PAD area of responsibility was to give directives concerning the political and cultural newspapers, magazines, and radio etc. Of course, these directives had to follow the political line assigned by the party's Central Committee. The Agitprop had to prepare different materials (assignments, reports, analyses) regarding the cultural sphere as well as the documents being sent to the Secretariat of the Party Central Committee and to the other higher political bodies (Politbüro, OrgBureau). The tentacles of the Agitprop stretched across all Romanian counties, regions, and governmental departments. Each Ministry had its own Department or Section of Agitation and Propaganda that pursued "the strengthening of class conscience" at the personnel level. These subsidiary agitprops regularly informed the central Agitprop, warning of the possible danger of "heretical" ideological trends and hostile attitudes demonstrated within different unions, universities, theatres, etc. Consequently, the Agitation and Propaganda Department was compelled to check and analyze these intimations and reports, in order to provide the needed "guidance." For example, in the summer of 1952, a team of Agitprop instructors descended on Cluj, a Transylvanian multinational town inhabited both by Romanians and Hungarians. The communist activists were to check information about displays of "wrong" political views, as well as nationalistic and chauvinist positions among the students of the two nationalities.[19] During these types of inspections, the ideological team fished for information from the local party leadership, university professors, and students, and held several meetings to analyze the existent political errors. Only upon the

---

[18] Nicoleta Ionescu-Gură, "Reorganizarea PMR–ului după modelul PC (b.) al URSS şi crearea nomenclaturii CC al PMR în Republica Populară Română (1949–1954)," in Gheorghe Onişoru ed., *Totalitarism şi rezistenţă, teroare şi represiune în România comunistă*, preface by Sabine Habersack (Bucharest: Consiliul Naţional pentru Studierea Arhivelor Securităţii, 2001), p. 224.

[19] ANIC, Fund Central Committee of the Romanian Communist Party—Propaganda and Agitation Section, File no. 58/1952, p. 1.

completion of all these stages did the PAD representatives make the final decision.

After 1947, the Romanian professorial body was purged as well. The objective of this campaign was to adjust the higher and public school education to the needs of the communist ruling Party. The old institutional structures, such as the students associations, were dissolved and replaced with pro-communist organizations. Although the student bodies grew after 1948, many students were discriminated against and even expelled from universities due to their bourgeois social origins and "reactionary" views. The technical departments of the universities became predominant and the social origin of the students changed gradually in favor of the peasants and workers. At the pre-university level one can see the efforts of the Agitprop to quickly enforce the Soviet model and to overcome important problems such as illiteracy, or the attachment of the common people to the religious values that were transmitted also through public education.[20]

The children of the *kulaks* (*chiaburi* in Romanian) suffered discrimination because at this moment the Communist leadership raised the question of expelling them, based only on class, from important educational institutions. The governmental decision-makers considered that these children had to be guided only towards industrial production and physical labor in order to change their inherited social and political "wrong views." Gheorghe Gheorghiu-Dej, the First Secretary of RCP—named Romanian Workers' Party (RWP) at the end of February 1948—in the postwar era, admitted that sometimes a natural *dekulakization* is preferable. "There are some cases, a few—Dej said—when they [the children with *kulak* fathers] break [the bonds] with their [*reactionary*] families or when they could have a good influence over their parents." However, the situation of those stigmatized teenagers worsened because such a natural dekulakization process was not pursued.

Theoretically, the cohesion of the Romanian families was hard to break even under major pressure. Nevertheless, discord among relatives was unavoidable and surfaced soon after 1948. The PAD and other Communist authorities encouraged the physical separation of children

---

[20] Cristian Vasile, "Imposing Control and Mechanisms of Escape: Education in Communist Romania during the Stalinist Period," *Historical Yearbook* (2004): 215.

from those parents presumably more hostile to the political system.[21] In such conditions of systematic discrimination, many young people wanted to get rid of this mark of disgrace (i.e., the stigma of social origin). They wanted to exculpate themselves. Usually, the children who came from bourgeois families or other alleged *enemies of the people* could not become members of the Union of Working Youth (UTM—*Uniunea Tineretului Muncitoresc*). There were cases when some pupils and students with problematic social origins denied their roots so that they could more easily adapt to or integrate into the social and political system.[22]

In order to limit and undermine the teachers' moral authority and autonomy, the official propaganda also decided to control them through school children organizations, thus replicating the Soviet model. Immediately after 1947, the opponents of the communist school reform noticed that the newly founded Romanian Pupils' Associations Union (UAER—*Uniunea Asociațiilor de Elevi din România*) showed anarchist tendencies in their confrontations with teachers, schoolmasters, and parents. For example, the PAD needed the help of the Pupils' Union in order to track down the bourgeois teachers who still used the old, forbidden textbooks in classes and ignored the official Marxist-Leninist oriented manuals. The Ministry of Education nominated inspectors served this very same purpose. The use of the prohibited textbooks was both a sort of escape mechanism and an act of defiance under the totalitarian regime. In the first year after the beginning of the Education Reform, however, the textbooks approved by the communists were either not printed or the publishing houses did not deliver them to the school storehouses.

After 1920, the foremost priority of the Soviet Ministry of Education was to introduce teachers to progressive methods of education. The political confrontation or ideological coercion of the teachers was to be avoided at all costs.[23] Sheila Fitzpatrick accurately noticed

---

[21] For the Czechoslovakian case, see Otto Ulč, "The Communist Party of Czechoslovakia and the Young Generation," *East European Quarterly*, Vol. 6, No. 2 (June 1972): 210.

[22] ANIC, Fund Central Committee of the Romanian Communist Party—Chancellery, File 149/1950, pp. v–14.

[23] Sheila Fitzpatrick, *Education and Social Mobility in the Soviet Union 1921–1934* (Cambridge: Cambridge University Press, 2002), p. 19.

that this approach was too subtle for many local soviets and education departments, which often put much cruder political pressure on the school than the Education Ministry desired. Most importantly, this policy offended militant communist organizations like the Comsomol—which constantly provoked political confrontation with the teachers—and the League of the Militant Godless.[24] Unlike the situation in the USSR, the UTM, the Romanian homologue for Comsomol, and the UAER did not assume independent significant actions that could defy the PAD, the Minister of Education authority's or the RWP's Central Committee's pronouncements. In the overwhelming majority of cases, they were mere obedient executioners. Moreover, in Romania, the communists did not find anything similar to the Association or League of the Militant Godless. There was only a Society for the Spreading of Scientific Knowledge (SRSC—*Societatea pentru Răspândirea Ştiinţei şi Culturii*). Its purpose was to bring into question and to compromise the Christian Church's views especially in regard to science and nature.

According to Randolph L. Braham, the Campaign for Literacy assumed paramount importance after the nationalization and collectivization programs had been launched (1948–49). The ever-increasing need for skilled and semi-skilled workers in the field and the factory prompted the communist party and the government to reorganize the literacy campaign on a more rational and institutionalized basis.[25] However, it must be stressed that this initiative did maintain an important political and ideological dimension. It was a part of the so-called communist Cultural Revolution. The Romanian communists did not deny that through means of such policies, allegedly aimed at significantly diminishing and even totally liquidating illiteracy, they were also eliminating the last obstacles to the complete imposition of a communist regime and the creation of a "new man." "The illiterate man cannot be influenced by our politics"—was an often-used slogan by the official propaganda at that time.

This campaign, prepared in accordance with the Ministry of Education's guidelines, encountered the reluctance and even the hostility

---

[24] *Ibid.*
[25] Randolph L. Braham, *Education in the Romanian People's Republic* (Washington: U.S. Department of Health, Education, and Welfare, 1963), p. 15.

of some schoolmasters and teachers.[26] Many of them were removed immediately after 1945 from city schools on a political basis and transferred to rural areas where the illiteracy rate was much higher. Here they could hardly find a decent dwelling and were poorly paid. They were therefore compelled to hold, without being paid, multiple classes for the illiterate population. Young and politically "reliable" teachers were sent to the rural areas, but they, like the reactionary teaching cadres, did not wish a repartition at these peripheral schools and thus were left with no financial support. Probably the total number of the teachers transferred to countryside schools, between 1948 and 1949, exceeded 10,000.[27] Often, they refused the appointment and resigned or were dismissed. The leadership of the Ministry of Education labeled such behavior as grave defiance, even "sabotage."[28] The communist leadership used the situation as a pretext to resort to another purge among the teaching body. These disobedient teachers therefore became collateral victims of the literacy campaign.

The propaganda did not mention anything about the enormous price of the Literacy Campaign: the great disturbance generated by the large-scale resignations, dismissals, abusive or punitive transfers, and the voluntary work. Moreover, that these reprisals produced a climate of fear, facilitating the political control over public education. Even if the official statistics detailing the educational level from the 1950s onwards were forged, an expansion of general schooling cannot be denied. The compulsory schooling years increased after 1948, while the teaching was consistently imbued with Communist ideology. However, due to the teachers from the old bourgeois school, some of the pupils managed to avoid the influence of the propaganda and maintained their personality and spontaneity.

The mandatory reading list for school children encompassed only the works on Socialist Realism. Some teachers, however, discretely

---

[26] ANIC, Fund Central Committee of the Romanian Communist Party—Chancellery, File 58/1948, p. 18.

[27] *Stenogramele ședințelor Biroului Politic și ale Secretariatului Comitetului Central al PMR 1949* [The Minutes of the RWP Political Bureau's and Secretariat's meetings 1949; hereafter: *Stenogramele*], vol. 2 (Bucharest: Romanian Național Archives, 2003), p. 52.

[28] ANIC, Fund Central Committee of the Romanian Communist Party—Chancellery, File 58/1948, p. 24.

recommended forbidden readings, especially the interwar Romanian
literature that was considered "decadent" by the communist establishment. By such means, at least a part of the young generation was offered an alternative to the official ideology. For example, in the 1950s,
Tudor Vianu, a well-known philosophy and philology professor, held
classes and gave examinations in private for a few select students.[29] But
these seminars were limited only to a small group of Romanian teenagers with very specific socio-cultural backgrounds. It did not, unfortunately, develop into an alternative culture capable of defying the communist system, as in Hungary (1956) or in Czechoslovakia (1968).

Although the philology departments were purged, some "reactionary" professors survived. The communist leadership and the PAD
needed a special school for the creation of new and re-educated writers.
Thus, at the beginning of the 1950s, the "Mihail Eminescu" Literature and Literary Critics School was opened. This institution of higher
education looked like a garrison with high walls and barbed wire. The
literary milieus of those years perceived it as a system of brainwashing.
Its students were lavishly stuffed both with food and ideology, being
forced to deal with huge mandatory bibliography, predominantly socialist realism literature. However, with the exception of a few zealous
individuals, who wished to entirely integrate themselves into this brainwashing system, many of the young students were hesitant and had irk-
some second thoughts. One such case was Marin Ioniţă. In his memoirs he confessed: "I discovered that some of my colleagues showed a
sort of an unspoken and hidden resistance to the system which probably was noticed by our supervisors, too."[30]

In its effort to destroy the former social structures, the RWP leadership did not neglect the academic and university milieus. The status
of the professorial body decreased as a result of state pressure. The
autonomy of the universities was suppressed to such an extent that
even Mihai Ralea, one of the most obedient and opportunistic intellectuals, decided in 1955, during a period of cultural "thaw," to send
a report to the leadership of the RWP, lamenting the appointment of

---

[29] Matei Călinescu and Ion Vianu, *Amintiri în dialog* [Recollections through
dialogue] (Bucharest: Litera, 1994), p. 69.
[30] Marin Ioniţă, *Kiseleff 10: Fabrica de scriitori* [10, Kiseleff Boulevard. Writers's
Factory] (Piteşti: Paralela 45, 2003), p. 20.

the educational institutions' principals exclusively on political criteria.[31] Mihai Ralea also brought up the decline of the scientific production due to the fact that the main university had only one publication for all its departments and that its issues were not published at regular intervals.[32] The situation was even worse than the case of Soviet university professors at the beginning of the 1920s. The Soviet government exercised censorship, but permitted the re-establishment of private publishing in the early 1920s. Seemingly, the Soviet scholars appear to have been comparatively little affected by the censorship, in contrast to Soviet writers of fiction and drama.[33] In Stalinist Romania all these categories of intellectuals had to be at the censor's beck and call. Additionally, they had to extensively emulate Russian and Soviet Literature.

Immediately after the suppression of the traditional students associations almost all students joined, either under pressure or for mere opportunism, the National Union of Romanian Students (UNSR—*Uniunea Națională a Studenților din România*). This body was the only one of its type officially endorsed by the regime. Many of them fell into this trap due to the sly tactics of the communist authorities. The latter encouraged them to cherish illusions concerning the apolitical character of the UNSR. In fact, the government and the Party never allowed free play in the case of the UNSR, an association which actually lasted only one year. At the beginning of 1949, significant communist leaders claimed that almost all of the Romanian fascist youth had enlisted in the UNSR,[34] and that others joined the organization just for material advantages (e.g., ration cards).[35] These charges provoked the dissolution of UNSR and the founding of a class-based association: the Union of the Working Youth. Afterwards, the communist officials launched a threat: "Those who do not enter UTM must be re-educated and forced to form cultural circles."[36]

---

[31] ANIC, Central Committee of the Romanian Communist Party—Propaganda and Agitation Section Fund, File 76/1955, pp. 14–5.

[32] *Ibid.*

[33] Sheila Fitzpatrick, *Education and Social Mobility in the Soviet Union 1921–1934*, p. 83.

[34] ANIC, Fund Central Committee of the Romanian Communist Party—Chancellery, File 1/1949, p. 5.

[35] *Ibid.*, File 45/1949, p. 9.

[36] *Ibid.*

The so-called "improvement of class composition in schools and universities" became an obsession for the Agitprop. In 1949, the Ministry of Education forbade the admission to institutions of higher learning of children who belonged to the so-called "capitalist exploiting elements." The same happened two years later in the case of pupils' admission to the eighth grade. Despite this absurd class-based discrimination, the enrollment rate of poor peasant and working class students' did not significantly increase between 1948–52. Under the circumstances, in the summer of 1952, the acute problem of the improvement of class composition in schools and universities again seized the attention of the communist leadership. They were worried about the fact that the "healthy" youth (from the political point of view) could be contaminated by the presence of "undesirable" children—sons and daughters of "capitalist exploiters." Gheorghe Gheorghiu-Dej warned that the Communist Party could not rely on these undesirable elements after their graduation. He expressed the fear that these "inimical elements", upon graduating from institutions of higher learning, would penetrate the state bureaucracy and they would sabotage the building of socialism.[37] Dej also pointed to those guilty for this situation: one of the scapegoats was Gheorghe Vasilichi, a member of the party's pre-1945 "old guard."

In order to prevent the admission of "undesirables," the authorities divided the children in sociopolitical categories. Initially, in a report prepared by Leonte Răutu expressing most drastic limitations, there were four categories. His radical proposals for restrictions provoked even the reaction of Dej himself who declared: "it is not advisable to lay it on with a trowel." Although, in the end, the First Secretary of RWP imposed only three categories of children the effects were nevertheless drastic. The surveys and the other statistics prepared by Ministry of Education officials already anticipated that putting into practice these restrictive measures would cause dramatic results. The proportion of "undesirable" children admitted to the eighth grade severely decreased: from almost 21,000 pupils only four (0.01 percent) belonged to the third category.[38] Probably, in order to protect the international

---

[37] *Ibid.*, File 66/1952, p. 13.

[38] *Ibid.*, Central Committee of the Romanian Communist Party—Propaganda and Agitation Section Fund, File 37/1953, pp. 18–19.

image of the regime, these severe and absurd limitations were not included in the law adopted by the Great National Assembly, Romania's pseudo-parliament during the communist times. Although the discriminatory provisions did not appear in the Official Gazette (*Buletinul Oficial al Republicii Populare Române*), the party included it in a directive concerning the necessary measures for the improvement of pupils and students' class composition, a top secret document which remained unpublished.

The school inspectors and principals strictly observed this directive. After 1947–48, the principals of the country's most prestigious high schools were either removed or, at best, coupled with deputies who were loyal to the totalitarian regime. A few old and skilled principals who kept their jobs after this purge admitted shamefully that "we accustomed ourselves [to the new political circumstances] and we made compromises against our conscience in order to save little things we could still do. Now we have nothing: we lost both the school and our honor." Only Stalin's death in March 1953 brought a slight relaxation of these restrictive measures. Nevertheless, it was only in August 1953 that the Party leadership tried to find a way out and decided that a change of the discriminatory directive was necessary in order to create the possibility of admission for the deserving pupils whose origins were problematic.[39] The crucial importance of the Education Reform was emphasized by Gheorghiu-Dej himself: "The Ministry of Education is not a part time job of four hours. It is more important than the State Security Ministry because we had to destroy the enemy from the cultural domain. We had to train the future teaching cadres and also to educate the working class."[40]

On 31 January 1949, during a session of the Central Committee of the Communist Party Secretariat, Vasile Luca, one of the most influential leaders of the RWP, estimated that Gheorghe Vasilichi, the Minister of Education at the time, viewed with "sentimentalism" the class enemy and was entirely wrong when he imagined that the character of "unreliable" intellectuals could change for the better. Vasile Luca added: "The cadres problem is one of the most important because there [at the Ministry of Education] the Department maintained

---

[39] *Ibid.*, p. 1.
[40] *Stenogramele*, Vol. 2, p. 39.

the old reactionary staff that put into practice our Education Reform. It would be better to appoint and hire unskilled but devoted personnel, which can be and is good at imposing the educational reform."

These statements were almost identical with the Stalin's 1935 slogan—"Cadres decide everything."[41] The similarity also shows how extensive Romania's dependence was on the Soviet model during the first decade of Communism. The successes of the Party in enforcing the Soviet pattern were due mainly to the pre-existence of this model.

Since the autumn of 1944 the Romanian communists showed a particular interest in the use of visual propaganda as part of the political battle against its enemies. They also focused upon winning the painters' and sculptors' favor in order to strengthen the so-called National Democratic Front (FND—*Frontul Naţional Democrat*), a pro-communist and pro-Soviet coalition of parties. This subtle initiative of head hunting fell within the competence of two avant-garde artists, sympathizers of the Romanian Communist Party—Maximilian Hermann Maxy (better known as M.H. Maxy) and Jules Perahim, a graphic artist who took refuge in the USSR during World War II and returned to Romania with the Red Army in 1945. The main task of M.H. Maxy was to generate an affable attitude amongst the salient representatives of the Fine Arts towards the RCP. According to art historian Radu Bogdan, M.H. Maxy "succeeded very quickly in his duty because [...] during those years [1945–46] the Communist Party did not exert censorial pressure on the artistic works. The Party representatives were satisfied both with their position of persons who advised with benign critical allusions and with the privilege of demanding from artists a thematic approach to the present."[42]

Under circumstances of political transition, Romania experienced a brief artistic revival that quickly ended by the autumn of 1947. During this short period the avant-garde re-activated its old connections with French surrealism. Sadly though, the Romanian avant-garde was disunited: some painters wholeheartedly embraced socialist realism either as true-believers or out of opportunism in order to become socially

---

[41] Sheila Fitzpatrick, *The Cultural Front: Power and Culture in Revolutionary Russia* (Ithaca and London: Cornell University Press, 1992), p. 149.
[42] Radu Bogdan, "Un martor al realismului socialist" (XV), in *Dilema*, Vol. 3, No. 128, 23–29 June 1995.

successful. Others, however, left the country foreseeing the all-out imposition of the party censorship on the arts.

In general, the most famous painters and sculptors came to terms with the new regime. Among the reasons for such a *modus vivendi* was the fear of an abusive and tendentious enforcement of the law regarding administrative purges. This document was promulgated by the Groza Government on 30 March 1945 in order to eliminate fascist elements from public offices. Until 1947, though, the Party exerted its ideological influence cautiously even in the RCP newspapers, for it wished to avoid widespread media aggression against reputable artists.[43] As I already suggested, October 1947 was a turning point in the history of Romanian culture: from this moment on the angry tone of the propaganda became increasingly louder. The hardening of the line concerning the independent works of art became clear on 18 and 19 October 1947, at the congress of the Trade Union Association of the Artists, Writers, and Journalists (USASZ—*Uniunea Sindicatelor de Artişti, Scriitori şi Ziarişti*). On this occasion, Lucian Grigorescu, a well-known painter, criticized the impressionist and surrealist tendencies in the arts, called white black, and rejected any significant Western influences upon his career.[44]

This was not an act of political adherence or a concession of an avant-garde artist: Lucian Grigorescu belonged to the mainstream. Unlike the Russian avant-gardists, M.H. Maxy and Jules Perahim did not take a firm and aggressive position against the old artistic school. They did not confront the conservative academic artists with the energy of their Russian colleagues immediately after October 1917.[45] Moreover, one cannot distinguish any domination by the artistic left over the Ministry of Arts from 1945 to 1947. For example, M.H. Maxy acted only as a minister's advisor. In order to impose its cultural program for changing the structure of the painters' creative union, the PAD used both the avant-garde and the conservative artists.[46]

---

[43] *Ibid.*, *Dilema*, Vol. 3, No. 113, 10–16 March 1995.

[44] In 1948 Lucian Grigorescu was appointed head of the Fine Arts Department of the Ministry of Arts and Information.

[45] Sheila Fitzpatrick, *The Commissariat of Enlightenment: Soviet organization of Education and the Arts under Lunacharsky October 1917–1921*, p. 123.

[46] Magda Cârneci, *Artele plastice în România 1945–1989* (Bucharest: Editura Meridiane, 2000).

In conclusion, the Propaganda and Agitation Department emerged when *Zhdanovschina* was at its highest point. Few artists resisted reaching some sort of compromise with party propaganda and its forced-mobilization techniques. The RCP/RWP Agitprop focused on specific ideological tasks regarding the cultural sphere, such as eliminating reluctant intellectuals and transforming the creative unions. All in all though, intellectuals and artists accustomed themselves to the communist regime. By 1948, only a minority of refractory writers and scholars existed, namely, those who rejected professional enrollment conditioned by ideological ends.

The Romanian case is somewhat similar to the East German case. Both in Romania and East Germany, in contrast with the Polish and Czech situation, the intellectuals, artists, students, and professors failed to contribute to the destabilization of the regime. Some scholars have attempted to show that behind a façade of uniformity separate national traditions continued through the Stalinist period, creating different contexts for politics and for societal experience.[47]

Why did so many Romanian intellectuals accept the terms of the communist propaganda and why did they not rebel after 1953? Romanian historians have yet to find adequate and convincing answers. But Dennis Deletant did signal out, after 1989, three explanations for this Romanian passiveness. First, Romanians are by nature timorous, conditioned by their history under the foreign imperial rule of the Ottoman Turks, the Habsburgs, the Russians, and the Soviet communists. They show a propensity to adopting a defensive stance rather than open revolt. Second, this passiveness is engendered by the Orthodox Church. And third, the secrete police, the *Securitate*, was extremely efficient.[48] Dennis Deletant and other historians underlined the fact that communist Romania was one of the harshest dictatorships in Eastern Europe and that the intellectual elite suffered large-scale repressions. However, as Deletant concluded, while all three explanations have

---

[47] See for example John Connelly, *Captive University: The Sovietization of East German, Czech, and Polish Higher Education, 1945–1956* (Chapel Hill and London: The University of North Carolina Press, 2000).

[48] Dennis Deletant, "Fatalism and Passiveness in Romania," in Dennis Deletant and Maurice Pearton, *Romania observed: Studies in Contemporary Romanian History* (Bucharest: Encyclopaedic Publishing House, 1998), p. 333.

some truth in them, they are not entirely valid either in themselves or as a complete answer to the question. Probably one must add that the Party tried both to change the way intellectuals thought and to devote more financial resources to artists.

Moreover, the political culture of Romanian socialism was different in comparison with that of other East European countries (e.g., Czechoslovakia, Bulgaria, even Poland). The Romanian Social Democracy was weak and therefore easily cowed by communists in 1948. Consequently, the voice of the former social democrat intellectuals could be barely heard in the 1950s. Romania was not an urban society; on the contrary, a significant section of the country's intellectuals was of rural origin. The PAD manipulated them and by the beginning of 1960s this group of intellectuals saw the RWP/RCP leaders as agents of a national revival. This group along with other writers and artists tended to view Marxist ideology as a foreign entity for the Romanian soul. They adhered to the communist political objectives from the national and anti-Soviet side. The lack of a true Marxist tradition is somehow responsible for the intellectuals' inability to elaborate demands for political and ideological change. They simply found it hard to learn this part of the language of power.[49]

In Poland a relatively cohesive professoriate remained in place and frustrated the communists' attempts to instill a new consciousness in the working class and peasant students. Unlike the Polish case, in Romania the old professoriate was severely purged and those who survived were not necessarily united by a common political and intellectual culture. The lack of solidarity also characterized the student milieus in the 1950s. Ultimately, as it has been already suggested in Romania, during the communist period, intellectuals remained caught in the trap of their own trite postulates about national fatalism. Such a state of affairs became synonymous with the resolution: "It can always get worse."[50]

---

[49] See Michael Shafir, "Political Stagnation and Marxist Critique: 1968 and Beyond in Comparative Perspective," *British Journal of Political Science*, Vol. 14, No. 4 (October, 1984): 435–59.

[50] Cited by Carmen Firan, "Survival through Culture in a Surreal Romania," *East European Quarterly*, Vol. 34, No. 2 (Summer 2000): 260.

SVETOZAR STOJANOVIC

Varieties of Stalinism in Light of the Yugoslav Case

"What's the time now in Moscow?" (D. Ćosić in the novel *The Sinner*) is one of the best metaphors for international Stalinism. The time in Moscow did, indeed, change continually and unforeseeably in rhythm with the super-despot's twists and turns, while all the other communist parties set their own clocks in tune with the Kremlin's (until the Yugoslav communists began, so to say, asking "What's the time now in Belgrade?").

Diffuse Stalinism

Stalinism was a somewhat diffuse phenomenon. A long time ago I put forward some conceptual and other distinctions for it, relying on the specific example of the Yugoslav Communist Party (YCP). In the following paper, I will elaborate once more and revisit my earlier observations on the topic.

From the time of their inception, communist parties in Eastern Europe were for almost three decades *in opposition, underground, under foreign occupation,* and *not in power,* as was the Communist Party of the Soviet Union (CPSU). The former were able to realize their full Stalinist potential only after assuming total control of the state in their countries. One should also not underestimate the difference between the Stalinism of the YCP during the anti-fascist and civil war, and revolution (1941–45), on the one hand, and the ruling Stalinism in Yugoslavia once that Party assumed power. Furthermore, Stalinism in power was one thing and the Stalinism of the communist parties in Western democracies was another. *Parliamentarism* lay at one end of the Stalinist spectrum, while *totalitarianism* was at the opposite one.

Stalinism was the result of a *process* and therefore *its phases and degrees* have to be differentiated. In that process even the incomplete Stalinists were eliminated. For this reason, the key question fueling the present paper is "To what degree had the YCP become Stalinized prior to Stalin's onslaught in 1948?" Three years in power had apparently not been sufficient for that party to complete the stalinization process. It is also important to note that while in 1948 the YCP's *ideology* was completely Stalinized, *in practice* some important differences with Moscow had already accumulated. In Yugoslavia, as in other countries as well, there was a pronounced difference between the Stalinists as initiators, orderers, and executors of mass terror and the Stalinists who were naive believers. Let me say that the political regimes in the first Yugoslavia actually abetted the hardcore Stalinists (a special type being the *convict-Stalinists*) through their policies of harsh persecution of communists. It would also be unjustified to equate the uninformed Stalinists with those who became Stalinists even though they were well informed. Up until the end of World War II, there were only a minuscule number of Yugoslav communists who knew what the real situation was like in the USSR. The rest, living at a great distance and possessing scant knowledge of Soviet affairs, were Stalinists in the sense that they blindly supported Stalin, the CPSU, and the Soviet Union, in their belief that *communist ideals* were genuinely being materialized there. These were mostly young, virtually still teenagers, who joined the Communist Youth League and the YCP only in 1941, and unlike some of their elder comrades, were not genuinely tormented by the late 1930s Moscow trials or the Hitler–Stalin Pact. After all, such problems were being rapidly pushed into the background, even by the experienced communists, especially when the German occupation and the liberation struggle began. This is hardly surprising, considering that even a section of the Russian anti-communist *émigrés* in the West altered their stance *vis-à-vis* the USSR, when Hitler attacked that country. It would also be unjust to lay special blame on the young and inexperienced Yugoslav communists for their loyal devotion to Stalin and the USSR, when we know that some of the most prominent intellectuals in the West nurtured similar illusions. Tito himself believed that the USSR would defeat Germany within six months. The Yugoslav Partisans hoped they would receive military assistance from the USSR, even when that country was on the brink of defeat. After the war, Yugoslav communists also expected economic aid from the USSR although its territory was even more devastated than Yugoslavia's.

Neither should we pass *over*generalized judgments on the Stalinists because of the generational differences. An important component of idealistic as opposed to realistic Stalinists was the *utopian* nature of the communist youth. The "highly developed" Soviet Stalinism was marked by terrorist industrialization, terrorist etatisation of agriculture, and terrorist purges in the Communist Party of the Soviet Union (Bolshevik) itself. The conflict between the YCP and Stalin, however, occurred at a time of a fairly enthusiastic (not mass terrorist) industrialization of Yugoslavia. More importantly, it occurred at a time when the YCP had not yet irreversibly plunged into the mass terrorist collectivization of the countryside. How significant this was is evident from the fact that such terrorization of the peasantry in the USSR, starting from 1928 onwards, marks the watershed between Leninism and Stalinism. Prior to Stalin's offensive in 1948, the YCP likewise had not engaged in mass terrorist purges in its own ranks. By a curious play of chance, every 10 years—1928, 1938 (the completed stalinization in the USSR), and 1948—crucial events took place in the history of Stalinism. Just as the CPSU had 20 years earlier, the YCP in 1948 reached a crossroads but—in contrast to the Soviet case—it turned to its own type of NEP, after a period of forcing the peasants into the so-called work cooperatives.

Stalinism moved in a vicious circle of self-enlarging and self-justifying mass terror. Even the most active manifestation of loyalty to Stalin was not enough to save anyone from wholly arbitrary terror. Under such circumstances, a mood of panic spread rapidly and even penetrated intimate human relations. In a certain sense, the family was the basic foundation of the expanded reproduction of Stalinist totalitarianism. In those days, school children brought home a godlike image of Stalin. Distraught parents most certainly dared not call this image into question in front of their children, but sometimes even bent over backwards to uphold and strengthen it. And in order not to collapse under the burden of self-debasement, many parents convinced themselves that the super-cult of Stalin was justified. A similar totalitarian mechanism was operative in Yugoslavia with regard to Tito and his leadership, both before the break with Stalin and, even more so, with the heightened terrorization after the break.

Stalinist terror constantly produced its own justification as well. The harsher the consequences of Stalinism, the more it considered itself indispensable. For instance, when the private peasants did not have sufficient farm produce for the requisitions, the repressive measures had to increase in intensity because the towns were threatened with greater danger of starvation; and, since even the intensive terrorization did not augment agricultural yields, the only solution was the forced collectivization of the peasants' farms. This resulted in an upward spiral of shortages of agricultural products. Subsequently, a vicious circle of violence was institutionalized. This is also an approximate picture of Titoist policy before the peasants were allowed (on small holdings) to produce for the market, after the break with Stalin. But the latter change was already a *Bukharinist turn in Titoism*.

Unless one perceives the differences among the Stalinists, it is impossible to understand what was to happen later during the de-Stalinization process, the liberal communist reforms, or, finally, during the recent implosion of communism. Some idealistic and naively loyal Stalinists, such as for example Gorbachev and his associates, became later transformed into the principal initiators and leaders of communist reformism and even into decisive actors in the process of the self-negation of communism.

Stalinist Anti-Stalinism in Yugoslavia

The biggest irony in the YCP's history, however, was that its most Stalinist potential was manifested only at the time it openly resisted Stalin. This is why I have described, more than 40 years ago, Tito's initial "no" to Stalin as a form of *Stalinist anti-Stalinism*. In doing so, I primarily had in mind the forced establishment of the so-called peasant work cooperatives that were dissolved only after Stalin's death. Another reason for my statement was the imprisonment of "bourgeois elements" within the Popular Front, the annihilation of the last remnants of small private businesses and trades, the brutal terrorization of real or imputed cominformists, the convictions (based on earlier Soviet denunciations) and even the execution in Slovenia of a group of former Dachau and Buchenwald concentration camp inmates. My own father, a pre-war merchant, a "bourgeois fellow-traveler" of the communists (though never a member of the YCP) from the very outset of the uprising against the occupiers in 1941, was a candidate on the Democratic Party's list for deputy within the framework of the Popular Front in the first post-war elections. He was arrested soon after Stalin's first letter to Tito, in the spring of 1948, and sentenced to 14 years of hard labor, of which he spent more than three years in prison. This was one in a series of actions which in practice meant implicit acceptance of the "criticism" by Stalin, but which was rejected at an official declarative state level. One can draw the following conclusion from the above analysis: it was a typical feature of our Stalinist anti-Stalinism to intensify repression, especially by the secret political police, the latter phenomenon being a lasting hallmark of Titoism.

When we observe the Titoists' treatment of the cominformists within their own ranks, from 1948 onwards, we must also bear in mind the distinctions among the Stalinists. Many good communists were imprisoned as being cominformists only because they insisted that their leaders should have attended a Cominform meeting in Bucharest in order to defend themselves from the accusations leveled against them. They had no inkling of the possibility that such a delegation would not have returned to Yugoslavia alive. The leadership, headed by Tito (who, in his own words, experienced Stalin's attack with great astonishment) was thoroughly acquainted with the situation in the USSR. Yet, that leadership required communists who were quite ignorant of all this to take up the proper attitude straightaway. Such communists were not even aware of the real nature of their own leadership and naively responded to the call to freely voice their opinions about the Cominform Resolution against the YCP, at their Party meetings. The top-rank leadership of the YCP was quite patient with some of the leaders who were hesitant. But, at the same time, the leadership hurriedly arrested the young and ill-informed cominformists. Incidentally, Stalin committed a serious blunder in 1948 by disparaging the YCP and its wartime and revolutionary contribution, thereby alienating numerous idealistic Stalinists in the Communist Youth League and in the YCP. The Titoist leadership that had taught the communists to worship Stalin now required them, virtually overnight, to turn against him. The realistic Stalinists, Tito and Kardelj, before all others, who had sojourned in Moscow before the War and were best acquainted with Stalinism, began dealing brutally with even the youngest of Stalinist idealists.

In the Bare Island (*Goli otok*) concentration camp (our anti-Gulag), as in other such camps as well, real and imputed cominformists were subjected to appalling terror, at a time when Tito and his closest associates enjoyed the pleasurable amenities of the Brioni Islands and even sailed past the torture sites in his floating palace, the cruise ship "Galeb," as he travelled on his "missions of peace" around the world. Aleksandar Ranković, Tito's right-hand man, was later to admit that almost half of the imprisoned cominformists were innocent. He did not, however, feel the need to draw any political conclusions from this fact as to the possible consequences for the YCP leadership. The latter continued claiming successes while distancing itself from all responsibility for its misdeeds and crimes, as though they had been caused by natural disasters. The fact that at least one-fifth of the YCP membership declared itself in favor of the Cominform Resolution seemed not to have had any connection with the previous policy of unquestioning loyalty to Stalin. Not to mention the treatment in the concentration camps for the cominformists that, in some sense, was even more inhumane than that in the Soviet camps. Some cominformists were cynically given the freedom to exercise "self-management and self-reeducation" in the camps, which led to brutal physical and psychological torture amongst the inmates who in this way competed to deserve being paroled. One must also not forget that, in Yugoslavia, some communists, even some non-communists and anti-communists, who criticized the Yugoslav leadership from liberal and democratic positions, were deliberately incarcerated in perfect Stalinist style, as being cominformists. Not only were these people subjected to torture but their families, friends, and even some chance acquaintances were also persecuted. Even if we agree that the physical isolation of genuine cominformists was necessary, this certainly could not justify the brutality toward them. I want to add, as a side note, a tale which shows the grotesque and contradicting leadership's attitudes at the time: Tito decided to confine the cominformists to a wooded Adriatic island (that was far from the Eastern and Northern borders of Yugoslavia, so as to prevent their liberation in the event of a Soviet military intervention), while also sending selected communists, who rejected Stalin's accusations with the right arguments, to work among the inmates for the purpose of patient persuasion without torture. And as we are speaking of the suffering cominformists, it should be emphasized that very few of them recognized the organic link between their own fate and the mass terror perpetrated on the anti-communists and non-communists in which they themselves had earlier actively or passively participated.

What course would our history have taken had Stalin not demanded the overthrow of Tito and his trio (Kardelj, Rankovic, and Djilas), but had continued setting them up as models to other communist leaders and had then craftily induced them to forge ahead into the mass terrorist collectivization of agriculture, into a more rapid and more radical nationalization of private property, into still more brutal persecution of "bourgeois elements," into the organization of countless trials similar to the so-called Dachau and Buchenwald trials? In a word, if he had urged them to turn the whole of Yugoslavia into a specific "Gulag Archipelago"? After all, Stalin's emissaries at the first Cominform Meeting in 1947 had already persuaded the Yugoslav delegation to arrogantly criticize the French and Italian communist parties and thus unwittingly contribute to its own isolation when its turn came the following year. Another counterfactual question is what would have ensued if Stalin had allowed Tito to create a Balkan federation with Bulgaria and Albania, to integrate it straightaway into a kind of Warsaw pact (which was established only in 1949 after Tito had already successfully defected) and then had militarily intervened against Yugoslavia by invoking these "international" institutions?

However, nothing of all this would have been necessary for Stalin in his younger days. He would have known how to invite Tito and his trio to some celebration, give them a handful of medals and decorations and then arrange for them to perish in an airplane accident on their way home. He would then have had the occasion to "mourn" them at their funeral just as he did at Kirov's. True, Stalin "missed" doing this as early as mid-1946 when Tito last visited the USSR, before the rift between the two leaders. Subsequently, using various pretexts, Tito preferred to send others from among the leadership to the Soviet Union.[1] This is one of reasons for the "paradoxical"

---

[1] Djilas was in Moscow at the last meeting before the conflict broke out. On that occasion something occurred that he has never made public but which I learned from him personally. Namely, in January 1990 the Moscow journal *Literary-Gazette* and the Belgrade weekly *NIN* arranged in Moscow a Soviet–Yugoslav discussion on the "Stalin–Tito Conflict." Of the Yugoslavs, among others, Djilas and I participated. After Djilas spoke I asked him whether Sta-

conclusion that the YCP could not have successfully resisted Stalin had it not been led by a Tito with his Stalinist characteristics and experience.

After the break with Stalin, Tito and his ideologists re-styled earlier differences, even lifting them to mythic proportions by means of hindsight projections. We were to believe that when Tito assumed the leadership of the YCP on the eve of World War II, the YCP was a non-Stalinist, almost anti-Stalinist, party. This was a case of retroactive metaphysics: the "essence" of the YCP was the same both when it obsequiously followed Stalin and when it wrenched itself free from his coattails! During the war, the Soviet leadership secretly rebuked Tito for calling his military detachments "proletarian" and for setting up a temporary government at the second session of the Anti-fascist Council of National Liberation of Yugoslavia (AVNOJ), in November 1943. Furthermore, in a speech on 27 May 1945 in connection with the forced withdrawal of his troops from Trieste, Tito criticized the policy of spheres of influence, which the USSR considered an insult and therefore protested. In addition, the Titoist leadership obstructed Soviet intelligence services in their efforts to recruit agents within the YCP, even after the end of the Second World War. Finally, while the war was still in progress and, particularly in its aftermath, the Soviet side looked askance at the equal glorification of Stalin and Tito by the Yugoslav communists. Nevertheless, the fateful discord between the Soviet and Yugoslav leaderships cropped up only after Tito attempted to create a Balkan federation under his leadership.

---

lin had ever suggested in one way or another that he (Djilas) should assume Tito's position. Djilas responded by describing the following scene. In Stalin's dacha, during a working dinner, attended by the highest Soviet leaders, and from among the Yugoslavs only by Djilas, at a certain moment the conversation lapsed and was followed by a long silence. All those present fixed their eyes on Djilas, who intuitively felt that Stalin was about to suggest a change in the Yugoslav leadership. So he (Djilas) broke the silence by an abrupt warm praise of Tito. After a while, Stalin cut Djilas short with an energetic, dismissive wave of his hand and a sharp look, returning to topics from the previous conversation.

Jugo-Stalinism and Anti-Fascist Patriotism

On the eve of Hitler's attack on Yugoslavia, the YCP was a fully disciplined section of the Communist Internationale. The leading Yugoslav Stalinists endeavored primarily to assist the Soviet Union, overthrow the government in their country and integrate it into the USSR as one of the republics. They supported Stalin's pact with Hitler. We need to look only as far as the Resolution of the Fifth National Conference of the YCP, dated 1940, which defined World War II as an "imperialist" war and stated that the "English and French imperialists sparked a new conflict." When he saw how enthusiastically the Ustasha government was welcomed in Zagreb in April 1941, Tito moved the central headquarters of the YCP to Belgrade. His first thought undoubtedly was to survive, but his decision was also motivated by the prospects for eventual resistance to the occupational forces. The bulk of the partisan units that launched the uprising in July 1941 were made up of young persons who had just joined the Communist Youth League and the YCP. True, they did aspire to come to power, no less than did the older communists, but they were at least equally motivated by patriotic anti-fascism. The culture of resistance and revolt against foreign invaders, so pronounced in the Serbian territories of Yugoslavia, exerted great influence on them. I believe that a few autobiographical details can provide some idea of the reality of those times. During the German occupation of Serbia (1941–45), I was 10–14 years old. My post-war decision to join the Communist Youth League was decisively influenced by the fact that several young communists passed through our home on their way to join the Partisans. I was also influenced by the fact that my father, as a patriot, cooperated with the Partisans— for which his life had hung on a thread on several occasions. Likewise, another circumstance that left an impression on me was that a Jewish woman, who managed to survive the war, was hidden in our home for a period of time.

Going back to my argument, I believe that unless one clearly differentiates the motivation of the leading communists from that of the younger ones, one cannot understand the relationship between Stalinism and patriotic anti-fascism. These two components of Yugo-communism were in a state of tension, but Stalinism became dominant as soon as the question of priority was raised, because for the communist leaders patriotic anti-fascism possessed an instrumental and not intrinsic value. After all, the essential feature of Stalinist totalitarianism was to treat everyone and everything as a means to its end. Thus, for example, by subsequent ideologization, it was "established"' that the communists played the decisive role in the 27 March 1941 overthrow of the Yugoslav government's pact with Hitler, signed two days earlier. However, the real communist contribution to this event was negligible. During the whole time they ruled, the communists concealed from the people the fact that Tito had immediately rebuked the then communist leadership in Serbia for surrendering to the mass anti-fascist enthusiasm.

The YCP sent out a call for an uprising against the occupiers on 4 July 1941 only after Hitler's attack on the USSR, which was launched on 22 June of that year. This was in line with Stalin's appraisal that the attack radically changed the nature of World War II from being an imperialist war to a liberation war. One of the first moves of the Yugoslav Stalinist war leadership was to kill those communists who had earlier opposed the "Bolshevization" of the YCP. Thus, Živojin Pavlovic, author of a book entitled *The Soviet Thermidor*, in which he criticized Tito for Stalinizing the YCP, was killed on the liberated territory (the Užice Republic) in the fall of 1941. As the liberation war in Yugoslavia gained momentum, so did the aspirations of the communists to monopolize anti-fascism. For this reason, 4 July 1941 was finally selected to mark the beginning of the uprising, as it was on that day that the YCP called for the armed struggle. As long as it could, the leadership glossed over the fact that the armed struggle had been launched before that date by the non-communist Serbs in Croatia and in Bosnia-Herzegovina, in their efforts to save themselves from the Ustasha genocidal assault.

My thesis on the instrumentalization of anti-fascism is also confirmed by the negotiations conducted in March 1943 in Zagreb, by a partisan delegation led by Milovan Djilas. This delegation proposed to the German command that the mutual hostilities should cease for the purpose of concentrating their forces on their conflict with the Chetniks, before the expected landing of the Western Allies on the Adriatic coast. To the very end of his life, Tito denied that these negotiations were conducted on his orders because he knew that the truth would cast doubt on the proclaimed anti-fascist purity of the Partisans, a matter of key significance for the assertion of their patriotic moral superiority over that of Draža Mihajlović's Chetniks. The official history of the National Liberation War did not ascribe any significant differences to what the Chetniks represented, on the one side, and the Nedić, Ljotić, and even the Ustashi formations, on the other. In order to understand what I mean by this, I must first remind the reader of the existence of two crucially different dimensions in Serbian tradition. One such tradition is the *rebel-deontological* one and the second is the *opportunist-utilitarian* tradition. The first was manifested, for example, in the desire to reject in entirety the Austro-Hungarian ultimatum in 1914, in the refusal to accept the Yugoslav government's pact with Hitler in 1941, as well as in the outbreak of the Partisan and Chetnik uprisings against the occupiers in that same year. The second tradition was manifested in the partial acceptance of the Austro-Hungarian ultimatum by the Serbian government, in the signing of the accord with Hitler on March 25, 1941, in the goodwill shown to him by the new Simović government as soon as it assumed power after the 27 March 1941 coup d'etat, in the Chetnik decision to refrain from continuing the uprising and, most of all, in the Nedić quisling government and its armed struggle against the Partisans up to the end of the War.

In Serbian history these two dominant tendencies constantly conflict and interplay, while occasionally also mitigating each other's effects. When a fatal danger appears to threaten their national dignity or independence, the rebel-deontological elite often prevails by bestowing its voice and their actions to the masses, and by conveying the impression that the majority of the Serbs are ready to sacrifice their lives for higher values. In fact, the Serbs are generally educated to feel shame if they evince fear or the readiness to be flexible. But, when due to the activities of a relatively small uncompromising avant-garde, huge sacrifices ensue, a decisive role is then taken up by the opportunist-utilitarian camp and even, in some instances, by those who pursue a *collaborationist orientation*. It is in this light that I see what happened in Serbia during the 1941–1944 occupation. As is already well known, the Partisans and the Chetniks rose against the German occupying forces and succeeded in freeing a considerable area of Serbia in the second half of 1941. However, the two groups soon separated not only because of their ultimate wartime aims, but also by dint of the defeat of the uprising and especially because of their attitudes to the mass reprisals against the civilian population.

The bulk of the Partisans fled beyond Serbia while the few remaining ones did not cease harassing the enemy, despite the subsequent civilian casualties. These sacrifices, however, shocked the Chetniks of Draža Mihajlović and marked them psychologically and politically until their final collapse. "It is not yet time to fight," became the Chetnik watchword. They waited, more or less, for the Allied victory over Hitler, and then only to participate in the war during the concluding military operations and in this way impose a solution to the problem of the post-war rulers in Yugoslavia. The Chetniks, however, continued fighting the Partisans with the latter paying them in the same coin. In this ostensibly winning combination, there was "only" one oversight: Churchill was no less an opportunist and utilitarian than Draža Mihajlović. He therefore withdrew his support from the Chetniks and extended it to the Partisans. Mihajlović's position was quite fragile from the moral standpoint as well: he ultimately wanted to save his people at the cost of the wartime losses from the leading anti-fascist powers. If we compare the two anti-fascist formations in Yugoslavia, we can note that the main cause for the Mihajlović movement's collapse was the leader's unwillingness to continue fighting the occupying forces. The moral decadence of Titoism manifested itself primarily in the continuation of the worst dimensions of the civil war even after its victory had been attained.

More light is thrown on the relationship between communism and anti-fascism in former Yugoslavia if one turns to the main patterns that were taken over at the local level from the Stalinized history of the Bolshevik revolution and the USSR. This is how one can explain, in my opinion, the fact that anti-fascism was no obstacle to the Yugoslav communists in their "sharpening of the class struggle" as well as in their rapid shift from the "bourgeois phase" of the revolution to the "proletarian" one. In doing this, they annihilated actual and potential enemies and rivals, particularly those anti-fascists who competed for recognition, both at the level of the populace and on the international scene. When the communist terrorization led to grave defeats, the leadership of the YCP and the National Liberation War distanced themselves in true Stalinist fashion from the acts of terror as from "leftist deviations," although the terror was inspired by leadership itself.

Another evidence of the official ideologization regarding the "intrinsic" anti-fascism of yugo-communism was the declaration that every form of anti-communism in Yugoslavia was pro-fascist or even fascist, at least "objectively" so, if not by deliberate choice. All potential rivals of the communists, not to mention the real enemies, were proclaimed "fascists," "the servants and helpers" of fascism, or "enemy collaborators" and the like. These terms were used to justify the mass arrests and executions that incurred when the communists assumed power. They also made use of the confiscation of the property of "enemy collaborators" (often falsely accused as such), one of the YCP's favorite forms of etatization. There was also a close link between the instrumentalization of anti-fascism and the absence of an enlightened de-nazification in Yugoslavia, after the end of World War II, despite the fact that in Bosnia-Herzegovina and in Croatia numerous Ustashi and their accomplices were to be found. Let me add: more Nazis and fascists were imprisoned and executed in Yugoslavia than in Germany, Austria, or Italy, but unfortunately much less effort was exerted to explain why there was such a large number of them in our country. The communist leaders and ideologues were guided by the tacit premise that Nazism and fascism was, in some of national communities in Yugoslavia, just a kind of "accident" in comparison with their "essence," personified by the communists and the National Liberation War.

Dragoş Petrescu

Community-Building and Identity Politics in Gheorghiu-Dej's Romania, 1956–64

Numerous scholars have been concerned with Nicolae Ceauşescu's flamboyant display of chauvinistic nationalism. Indeed, under the reign of Ceauşescu (1965–89), the Romanian Communist Party (RCP) adopted coherent strategies explicitly aimed at reinforcing the ethnic ties among the Romanian majority and assimilating the historic ethnic minorities.[1] This project was heralded by the launch of the so-called "Theses of July 1971" and was followed by concrete measures for building an ethnically homogeneous "socialist nation" in Romania. Nonetheless, it was Gheorghe Gheorghiu-Dej, Ceauşescu's predecessor, who initiated, after 1956, a return to the local traditions and thus to an ethnic understanding of the nation.

However, the context in which this nationalistic turn occurred under the rule of Gheorghiu-Dej is less discussed. We now know that the Stalinist power elite in Bucharest was appalled by Nikita Khrushchev's condemnation of the crimes perpetrated by Stalin against Party members. It goes without saying that Romanian Stalinists were not scandalized by the evidence provided by Khrushchev to support his statements: after all, the communist elite in Bucharest did exactly the

---

[1] Over the period 1948–65, the official name of the communist party in Romania was *Partidul Muncitoresc Român—PMR* (Romanian Workers Party—RWP); from 1965 to 1989 the official name was *Partidul Comunist Român— PCR* (Romanian Communist Party—RCP). Throughout this study, the two terms are used in accordance with the period discussed and are not interchangeable. The abbreviation RWP/RCP has been used when patterns of continuity between the two periods, i.e., 1948–65 and 1965–89 needed to be stressed. RCP is also used for the period spanning from its establishment in 1921 to 1948.

same things Stalin did in order to get rid of their political enemies from within the Party, only that the number of victims was smaller due to the size of the Romanian Workers Party (RWP). For Gheorghiu-Dej and his men, truly appalling was the prospect of a Soviet-backed party coup meant to replace them with a Khrushchevite faction at a moment when they were, finally, in full control of the Party and the Romanian society.

The main argument of the present paper reads as follows: Confronted with Khrushchev's de-Stalinization campaign, the Romanian communist elite headed by Gheorghiu-Dej discovered that national identity is a crucial social and political resource and made use of it in order to ensure their political survival. This is not to say that in terms of their conceptualization of the nation the Romanian Stalinists were of an "instrumentalist persuasion"—to quote Anthony D. Smith,[2] and therefore knew perfectly well how to make use of nationalism, all of a sudden, as a most powerful instrument of political mobilization. On the contrary, it took them some eight years (1956–64) to understand fully the extraordinary force of nationalism as an instrument for controlling the state, as well as for maintaining and using state power.[3] After 1956, the Romanian Stalinist elite engaged cautiously in a process of "selective community-building,"[4] which was aimed at building a new political community after a period of random terror conducted by the state itself against a majority of its citizens. Nevertheless, it was only from 1964 onwards that the process of selectively building a political community was turned into an all-encompassing nation-building process. To sum up, one can argue that somewhere on the road to the party-

---

[2] Anthony D. Smith, *Myths and Memories of the Nation* (Oxford: Oxford University Press, 1999), p. 99.

[3] As Breuilly wonderfully puts it: "To focus upon culture, ideology, identity, class or modernization is to neglect the fundamental point that nationalism is, above and beyond all else, about politics and that politics is about power. Power, in the modern world, is principally about control of the state." See John Breuilly, *Nationalism and the State*, 2nd ed. (Chicago: The University of Chicago Press, 1994), p. 1. Breuilly, however, is concerned with nationalism as a movement, which is not applicable in the case of communist Romania. Nonetheless, what is useful for the present analysis is his emphasis on nationalism as a political argument.

[4] I am indebted to Professor Kenneth Jowitt who drew my attention to the selective nature of this process of community-building.

state fusion, the nation surfaced in the mental structure of Gheorghiu-Dej's "socialism," without being properly referred to as such. Ironically enough, the way the nation came to be understood by the end of Dej's rule recalls very much the way it was conceptualized in the interwar period. It is the purpose of this paper to shed some light on the process that led to such an outcome.

Party-State Fusion:
A New Political Culture in the Making

Following Robert C. Tucker, who has studied the "mental structure" of Lenin's Bolshevism as a "party-state political culture" that came into being after the 1917 October Revolution,[5] this paper examines Dej's "socialism" as a heavily context-dependent "party-state political culture" in the making. When analyzing the particular features of the political culture of the Romanian communist elite, three elements need a closer examination: 1) ideology; 2) cohesion; and 3) Gheorghiu-Dej's vision of politics and leadership style.

1) Ideology. The "tiny sect" of Romanian communists numbered some 900–1,000 members in August 1944. This group took power with the backing of the Red Army and had no other chance of staying in power than to be completely subservient to Stalin and frantically emulate the Soviet model. As Kenneth Jowitt perceptively argued: "On coming to power, the Romanian [communist] elite possessed and was committed to a Leninist consensual ideology, but it did not have a set of politically and situationally relevant definitions derived from that ideology. In short, it lacked a 'practical ideology'."[6] Indeed, the official Party documents from the early Gheorghiu-Dej period show little, if any, theoretical sophistication. These documents reveal that the RWP was rigidly

---

[5] Robert C. Tucker, *Political Culture and Leadership in Soviet Russia: From Lenin to Gorbachev* (New York: W.W. Norton & Co., 1987), p. 34.

[6] As Jowitt puts it: "A 'practical ideology' is not synonymous with a pragmatic orientation. Rather, it refers to a set of action-oriented beliefs that are defined in terms which in significant respects reflect and are congruent with a given social reality and political situation." See Jowitt, *Revolutionary Breakthroughs and National Development*, p. 76.

and forcefully imposing the Soviet model upon the Romanian society, with no concern whatsoever for social realities.

As the "Resolution of the plenary meeting of the Central Committee of the RWP of 3–5 March 1949" explicitly states, in the aftermath of WWII the Romanian communists had two major objectives: the seizure of political power and the building of socialism.[7] In practice, this meant the institutionalization of the Party and the industrialization of the country. The Party grew from the initial figure of some 1,000 members in 1944 to around 257,000 in October 1945 and to over 1,000,000 in February 1948. In 1948, it was claimed that "unsound" elements entered the Party, which had to undergo a "verification campaign." As a result, 192,000 Party members were purged, and until 1952 admissions of new members were suspended. Consequently, in December 1955 the RWP numbered approximately 539,000 members.[8]

As the Resolution mentioned above stated, the focus on extensive industrialization was an axiom: the economic strategy of the RWP was based on the development of "socialist industry," with a special emphasis on heavy industry and the "planned organization of national economy." With regard to the "peasantry problem" the same document read: "Guided by the Marxist-Leninist teaching, our party sees in the

---

[7] See *Rezoluţia şedinţei plenare a Comitetului central al P.M.R. din 3-5 martie 1949 asupra sarcinilor partidului în lupta pentru întărirea alianţei clasei muncitoare cu ţărănimea muncitoare şi pentru transformarea socialistă a agriculturii* [Resolution of the plenary meeting of the Central Committee of the RWP of 3–5 March 1949 regarding the party tasks in the struggle for strengthening the alliance of the working class with the working peasantry for the socialist transformation of agriculture] (Bucharest: Editura Partidului Muncitoresc Român, 1949), p. 7. Hereafter quoted as *Resolution of the plenary meeting of the CC of the RWP of 3–5 March 1949*.

[8] For an analysis of RWP membership over the period 1945–89, see Nicoleta Ionescu-Gură, "Introductory Study" to Florica Dobre *et al.* eds., *Membrii C.C. al P.C.R., 1945–1989* [The members of the Central Committee of the Romanian Communist Party, 1945–1989] (Bucharest: Editura Enciclopedică, 2004), pp. 20–2. With regard to the verification campaign of 1948–50 and the number of purges, see Gheorghe Gheorghiu-Dej, "Raportul de activitate al Comitetului Central al Partidului Muncitoresc Român la Congresul al II-lea al Partidului—23 decembrie 1955" [Activity report of the CC of the RWP to the Second Congress of the Party—23 December 1955] in *Idem, Articole şi cuvîntări, decembrie 1955—iulie 1959* [Articles and speeches, December 1955—July 1959] (Bucharest: Editura Politică, 1960), p. 117.

peasantry problem a part of the general problem of the dictatorship of the proletariat, namely the problem of the main ally of the working class."[9] The "socialist organization of agriculture" meant in fact collectivization of agriculture, which was carried out with great brutality, like any Stalinist "revolution from above," and was launched in the aftermath of the above-mentioned plenary meeting of the CC of the RWP of 3–5 March 1949.

As far as Gheorghiu-Dej was concerned, he did not elaborate on the building of a classless and stateless communist society or on the transformation of human nature under "socialism," but simply praised the "triumphant ideas" of the official ideological forefathers. A telling statement can be found in his speech, delivered on 8 May 1951 and occasioned by the 30th anniversary of the Party:

> The endless source of our Party's strength is its unabated fidelity to the triumphant ideas of Marx, Engels, Lenin, and Stalin. Our Party faced the most difficult challenges and went forward through the storms of the underground years due to its belief in the triumph of the proletarian cause instilled to it by the glorious Bolshevik Party and the brilliant teachings of the leader of world communism—comrade Stalin.[10]

At the Party apparatus level, the lack of a "practical ideology" determined a mechanical learning of Lenin's interpretation of Marxism, centered on economic determinism and party control over each and every segment of society. As Vladimir Tismăneanu perceptively puts it, the political credo of the Romanian communist elite "derived from the simplistic, Manichean worldview of the Comintern," which did not allow for a Romanian Lukács or Gramsci to appear from within the

---

[9] *Resolution of the plenary meeting of the CC of the RWP of 3-5 March 1949*, pp. 7–8.

[10] Gheorghe Gheorghiu-Dej, *30 de ani de luptă a Partidului sub steagul lui Lenin și Stalin: Raport prezentat în ziua 8 Mai la adunarea solemnă în cinstea celei de a 30-a aniversări a întemeierii Partidului Comunist Român* (30 years of struggle under the flag of Lenin and Stalin: Report presented to the solemn meeting dedicated to the celebration of 30 years from the creation of the RCP) (Bucharest: Editura Partidului Muncitoresc Român, 1951), p. 6. Hereafter quoted as *30 years of struggle under the flag of Lenin and Stalin.*

ranks of the RWP/RCP.[11] This hampered the appearance of a faction of softliners within the Party and thus prevented a negotiated transition to democracy in Romania in December 1989. The issue of Party cohesion deserves further elaboration and is discussed below.

2) Cohesion. As far as the political culture of the Romanian communist elite is concerned, there were two major elements of continuity between the Gheorghiu-Dej and Ceauşescu regimes. These elements can be identified as the two major features of the political culture of Romanian communism: *Party monolithism* and *Party emancipation*. It is this author's opinion that eventually these two features were transformed into the most powerful myths of Party "regeneration" or "rebirth," and were shared by the group of communists that stayed together in prisons during WWII. These two Party myths determined the particular way in which national-communism was born in Romania: not as a direct return to the interwar conceptualization of the nation, but as a process that spanned over some eight years (1956–64) and was launched as a "selective community-building" process in the very special political context of the year 1956.

Preserving the Party's monolithism was a central element of the political cultures of both Gheorghiu-Dej and Ceauşescu regimes. Factions within the party had to be avoided at all costs. In this respect, one can grasp from Gheorghiu-Dej's official speeches what the supreme leader of the Romanian communists thought of the need to preserve the unity of the Party. For instance, in his speech delivered at the "solemn meeting" dedicated to the celebration of 30 years from the creation of the RCP, Gheorghiu-Dej stated that the most precious asset of the Party was its unity:

> The unity of Party's ranks is its most precious asset. Without this unity, characteristic to a new type of Marxist-Leninist Party, we could

---

[11] See Vladimir Tismăneanu, *Stalinism for All Seasons: A Political History of Romanian Communism* (Berkeley: University of California Press, 2003), pp. 117–8; page numbers are to the Romanian edition (Iaşi: Polirom, 2005). This author also follows Tismăneanu's conceptualization of the "three centers" of power from within the RCP during the WWII period: 1) the underground Central Committee; 2) the center from prisons; and 3) the center in Moscow. For a detailed discussion, see Tismăneanu, pp. 119–25.

not obtain successes in fulfilling the historical tasks that stayed ahead of us. The preoccupation for the unyielding unity of the Party, for the purity of its ranks, for the education of the Party members in the spirit of vigilance against the class enemy from inside and outside the Party and of intransigence towards deviations from the Party line, is a permanent duty for every Party organization.[12]

Similarly, a massive work published in 1960 by the Institute for Party History affiliated with the CC of the RWP (*Institutul de istorie a partidului de pe lîngă C.C. al P.M.R.*) defined one of the basic principles of a Marxist-Leninist party as follows: "The Party represents *a unity of will that is incompatible with the existence of factions.*" [emphasis added][13] Under Gheorghiu-Dej's rule, the observance of this basic principle led to assassinations, purges, and marginalization of Party veterans. In fact, the most significant, though unsuccessful, attempt at creating a split at the top of the RWP hierarchy under Gheorghiu-Dej's rule was that of Miron Constantinescu—supported by Iosif Chişinevschi—in the aftermath of Khrushchev's 1956 secret speech. It was precisely this feature of Romanian communist regime that permitted the group from prisons to fully control the party from 1952 onwards. As already mentioned, it was the same feature that made a negotiated solution involving an "enlightened" faction from within the Party and the opposition elites impossible, and determined the sudden, bloody collapse of the regime in December 1989.

Party emancipation was an equally powerful RWP/RCP myth, born of the interwar years when the Party was compelled to follow unabatedly the orders coming from Kremlin; this also led to its profound political marginalization during this period. This was due to the fact that the RCP propaganda had little success in reaching the hearts and minds of the overwhelming majority of the population of Greater Romania since the Party militated, as far as ethnic minorities were concerned, for "self-determination up to complete secession." In terms of leadership, the RCP—which was founded in May 1921—had during the period 1922–44 only one general secretary of Romanian ethnic origin, Gheorghe Cristescu (1922–24), while all the others were of non-Romanian ethnic

---

[12] Gheorghiu-Dej, *30 years of struggle under the flag of Lenin and Stalin*, p. 59.

[13] Institutul de istorie a partidului de pe lîngă C.C. al P.M.R. [The institute for Party's history affiliated with the CC of the RWP], *Lecţii în ajutorul celor care studiază istoria P.M.R.* [Lessons to help those who study the history of the RWP] (Bucharest: Editura Politică, 1960), p. 620.

origin: Elek Köblos (1924–28); Vitali Holostenko (1928–31); Aleksandr Danieluk Stefanski (1931–34); Boris Stefanov (1934–40), and Ştefan Foriş (1940–44).[14] Such a situation created a deep frustration among the ethnic Romanian members of the Party, whose salience could be grasped from witness accounts, testimonies and even Party documents, long after the "group from prisons" took control over the Party.

When examining the identity-forming experiences of the post-war RWP elite, a truly significant aspect relates to the common socialization, in the prisons, of those who would compose the future Party elite. Sociologist Pavel Câmpeanu provided an insightful analysis of the period spent in prisons by the group of communist militants that included, among others, Gheorghe Gheorghiu-Dej, Gheorghe Apostol, Emil Bodnăraş, Iosif Chişinevschi, Miron Constantinescu, Chivu Stoica, Nicolae Ceauşescu, and Câmpeanu himself.[15] From Câmpeanu's detailed account, one can grasp how important the period of common socialization in prisons was in determining the nature of the political culture of the Romanian communist elite and thus its cohesion. Marginalization, humiliation and harassment by the interwar authorities—Gheorghiu-Dej stayed eleven years in prison, between 1933 and 1944—all these explain the determination of Gheorghiu-Dej and his "group from prisons" to eliminate their rivals from within the Party and, after the takeover, their former political opponents (especially the members of the historic political parties—National Peasant Party, National Liberal Party, and Social Democratic Party).

Furthermore, the members of the "group from prisons" went through a process of common socialization that enabled them to draw sharp distinctions between in-group and out-group individuals. Jowitt observes that Gheorghiu-Dej had a major interest in ensuring a high degree of Party cohesion. The same author refers to the concepts of "peer cohesion" and "hierarchical cohesion" and argues that

---

[14] For the purpose of the argument developed in this section it is important to mention the ethnic origin of these RCP general secretaries: Holostenko was Ukrainian, Stefanski was Polish, Stefanov was Bulgarian, and Foriş was a Hungarian from Romania. See Florin Constantiniu, *P.C.R., Pătrăşcanu şi Transilvania, 1945–1946* [RCP, Pătrăşcanu, and Transylvania, 1945–46] (Bucharest: Editura Enciclopedică, 2001), p. 34.

[15] Pavel Câmpeanu, *Ceauşescu: Anii numărătorii inverse* [Ceauşescu: The countdown years] (Iaşi: Polirom, 2002). Hereafter quoted as *Ceauşescu: The countdown years.*

Gheorghiu-Dej was primarily oriented towards hierarchical cohesion, which refers to "bonds linking actors of different ranks."[16] Câmpeanu's witness account tends to support such an assertion. As he puts it, the communists learned in prison a lesson of crucial importance: "*It was not the doctrine or the class relations that really counted, but the relationships based on personal subordination.*" [emphasis added][17] However, Câmpeanu also stresses the dual character of the relationships established between communists during their prison term, generated by the "equality of their condition:" "While Dej's infallibility was taken for granted, even the younger [communist] prisoners were allowed to address him informally as 'Ghiță'."[18] Therefore, it may be argued that it was in fact a complex blend of peer and hierarchical cohesion that determined the unity of the "group from prisons," which permitted it to avoid a major split at the top of the RWP/RCP until the issuance of the "Letter of the six" former *nomenklatura* members in March 1989.[19]

3) Gheorghiu-Dej's leadership style. Ironically enough, it was Mihail Hașeganu, one of Gheorghiu-Dej's ambassadors to former Czechoslovakia and the United Nations that provided an insightful characterization of a communist supreme leader. True, the portrait was that of the Albanian supreme leader, Enver Hoxha, but it is this author's opinion that such a characterization could be very well applied to Gheorghiu-Dej himself.

> Personally, I perceived in him the specific traits of a Stalinist activist that was actually not the product of specific Russian abnormal outgrowths, neither of French left-wingers, nor of Chinese Maoism, but a synthesis of all these. *For this type of activist the central problem remains the power struggle, and he is able to walk over any creed or principle in order to fulfill his goals.*[20]

---

[16] Jowitt, *Revolutionary Breakthroughs and National Development*, p. 143.

[17] Câmpeanu, *Ceaușescu: the countdown years*, p. 101.

[18] *Ibid.*, p. 58.

[19] For more on the significance of the "Letter of the Six" and the context in which it was issued, see Cristina Petrescu, "The Letter of the Six: On the Political (Sub)Culture of the Romanian Communist Elite," *Studia Politica* (Bucharest), Vol. 5, No. 2 (2005): 355–83.

[20] Mihail Hașeganu, *Din culisele diplomației: Memoriile unui ambasador* [Backstage diplomacy: Memoirs of an ambassador] (Bucharest: Casa de Editură și Presă "Viața Românească," n.d.), p. 35, emphasis added.

Câmpeanu argues that Dej became a natural leader of the impris-oned communists for at least three reasons. First, it was due to his long period of internment, which, according to an unwritten rule, calls for respect on the part of the other political convicts. Second, he was living proof of the abuses of the interwar "bourgeois" regime that convicted a communist militant to a ten-year term in prison for organizing a strike. Third, Dej possessed a charismatic personality, coupled with a ruthless determination to achieve "unlimited power."[21] It should be added that after Stalin's death Gheorghiu-Dej managed to impose upon the Party a particular political style that can be defined as follows: Under Dej's rule, RWP's immediate political goals were contextually defined and the strategies devised to pursue them were context-dependent.[22] Such a political style enabled Dej to maintain his personal power in spite of the major challenges he faced during the year 1956.[23]

Power, Identity, and Contingency: The Lessons of 1956

At the end of 1955 Gheorghiu-Dej was already the undisputed leader of the RWP. By that time, his major rivals from within the Party, i.e., Ştefan Foriş, Lucreţiu Pătrăşcanu, and Ana Pauker, had been either assassinated or purged. Nonetheless, one cannot predict the unpre-dictable. Consequently, Gheorghiu-Dej and his men could not predict the events that would deeply affect world communism during the year 1956, i.e., Nikita Khrushchev's condemnation of Stalin's personality cult in front of the 20th Congress of the CPSU, and the Hungarian Revolution of 23 October–4 November. This time, Dej's unlimited personal power was not threatened by domestic factors, but by the very

---

[21] Câmpeanu, *Ceauşescu: the countdown years*, p. 62.

[22] This definition has been inspired by Ross' reflections on the cultural analysis of politics. See Marc Howard Ross, "Culture and Identity in Comparative Political Analysis," in Mark Irving Lichbach and Alan S. Zuckerman eds., *Comparative Politics: Rationality, Culture, and Structure* (Cambridge: Cambridge University Press, 1997), p. 44.

[23] For more on Dej's political biography, see Florica Dobre *et al.* eds., *Membrii C.C. al P.C.R., 1945–1989* [The members of the Central Committee of the Romanian Communist Party, 1945–1989] (Bucharest: Editura Enciclopedică, 2004), pp. 291–2. Hereafter quoted as *Members of the CC of the RCP.*

source of RWP's authority: the Kremlin. Such a new context called for a rapid adoption of a strategy of political survival, and the Romanian communists managed to devise one that had at its core a slow and cautious return to autochthonous values.

Khrushchev's attack on Stalin's crimes against Party members came as a shock for Gheorghiu-Dej. The RWP delegation to the 20th Congress of the CPSU was composed of four members: Gheorghiu-Dej (head of the delegation), Miron Constantinescu, Iosif Chişinevschi, and Petre Borilă.[24] Paul Sfetcu, who served as Dej's secretary from 1952 until the death of the RWP supreme leader on 19 March 1965, accompanied the delegation and has provided valuable details on the atmosphere of great tension that persisted within the Romanian delegation during the Congress. True, Sfetcu's volume of memoirs is intended to rehabilitate Gheorghiu-Dej and praise his leadership, but at the same time it provides useful details regarding the reactions of the members of the Romanian delegation to Khrushchev's speech. According to Sfetcu, one could detect a latent hostility towards Gheorghiu-Dej in the way Constantinescu and Chişinevschi behaved in those days.[25] What is important for the present analysis is that upon his returning to Romania, Gheorghiu-Dej managed to buy some time in order to devise a political strategy of opposing de-Stalinization. Miron Constantinescu, supported by Iosif Chişinevschi, launched an attack on Dej's "personality cult" at a Politbüro meeting in April 1956.[26] However, the two *nomenklatura* members did not manage to convince other prominent Party members to support them. Nonetheless, Dej's position was difficult at the time, and therefore it took him until the next year to oust both Constantinescu and Chişinevschi from the positions they held at

---

[24] On the political biographies of Constantinescu, Chişinevschi, and Borilă, see Dobre *et al.* eds., *Members of the CC of the RCP*, pp. 175–7, 149–50, and 108–9, respectively.

[25] See Paul Sfetcu, *13 ani în anticamera lui Dej* [Thirteen years in Dej's antechamber] (Bucharest: Editura Fundaţiei Culturale Române, 2000), pp. 272–83.

[26] For details regarding the Constantinescu-Chişinevschi attack on Dej, see Elis Neagoe-Pleşa and Liviu Pleşa, "Introductory Study" to *Idem* eds., *Dosarul Ana Pauker: Plenara Comitetului Central al Partidului Muncitoresc Român din 30 noiembrie—5 decembrie 1961*, Vol. 1 [The Ana Pauker file: The Plenum of the CC of RWP of 30 November—5 December 1961] (Bucharest: Editura Nemira & CNSAS, 2006), pp. 41–9.

the top of the Party. This happened on 28 June–3 July 1957, at a plenary meeting of the CC of the RWP.

Contingency played a major role in saving Dej's political career. It was the Hungarian Revolution of 1956 that contributed decisively to Dej's political survival. The Romanian communists immediately condemned the Hungarian revolution and adhered to the counter-revolution thesis. Moreover, they succeeded in convincing the Soviets of their profound loyalty. Actually, the 1956 events in Poland and Hungary, i.e., the Poznań uprising for "bread and freedom" in June and the revolution that was sparked in Budapest in October, provided unexpected support for Dej's efforts aimed at preserving his personal power by avoiding de-Stalinization. The communist elite in Bucharest took rapid measures to contain the spread of information about the real meaning of the events in Hungary. Thus, on 24 October 1956, at a meeting of the Politbüro of the CC of RWP, an eighteen point plan meant to keep the situation under strict control was put forward. Prominent *nomenklatura* members were sent to Transylvania to provide an official interpretation of the situation in Hungary. For instance, Miron Constantinescu was sent to Cluj, while János Fazekas was sent to the Hungarian Autonomous Region. There is, nonetheless, an important aspect that needs to be stressed. The RWP leadership was facing for the first time after the takeover a major problem: they did not really know the state of mind of the population and feared that the unrest could spread to Transylvania. In this respect, point thirteen of the above mentioned plan devised by the Politbüro stated that the situation in Hungary had to be explained to the workers via the trade unions and in such a way as to avoid sparking unrest. Special attention was to be paid to young audiences, especially the students. Also, the said plan specified that it was crucial to supply the population with basic foodstuffs such as bread, meat, and edible oil.[27]

From 26 October 1956 onwards, the Romanian official reaction to the events in Hungary became resolute: it was decided to organize meetings throughout the country, in which workers and clerks, young

---

[27] See "Protocol No. 54 al Şedinţei Biroului Politic al CC al PMR din 24 octombrie 1956" [Minutes of the CC of RWP's Politbüro Meeting of 24 October 1956] in Mircea Stănescu ed., *Organismele politice româneşti, 1948–1965* [Romanian Political Organizations, 1948–1965] (Bucharest: Editura Vremea, 2003), pp. 396–402.

and old, would condemn the "reactionary and fascist forces in Hungary and would express solidarity with the heroic struggle of the Hungarian working class for crushing the counter-revolution as soon as possible."[28] Thus, the RWP sided without hesitation with the Soviets and provided immediate support. Consequently, at the Politbüro meeting of 1 December 1956, Gheorghiu-Dej could proudly claim:

> We are happy to say that we did not look on passively, as spectators, at the events in Hungary. We were directly interested that the unfolding of events be in the interest of the Hungarian people and the future of socialism in Hungary, as well as in the interest of our camp; thus we did not stay passive and let the Soviet Union manage as it could, and therefore we contributed a lot.[29]

Nevertheless, one of the most telling documents related to the reaction of the Romanian communist elite to the Hungarian revolution is the report of two high ranking officials, Aurel Malnăşan and Valter Roman, concerning the visit of the RWP delegation to Hungary in order to assess the course of events in Budapest. On 2 November 1956, in front of the RWP's Politbüro, Valter Roman emphasized two major elements that, in his opinion, led to "counter-revolution:" 1) under the leadership of Mátyás Rákosi, the Hungarian Workers' Party was not accepted by the Hungarian people due to its arrogance and disregard for national traditions, as well as for its total subservience to Stalin and the Soviet Union; and 2) the leadership of the Hungarian Workers' Party displayed an "anti-Romanian spirit" and "never took a just stance with regard to Transylvania;" in this respect, Valter Roman quoted the words of János Kádár, whom he met in Budapest during his visit: "Give autonomy to Transylvania!"[30] These two conclusions with regard to the causes of the revolutionary events in Hungary, presented

---

[28] This was expressed clearly on 26 October 1956. See "Protocol No. 55 al Şedinţei Biroului Politic al CC al PMR din 26 octombrie 1956" [Minutes of the CC of RWP's Politbüro Meeting of 26 October 1956] in *Ibid.*, p. 403.

[29] See "Stenograma Şedinţei Biroului Politic al CC al PMR din data de 1 decembrie 1956" [Minutes of the CC of RWP's Politbüro Meeting of 1 December 1956] in *Ibid.*, p. 472.

[30] See "Stenograma Şedinţei din data de 2 noiembrie 1956 cu tov. Aurel Mălnăşan şi Valter Roman" [Minutes of the Meeting of 2 November 1956 with comrades Aurel Mălnăşan şi Valter Roman] in *Ibid.*, pp. 409–27.

in front of the RWP Politbüro, would nurture two other important elements of the political culture of Romanian communism: *fear of Moscow and distrust towards Budapest.*[31]

As shown above, Party *monolithism* and Party *emancipation* are concepts that enable one to understand better the particularities of the political culture of Romanian communism. Furthermore, two major features related to Romanian communist elite's perception of its enemies from within the communist camp—*fear of Moscow* and *distrust toward Budapest*—were reinforced by the lessons of the year 1956. To be sure, these features were shaped by a long process of building the Romanian identity in opposition to two strong identities from neighboring empires—Russian and Hungarian—from the mid-19th century onwards. However, the strategy of political survival—based on a return to the traditional values associated with the Romanian identity and extensive industrialization—devised by Gheorghiu-Dej in 1956, in the aftermath of the 20th Congress of the CPSU and the Hungarian Revolution, strongly reinforced these elements. Gheorghiu-Dej's political strategy was strictly followed by Ceauşescu who internalized the crucial elements mentioned above through a long process of political socialization within Gheorghiu-Dej's inner circle of power. Ceauşescu, though, was less imaginative and capable of adopting flexible policies according to the domestic and international contexts in comparison to Gheorghiu-Dej.

As an American scholar observed, "Romanian leaders have successfully capitalized upon the non-Slavic identity of the population."[32] But this did not happen overnight: things changed in the direction desired by the Party during the period 1956–64. It should be added to this that it was also a slight improvement of the standard of living that found an echo in the hearts and minds of a majority of Romania's

---

[31] For a detailed analysis of the impact of the 1956 Hungarian Revolution on the political culture of Romanian communism, see Dragoş Petrescu, "Fifty-Six as an Identity-Shaping Experience: The Case of the Romanian Communists," in János M. Rainer and Katalin Somlai, eds., *The 1956 Hungarian Revolution and the Soviet Bloc Countries: Reactions and Repercussions* (Budapest: The Institute for the History of the 1956 Hungarian Revolution, 2007), pp. 48–68.

[32] Ronald H. Linden, "Romanian Foreign Policy in the 1980s," in Daniel Nelson, ed., *Romania in the 1980s* (Boulder, CO: Westview Press, 1981), p. 229.

population. If one looks attentively at the shares allotted to accumulation and consumption over the entire communist period, one observes that it was in the aftermath of the Hungarian Revolution that the RWP decided to raise significantly the share of consumption. During the period 1956–60, 82.9 percent of the national income went to the consumption fund while only 17.1 percent went to the accumulation fund. This was the largest share ever allotted to the consumption fund under communist rule in Romania.[33] Thus, due to a particular conjuncture, *fear of Moscow* and *distrust towards Budapest* were reinforced as major shared understandings of intra-bloc politics at the level of the Romanian communist elite. Ironically enough, these two features also characterized the political culture of the Romanian elite in the interwar period, as a direct result of the Soviet and Hungarian claims against Romania.

Paradoxically, it was also a Soviet political decision that served, quite unexpectedly, Romanian communists' efforts of opposing de-Stalinization: the decision to withdraw their troops from Romania. A former high-rank official of the RWP/RCP, Gheorghe Apostol, remembers that the issue was first raised in 1955, after the Soviet army withdrew from Austria. Although the Romanian communists' request enraged Khrushchev on the spot, later on he decided to order the withdrawal of the Soviet troops. No matter how the decision was made, the 1958 Soviet troops' withdrawal from Romania represented the coming of a new era in RWP's history. Western sources, such as the US legation in Bucharest, perceived the withdrawal from Romania at the time as an initiative of the Soviet Union, and recent scholarship supports such an assertion.[34] That Dej was extremely pleased with the withdraw-

---

[33] For the entire 1951–89 period, the national income was divided into consumption and accumulation as follows: 1951–55—75.7% consumption, 24.3% accumulation; 1956–60—82.9% consumption, 17.1% accumulation; 1961–65—74.5% consumption, 25.5% accumulation; 1966–70—70.5% consumption, 29.5% accumulation; 1971–75—66.3% consumption, 33.7% accumulation; 1976–80—64% consumption, 36% accumulation; 1981–85—69.3% consumption, 30.7% accumulation; and 1986–89—74.3% consumption, 25.7% accumulation. See Maria Mureşan, *Evoluţii economice, 1945–1990* [Economic evolutions, 1945–1990] (Bucharest: Editura Economică, 1995), p. 87.

[34] See Sergiu Verona, *Military Occupation and Diplomacy: Soviet Troops in Romania, 1944–1958* (Durham: Duke University press, 1992), pp. 122–40.

al of the Soviet troops, one can grasp—as historian Vlad Georgescu noted—from his servile speech of 25 July 1958, on the occasion of the departure of the last echelons of Soviet troops from Romania.[35] Thus, by the end of 1958 Gheorghiu-Dej had good reason to congratulate himself for his political ability. He had managed not only to demote his main critics from within the Party, but also to survive the first wave of de-Stalinization. On top of this, the Soviet troops had left the country. Yet, there was something that he did not manage to achieve: the full support of his own people. The way he managed to partially fulfill this task is discussed below.

A Process of "Selective Community-Building," 1956–64

As already mentioned, the strategy of political survival devised by Dej and his men was not centered from the very beginning on a skillful instrumentalization of nationalism. There is little evidence that the Romanian communist elite mastered the main elements of traditional Romanian nationalism. Nonetheless, once Khrushchev inaugurated his de-Stalinization campaign, Romanian communists had to look elsewhere for legitimacy and thus were compelled to initiate a process of "selective community-building," that is, to create new political meanings, shared by the communist ruling elite and the population concerning the relationship between the Party and the society.[36] Such a process was launched as an expansion of the within-group, i.e., within-the-group-from-prisons vision of politics. In other words, it was not a dormant sense of national identity that was awakened in the political conjuncture of the year 1956. On the contrary, the context of 1956 implied the devising of a new political strategy and that strategy was also designed as a "tacit deal" offered to a majority—but by no means to all—of the Romanian society. The selective nature of the community-

---

[35] For documents related to the withdrawal of the Soviet troops from Romania, see Ioan Scurtu ed., *România: Retragerea trupelor sovietice—1958* [Romania: The withdrawal of the Soviet troops—1958] (Bucharest: Editura Didactică și Pedagogică, 1996). For Gheorghiu-Dej's speech of 25 July 1958, see pp. 355–61.

[36] Jowitt, *Revolutionary Breakthroughs and National Development*, p. 74.

building process launched in the aftermath of the 1956 events needs to be stressed once more. Not all segments of Romanian society were allowed to take part in the process. Up to the year 1964, numerous Romanian citizens were imprisoned on political grounds, while their offspring were denied basic civil rights.[37] Obviously, they were considered "enemies of the people" and the community building process was not aimed at them.

However, Khrushchev's de-Stalinization was a threat to Dej and his men, and a return to the people—"enemies of the people" excluded—as the ultimate source of legitimacy was the only solution at hand. This is how a worldview developed within the ranks of the Party (i.e., the illegal RCP) during the interwar years and subsequently in Greater Romania's prisons was extended to the Party-State level. Marginalization, humiliation, external control, reliance only on the inner circle of power made of *monolithism* and *emancipation* fundamental values shared by Dej and his inner circle of power. Valued at the Party level, monolithism and emancipation were nevertheless synonymous with *unity* and *independence*, arguably the most powerful historical myths (alongside ancient roots and continuity) that were instrumental in establishing the modern Romanian nation-state in the mid-19th century.

Again, this is not to say that Dej knew the language of nationalism perfectly. Actually, he did not. Câmpeanu, himself a member of the group from prisons, speaking of the period spent in prison, argues that the said group was not xenophobic or ethnocentric: "Over the years, I did not observe in that multinational community the slightest sign of interethnic prejudices."[38] In fact, Dej never referred to the "Romanian nation" in his official speeches. The RWP first secretary did refer to "people" or "motherland," but never to the "nation" as

---

[37] The most recent estimate places the number of political prisoners at around 600,000. However, if one adds the persons deported, placed under house arrest, interned in labor camps in the Soviet Union, etc., the total number of the direct victims of the communist repression rises to approximately 2,000,000 persons. For more on this issue, see Romulus Rusan, *Cronologia şi geografia represiunii comuniste din România: Recensămîntul populaţiei concentraţionare, 1945–1989* [Chronology and geography of communist repression in Romania: A census of detained population, 1945–1989] (Bucharest: Editura Fundaţiei Academia Civică, 2007), pp. 61–2. Hereafter quoted as *Chronology and geography of communist repression in Romania*.

[38] Câmpeanu, *Ceauşescu, the countdown years*, p. 101.

such, although mentions were made to "national economy"[39] or "national independence."[40] Nonetheless, his recourse to Party-State building in the guise of selective community-building created the basis for Ceauşescu's program of party-state building in the form of an all-embracing nation-building project. As Jowitt aptly puts it: "Given the highly concrete, rigid, hence superficial nature of Gheorghiu-Dej's Marxist-Leninist beliefs, there was a chance that his regime could become nationalistic in the style of historic Romanian nationalism."[41]

It took however a rather long time until the Party learned the language of nationalism and fully understood the importance of national ideology. In this respect, the story of Marx's writings about Romanians is telling. The manuscript was discovered in Amsterdam in 1958 but it was published only in 1964, when it became clear that it could serve the Party's policy of independence from Moscow.[42] Pavel Ţugui, a former head of the Scientific and Cultural Section of the CC of the RWP (1955–60) states clearly in his memoirs that the publication of Marx's writings was part of the new "political strategy and tactics" pursued "discretely but perseveringly by some members of the CC of the RWP" after 1956.[43] The fact that in 1958 the regime launched a second wave of repression—during which the collectivization process was completed (1962)—meant to further tame the population supports the argument that the Party was not sure of the effects the emerging nationalistic rhetoric would have on the population.[44] Actually, it was only on

---

[39] See *Resolution of the plenary meeting of the CC of the RWP of 3–5 March 1949*, p. 7.

[40] See Gheorghiu-Dej, *30 years of struggle under the flag of Lenin and Stalin*, p. 5.

[41] Jowitt, *Revolutionary Breakthroughs and National Development*, p. 224.

[42] Karl Marx, *Însemnări despre români—Manuscrise inedite* [Notes about Romanians—Unedited manuscripts] (Bucharest: Editura Academiei Republicii Populare Române, 1964).

[43] See Pavel Ţugui, *Istoria şi limba română în vremea lui Gheorghiu-Dej: Memoriile unui fost şef de Secţie a CC al PMR* [History and Romanian language in Gheorghiu-Dej's times: The memoirs of a former head of Section of CC of the RWP] (Bucharest: Editura Ion Cristoiu, 1999), pp. 185–6.

[44] For details regarding the wave of repression launched in 1958, see Rusan, *Chronology and geography of communist repression in Romania*, pp. 31–4. For more on the forced collectivization process, see Gheorghe Iancu, Virgiliu Ţârău, and Ottmar Traşcă eds., *Colectivizarea agriculturii în România: Aspecte legislative, 1945–1962* [Collectivization of agriculture in Romania: Legislative aspects, 1945–1962] (Cluj: Presa Universitară Clujeană, 2000); and Octavi-

21 August 1968, when Ceauşescu publicly condemned the invasion of former Czechoslovakia by troops of the Warsaw Treaty Organization that the Party could evaluate the force of the nationalistic argument. The immediate result of that event was that the RCP gained widespread popular support almost overnight.

Until Gheorghiu-Dej's death in March 1965, there were two major domestic political events that deserve a closer look: the Plenum of the Central Committee held on 28 November–5 December 1961 and the Declaration of April 1964. The CC Plenum of November–December 1961 provided a simple but effective description of the Party's history since the end of WWII, seen as a struggle between two camps: an autochthonous and patriotic one, and a Soviet-oriented one. Thus, Gheorghiu-Dej claimed that the purges of 1952 (the Pauker–Luca–Teohari group) and 1957 (the Constantinescu–Chişinevschi faction) were the result of a struggle between the proponents of two visions. A first group, led by Dej himself, put Romania's interests above everything else. That group was fiercely opposed by a so-called Muscovite group, which served only the interests of the Soviet Union. Subsequent to Dej's speech, all the participants to that Plenum were called to reiterate the interpretation of their leader.[45]

Nonetheless, it is important to stress that at the same plenary session of November–December 1961 top communist officials made recurrent references to their "just" stances with regard to Transylvania. Gheorghiu-Dej himself stated bluntly that immediately after WWII, "the chief preoccupation of Rákosi and his group was: 'To whom would Transylvania belong'."[46] This indicates that the Romanian com-

---

an Roske, Florin Abraham, and Dan Cătănuş eds., *Colectivizarea agriculturii în România: Cadrul legislativ, 1949–1962* [Collectivization of agriculture in Romania: The legal framework, 1949–1962] (Bucharest: Institutul Naţional pentru Studiul Totalitarismului, 2007).

[45] After the fall of the Ceauşescu regime in December 1989, Paul Niculescu-Mizil was one the most vocal former *nomenklatura* members in praising Ceauşescu's independent line. Nonetheless, he concedes that the Plenum of 1961 was meant primarily to praise Dej and mentions that Ceauşescu was among those who excessively glorified Dej. See Paul Niculescu-Mizil, *De la Comintern la comunism naţional* [From Comintern to national-communism] (Bucharest: Editura Evenimentul Românesc, 2001), pp. 244–5.

[46] Elis Neagoe-Pleşa and Liviu Pleşa, eds., *Dosarul Ana Pauker: Plenara Comitetului Central al Partidului Muncitoresc Român din 30 noiembrie—5 decembrie*

munist elite was discovering the main ingredients of the nationalist discourse; the reference to the contested territory of Transylvania and the allegedly irredentist stances of Hungarian Stalinists was meant to stress once more the increasingly national line adopted by the RWP after 1956. Transylvania was already conceptualized as an "ethnoscape." As Anthony D. Smith puts it: "Historic 'ethnoscapes' cover a wider extent of land, present a tradition of continuity and are held to constitute an ethnic unity, because the terrain invested with collective significance is felt to be integral to a particular historical culture community or *ethnie*."[47] Thus, it may be argued that in 1961 the shift from a selective community-building to a nation-building process was only a matter of inclusion, i.e., of including in the process those citizens who were previously excluded on ideological grounds.

The document that epitomizes Dej's policy of independence from Moscow was issued in April 1964. Known as the "Declaration of April 1964," the document is one of the RWP's most important official documents. Simply put, the Declaration proclaimed that all communist parties were equal within the international communist movement, and therefore they were free to choose their own path toward communism:

> It is the exclusive right of each communist party to elaborate independently its political line and specific objectives, as well as the ways and methods to reach them, by applying creatively the general truths of Marxism-Leninism and the conclusions it draws from the thorough study of the experience of other communist and workers parties. *There is no "parent" party and "offspring" party, "superior" and "subordinated" parties, but there is the large family of communist and workers parties having equal rights.*[48]

1961 [The Ana Pauker file: The Plenum of the CC of RWP of 30 November–5 December 1961] Vol. I (Bucharest: Editura Nemira & CNSAS, 2006), p. 251.

[47] Anthony D. Smith, *Myths and Memories of the Nation*, p. 150.

[48] See *Declaraţie cu privire la poziţia Partidului Muncitoresc Român în problemele mişcării comuniste şi muncitoreşti internaţionale, adoptată de Plenara lărgită a C.C. al P.M.R. din aprilie 1964* [Declaration concerning the position of the Romanian Workers' Party with regard to the problems of the international communist and workers' movement adopted by the enlarged Plenum of the CC of the RWP of April 1964] (Bucharest: Editura Politică, 1964), p. 55., emphasis added.

After claiming the right of each and every communist party to decide upon its own strategy of building "socialism," the RWP elite took the major step towards a decisive shift from selective community-building to nation-building: the liberation of political prisoners. The general amnesty led to the liberation of the overwhelming majority of political convicts by the end of August 1964.[49] However, Dej did not live long enough to see the results of this major shift. It was his successor, Nicolae Ceauşescu, who turned Dej's incipient ethnic nationalism into consistently chauvinistic policies.

Concluding Remarks

The unexpected de-Stalinization campaign launched by Khrushchev took the Stalinist elite in Bucharest by surprise. Having eliminated his most redoubtable enemies from within the Party—most prominently Lucreţiu Pătrăşcanu and Ana Pauker—it seemed that nothing could hamper Gheorghiu-Dej's "group from prisons" from fully controlling the Party and the State. By 1956, a decisive shift occurred in the *party institutionalization* process. A "verification campaign" was launched in 1948 and led to massive purges that amounted to 192,000 persons. This allowed the reorganization of the Party through subsequent formalization, infusion of values and emotional attachment. However, contingency played a major role in changing fundamentally the short-term objectives of the Romanian communist elite. Avoiding de-Stalinization became a crucial task of Dej's inner circle of power. Thus, Gheorghiu-Dej and his men were compelled to adopt a strategy of political survival based, on the one hand, on a return to the people as the ultimate source of legitimacy and, on the other hand, on a continuation of the process of extensive industrialization. The return to the people meant, in fact, the building of a new political community, but this was by no means easy. The country had gone through a period of random terror and numerous citizens were imprisoned on political grounds while their offspring and relatives were denied basic civil rights. What emerged was a process of "selective community-building" that spanned over the period 1956–64, which constituted basically an expansion of

---

[49] Rusan, *Chronology and geography of communist repression in Romania*, p. 35.

the vision of politics of the within-group, i.e., within-the-group-from-prisons to a large part of the Romanian society. Such a vision of politics was born during the interwar period and crystallized in prisons during the WWII period. Exclusion, political marginalization, harassment by the interwar police, subordination to Moscow and to the local leadership of non-Romanian ethnic origin, all these made of *monolithism* and *emancipation* powerful myths of "regeneration" or "rebirth" of the Party under the lead of Gheorghiu-Dej and his group.

This is how a worldview that developed within the ranks of the underground Party, gradually expanded to the Party-State level after the communist takeover. Valued as the most powerful "myths of rebirth" by the group from prisons, *monolithism* and *emancipation* were synonymous with *unity* and *independence*. But unity and independence were, alongside *ancient roots* and *continuity*, the four most powerful "myths of ethnic descent" that contributed to the establishment of the modern Romanian nation-state in the mid-19th century.[50] Appeals to such myths after the change of legitimating strategy in 1956 resonated in the hearts and minds of a majority of Romania's population. Arguably, Gheorghiu-Dej did not master the language of Romanian traditional nationalism. Although he never referred to the "Romanian nation" in his speeches, his recourse to party-state building in the form of a selective community-building process, that is, infusion of new political meanings concerning the party–masses relationship—since the community became after 1956 his only source of legitimacy—created the basis for Ceauşescu's party-state building in the form of an ethnocentric nation-building process.

---

[50] The term is used in the sense given by Smith. See Anthony D. Smith, *Myths and Memories of the Nation*, pp. 62–71.

APPENDIX

List of Contributors

KENNETH JOWITT is the President and Maurine Hotchkis Senior Fellow at the Hoover Institution and the Emeritus Professor at the University of California, Berkeley. He is the author of *The New World Disorder: The Leninist Extinction* (University of California Press, 1992). He is presently working on *Frontiers, Barricades and Boundaries,* a book dealing with the changes in international political geography and the challenges to American and Western institutions.

VLADIMIR TISMANEANU is professor of politics and director of the Center for the Study of Post-communist Societies at University of Maryland (College Park) and President of the Presidential Commission for the Analysis of the Communist Dictatorship in Romania. Among his publications in are: *Reinventing Politics: Eastern Europe from Stalin to Havel* (The Free Press, 1992, paperback with a new epilogue, 1993); *Stalinism for All Seasons: a Political History of Romanian Communism* (University of California Press, 2003). He was also co-author and co-editor of the *Final Report of the Presidential Commission for the Analysis of the Romanian Communist Dictatorship* (2007). He recently finalized the manuscript for a forthcoming book entitled *The Devil in History. Lessons of the 20th Century.*

MARK KRAMER is director of the Cold War Studies Program at Harvard University and a senior fellow of Harvard's Davis Center for Russian and Eurasian Studies. Professor Kramer is the author of *Crisis in Czechoslovakia, 1968: The Prague Spring and the Soviet Invasion* (Oxford UP, 2001) and two forthcoming titles: *The Collapse of the Soviet Union* and *Crisis in the Communist World, 1956: The Soviet Union, the Warsaw*

Pact, and Upheavals in Poland and Hungary. He was the translator and American editor for *The Black Book of Communism: Crimes, Terror, Repression* (Harvard University Press, 1999). He is completing another book titled *From Dominance to Hegemony to Collapse: Soviet Policy in East-Central Europe, 1945–1991.*

ALFRED J. RIEBER is professor Emeritus, University of Pennsylvania and University Research Professor at the Central European University. His major publications are *Stalin and the French Communist Party, 1941–1947* (Columbia UP, 1962), *The Politics of Autocracy* (Mouton & Co., 1966), *Merchants and Entrepreneurs in Imperial Russia* (University of North Carolina Press, 1982), *Zhdanov in Finland* (Center for Russian and East European Studies, 1995), and *Imperial Rule,* co-edited with prof. Alexei Miller (CEU Press, 2004). He is presently working on the book project *Struggle over the Borderlands.*

THOMAS W. SIMONS JR. is currently a Lecturer in Harvard University's Department of Government and Visiting Scholar at Harvard's Davis Center for Russian and Eurasian Studies. He is the author of three books: *The End of the Cold War?* (St. Martin's Press, 1990), *Eastern Europe in the Postwar World* (2nd revised edition, St. Martin's Press, 1993), and *Islam in a Globalizing World* (Stanford UP, 2003).

AGNES HELLER is Hannah Arendt Professor of Philosophy and Political Science at the New School for Social Research in New York. She has extensively written on the philosophy of history and morals, or the theory of modernity: *The Time Is Out of Joint: Shakespeare as Philosopher of History* (Blackwell, 2002); *A Theory of Modernity* (Blackwell, 1999); *An Ethics of Personality* (Basil Blackwell, 1996); *General Ethics* (Basil Blackwell, 1988); *Beyond Justice* (Basil Blackwell, 1987); *The Theory of Needs in Marx* (Allison and Busby, 1976). She is presently working on two books: *Immortal Comedy: The Comic Phenomenon in Art, Literature, and Life* and *The Concept of the Beautiful.*

JOHN CONNELLY is associate professor at University of California, Berkeley, Department of History. Member of the Institute for Advanced Study, Princeton (2002–3) and co-director, UC Berkeley History Social Science Project. He is the author of *Captive University: The Sovietization of East German, Czech, and Polish Higher Education, 1945–1956* (University of North Carolina Press, 2000) and of many important articles dealing with the politics of higher education under Stalinism in Central Europe. Prof. Connelly is currently working on the relation between anti-Semitism and racism in Catholic thought from the 1930s to 1960s, with focus on Central Europe and the US.

ANTONI Z. KAMINSKI is a senior researcher at the Institute of Political Studies, Polish Academy of Sciences and lecturer at Collegium Civitas in Warsaw. He has published extensively on international security and governance issues including corruption. He was a President of the Polish Chapter of Transparency International. His most recent publication was *Korupcja rzadow: kraje postkomunistyczn wobec globalizachi* (Corruption of governance: post-communist countries and globalization), (co-authored with Bartłomiej Kaminski, Trio, 2004).

BARTŁOMIEJ KAMINSKI teaches International Political Economy, Global Economic Governance and Political Economy of Transition at the Department of Government, University of Maryland at College Park. His most recent publications include *The Caucasian Tiger: Sustaining Economic Growth*, co-authored with S. Mitra, D. Andrews, G. Gyulumyan, Paul Holden, Y. Kuznetsov and E. Vahskakmadze, (The World Bank, Washington D.C., 2007), and *Korupcja rzadow: kraje postkomunistyczn wobec globalizachi* (Corruption of governance: post-communist countries and globalization), (co-authored with Antoni Kaminski, Trio, 2004).

JÁNOS RAINER is director of the Institute for the History of the 1956 Hungarian Revolution. He is also a lecturer at Budapest University of Theater and Film Arts. His publications are: *Imre Nagy. Political Biography 1896–1953* Vol. 1 and 2 (2002), *The Hungarian Revolution of 1956. Reform, Revolt and Repression 1953–1963* (1996) (co-authored with György Litván and János M. Bak). Along with Csaba Békés and Malcolm Byrne, prof. Rainer compiled, edited and introduced *The 1956 Hungarian Revolution: A History in Documents* (CEU Press, 2002).

BOGDAN CRISTIAN IACOB is Ph.D. candidate at Central European University, History Department, completing a dissertation with the title "Stalinism, Historians and the Nation in Romania (1955–1977)." He was research fellow at the Center of Advanced Studies in Sofia, Center for Advanced Studies at Leipzig University, and the Center for the Study of Post-communist Societies at University of Maryland (College Park). He is author of multiple articles in Romanian and English on the history of communism, comparative ideologies, and transitional justice.

EKATERINA NIKOVA is Senior Research Associate, Institute for Balkan Studies at the Bulgarian Academy of Sciences. Major publications: *The Balkans and the European Community* (1992), *Bulgaria in the Balkans* (1999), *Balkan Regional Cooperation Revisited* (2001), *Balkan Politics at the Cusp of Two Centuries* (2003), *The Balkans: Modernization Unfulfilled* (forthcoming).

DORIN DOBRINCU is General Director of National Archives of Romania and associate professor at the Department of History at "Alexandru I. Cuza" University (Iași, Romania). Among his publications is *Transforming Peasants, Property, and Power. The Collectivization of Agriculture in Romania (1949–1962)* (co-editor with Constantin Iordachi, CEU Press, 2009). Professor Dobrincu was also co-author and co-editor of the *Final Report of the Presidential Commission for the Analysis of the Romanian Communist Dictatorship* (2007).

BRADLEY ABRAMS has taught modern Eastern European history at Copenhagen University and, from 1997–2007 in Columbia University's Department of History. He is the current President of the Czechoslovak Studies Association. He is the author of *The Struggle for the Soul of the Nation: Czech Culture and the Rise of Communism* (Rowman & Littlefield, 2004). He is currently working on a project entitled "Normalizing the Socialist Good Life: Consumption, Consumerism and Political Legitimacy in Czechoslovakia after the Prague Spring," and is under contract with Oxford University Press for a book on interwar Eastern Europe.

CRISTIAN VASILE is Coordinator of the Advisory Presidential Commission for the Analysis of the Communist Dictatorship in Romania and researcher at the „Nicolae Iorga" History Institute of the Romanian Academy (Bucharest). He was also co-author and co-editor of the *Final Report of the Presidential Commission for the Analysis of the Romanian Communist Dictatorship* (2007). His most recent publications are: *Per-*

fectul acrobat. Leonte Răutu și măștile răului (co-author with Vladimir Tismaneanu, Editora Humanitas, 2008); *Biserica Ortodoxă Română în primul deceniu comunist* [The Romanian Orthodox Church in the first communist decade] (Curtea Veche, 2005).

SVETOZAR STOJANOVIC is founder and president of the Serbian–American Center, Belgrade, president of its Forum for National Strategy. He was editor-in-chief of the journal *Praxis International* (Oxford) along with Seyla Benhabib (1987–1990). Books in English: *Between Ideals and Reality* (Oxford UP, 1973); *In Search of Democracy in Socialism* (Prometheus Books, 1981); *Perestroika: From Marxism and Bolshevism to Gorbachev* (Prometheus Books, 1988); *The Fall of Yugoslavia: Why Communism Failed* (Prometheus Books, 1997); and *Serbia: The Democratic Revolution* (Prometheus Books, 2003).

DRAGOȘ PETRESCU teaches modern European history and comparative communism at the Faculty of Political Science, University of Bucharest. He is also a member of the Board of the National Council for the Study of the *Securitate* Archives (CNSAS) in Bucharest. He was co-author of *Final Report of the Presidential Commission for the Analysis of the Romanian Communist Dictatorship* (2007). He is author of multiple articles and chapters in collective volumes.

Index